HISTORICAL DICTIONARIES OF INTELLIGENCE AND COUNTERINTELLIGENCE

Jon Woronoff, Series Editor

1. *British Intelligence*, by Nigel West, 2005.
2. *United States Intelligence*, by Michael A. Turner, 2006.
3. *Israeli Intelligence*, by Ephraim Kahana, 2006.
4. *International Intelligence*, by Nigel West, 2006.
5. *Russian and Soviet Intelligence*, by Robert W. Pringle, 2006.
6. *Cold War Counterintelligence*, by Nigel West, 2007.
7. *World War II Intelligence*, by Nigel West, 2008.
8. *Sexspionage*, by Nigel West, 2009.

The use of sex is "a common practice among intelligence services all over the world. This is a tough dirty business. We have used that technique against the Soviets. They have used it against us."

—Former Assistant FBI Director William C. Sullivan in testimony before the Church Committee, United States Senate, 1 November 1975.

I hope you are not a spy.

—President John F. Kennedy to Enüd Sztanko, October 1962

The Soviets cannot eliminate love and sex and greed from the scene . . . they use them to ensnare people.

—Allen Dulles in *The Craft of Intelligence*

I am no believer in what might be described as Mata Hari tactics.

—Max Knight in MI5 memorandum, 1940

Those who seduce to treason have at least as often been glamorous females like Mata Hari, and their prey the most committed heterosexuals.

—Tom Driberg in *Ruling Passions*

There are many brave men we ask to lay down their lives for their country. But for brave women we simply ask them to lay down.

—KGB General Oleg Kalugin

Historical Dictionary of Sexspionage

Nigel West

Historical Dictionaries of Intelligence and Counterintelligence, No. 8

The Scarecrow Press, Inc.
Lanham, Maryland • Toronto • Plymouth, UK
2009

SCARECROW PRESS, INC.

Published in the United States of America
by Scarecrow Press, Inc.
A wholly owned subsidiary of
The Rowman & Littlefield Publishing Group, Inc.
4501 Forbes Boulevard, Suite 200, Lanham, Maryland 20706
www.scarecrowpress.com

Estover Road
Plymouth PL6 7PY
United Kingdom

Copyright © 2009 by Nigel West

All rights reserved. No part of this publication may be reproduced, stored in a retrieval system, or transmitted in any form or by any means, electronic, mechanical, photocopying, recording, or otherwise, without the prior permission of the publisher.

British Library Cataloguing in Publication Information Available

Library of Congress Cataloging-in-Publication Data

West, Nigel.
 Historical dictionary of sexspionage / Nigel West.
 p. cm. — (Historical dictionaries of intelligence and counterintelligence, no. 8)
 Includes bibliographical references and index.
 ISBN-13: 978-0-8108-5999-9 (cloth : alk. paper)
 ISBN-10: 0-8108-5999-8 (cloth : alk. paper)
 ISBN-13: 978-0-8108-6287-6 (ebook)
 ISBN-10: 0-8108-6287-5 (ebook)
  1. Sex in espionage–History–Dictionaries. 2. Spies–Biography–Dictionaries.
 3. Intelligence officers–Biography–Dictionaries. I. Title.
 UB270.W45 2009
 327.12009–dc22   2008037597

∞™ The paper used in this publication meets the minimum requirements of American National Standard for Information Sciences—Permanence of Paper for Printed Library Materials, ANSI/NISO Z39.48-1992.
Manufactured in the United States of America.

Contents

Editor's Foreword *Jon Woronoff*	vii
Acknowledgments	ix
Acronyms and Abbreviations	xi
Chronology	xv
Introduction	xxiii
THE DICTIONARY	1
Bibliography	321
Index	335
About the Author	367

Editor's Foreword

As long as people have gone to war—and that is a very long time—they have engaged in espionage to uncover their enemies' weaknesses and to obtain crucial information. And, during that entire time, they have found that sex, no matter how defined or used, can be an essential tool to achieve their ends. Indeed, some spymasters and intelligence agencies have placed particular emphasis on "sexspionage," and it could hardly be claimed that they were wrong. They did achieve results, no matter how many lives were shattered. Of course, this use of sex can take many forms, whether through the use of call girls, prostitutes, or professional agents, the genuine love of husband and wife, or simply good friends who do not want the other to suffer. It can come into play between men and women as well as between members of the same sex, and a disproportionately large share of past cases of sexspionage revolved around homosexuality. Oddly enough, even with the current abundance of technical gadgetry, old-fashioned methods of obtaining crucial information have not actually disappeared; far from it. Thus, a tradition going back to the Bible (and doubtlessly before) continues into this day and age.

This *Historical Dictionary of Sexspionage* covers the whole scope of the phenomenon, covering its long and continuing practice, the large numbers of countries and organizations that have applied its use or had to fend it off, and the many forms and varieties it can take. Just how long sexspionage has been around—and in how many different contexts it has emerged—immediately becomes clear when one glances through the chronology. The motivation, techniques, and results are summed up analytically in the introduction. Bur the most significant (and occasionally raciest) parts are the numerous case histories in the dictionary section. They shed light on the actions of an often gaudy cast of characters— those who came into the spotlight and others who manipulated them from the shadows, the intelligence agencies they worked for or led, and some exceptional individuals who have gone down in history, from Delilah to Mata Hari to the Cambridge Five. Other entries deal with very dubious techniques such as the bra camera, swallows and ravens, and the honeytrap. For those whose appetite is whetted by this book, further reading can be found in the bibliography.

This volume was written by Nigel West, a historian who specializes in intelligence, and who is certainly one of the best such authors. In 1989 he was voted the "Expert's Expert" by a panel of spy writers selected by the *Observer*. In October 2003 he was given the first Lifetime Literature Award by the U.S. Association of Former Intelligence Officers. This was due to a long series of books, articles, and reference works on intelligence, starting with his first publication in 1980 and with a list that is still growing. These books cover especially British intelligence but also American, Soviet, and other strands, and deal mainly with World War II and the Cold War. This is now his fifth historical dictionary in our series on intelligence and counterintelligence; West previously produced the volumes on British intelligence, international intelligence, Cold War counterintelligence, and World War II intelligence.

Jon Woronoff
Series Editor

Acknowledgments

During the course of my research, I spoke to numerous intelligence officers and their agents, and I owe a debt of gratitude to Charles Elwell, Gabrielle Gast, Rufina Philby, Rainer Rupp, John Symonds, and the late Anthony Blunt, Tony Brooks, Elvira de la Fuentes, Dusko Popov, John Profumo, Michael Straight, Halina Szymanska, John Vassall, Dr. Michael Bialoguski, and Markus Wolf.

Acronyms and Abbreviations

ASIO	Australian Security Intelligence Organisation
AVH	Allami Vedélmi Hatosag (Hungarian Intelligence Service)
BfV	Bundesamt für Verfassungsschutz (West German Security Service)
BND	Bundesnachrichtendienst (West German Intelligence Service)
BOSS	Bureau of State Security (South Africa)
BSC	British Security Coordination
BUF	British Union of Fascists
CDU	Christian Democratic Union
CPA	Communist Party of Australia
CPC	Communist Party of Canada
CPGB	Communist Party of Great Britain
CPI	Communist Party of India
CPSU	Communist Party of the Soviet Union
CPUSA	Communist Party of the United States of America
CSIS	Canadian Security Intelligence Service
DCI	Director of Central Intelligence
DDO	Deputy Director for Operations
DGI	Dirección General de Inteligencia (Cuba)
DGSE	Direction-General de Securité Exterieure (France)
DIA	Defense Intelligence Agency
DIE	Departamentul de Informatii Externe (Romania)
DIO	Defense Intelligence Organization
DO	Directorate of Operations
DPRK	Democratic People's Republic of Korea
DST	Direction de la Surveillance du Territoire (France)
FBI	Federal Bureau of Investigation

FIU	Florida International University
FRG	Federal Republic of Germany
GC&CS	Government Code & Cypher School
GCHQ	Government Communications Headquarters
GDR	German Democratic Republic
GRU	Glavnoe Razvedyvatel'noe Upravlenie (Soviet Military Intelligence Service)
HCUA	House Committee on Un-American Activities
HVA	Hauptverwaltung Aufkrarung (East German Intelligence Service)
IB	Intelligence Bureau (India)
ISI	Inter-Services Intelligence (Pakistan)
ISRO	Indian Space Research Organization
KGB	Komitei Gosudarstevnnoi Bezopasnosti (Soviet Intelligence Service)
KPD	Kommunist Partei Deutschland (German Communist Party)
MfS	Ministerium für Staasssicherheit (East Germany)
MI5	British Security Service
MI6	British Secret Intelligence Service
MI19	British Combined Services Detailed Interrogation Centre
MSS	Ministry of State Security (China)
NKVD	Narodni Kommisariat Vnutrennih Dei (Soviet Intelligence Service)
NSA	National Security Agency
NTS	Narodnyi Trudovoi Soyuz (Union of Ukrainian Nationalists)
NZSIS	New Zealand Security Intelligence Service
OGPU	Obyeddinenoye Gosudarstvennoye Politischekoye Upravlenie (Soviet Intelligence Service)
ONI	Office of Naval Intelligence
OSS	Office of Strategic Services
OUN	Organization of Ukrainian Nationalists
PCD	Postal Censorship Department
PIRA	Provisional Irish Republican Army
POW	Prisoner of War
PRC	Peoples Republic of China

RAW	Research and Analysis Wing (Indian Intelligence Service)
RCMP	Royal Canadian Mounted Police
RHSA	Reichsicherheitshauptamt
ROVS	Rossiiskii Obshchevoennyi Soyuz (Union of Russian Veterans)
RUC	Royal Ulster Constabulary
SCD	Second Chief Directorate
SD	Sicherheitsdienst
SDECE	Service de Documentation Exterieure et de Contre-Espionage (France)
SE	Soviet/Eastern Europe Division
SEAC	South-East Asia Command
Shin Beth	General Security Service (Israel)
SIM	Servicio di Informazione Militar (Italy)
SIME	Security Intelligence Middle East
SIS	Secret Intelligence Service
SOE	Special Operations Executive
Stasi	Staatssicherheit (East German Security Service)
StB	Statni Bezpecnost (Czech Intelligence Service)
SVR	Sluzhba Vnezhney Razvedki (Russian Federation Intelligence Service)
TASS	Telegrafnoje Agentstvo Sovietskovo Soïuza (news agency of the former Soviet Union)
UB	Urzab Bezpieczenstwa (Polish Intelligence Service)
UN	United Nations
UNSCOM	United Nations Special Commission
UpDK	Upravlenie podelam Diplomaticheskogo Korpusa (Main Directorate for Services to the Diplomatic Corps)

Chronology

1857 Rosie Greenhow recruited by Captain Thomas Jordan.

1859 Ginnie and Lottie Moon are engaged to 38 Union soldiers.

1860 Wilhelm Stieber appointed Prussia's spymaster.

1861 Belle Boyd passes information to General "Stonewall" Jackson.

1862 Emma Edmonds reconnoiters Yorktown. Augusta Morris released from prison.

1867 The Hall of Pleasurable Delights opens in Hankow.

1872 General de Cissy comforted by the Baroness de Kaulle while a prisoner in Hamburg.

1893 Richard Burton, translator of the *Kama Sutra*, is knighted.

1897 Paulene Cushman dies of an overdose.

1912 George Parrott convicted of passing secrets to his German mistress.

1913 Alfred Redl confronted with evidence of his espionage.

1914 Maud Gould acquitted.

1915 Lizzie Wertheim arrested and imprisoned. Marthe Richard becomes Major von Krohn's lover. Edith Cavell executed. Mata Hari recruited in Amsterdam.

1916 Eva de Bournonville sentenced to death and reprieved. Sir Roger Casement arrested in Ireland.

1917 Marguerite Francillard shot by a French firing-squad. Mata Hari arrested and executed.

1918 Moura Budberg becomes Robert Bruce Lockhart's mistress. Agnes Smedley indicted on espionage charges.

1919 Jules Silber leaves the Postal Censorship Department.

1920 Lizzie Wertheim dies insane at Broadmoor.

1921 Tom Driberg recruited by Max Knight.

1922 Wilhelm Reich appointed deputy director of Sigmund Freud's Psychoanalytic Polyclinic in Vienna.

1923 Lydia Stahl takes Professor Louis Pierre Martin as her lover.

1924 Arnold Deutsch joins the Austrian Communist Party.

1925 Sir Basil Thomson arrested with Thelma de Lava.

1926 Noel Field joins the State Department.

1927 Averell Harriman is alleged to have fathered an illegitimate child in Georgia. MI5 investigates Nellie Williams.

1928 Hede Massing recruited by Richard Sorge. Agnes Smedley travels to Shanghai.

1929 Edith Suschitsky visits Great Britain on a secret mission.

1930 Ernest Oldham sells information to the Soviets in Paris. Wilhelm Reich publishes *The Sexual Revolution*.

1931 Jules Silber publishes *Invisible Weapons*. Olga Gray recruited by Max Knight.

1932 Fred Rose elected to Parliament in Canada. George Hill publishes *Go Spy the Land*.

1933 Norman Baillie-Stewart convicted of Official Secrets offenses. Ernest Oldham commits suicide. Robert and Marjorie Switz move to Paris.

1934 Edith Suschitsky introduces Kim Philby to Arnold Deutsch.

1935 Herman Goertz arrested at Harwich. Wallis Simpson placed under surveillance by MI5.

1936 Anthony Blunt recruited by the NKVD. The Salon Kitty opens in Berlin.

1937 Betty Pack recruited by Jack Shelley in Warsaw. Gertrude Schilbeck lures Ignace Reiss into a trap in Lausanne. Ignatz Greibl and Kay Moog recruited by the Abwehr on the *Europa*.

1938 Elizabeth Bentley meets Jacob Golos. La Plevitskaya confesses to the murder of General Skoblin. Olga Gray gives evidence against Percy Glading.

1939 Tyler Kent posted from Moscow to London. John King arrested.

1940 Henry Antheil killed over the Baltic. Vera Schalburg arrested in Scotland. Anna Wolkoff convicted in London. Ursula Kuczynski falls in love with Len Beurton. Dusko Popov arrives in London.

1941 Mollie Hiscox and Nora Briscoe convicted of breaches of the Official Secrets Act. Alberto Lais expelled from the United States. Richard Sorge arrested in Tokyo. Inga Arvad and John F. Kennedy investigated by the FBI.

1942 Anthony Courtney posted to the Soviet Union. Mary Bancroft recruited by Allen Dulles in Bern. Ilse Stoebe arrested in Berlin. TATE meets Mary. Denis Rake falls in love with Max Halder in Paris.

1943 Mildred Harnack executed in Berlin. Death of Jacob Golos in New York. Viviana Diaz arrested in Trinidad.

1944 Nellie Kapp defects to OSS in Ankara. Adrienne Molnar persuades Willi Hamburger to defect. Victor Kravchenko defects in the United States. Theresa Jardine posted to Kandy. Richard Sorge executed in Tokyo.

1945 Death of Monica de Wichfeld in Waldheim Prison. Elizabeth Bentley defects in New York. Igor Gouzenko defects in Ottawa.

1946 Markus Wolf attends the Nuremberg trials as a journalist. Ted Hall marries Joan Krakover.

1947 Edward Scott joins the Foreign Office. Annabelle Bucar begins an affair with Konstantin Lapshin. Anne-Marie Snellman recruits her lover, Urho Kekkonen.

1948 FBI begins a molehunt for SIMA. The CIA introduces polygraph tests.

1949 Jacques Abrey publishes *The Secret War of Josephine Baker*. Judith Coplon and Valentin Gubitchev arrested in New York.

1950 Elli Barczatis investigated by the East German MfS. Guy Burgess appointed to Washington, D.C.

1951 Roy Rhodes compromised in Moscow. Susanne Sievers arrested in Leipzig. Frank Bossard posted to Germany.

1952 Nikolai Khokhlov marries Yania Timashkevits. Annabelle Bucar publishes *The Truth about American Diplomats*.

1953 Piotr Popov approaches the CIA in Vienna. Heinz Helfmann persuades Irmgard Roemer to copy German Foreign Ministry documents.

1954 Nikolai Khokhlov defects in Germany. John Vassall posted to Moscow. Vladimir and Evdokia Petrov defect in Australia. Piotr Deriabin defects in Austria.

1955 Roy Rhodes discharged from the U.S. Army. Elli Barczatis and Karl Laurenz beheaded.

1956 Victor Grayevsky acquires Khrushchev's secret speech from Lucia Baranowski. James Mintkenbaugh discharged from the U.S. Army. Tom Driberg interviews Guy Burgess in Moscow. E. P. Lutsky cultivates a passport clerk in Wellington.

1957 Roy Rhodes confesses. Death of Walter Duranty. Kenneth Alsop blackmailed in Moscow. Lee Harvey Oswald begins to frequent the Queen Bee in Tokyo.

1958 Edward Scott compromised in Prague. Maurice Dejean honeytrapped in Moscow. Ion Pacepa deploys MIMI in Wiesbaden to entrap KONRAD.

1959 Piotr Popov arrested in Moscow. Bernon Mitchell and William Martin visit Cuba.

1960 John Stonehouse compromised in Prague. Irwin Scarbeck compromised in Warsaw. Marianne Lenzkow recruited under a false flag. Oleg Penkovsky approaches an SIS courier in Moscow.

1961 Anthony Courtney compromised in Moscow. Margarethe Lubig recruited by the Hauptverwaltung Aufkrarung. Stephen Ward introduces John Profumo to Christine Keeler.

1962 John Vassall arrested. Louis Guibaud shoots himself after being honeytrapped in Moscow. Dmitri Polyakov compromises Maria Dobrova.

1963 Eugene Ivanov recalled to Moscow. Ivan Skripov expelled from Canberra. Yuri Krotkov defects in London. John Profumo resigns. Stephen Ward commits suicide. Eleanor Philby joins Kim in Moscow. Ivor Rowsell withdrawn from Moscow after an attempt to honeytrap him.

1964 Bernard Boursicot posted to Paris. Yuri Nosenko defects in Geneva. Mary Meyer murdered in Washington, D.C.

1965 Geoffrey Harrison posted to Moscow. Robert Johnson confesses. James Mintkenbaugh arrested. MIDNIGHT CLIMAX closed down.

1966 Helge Berger meets Peter Krause in Bonn. Munir Redfa persuaded to fly his Iraqi MiG-21 to Israel.

1967 Evgenni Runge defects in Berlin. Florentino Azpillaga defects in Vienna with his girlfriend.

1968 Sir Geoffrey Harrison recalled to London. Dovie Beams meets Ferdinand Marcos.

1969 Natasha Makhotina is approached by the RCMP Security Service over her affair with JOKER.

1970 Monique Rousseau's father convicted of espionage in France. Nikolai Ogorodnikov and his wife granted political asylum in Vienna.

1971 Zoltan Szabo recruited by the Hungarian AVH. Karl and Hana Koecher granted American citizenship.

1972 Oleg Lyalin defects in London. Ann-Christine Bowen marries Rainer Rupp. Philip Agee meets Janet Strickland. John Symonds recruited by the KGB.

1973 Dieter Will and Ursel Lorenzen defect to East Germany. TRIGON recruited by his Spanish girlfriend.

1974 Felix Bloch posted to East Berlin. John Stonehouse fakes his own death in Florida.

1975 Dagmar Kahlig-Scheffler joins Helmut Schmidt's staff. Jack Anderson reveals "CIA love-nests" in Greenwich Village.

1976 Renate Lutz arrested in Bonn.

1977 Guvnor Haavik arrested in Oslo. Gabriele Albin recruited in Bonn.

1978 Defection of Arkadi Shevchenko. Arrest of Jeremy Thorpe.

1979 Defection of Werner Stiller. Robert Hanssen sells FBI secrets to the GRU in New York. Anthony Blunt exposed publicly as a Soviet spy.

1980 David Barnett arrested.

1981 Vladimir Potashov recruited by the CIA.

1982 Edward Ellis Smith killed in San Francisco. Rhona Ritchie convicted of passing secrets to Rafaat El-Ansary. Geoffrey Prime arrested on pedophile charges.

1983 Aldrich Ames appointed chief of counterintelligence in the CIA's Soviet/Eastern Europe Division.

1984 Clayton Lonetree posted to Moscow. Robert Hanssen contacts the KGB in Washington, D.C. The Koechers are arrested in New York.

1985 Aldrich Ames sells CIA secrets to the KGB and marries Rosario Casas. Margarete Höke arrested in Bonn. Richard Miller convicted of passing secrets to Svetlana Ogorodnikova.

1986 Viktor Gundarev defects in Athens. Boris Yuzhin arrested in Moscow. Mordechai Vanunu abducted in Rome. Earl Pitts arrested in New York.

1987 Felix Bloch recalled to Washington, D.C., from Vienna. Margarete Hoeke convicted of spying for the KGB.

1988 William Cleveland begins affair with Katrina Leung.

1989 Felix Bloch makes a limited confession.

1990   Clyde Conrad sentenced to life imprisonment. Felix Bloch dismissed from the State Department. Magarethe Lubig arrested.

1991   Katrina Leung contacts the Chinese MSS. Robert Hanssen abandons Priscilla Galey.

1992   Helen Anderson arrested in Berlin. Natalia Ljuskova arrested in Finland.

1993   William Cleveland retires. Rainer and Ann-Christine Rupp arrested. Iraq's Mukhabarat attempts to compromise UNSCOM helicopter pilots.

1994   Aldrich and Rosario Ames arrested.

1995   Conviction of Markus Wolf quashed by Germany's Constitutional Court. CIA station chief Dick Holm expelled from France.

1996   Clayton Lonetree released from prison.

1997   Katrina Leung takes secret document from J. J. Smith.

1998   Death of Arkadi Shevchenko. Arrest of the RED AVISPA spy ring in Miami.

1999   Therese Squillacotte imprisoned.

2000   Simon Lappas passes secrets to Sherryll Dowling, a Canberra prostitute.

2001   Robert Hanssen arrested. Ana Montes arrested.

2002   Katrina Leung's home searched.

2003   Edward Lee Howard dies in an accident in Moscow. Nada Nadim Prouty joins the CIA.

2004   Death of Michael Straight. Amir Laty withdrawn from Australia.

2005   Brigadier Andrew Duncan withdrawn from Islamabad.

2006   Carlos and Elsa Alvarez arrested in Miami. Ariel Weinmann arrested in Dallas.

2007   Donald Keyser convicted of passing secrets to Isabelle Cheng.

2008   Philip Agee dies in Havana.

Introduction

The motives that drive individuals to engage in espionage are many, and very often those involved are reluctant to admit precisely what it was that propelled them into it. Ideology is frequently cited as a reason for someone having betrayed his or her country, often on the basis that a political commitment is easier to acknowledge than sheer greed or some monetary consideration. Counterintelligence analysts, of course, are always anxious to learn more about motives, partly so they can attempt to develop a profile that will assist them in detecting a betrayal before serious damage is incurred, but also to enable them to recognize the traits in an adversary who perhaps might usefully be exploited.

During the Cold War there was a concentrated effort by all the protagonists to persuade intelligence professionals to defect, and many did so. Some simply fled to escape arrest, such as the CIA's Edward Lee Howard in 1985, just as the Federal Bureau of Investigation was closing in on him, while others like Vitali Yurchenko wanted to cash in on the widely publicized figure of a million dollars supposedly available to senior KGB personnel willing to be resettled in the West in return for the disclosure of valuable information.

The lure of wealth is well understood as a powerful incentive for some to sell classified material, and it may well be that the person concerned has fallen into debt or considers that his talents have not been sufficiently rewarded, and his privileged access to a highly saleable commodity looks like an attractive alternative to penury or disgrace. Others may have quite straightforward economic reasons for switching sides, but it is a common characteristic that whatever the underlying influences, they invariably justified their actions by claiming to have been politically inspired, apparently in the belief that an ideological conversion is a nobler motive. Thus Oleg Gouzenko, the GRU cipher clerk in Ottawa who fled his embassy in September 1945, insisted that he had become a convert to the principles of democracy, whereas others who came to know him well concluded that he simply wanted a better life for his pregnant wife and their daughter, or certainly better prospects than were likely to await him in Moscow, having been recalled home on disciplinary grounds. Forty years later Oleg Gordievsky claimed that his loyalty to the Soviet cause had been undermined by the brutal suppression of Alexander Dubcek's 1968 Prague spring, yet his decision to collaborate with the British Secret Intelligence Service coincided with a warning from his *rezident*, Mikhail Luibimov, that his affair with Leila, an embassy secretary, would jeopardize his chances of future advancement in the KGB. It is indeed noticeable that some of the Cold War's most important defectors underwent professional setbacks shortly before they had made their move and approached the other side. Anatoli Golitsyn had been involved in a career-threatening row with his *rezident* in Helsinki shortly before he presented himself to the local CIA station chief in December 1961. Vladimir Petrov had fallen into his ambassador's disfavor in Canberra before he accepted an invitation in 1954 from the Australian Security Intelligence Organization, which had been cultivating him for months. Similarly, Vladimir Kuzichkin feared being disciplined for having mislaid some sensitive documents, and Viktor Gundarev was anxious to start a new life with his mistress.

Clearly, ideology and money can play a large part in creating the circumstances in which someone opts to betray a country, employer, family, tribe, nationality, or religion, but one frequent common denominator is the role of "sexspionage," a term memorably coined by British author David Lewis in 1976. It is a fact, as will be demonstrated in the pages that follow, that love and sex are often cited as factors in the transformation of an otherwise conscientious public servant into a traitor. There are examples of dedicated professionals, trapped in an unhappy marriage, who think they have found solace elsewhere; the lonely homosexual, caught in a classic honeytrap and coerced into compromising classified material to satisfy his blackmailers; the vulnerable secretary, seduced by the handsome "raven"; the besotted ingénue, anxious to retain the affections of his quest. In a surprising number of espionage cases, sex has played a significant role, perhaps only in the background, possibly as a reason why a particular individual has lived beyond his means and in desperate need of cash. Looking behind the obvious financial motive, one can sometimes find traces of sexspionage.

Aldrich Ames, for instance, admits he first approached the KGB because his divorce had left him unable to meet his second wife's expectations. Having left his first wife for Rosario, his offer to sell the CIA's secrets for $50,000 was intended, so he said in his confession, to be a one-off opportunity to meet his lawyers' bills, settle his divorce obligations, and repay his credit card debt. As it turned out, Ames's first sale proved insufficient, and by the time of his arrest he had received an estimated $3 million, but the surveillance audiotapes of his conversations with Rosario show conclusively not just her involvement in his espionage but also her depressingly eloquent role as a motive for him to have engaged in treason in the first place. Although Ames conceded his financial predicament, he did not attempt to shift the blame to Rosario, perhaps another manifestation of his commitment to her.

Similarly, Bob Hanssen cited his poor pay as an FBI special agent in New York as a reason for his first sale of secrets to one of his GRU surveillance targets, but it is now known that he was indebted beyond the familiar burdens of a mortgage and six children to educate. His bizarre relationship with a stripper and his need to shower her with expensive gifts, including a car, jewelry, and a vacation in Hong Kong, suggest that here too sex played some part in the events that eventually would culminate in his arrest in February 2001. Another of Hanssen's colleagues, Earl Pitts, also sold the FBI's secrets to the Soviets, and his habitually heavy use of male and female prostitutes contributed to the financial crisis he blamed for his behavior. Such vulnerabilities led Yuri Nosenko to collaborate with the CIA, having misappropriated KGB funds to entertain expensive women while on official duties in Geneva, and Aleksandr Ogorodnik of the Soviet Foreign Ministry was persuaded to become a spy by his pregnant Spanish lover, an agent recruited by the CIA.

In the realm of human behavior, sex can be the catalyst for risky or reckless conduct, and this applies to both genders. Just the prospect of a few brief moments of gratification can prompt perilous self-indulgence that can have a wholly disproportionate, lasting impact. These are not necessarily the follies of "Type A" personalities, of men undergoing midlife crises, or the lack of judgment manifested by a lonely spinster besotted with a younger lover, but more a compulsion that drives otherwise entirely rational, sensible people to abandon good sense. In politics, the professions and jurisprudence of such instances provide the tabloids with great copy and their readership with voyeuristic confirmation of the universal frailty of the human condition. In the context of classified information, it is sexspionage, and adds an extra dimension to the scandal. In the case of Jack Profumo, the fact that Harold Macmillan's secretary of state for war was seeing a beautiful call girl ensured newspaper headlines. The fact that she was also seeing the Soviet assistant naval attaché turned a resignation issue into a national trauma.

Sexspionage is not a new phenomenon, nor was it restricted to the era of the Cold War. Women could not have engaged in what has been termed the "second oldest profession" without a ready clientele, and it could be argued that Delilah is an early example of a woman exercising her sensual power for an ulterior motive, in her case on behalf of Samson's adversaries. More recently, the Prussian spymaster Wilhelm Stieber sponsored a bordello to acquire information from French officers, and during the American Civil War both sides employed female agents to infiltrate enemy positions, conduct clandestine reconnaissance missions, act as couriers, and seduce vulnerable personnel with a knowledge of future plans.

Arguably the most famous spy of all time, Mata Hari, is credited with having used her considerable womanly wiles to extract vital information from French officers during World War I. One of history's most notorious turncoats, Alfred Redl, was persuaded to pass his country's secrets to the enemy after he had been sexually compromised. Typically, the Nazis almost institutionalized sexspionage by establishing the notorious Salon Kitty in Berlin, a brothel where the clients were blackmailed when they were most disadvantaged. We now know that the head of the German Abwehr, Admiral Wilhelm Canaris, was romantically involved with a glamorous Polish lady, Halina Szymanska, and that during their trysts in Switzerland and Italy he confided Hitler's future plans to her, knowing she would relay them to the Allies.

Apart from his relationship with Madame Szymanska, Canaris had no other direct contact with the Allies, despite speculation to the contrary, and plenty of opportunity to do so. The exercise of influence, of course, can also be a facet of espionage, and during the war some in Washington were uneasy about the extent to which prominent Americans had fallen under a nefarious spell cast by the British. Ambassador John Winant would be entranced by Churchill's daughter Sarah, and

Averell Harriman would have an affair with Pam Digby, then married to Churchill's son, Randolph. Even General Dwight D. Eisenhower took an English mistress, Kay Summersby, even if FDR's son was also in pursuit of her. Although there was no evidence of a sexual conspiracy to entrap unwary Americans and perhaps influence official policy, there were those who put a more sinister interpretation on such illicit liaisons.

In the postwar era, sexspionage was adopted by the Soviets as a method of penetrating diplomatic missions in Moscow. Even before World War II, the NKVD had compromised two American embassy cipher clerks, Tyler Kent and Henry Antheil, by procuring for them beautiful mistresses whose affections were dependent on their acquisition of codes and copies of secret telegrams. As a method of penetrating Western premises, the use of entrapment techniques proved highly effective; Norwegian, Swedish, British, American, French, and Canadian diplomats reported attempts to compromise their staff. At least three ambassadors succumbed to the temptation, and numerous other attachés and more junior envoys were caught in honeytraps and blackmailed. The KGB's Second Chief Directorate (SCD), the branch responsible for monitoring the activities of foreigners in the Soviet Union, even controlled UpDK, the agency that supplied clerical and domestic staff to the foreign missions, and ensured that some of the more attractive employees were assigned to target personalities deemed vulnerable. Thus Sir Geoffrey Harrison began an affair with Galyna, his beguilingly attractive housekeeper; John Vassall was photographed in bed with his athletic homosexual lover; and Maurice Dejean was seduced by his beautiful Russian mistress. As the UpDK maintained sources inside almost every Western mission, it was easy for the SCD to develop profiles of susceptible personalities, prey on the weaknesses of isolated bachelors or lovelorn secretaries, and mount sophisticated schemes to coerce the unwary. The techniques became so sophisticated that sometimes the victims were the last to realize the true nature of their predicament, believing the "kindly uncle" role adopted by some of the more skilled practitioners, who pretended to act as an intermediary, using their supposed influence or negotiating talents to keep the vengeful authorities from exacting the necessary consequences of some supposed infraction of the criminal code. In such circumstances, the wretched victims often went to considerable lengths to protect the very architects of their misfortune. In John Vassall's case, it took him a long time to realize that Nikolai Karpekov was not his protector but truly his tormentor.

At the height of the Cold War, the hazards of conducting business in Moscow or of working there as a diplomat became so great that the British Security Service, MI5, produced *Their Trade Is Treachery*, a document outlining the perils of apparently casual encounters with local women in hotel bars, and the consequences of inviting late-night visitors back to a hotel room that probably was wired for sound and cine. After numerous incidents, MI5 concluded that the best way of alerting travelers to the pitfalls inherent in Eastern bloc countries was a limited distribution of a series of case histories describing the experiences of the unwary. Despite this precaution, some people still found themselves entrapped, but at least upon their return home they knew how to approach the appropriate authorities, and MI5 attempted to turn the discomfort of the victims to the organization's advantage by encouraging them to appear to cooperate with their blackmailers in an effort to identify their contacts and perhaps turn the tables on their adversary by recruiting them. Years later, having failed to make a single successful recruitment through this double-agent ploy, MI5 learned that the KGB's SCD had targeted individuals it had been confident would report their predicament and, through surveillance, spot their MI5 case officers, and then pitch them! To MI5's dismay, it was discovered that not a single member of the counterintelligence teams engaged in these high-risk operations had reported such an approach, suggesting either that the KGB had not followed through on the plan, or more likely that it had been successful and had accomplished its goal.

A definition of sexspionage should include not just the tendency to exploit sexual weakness but also the willingness of spies to engage in espionage to please their partners. The legendary Markus Wolf proved adept at deploying some of his agents to take advantage of lonely West German secretaries, and there are also a few cases of wives participating in their husband's spying, although in the United States the cases are limited to Rosario Ames and the Cuban spies Linda Hernandez and Amarilys Santos, who were arrested in Miami in 1998. In fact, by an analysis of such statistics as exist, gender would seem to play a relatively significant role in collaborative espionage where a husband-and-wife team operates overseas, especially when the KGB sent illegals on missions into the West. In several cases, notably the Sokolovs, Cohens,

Ogorodnikovs, Koechers, and the Tairovs, the decision to send agents in pairs may have been taken in an effort to enhance their chances of success and limit their vulnerability to entrapment or simply reduce the possibility of developing a relationship that might compromise their assignment.

Behavioral scientists relish the opportunity to study aberrant conduct, and counterespionage specialists are particularly attracted to patterns that offer potential clues to breaches of security. Accordingly, this study takes the broadest interpretation of sexspionage to include the impact the fairer sex has made on the arcane arts.

In the pages that follow, we examine some of the cases of sexspionage that have occurred throughout history, look at the organizations responsible for exploiting human frailty, and assess the impact of relationships conducted in an adversarial environment. We also widen the area of scrutiny to cover the role gender plays in counterintelligence, and there is some fascinating evidence concerning the performance of women operating under cover, their involvement in relationships where espionage is a major part of their life, and their historical contribution to clandestine operations. What emerges is a complex picture that ranges at one extreme from the cynical manipulation of the weak, to the other end of the spectrum where loyalty to an individual outweighed patriotism. In between are the often-tragic case histories of people in positions of trust who either betrayed their responsibilities or were themselves hideously betrayed.

The Dictionary

– A –

AGEE, PHILLIP. A **Central Intelligence Agency** (CIA) officer formerly based in Mexico, Agee volunteered his services to the KGB in Mexico City following his divorce and a refusal by the CIA to his request for financial assistance. However, Agee was turned away by a Soviet security officer who did not believe such a scruffy individual could really be an authentic CIA officer. Allegedly, he was also rejected by Colonel Krepkogorsky, a KGB officer in the United States who suspected a provocation. Agee subsequently flew to Cuba where his offer was accepted with alacrity, and he was subsequently handled by Directorate K's Oleg Nichiporenko. Under his guidance, Agee wrote *Inside the Company: A CIA Diary* and contributed to the *Covert Action Information Bulletin*.

While preparing his book in Paris in July 1971, Agee met a wealthy American, good-looking, blonde heiress calling herself Leslie Donegan, who offered to finance his research and supplied him with a portable typewriter that contained an electronic beacon concealed in the lid. At the time, Agee never suspected that his apparently generous sponsor was actually Janet Strickland, a CIA agent whom he encountered four years later when she was employed by the International Labor Organization in Geneva.

Donegan claimed to be a graduate of Boston University, the daughter of a Venezuelan who had married her American father in Caracas, and said she had studied French at Geneva University before reaching Paris, where she had been introduced to Agee in an English pub, the Mayflower. Over dinner a few nights later, she offered to finance his book venture and accepted a copy of the work he had completed. She then offered to pay for a professional typist and gave him the use of

1

her studio apartment on the 20th floor of a modern block near the Plaisance metro station, saying she would be spending the next two months with her boyfriend in Spain. When she returned, she began an affair with Salvatore Ferrera, a freelance American journalist who had befriended Agee and had often expressed an interest in learning his address. Years later, Agee learned that Janet Strickland, whose father had headed Exxon's Latin American Division and then moved to Palm Beach, Florida, had adopted the identity of Leslie Donegan, whom she had known as a school friend in Caracas. He also came to suspect that Salvatore Ferrera, too, had been a CIA agent, part of a large operation to monitor his activities.

The son of a wealthy businessman from Tampa, Florida, Philip Agee studied business administration and then philosophy at Notre Dame University but left law school before graduating. In 1956, he was drafted into the U.S. Army and while undergoing his military training he wrote and volunteered for service with the CIA. His application was accepted in 1957. In 1960, he was sent on his first overseas assignment, under diplomatic cover to Ecuador and then Uruguay, during which he married and had two sons. In 1966, he returned to Washington, D.C., to join the Mexico branch of the Western Hemisphere Division but in the middle of the following year he was sent to Mexico City under Olympic attaché cover, in anticipation of the Olympic Games scheduled for 1968.

In Mexico, Agee began an affair with an American divorcée with strong leftist political sympathies. Under her influence, he resigned from the CIA in the autumn of 1968 but remained in Mexico, working for a local company manufacturing mirrors. In early 1970, more than a year after he had left the agency, Agee went to New York to interest publishers in a book project; nothing materialized, so he enrolled in a university course in Mexico, and the following year traveled to Cuba, on the recommendation of the French publisher Francois Maspero, who had released Che Guevara's diaries. There, he started work on a book that was to be published as *Inside the Company: CIA Diary*. He finished writing it in Paris, under continuous CIA surveillance, but not before he received a warning from the agency's lawyers reminding him of his secrecy agreement, and notification of a federal court judgment against Victor Marchetti, reinforcing the CIA's right to scrutinize and censor anything written by an ex-employee.

Agee's book was published in London in January 1975, coinciding with an article Agee had contributed to *CounterSpy*, a radical magazine founded by Norman Mailer that also produced a list of what it claimed were the names of 100 CIA station chiefs based under cover around the world. From his new home in Cornwall, Agee encouraged journalists to research embassy lists to spot the biographical entries of CIA personnel working under diplomatic cover. In December, Richard Welch, the CIA station chief in Athens who had been mentioned by *CounterSpy* as having served in Lima, was shot dead outside his home.

Undeterred by Welch's murder, Agee planned further revelations but in November 1976, while living in Cambridge, England, he was served with deportation papers and in June the following year he moved to Amsterdam. Soon afterward, he was expelled from France and excluded from West Germany and Holland. In 1977, Agee launched a new periodical, the *Covert Action Information Bulletin*, at a press conference in Cuba, together with a group of supporters that included two disaffected former CIA employees, Jim and Elsie Wilcott. The journal was intended to expose CIA staff and operations; in June 1980, it named the CIA station chief in Kingston, Jamaica, as Richard Kinsman, whose house was promptly the subject of an attack.

The *Bulletin*'s objective was shared by Agee's next publishing venture, an edited compendium of articles entitled *Dirty Work: The CIA in Western Europe*, which included the biographical data of hundreds of purported CIA officers. In 1979, a sequel followed, *Dirty Work II*, concentrating on the CIA's operations in Africa. None of these publications were the subject of criminal prosecution in the United States because, as the U.S. Justice Department confirmed, the CIA could not undergo the usual discovery proceedings associated with a trial. Instead, Agee's U.S. passport was revoked, and he was issued with a Grenadian one by Maurice Bishop, the premier of that tiny Caribbean island, who was himself to be deposed and assassinated by even more extreme radicals. Later, Agee acquired a Nicaraguan passport that he used to maintain his residency in Hamburg, and later to enter Canada and slip back into the United States, before settling in Cuba to run a travel agency. He died in Havana in February 2008.

AGIRAKI, ANNA. The Greek mistress of the chief of the Italian Servicio di Informazione Militar (SIM) in Athens, Anna Agiraki was sent on an espionage mission in August 1942 by boat to Syria because her lover felt she was attracting too much attention from the Italian secret police. She was accompanied by George Liossis and a radio operator but was arrested by the Royal Navy off the Syrian coast. Liossis, a Greek Air Force officer and son of General Liossis, revealed that he had been in contact with the British Secret Intelligence Service before the war and volunteered to work for the British as a double agent. His offer was accepted and he was codenamed QUICKSILVER. Agiraki also agreed to become a double agent and, codenamed GALA, she notionally became a prostitute plying her trade to indiscreet Allied officers who supposedly confided secret plans to her.

Agiraki claimed to receive information from five regular clients: DENZIL, a Royal Air Force technician engaged in preparing plans for Allied airfields to be constructed in Turkey after the country had been occupied in early 1944; PAPADOPOULOS, a dockyard superintendent in Beirut; STEVEN, a liaison officer from the Royal Navy's base at Alexandria; TAKIS, a Greek submariner; and TOLLUS, who really was Brigadier George Tolhurst. The other four sources were entirely notional, and Agiraki remained an active source until October 1944, even though she spent the entire time in prison in Palestine. Of her two companions, only Liossis retained his freedom and would return to Greece with a promotion.

ALBIN, GABRIELE. A German employed as a clerk by the U.S. embassy in Bonn, in 1977 Gabriele Albin was seduced by a Hauptverwaltung Aufkrarung (HVA) **Romeo**, Rudolf Beck alias Frank Dietze, after her marriage to an American solder had failed. Codenamed GERHARD, she was run by the HVA's Colonel Heinz Keller until she entered a psychiatric hospital for treatment in 1980, but she returned to work two years later and was transferred to the Office of Defense Cooperation, where she had access to large quantities of classified information, for which she was paid more than $105,000.

Albin and Beck were arrested in March 1991 but he was killed in his car in a railway-crossing accident soon afterward, leaving his supposed fiancée to be tried alone. In August 1996, she was sentenced to two years' probation.

ALSOP, KENNETH. In 1957, while on a visit to Moscow, the well-known journalist Kenneth Alsop was photographed in bed with a young man and then approached by the KGB. Alsop declared the incident to the American ambassador, who advised him to tell the **Central Intelligence Agency**, and the matter was reported to the Federal Bureau of Investigation. Apparently aware that Alsop had reported the matter, the KGB made no further attempt to contact him. Alsop later pursued a successful career as a BBC television journalist, hosting the early evening news show *Tonight*. He died in Indiana in December 1997, aged 83.

ALVAREZ, CARLOS. In January 2006, 61-year-old Dr. Carlos M. Alvarez and his wife, 55-year-old Elsa Alvarez, were arrested by the Federal Bureau of Investigation (FBI) after a lengthy surveillance operation and charged with espionage on behalf of the Cuban Dirección General de Inteligencia (DGI) at Florida International University (FIU). The Cuban-born couple, codenamed DAVID and DEBORAH, had been recruited by the DGI in 1977 and had visited Cuba several times on educational trips sponsored by FIU's Cuban Research Institute and Cuban Bridges. In reality, Alvarez, an associate professor in the Department of Educational Leadership and Policy Studies since 1974, and his wife, an FIU administrator and counselor since 1999, passed information about the émigré community in south Florida to the DGI in Mexico, South America, and to post office boxes in New York, and confessed to the FBI in June and July 2005. Carlos Alvarez was sentenced to five years' imprisonment in a plea agreement, while his wife received a three-year prison sentence.

AMES, ALDRICH. A senior **Central Intelligence Agency** (CIA) officer arrested in February 1994 and sentenced to life imprisonment, Aldrich Ames approached the KGB in Washington, D.C., in May 1985 and received $50,000 for his information. He established his credentials by revealing that the KGB *rezident*, Stanislav

Androsev, was known internally within the KGB by his codename CRONIN.

When he heard of the arrest of John Walker, he feared his own betrayal was likely and held a further meeting on 13 June to identify all the Federal Bureau of Investigation and CIA assets he knew of inside the KGB. The result was a series of unpublicized arrests in Moscow, secret trials, and a dozen executions.

Fluent in Mandarin and the son of a CIA officer, Rick Ames had joined the CIA in 1967 and had turned in mediocre performances as a directorate of operations (DO) officer in Ankara and Mexico City. Nevertheless, he had participated in some significant cases, including those of the Foreign Ministry spy **Aleksandr Ogorodnik**, and two members of the United Nations, Arkadi Shevchenko and Sergei Fedorenko. He had also participated in a double-agent operation against an East German physicist, Alfred Zehe, then living in Mexico City, who would be arrested in Boston in December 1983 and convicted of espionage in July 1984.

In September 1983, Ames, by now fluent in Russian, was appointed chief of the counterintelligence branch in the Soviet/Eastern Europe (SE) Division, which had given him complete access to the DO's most closely guarded files on its most successful assets. Heavily in debt following his divorce in August 1985 from a fellow CIA officer, Nancy Segebarth, Ames convinced himself that his talents had gone unrecognized. He had married Segebarth in May 1969, after they had trained together and were posted to the same station in Turkey. They separated after 12 years of a childless marriage in 1981 when Ames went to Mexico and his wife remained in New York. Within nine days of obtaining a divorce, Ames married one of his agents, **Rosario**.

The damage caused by the Ames list was immense, and severely compromised AE/TICKLE, Britain's star agent inside the KGB's London *rezidentura*. As a direct consequence of the tip from Ames, Oleg Gordievsky was unexpectedly recalled to Moscow on 17 May 1985, supposedly for urgent top-level consultations three days later, but actually for a lengthy, hostile interrogation that included the use of drugs.

Another lucky escape was made by Sergei Bokhan, the CIA's GRU source in Athens. He had defected at the end of May, a fortnight before Ames delivered his list. Other agents working for the CIA suffered a rather dissimilar experience. Major Sergei M. Motorin and Colonel Valeri F. Martynov, both KGB officers who had been recruited by the FBI in Washington, D.C., were arrested and later executed. Although Ames never acknowledged precisely whom he fingered in his first letter, it is highly likely that he included the names of Motorin, Martynov, and Gordievsky, the KGB trio in the best position to warn the CIA of the existence of a well-placed traitor within its own ranks. As a matter of self-preservation, Ames would have been bound to warn the *rezident* that some of his colleagues were really working for the West. In his list of 13 June, he mentioned Adolf Tolkachev, who had just been arrested and was to be executed, and a group of other Soviet intelligence officers who had been recruited while under diplomatic cover in the United States: Leonid Poleschuk, recruited in Katmandu in the 1970s; a GRU officer, Gennadi Smetanin, and his wife, Svetlana, who had been recruited in 1983; and Gennadi Varenik, the son of a senior KGB officer under TASS cover when he was recruited in March 1985 in Bonn, who was arrested in November and shot in February 1987.

In addition, GT/BACKBEND, GT/GLAZING, GT/TAME, and GT/VEST showed signs that they had come under the KGB's intensive scrutiny, a development that indicated the Soviet/Eastern Europe (SE) Division had suffered a very comprehensive calamity. The scale of the catastrophe was not lost on Burton Gerber or his deputy, Milton Bearden, who instituted a major review of each case so as to establish whether operational blunders were to blame or if there was something altogether more sinister afoot. Gus Hathaway, who had returned from Bonn in January 1985 to run the Counterintelligence Staff, estimated that up to 45 separate cases had been placed in jeopardy. As the losses mounted from May 1985, Hathaway became increasingly convinced that SE had been penetrated at a high level.

The director of central intelligence, Bill Casey, was briefed on the SE Division's losses for the first time in January 1986 by the deputy director for operations (DDO) Clair George, Gerber, Hathaway, and Bearden, and Casey promptly instructed the former DDO, John Stein, who was then the CIA's inspector-general, to conduct an urgent investigation. As Stein reviewed each case, the DO suffered more inexplicable losses. On 10 March Sergei Vorontsov, codenamed

GT/COWL, who had spied since late 1984, was caught, and his CIA contact, Michael Sellers, was detained while on his way to a rendezvous in Moscow and expelled. Also in March, GT/VILLAGE was recalled from the Soviet consulate in Surabaja, Indonesia, and vanished. Two months later, on 7 May, another member of the Moscow station, Erik Sites, was ambushed while attempting to meet GT/EASTBOUND. On 1 July, Vladimir V. Potashov (GT/MEDIAN), an arms control negotiator at the Soviet Institute for the United States and Canada Studies who had spied since 1981, was taken into custody, and three days later Dmitri Polyakov was summoned unexpectedly to the Lubianka and arrested. Soon afterward Colonel Vladimir M. Piguzov (GT/JOGGER), who had been recruited in Djakarta and had been assigned to the KGB's Andropov Institute training academy, dropped from sight. This was an especially mysterious and sinister loss because Piguzov had not been in contact with the CIA since 1979 when he had returned to Moscow, and had proved himself to be an exceptionally useful source by identifying David H. Barnett, a contracted CIA retiree working on a training program, as a turncoat; Barnett had been arrested in April 1980 and sentenced to 18 years' imprisonment.

It was almost as if, having exhausted the current hot cases, someone was rifling the DO's dormant files to find less valuable spies to betray. Almost as confirmation, Boris Yuzhin (GT/TWINE), who had been the TASS correspondent in San Francisco in the 1970s and had returned to Moscow in 1982, was arrested on 23 December 1986. Almost simultaneously Colonel Vladimir M. Vasilev (GT/ACCORD), a GRU officer recruited in Budapest in 1983 who had identified a GRU network in which U.S. Army sergeant Clyde L. Conrad had been active in West Germany, was also caught. Vasilev's loss was significant, for he also enabled the Swedish security police to arrest Conrad's controllers, Dr. Sandor Kercsik and his younger brother Imre, and roll up a large Hungarian military intelligence network headed by a retired warrant officer, Zoltan Szabo. Originally a refugee from Hungary in the 1956 exodus, Szabo had joined the U.S. Army and had been decorated for gallantry in Vietnam. According to his confession, he had been recruited by the Hungarians in 1971 when he took his German wife and children on holiday to Lake Balaton. Although Vasilev had tipped off the CIA to the existence of Szabo's huge Hungarian spy ring in 1985, which extended into Italy, his role had been skillfully concealed, so it was a surprise when he was suddenly taken into the KGB's custody in 1986 and executed the following year. Conrad was allowed his liberty until August 1988 and was sentenced to life imprisonment in June 1990, but Szabo escaped to Budapest.

The damage caused by Ames was long lasting and, in terms of Soviet operations, was easily the worst case of penetration experienced by the CIA, which failed to notice the change in his circumstances following his divorce.

AMES, ROSARIO. The Colombian wife of **Aldrich Ames**, Rosario Casas was sentenced to five years' imprisonment at the end of April 1994, having been convicted on one count of conspiracy to commit espionage.

Maria del Rosario Casas Dupuy came from a politically prominent family in Bogotá where her father had been a government minister and her mother an academic. In October 1982, when she was introduced to her future husband, she was aged 30 and serving as the cultural attaché at the Colombian embassy in Mexico City. She spoke fluent French and Greek, was well traveled, but was somewhat naïve and inexperienced when she was recruited by a **Central Intelligence Agency** (CIA) officer, David Samson, so he could use her apartment as a safe house in which to meet sources. He passed her on to Rick Ames, then attempting to divorce his wife Nan, and they began an illicit relationship that culminated when he invited her to join him in Washington, D.C., in November 1983. They were married in August 1985 and she successfully gave birth to a son, Paul, in November 1988 after a miscarriage.

Although Ames first began supplying the KGB's Viktor Cherkashin with information in April 1985, he did not confide in his wife until August 1992, by which time he had already received some $2 million, money that she had been told had come from a friend in Chicago who supposedly appreciated his investment tips. In a letter in October 1992 addressed to his KGB contacts (recovered from the ribbon of his home printer), he revealed that his wife had adjusted to his news and was very understanding of his covert work for them.

The listening devices installed in the Ames' suburban home in Virginia by Federal Bureau of Investigation (FBI) Special Surveillance

Group personnel in October 1993 revealed numerous incriminating conversations in which the couple discussed signal sites and the other tradecraft associated with his clandestine links to the KGB, and she nagged him about the wisdom of placing large sums of cash in checked luggage when he returned from a rendezvous in Bogotá.

Rosario was arrested at home in February 1994 while her husband's car was stopped a few streets away, and she was taken to an FBI office at Tyson's Corner. Within three hours, she had begun to confess. Although initially the molehunters were suspicious of contacts she was known to have had with KGB agent Sergei Shurygin in Mexico City in 1982, they eventually concluded that she had not been recruited by him. Satisfied with the comprehensive nature of her confession, the charges against her were dropped as part of a plea bargain negotiated with her husband to obtain his cooperation so a full damage assessment could be completed by his former colleagues.

ANDERSEN, HELENE. Arrested in Marseilles in 1944 by the Americans as long-term German agents and members of a stay-behind network, Helene Andersen and her 36-year-old, London-born husband Svend were transferred to Camp 020 for interrogation. She eventually admitted that although her brother was a Royal Air Force pilot, she and Svend had been recruited to spy on their fellow countrymen in May 1940. At that time she had been Svend's mistress and assistant, but they had married in May 1942. Initially reluctant to confess, they were both persuaded to do so and were returned to France for trial.

ANDERSON, HELEN. Codenamed MARY by the Hauptverwaltung Aufkrarung (HVA), Helen Anderson believed that her lover, Dietmar Schumacher, was a peace activist named Olaf. Their relationship lasted for 12 years, and he persuaded her to stay in Germany and obtain a job at a U.S. Army base in West Berlin, where she stole classified NATO documents and passed them to him. She was arrested in March 1992 when Schumacher's HVA controller, Karl-Heinz Michalek, confessed, compromising Schumacher who was revealed as a man with a wife, Margarite, in East Germany, and a son. Because Anderson was able to demonstrate that she had no idea her lover had been a Communist spy, she was sentenced to just two weeks' community service before she settled down in Arbroath, while Schumacher received a suspended prison term of 12 months.

ANDERSON, JACK. In February 1975, the syndicated newspaper columnist Jack Anderson, who had edited the *Washington Merry-Go-Round* page since 1945, revealed that the **Central Intelligence Agency** (CIA) had been maintaining "love nests" in Greenwich Village, New York, where foreign diplomats were lured into **honeytraps**. He offered no evidence of the allegation but it was widely assumed that this claim was one of the items contained in the CIA "family jewels," the list of illegal activities compiled recently by the director of central intelligence, Bill Colby. When Anderson died in July 2004, the Federal Bureau of Investigation attempted to recover his private papers on the grounds that they might compromise national security.

ANTHEIL, HENRY W. Killed on 15 June 1940 when his Estonian airliner was attacked by Soviet fighters while flying from Tallin to Helsinki, Henry Antheil was a cipher clerk at the U.S. embassy who had previously served in Moscow and Berlin. However, when his apartment was cleared by a State Department colleague, dozens of secret telegrams were found, including letters that suggested that Antheil had acquired a girlfriend in Moscow whom he had wanted to bring to Finland. Also recovered were details of codes, notes of combination locks, and other sensitive documents. Other material showed that Antheil had been in correspondence with a Soviet official, Alexander Fomin, an alias adopted by Aleksandr S. Feklisov, a well-known NKVD handler. The suspicions concerning Antheil led to an undercover review of security at the U.S. embassy in Moscow, conducted by Special Agent Louis Beck of the Federal Bureau of Investigation. *See also* KENT, TYLER.

ANTON, NATASHA. The mistress of a former American consul in England named Fellner, in 1942 Natasha Anton acquired another admirer, Luis Calvo, who was an Abwehr spy working as press attaché at the Spanish embassy in London. A well-known journalist who had represented various newspapers in London since 1932, Calvo had been identified by MI5 from ISOS intercepts. He was arrested in February

1942, having been compromised by a double agent codenamed G. W., and he spent the remainder of the war at Camp 020, where he became the prison's librarian. After the war, he was released and later was appointed editor of *ABC*, Madrid's major daily newspaper. During MI5's surveillance on Calvo, it was learned that Natasha Anton was also sleeping with Fellner, who had returned to London as a representative of General Bill Donovan, President Franklin D. Roosevelt's coordinator of intelligence, and soon to be appointed head of the Office of Strategic Services. Although Fellner often boasted of his skills as a counterintelligence expert, he was unaware that his mistress was also seeing a Nazi spy until he received a discreet warning from MI5.

ARTAMONOV, NIKOLAI. In June 1959, Captain Nikolai Artamonov, the commander of a Soviet destroyer in the Baltic, abandoned his wife and family and defected to Sweden in a small boat from Gdansk with his Polish girlfriend, Ewa. In Stockholm, he applied for political asylum in the United States and, having been resettled with the new name Nikolai Shadrin, eventually worked for the Defense Intelligence Agency as a naval analyst while Ewa practiced as a dentist.

In 1966, Artamonov was asked by the Federal Bureau of Investigation (FBI) to act as a double agent if approached by the KGB, and he agreed to do so, traveling twice to Austria to make contact with members of the local *rezidentura* in Vienna. However, in December 1975 he was abducted, drugged, and driven to the Czech border, where it was discovered that he had succumbed to an accidental overdose.

Unaware that her husband had agreed to participate in a high-risk double-agent operation for the principal purpose of enhancing the status of a KGB officer recruited by the FBI, Ewa conducted a lengthy legal campaign to establish the truth about his fate. Eventually information from the defector **Vitali Yurchenko** in August 1985 confirmed that Artamonov had been killed by accident, an account subsequently verified by a KGB retiree, General Oleg Kalugin.

ARVAD, INGA. A devastatingly beautiful Danish blonde, Inga Arvad entered the United States as a student of journalism at Columbia University and worked as a columnist on the Washington *Times-Herald*. It was there she met Kathleen Kennedy, who in December

1941 introduced Arvad, a 28-year-old statuesque divorcée separated from her second husband, the Hungarian film director Paul Fejos, to her brother **John F. Kennedy**, for an interview subsequently published in the newspaper. Although Arvad was four years older than the U.S. Navy ensign, then working in the Office of Naval Intelligence, they began an affair that resulted in an espionage investigation conducted by the Federal Bureau of Investigation (FBI), who suspected Arvad of being a German spy. According to her FBI file, Arvad had interviewed numerous senior Nazis in Germany in 1936 while covering the Olympic Games, including Adolf Hitler, and her apparently easy access to them had led to speculation that she had engaged in espionage. At the Olympics, she had been photographed as a guest in the Fuhrer's private box, she had attended Hermann Göring's wedding, and she had been quoted as saying that Hitler "was not evil as depicted by the enemies of Germany" and was "without doubt an idealist." She had also been the mistress of Axel Wenner-Gren, the Swedish refrigerator tycoon who was Reichmarschal Göring's brother-in-law and the owner of the *Southern Cross*, the yacht formerly owned by Howard Hughes. Arvad had also been heard to boast that Jack Kennedy "has a lot to learn and I'll be happy to teach him."

When scandal about their relationship threatened to engulf him in Washington, D.C., Kennedy was transferred to the 6th Naval District headquarters at Charleston, South Carolina; Arvad followed him and took up residence on the weekends as "Barbara White" in the Fort Sumter Hotel and the Francis Marion Hotel. The FBI installed a microphone in her room and reported that the couple only emerged from their tryst for meals, and that "Kennedy and Mrs. Fejos engaged in sexual intercourse on a number of occasions while she was occupying room 132 at the Fort Sumter Hotel."

Although her torrid affair with Kennedy, who affectionately called her "Inga Binga," was closely monitored by the FBI through a wiretap placed on her Washington apartment telephone, it ended in March 1942 following unfavorable publicity by Walter Winchell in his newspaper column of 12 January 1942, but the couple remained friends for the remainder of the war. The FBI's reports indicated that the couple had occasionally discussed marriage, even though it would have required Arvad to obtain no less than two annulments, and she had raised the possibility of a pregnancy to extract a commitment from Kennedy, who seemed reluctant to rise to the bait.

The FBI's surveillance revealed that she was also having an affair with her old Danish lover Niks Blok and the financier Bernard Baruch, but after her divorce in Reno, Nevada, in June 1942 she moved to California and married Tim McCoy, then a star of cowboy movies. Ultimately, the FBI was unable to prove she had ever been a spy.

AZPILLAGA, FLORENTINO. The unexpected defection in June 1967 of the Cuban Dirección General de Inteligencia (DGI) *rezident* in Prague, Florentino Azpillaga Lombard, to his **Central Intelligence Agency** (CIA) counterpart in Vienna, Jim Olson, provided the CIA with a minor ethical problem when it was realized that his decision to switch sides had been prompted by his love for his underage girlfriend, who had accompanied him to the U.S. embassy. Despite considerable misgivings, Azpillaga's request for immediate political asylum and resettlement was granted because of the value of his information, and in particular his knowledge of the real names of most of the CIA case officers supposedly running agents against the DGI, thereby proving that they were all double agents who had succeeded in compromising the true identities of their handlers.

– B –

BAILLIE-STEWART, NORMAN. A Seaforth Highlander born in 1906, Lieutenant Norman Baillie-Stewart was arrested in March 1933, detained in the Tower of London, and charged with having supplied military secrets to a German contact, a "Herr Obst," during meetings held in Berlin, and with having received banknotes in letters from a woman in Germany named Marie-Louise for the information. Baillie-Stewart denied the charges and insisted that his trips to the Continent had been in pursuit of a 22-year-old unnamed blonde and that the payments had been for "services rendered of an immoral nature." The evidence against him consisted of a few potentially incriminating notes recovered from his regimental quarters at Aldershot, the texts of intercepted letters addressed to his home in Southsea, and the testimony of Lotte Geiller, a young woman he had met while on the train to Heidelberg.

Baillie-Stewart was convicted by a court-martial and sentenced to five years' imprisonment, but after his release in August 1937 he traveled to Berlin, where he took German citizenship and remained for most of the war. While Baillie-Stewart had been in Berlin, his German mistress had stayed in London and, much to MI5's embarrassment, had been detained in 1940 when it was discovered she had joined the Auxiliary Territorial Service.

In May 1945, he was arrested for a second time and he received a further prison sentence for having aided the enemy. Baillie-Stewart had been one of a small band of renegades who had supported the Nazis and either had contributed to anti-British propaganda or had persuaded British detainees to join the Legion of St. George, the Britische Freikorps branch of the Schutzstaffel.

After his release in May 1949, he moved to Dublin, where he adopted a new identity, that of "Patrick Stewart," and wrote a highly personal account of his experiences, *The Officer in the Tower*; he died in June 1966, only a few weeks after he had completed his book. According to his ghostwriter, John Murdoch, "he wanted to absolve his children from the stigma that had haunted him for more than 30 years—the stigma of a 'traitor.'"

BAKER, JOSEPHINE. In 1925, Josephine Baker, then a Broadway star who had made her reputation at the Cotton Club in Harlem, moved to Paris where she was an instant success as a singer, and in 1937 she took French citizenship. Born into a black family in St. Louis in 1906, she used her celebrity on the diplomatic circuit to cultivate unwitting sources in the Italian and Japanese embassies and passed her reports to Jacques Abrey of the Deuxième Bureau. She lived in great style in the Dordogne at the Chateau de Mirandes in Castelnau-Feyrac, where she ran a large household, and was one of the first Frenchwomen to qualify for a private pilot's license.

When the Nazis occupied Paris, Baker moved to Vichy, and in November 1940 was accompanied by Abrey, posing as her dance tutor, to Lisbon, where they delivered information to the British embassy concealed in her sheet music. Later, she would receive permission from the Vichy government to perform in Offenbach's *La Créole* in

Marseilles before moving to Algiers in January 1941. In subsequent months, she was in contact with political leaders and military officers in Marrakech, Agadir, Tunis, and Fez, collecting information that she passed back to Abrey in Lisbon. In early 1942, she fell ill in Casablanca, but when she had recovered she was sent on a mission to Beirut, where she played a role in the arrest of two Nazi spies, Paula Kock and Aglaya Neubacher.

Details of her undercover work for the Free French were eventually disclosed by Abrey in 1949 when he published *The Secret War of Josephine Baker*. Decorated with the Croix de Guerre, the Resistance Medal, and the Cross of Lorraine, Baker died in 1975, having adopted nine children.

BANCROFT, MARY. The mistress of Allen Dulles, the Office of Strategic Services (OSS) representative in Bern during World War II, Mary Bancroft also conducted an affair with one of his principal German sources, Hans Bernd Gisevius, codenamed GEORGE WOOD.

Born in Boston in 1903, Mary Bancroft graduated from South College and married a Swiss accountant. Bancroft was fluent in German and French, and her husband was often absent on business (he was living in Bern when she was recruited by Dulles in December 1942). With the apparent approval of Dulles's wife, Clover, the couple conducted a lengthy affair while she also acted as an intermediary with Gisevius, handling information he had removed from the Gestapo, for whom he worked as a senior official with permission to travel to Switzerland. After the war, Bancroft translated Gisevius's memoirs, and in 1983 wrote *Autobiography of a Spy*. She died in 1997.

BARCZATIS, ELLI. In 1949, two employees of the East German Ministry of Industry, Elli Barczatis (aged 37) and Karl Laurenz (aged 44) became lovers; her career prospered, and she was promoted to be secretary to the prime minister, Otto Grotewöhl, but Laurenz was expelled from the Communist Party for political unreliability. Unable to continue working as a lawyer, Laurenz became a freelance journalist and received information from Barczatis, but in January 1950 they were spotted passing documents surreptitiously and came under the Ministerium für Staatssicherheit (MfS)'s scrutiny. The subsequent investigation lasted five years, but eventually in March 1955 Laurenz was discovered attending a rendezvous in West Berlin with two known Bundesnachrichtndienst (BND) case officers. This was enough to justify the arrest of Barczatis, who was taken from her apartment in Köpenick and interrogated at Hohenschönhausen prison. She and her lover confessed, and in October 1955 they were beheaded in Frankfurt am Oder. Laurenz had insisted that Barczatis had been unaware of his role as a BND spy, but years later it was disclosed that her BND codename had been DAISY. According to her MfS file, Barczatis had been surrounded by informers, among them GRÜNSPAN, who had originally reported her suspicions, and LINA, who had been planted in her office.

BEAMS, DOVIE. Aged 38 when she was introduced to Ferdinand Marcos in Manila in 1968, she claimed to be a 23-year-old Hollywood actress; the president of the Philippines fell for the starlet from Nashville and began an affair that lasted two years. Many of their trysts took place in the presidential mansion in the seaside resort of Baguio. Marcos was one of the financial backers of a biopic starring the tall, leggy, busty blonde, who had recently appeared in the X-rated biker movie *Wild Wheels*, but he was unaware that some of their more passionate encounters had been recorded on tape by her. When he ended their relationship and declined to back the movie any further, Beams responded on 11 November 1970 by calling a press conference to play a selection of the tapes in which stunned journalists listened to Marcos singing her tuneless love songs and begging for oral sex. Having exposed the president, who had been in power for the past five years and would remain in control of the country until February 1986, she fled to Hong Kong, where there was a scuffle as the Philippines' consul-general attempted to prevent her from catching a flight to California. The incident attracted the attention of the local **Central Intelligence Agency** station and the MI5 security liaison officer, and Beams was placed in protective custody until she could be escorted to Los Angeles.

Marcos responded to the embarrassing disclosures by releasing some candid photos of Beams, apparently taken with her consent during their affair, but although his intention had been to discredit his blackmailer, the effect was to undermine his reputation. He would eventually be forced into exile in Hawaii, where he died in September

1989, while Beams, who appeared in the 1973 western *Guns of a Stranger*, married a nightclub owner and was later convicted of participation in an $18 million fraud.

BENTLEY, ELIZABETH. Codenamed CLEVER GIRL and then MYRNA by the NKVD, Elizabeth Bentley was a far-from-glamorous graduate of Vassar who was dubbed by the American tabloids who publicized her defection, and her subsequent evidence before Congress, as "the Red Spy Queen." Her important role as a Soviet agent came about as a result of her love affair with Jacob Rasin, alias Jacob Golos, the NKVD illegal *rezident* in New York.

Originally from Rochester, New York, Elizabeth Bentley joined the Columbia University branch of the **Communist Party of the United States of America** (CPUSA) in March 1935 while completing her master's degree in Italian and French. By then, she had visited Europe three times, studied at the University of Florence on a scholarship, and taken a summer course at the University of Perugia. After her graduation, she worked briefly as a shop assistant at Macy's Department Store, at an Amtorg summer school for Russian children, for the New York City Home Relief Bureau, and on Governor Dewey's election campaign committee. She encountered Jacob Golos in October 1938, having been interviewed at the CPUSA headquarters by Ferruccio Marini, a senior Party functionary who was later to edit the Communist *Unita del Popolo* in Italy. Marini used his Party work name "F. Brown" and prepared Bentley for underground work on behalf of the Comintern against the Fascists by introducing her to Golos. Golos had dispatched his wife Celia, a fellow student at Columbia, and their son Milton to Moscow in the mid-1930s, and since had lived with his mistress, Caroline Klein, in New York.

Bentley later recalled that her lover had been "powerfully built with a large head, very broad shoulders and strong square hands. His eyes were startlingly blue, his hair bright red, and I was intrigued by the fact that his mouth was very much like my mother's." By the time he succumbed to heart failure in November 1943, Golos had trained Bentley as a skillful courier, become her lover, and bequeathed to her the role of controller for a network that was concentrated in Washington, D.C. Among his many agents was Nathan Gregory Silvermaster, a Russian emigrant working in the Farm Security Administration; Silvermaster's wife Helen; and several highly placed subagents, including the assistant secretary of the Treasury, Harry Dexter White; White House counselor Lauchlin Currie; Victor Perlo of the War Production Board; and Major Duncan Lee, an aide to General Donovan of the Office of Strategic Services (OSS). In August 1945 Bentley made a tentative approach to the Federal Bureau of Investigation (FBI) in New Haven, and two months later submitted to a lengthy interrogation and made a statement dated 39 November 1945, naming dozens of her contacts.

Bentley was prompted to switch sides for a variety of motives, not all of which she subsequently set out in her memoirs, *Out of Bondage*, an account of her love for Golos, her enchantment with the CPUSA, and finally her disaffection. Her critics suggested that when Louis Budenz, formerly the editor of the *Daily Worker*, publicly renounced Communism and left the CPUSA, she would have known that it would have been only a matter of time before the FBI called on her, so she took the initiative. Budenz had been close to Golos and had acted as an intermediary between Bentley and an OSS source, Communist novelist Louis Adamic, who acted as an adviser regarding his native Yugoslavia. After Golos died, she had been supervised by Joseph Katz, and he had introduced her in early November 1944 to Anatoli Gorsky, the *rezident* at the Soviet embassy in Washington, D.C., who had taken up his post in September 1944.

Early in 1945 Bentley had been eased out of the NKVD's network and she had resented the loss of her dual role of courier and controller. Whatever her motives, she quickly followed Budenz to the FBI, making her initial tentative approach in New Haven in August 1945, and her value to the bureau was to act as a human encyclopedia, putting names and faces to members of the network. Her disaffection was complete by the time she approached the FBI in New York in October, which initially suggested she try and rejoin the organization by reestablishing contact with Gorsky. The first interview at which the topic of Soviet espionage was raised took place with Special Agent Edward J. Buckley on 7 November 1945, but she suspected that the FBI had been present when she had last met Gorsky, on 17 October. A further meeting took place at Gugganti's restaurant in New York on 21 November 1945, under heavy FBI surveillance, but the wily *rezident* was unwilling to let her return. Frustrated in her attempt to become a double agent, she signed a lengthy statement, covering 113 pages, on 30 November, and was given the FBI codename GREGORY. Eventually she provided the FBI with enough information to fill nearly half a million pages in 175 volumes, and identified more than 80 Soviet espionage suspects, including 27 in the administration.

Bentley died an alcoholic in 1963, unaware that much of her information had been verified by references contained in VENONA decrypts.

BERGER, HELGE. A buxom secretary in the Foreign Ministry of the German Federal Republic, Helge Berger believed that the handsome "Peter Krause" she met in Bonn in 1966 was a South African working for the British Secret Intelligence Service (SIS). He introduced her to his senior officer, who was actually a former Wehrmacht prisoner of war who spoke very fluent English, and he persuaded her to supply her boyfriend with thousands of copies of classified documents over the next six years, until she was arrested and sentenced to four and a half years' imprisonment.

BERIA, LAVRENTI. Born in the west of Georgia and trained as an architect, Lavrenti Beria replaced Nikolai Yezhov in November 1938 as head of the NKVD. Yezhov was eventually arrested and shot in January 1940, enhancing Beria's ruthless reputation that had made him widely feared and disliked. He was known to prowl Moscow in his limousine, grabbing young women off the streets and raping them at his home on Vspolny Pereulok, but his energetic efficiency ensured his immunity from any consequences of his debauchery. Beria's status and his rigid control over the NKVD would be enhanced when he supervised ENORMOZ, the highly successful joint NKVD-GRU operation created to steal the West's atomic secrets, which culminated in the successful detonation of a plutonium bomb in August 1949. Following the death of Josef Stalin in March 1953, Beria attempted to outmaneuver his Kremlin rivals and seize the leadership, but he was arrested in June on Nikita Khrushchev's orders, incarcerated in a secret underground bunker beneath Osipenko Street, and charged with espionage and moral degradation.

An internal NKVD investigation revealed that a senior officer, Colonel Ruben Sarkisov, had kept Beria supplied with women. His index contained the names of 2,000 women ranging from ordinary women to ministers' wives and included 200 victims who were well-known actresses and movie stars. Vardo Maksimilishvili was described as Beria's former secretary and mistress in Georgia who had a 12-year-old child by him. Beria had given her a position in the KGB's Emigré Department and had then had her sent to Paris to work against Georgian émigrés there. Anatoli Vlasov, a former officer of the KGB's Moscow branch, later revealed how he had tried to recruit a well-known Moscow actress as an agent. The woman asked if she might call her friend to ask for his advice. When Vlasov inquired who the friend was, she told him it was Beria. Vlasov hastily explained that there had been a misunderstanding and took his leave of her.

According to **Eugene Ivanov**, one of Beria's victims was Sofia Gorskaya, whom he had abducted while still a child. She had been set up in an apartment in Tverskaya-Yamskaya where he had called on her regularly, even after she had married. Appalled at Beria's persistence, Ivanona committed suicide. When Ivanov learned of the tragedy from a mutual friend, he contemplated denouncing Beria to Stalin's son Vasili but was persuaded against taking such a headstrong and dangerous step.

At his trial in December, the Soviet Supreme Court heard that when he had been searched one of Beria's pockets was found to contain a piece of paper bearing the names of four women he had abducted, raped, and murdered, one of them being just 16 years old. Upon his conviction, on 23 December, he was shot by an execution squad led by his chief guard, General Batissky, but the public announcement made no mention of his role as a rapist and murderer but only of his plotting to spy for the British.

BLAKE, GEORGE. Born George Behar in Holland, Blake received the longest prison sentence ever handed out by a British criminal court, a total of 42 years. However, he served less than six years before making a dramatic escape to the Soviet Union in October 1966.

His father was a Jewish businessman born in Constantinople who had served in the French Foreign Legion during World War I and had subsequently transferred to the British Army during the Mesopotamian campaign. He was decorated with the British Military Cross and the French Croix de Guerre and he also acquired British citizenship, marrying a Dutch wife, Catherine, in London before settling in Rotterdam. Upon his death in April 1934, when young George Behar was 13, the boy went to Egypt to live with his aunt, his father's younger sister, and learned for the first time of his Jewish origins.

In 1939, Blake returned to Holland to complete his education but war intervened and he was interned by the Nazis because of his British citizenship. After a month of detention, Blake was released and he became active in the anti-Nazi resistance, working as a courier delivering messages and helping distribute underground newspapers. After the death of his grandmother in 1942, Blake decided to escape to England to join his mother and sisters, who had already fled, and he made contact with the organizers of a route that guided *passeurs* from Paris to Lyons in the unoccupied zone, and then on to Spain. He crossed the frontier late in 1942 and, after being arrested by the Spanish police, was interned at the notorious Miranda del Ebro camp. He was released two months later, in January 1943, after the intervention of the British embassy in Madrid, and he then completed his journey to England via Gibraltar and a sea voyage aboard the *Empress of Australia*. He underwent the routine four-day screening process at the Royal Victoria Patriotic School at Wandsworth and, once cleared by the security authorities, found his family, who had found a house in the London suburb of Northwood and went to work for the Dutch government-in-exile. After five months of unremittingly dull clerical work in the Dutch Ministry of Economic Affairs, Blake anglicized his name by deed poll, together with his mother and two sisters, and in October 1943 joined the Royal Navy.

For the next year, Blake underwent an officers' training course and had a spell at sea aboard the cruiser *Diomede* but his naval career was to be short-lived. Assigned to submarine training, it was discovered that he had a medical condition that made him unsuitable for work underwater, and his name was passed to the Secret Intelligence Service (SIS); in August 1944 he enrolled as a member SIS's Dutch Section, where he was to escort agents as a conducting officer from one training school to another and process reports from SIS's networks in Holland. This was mainly office work in SIS's headquarters in

Broadway Buildings, where he was in close proximity to three very attractive secretaries who, he recalled, "were decidedly upper class and belonged to the higher strata of the establishment. There were among them daughters of Tory MPs and ministers, of bishops, of a Viceroy of India, of court dignitaries and some were even related to the Royal Family. . . . They were mostly pretty, some very beautiful, but inclined to be vague and incompetent in varying degrees, though to this there could be exceptions. They were pleasant to work with and helped create a cheerful, friendly atmosphere in the office. I was a beneficiary of this as I spent most of my time there."

Three of those who worked very closely with Blake were Diana Legh, Guinevere Grant, and the Honorable Iris Peake. Diana's father was Colonel the Honorable Sir Piers Legh, then Master of the King's Household, while Guinevere's father was Sir Alfred Grant, the twelfth to succeed to a Scottish baronetcy that had been created in 1688. Iris was the daughter of the Right Honorable Osbert Peake MP, a Tory minister later to be ennobled Viscount Ingleby. Blake quickly became infatuated with Iris Peake, and was embittered when her father told him one evening after dinner at their mansion in Yorkshire that there was no chance of his ever marrying his daughter. This incident would have a lasting impact on the younger man.

After the liberation, Blake stayed in SIS and opted for a Russian-language course at Downing College, Cambridge, following which he was posted to Seoul in October 1948. Eighteen months later, as the North Koreans unexpectedly invaded, the remaining employees of the British consulate-general, including Blake, were taken into custody, and for the next three years he was a prisoner.

In the autumn of 1951, he asked one of his guards to convey a message to the Soviet embassy in Pyongyang, and in due course, some six weeks later, he was interviewed by "a big burly man of about forty or forty-five with a pale complexion. What was remarkable about him was that he was completely bald, so that he looked very much like the film actor Erich von Stroheim." Blake made his pitch to "von Stroheim" and recalls that "he never told me his name, but many years later I learned that, at that time, he had been the head of the KGB in the Maritime Province." This initial encounter was followed by many more over the coming months, and Blake noticed that "while we were talking a young fair Russian with pleasant open features came in" who was "introduced as the man who would interview my companions."

Blake returned to London in March 1953, having been released by the North Koreans, determined to work for the KGB. His contact was to be Nikolai B. Korovin, the KGB *rezident* who had been operating under diplomatic cover in London since 1949. Korcvin was to stay in London until 1954, but returned from Moscow in 1956. In January 1961, he made a hasty departure following the arrest of **Harry Houghton**. Blake's initial meeting with Korovin had been in the customs building at Otpor, the frontier crossing point on the Trans-Siberian railway between Peking and Moscow. "He was a thick-set man of middle height aged about 50" says Blake. "He spoke English well but with a marked Slav accent." They arranged to meet again in The Hague in July 1953 and thereafter they met early in October outside Belsize Park tube station at seven in the evening "every month or three weeks." Blake recalled,

> I cannot say that Korovin was the kind of man who naturally evoked very warm feelings in me. There was too much of the iron fist in the velvet glove about him for that, but I had a great admiration for his skill.... Even though he was known to MI5 to be the KGB *rezident* in Great Britain and constantly followed by a highly experienced surveillance team, equipped with fast cars and modern radio communications, he always managed to get rid of his tail and meet me, punctually at the appointed time and appointed place. He once told me how it was done. In order to meet me at seven o'clock in the evening, he left his house at eight o'clock in the morning and was on the move all day. The operation involved several people and cars and a few safehouses. It was difficult and time-consuming, but it worked every time.

Blake revealed to Korovin in October 1953 that he had resumed working for SIS the previous month, and joined a section in which Gillian Allan, whom he would marry in October 1954, worked as a junior secretary.

Early in January 1955 Blake was transferred from what was essentially an eavesdropping post to the SIS station in Berlin. Here the KGB assigned him a new case officer, a man he knew only as Dick. "He was a thick-set man of about 50 with a pale complexion and a friendly twinkle in his eyes behind thick, horn-rimmed spectacles."

For nearly the next five years Blake held regular meetings with this man, handing over SIS's secrets on each occasion. Blake remained in Germany until he was posted back to London in the summer of 1959 when he resumed contact with Korovin, and another KGB officer whom he knew only as Vassili. He says that when Korovin "was away . . . his place was taken by a younger man called Vassili who differed from Korovin in that he had a much more cheerful disposition and looked typically English so that if he didn't open his mouth nobody would have dreamt of taking him for a foreigner."

In September 1960 Blake moved to Lebanon, where he started to learn Arabic on a Foreign Office language course at Shemlan, in the hills outside Beirut, and it was from here that he received a summons back to London at the end of March 1961. As soon as he reported as instructed to SIS's Personnel Department on Tuesday, 4 April, he was escorted across St. James's Park to an SIS office in Carlton Gardens for interrogation. There he was confronted by a panel of four SIS officers who conducted a series of interviews that lasted until Thursday evening. The four were Harold Shergold, a colleague from Germany; John Quine, the former head of station in Tokyo and now head of SIS's counterintelligence section designated R5; Terence Lecky, another veteran of the German stations who had recently ended a two-year tour in Zurich; and an ex-policeman named Johnson. Together, the four men took Blake through his career and confronted him with the mounting evidence that he had compromised virtually every operation he had been given access to.

According to Blake, he withstood the mounting pressure until Thursday afternoon when he was accused of having sold out to the KGB for money and of then having been the victim of blackmail. Blake says he was outraged at this suggestion and momentarily lost control, indignantly protesting that his collaboration with the Soviets had been ideologically motivated. The other version is that Blake successfully resisted the growing weight of evidence against him until Thursday lunchtime when, as usual, the participants broke for a midday meal. On the previous two days, Blake had been allowed to wander unaccompanied through the West End and eat alone in a restaurant. However, on this occasion he lost his nerve and decided to seek advice from his Soviet contact. He had an emergency telephone number for Korovin and a code word to summon help, but at the very last moment, after he had approached and then circled a telephone kiosk, he decided against making the call. Upon his return to Carlton Gardens, he had been informed that his every move had been watched, and his interrogators demanded to know whom he had been thinking of telephoning. Not realizing that he had been under surveillance, Blake panicked and confessed he had contemplated asking the Soviets to rescue him.

Blake spent the weekend with his colleagues at a country cottage while a decision was reached about what action should be taken, and on Monday, 10 April, he was arrested by two Special Branch detectives. His trial lasted just one day, on 3 May 1961, because he pleaded guilty to the charges, and he was sentenced to a total of 42 years' imprisonment.

After Blake's appeal had been rejected, he was visited again by Terence Lecky, representing his old service, and Tony Henley, MI5's principal interrogator, and he reconstructed each of the meetings he had held with the KGB and identified his three case officers, including Nikolai Korovin and Vassili S. Dozhdalev, a first secretary. The third turned out to be Sergei A. Kondrashev, first secretary at the Soviet embassy since 1955. The KGB defector Anatoli Golitsyn identified "Nikolai Korovin," the case officer who had met Blake on the Sino-Russian frontier, as General Nikolai Rodin, a skilled case officer who had been appointed *rezident* in 1949 in succession to Konstantin Kukin, who had held the post since 1943.

In October 1966 Blake escaped from Wormwood Scrubs prison with the help of a group of political activists and was smuggled to East Berlin, where he was reunited with Vassili Dozhdalev and escorted to Moscow, where he now lives. Although some of his former colleagues believe that he was originally motivated to betray his adopted country because of what he had interpreted to be Osbert Peake's anti-Semitism and his love for Iris, Blake insists he underwent an ideological conversion while in Korea. *See also* GOLENIEWSKI, MICHAL.

BLITS, HELENA. Arrested by the Americans in Montmartre, Paris, in 1944 as a suspected enemy agent, Helena Blits was interrogated at Camp 020, where she admitted having been the mistress of an Abwehr officer named von Poppel and having had a child by another

German agent, Fosseux. In her confession, Blits claimed that she had been recruited as a German spy under pressure because she was Jewish but had attempted suicide by gassing herself. According to her version, she had also tried to kill von Poppel by taking him to bed and leaving the bathroom gas tap on, but they had both awakened two days later, feeling very ill but suffering no lasting ill effects.

Blits was known as a member of the criminal underworld, reportedly had an illegitimate child in Lyons, and had a police record for extortion. Blits cooperated with her captors and identified several members of the Paris Abwehr, and in due course was returned to custody in France.

BLOCH, FELIX H. On 22 June 1989, Bloch, formerly the deputy chief of mission at the U.S. embassy in Vienna and currently director of regional economic and political affairs in the European bureau, received an early morning telephone call at his apartment in Washington, D.C., from "Ferdinand Paul" who warned him that Pierre was ill and that "a contagious disease is suspected." Thereafter, Reino Gikman, a suspected Soviet illegal masquerading as a Finnish businessman who had come under surveillance by the **Central Intelligence Agency** (CIA) and called himself "Pierre," disappeared from Austria. The Federal Bureau of Investigation (FBI) concluded that their investigation into a high-level leak from the State Department had been compromised. Gikman's relationship with Bloch had been under the FBI's scrutiny since 28 April 1989, following a tip from the CIA. Soon afterward, in May, he was identified in Paris by the French Direction de la Surveillance du Territoire as the person to whom Bloch twice handed over a briefcase. When Bloch returned to his home in Washington, D.C., his calls were monitored, and he received the somewhat transparent warning within five weeks of the FBI initiating its investigation.

Under interrogation by the FBI the same day as he received the warning call, Bloch explained his visits to Paris and Brussels as opportunities to buy stamps for his collection and to spend time with his girlfriend, Tina Jirousek, a woman he had met through the escort section of the Vienna telephone directory's yellow pages. Until this moment the FBI had no idea of her existence, and when the blonde was interviewed she revealed a bizarre relationship with Bloch over seven years in which he had paid her an estimated $70,000 to participate in sadomasochism and bondage rituals on Saturday mornings when he had told his wife he was working at his office. Neither the prostitute nor his wife Lucille had any idea that he had been engaged in espionage, and Bloch claimed that he hardly knew Gikman, who had introduced himself as a French stamp collector named Pierre Bart. According to Jirousek and Bloch, they had never engaged in sexual intercourse, and for the duration of the relationship she depended upon Bloch exclusively for her income. At the initial FBI interview, conducted by a rather overweight Hispanic special agent, Bloch denied having received an early morning telephone call, and when caught in the lie admitted to having passed information he had described as "sensitive" to the Soviets since 1976. Bloch subsequently was interrogated at length but he made no further admissions.

The son of Jewish parents in Vienna, Bloch had been taken to New York in 1939 at the age of four and, having graduated from the University of Pennsylvania, had met his American wife, Lucille Stephenson, while they were both studying in Bologna, Italy. They married in 1959, after Bloch had joined the State Department, and they had been posted to Dusseldorf. Two years later, they were transferred to Caracas, and upon their return to the United States, Bloch earned a master's degree at Berkeley. In 1977, he was sent to the embassy in Singapore and then, in 1980, to Vienna where he was to remain until 1987 when he was recalled to Washington, D.C., following disagreements with his ambassador, John Lauder, a political appointee.

Between 1980 and 1987, Bloch was the senior diplomat at the American Embassy in Vienna and had access to the very highest classifications of State Department telegrams. The molehunt, which had initially focused on Gikman, revealed that Bloch's sexual proclivities might have attracted the attention of the Hauptverwaltung Aufkrarung in 1974 when he was posted to East Berlin, after four years in West Berlin. According to KGB defector Vasili Mitrokhin, Bloch had been recruited while serving in Singapore.

In December 1990, after 30 years in the Foreign Service, Bloch was fired and denied a pension. He later moved to Chapel Hill, North Carolina, where he was twice convicted of shoplifting, was divorced by his wife, finally found work as a bus driver, and remarried. His application to regain Austrian citizenship was turned down. At various times, Bloch's wife and his two daughters were questioned and placed under surveillance as potential coconspirators, although there was never any evidence to implicate them. Indeed, they became convinced that Bloch had been the victim of some elaborate CIA operation masterminded by George Weisz, the CIA chief of base in West Berlin in 1975 who subsequently committed suicide.

Although Bloch was dismissed from the State Department and deprived of his federal pension, the case was to have wide ramifications, not least because it convinced the FBI and the CIA that there had been a high-level leak that had compromised the investigation at a very early stage. Ironically, the senior CIA counterintelligence officer, Brian Kelley, who had initiated and supervised the CIA's surveillance of Gikman, himself became the subject of a secret molehunt. The FBI's failure to bring the investigation to a successful conclusion was later blamed in part on **Robert Hanssen**'s interference and his apparent reluctant intervention on behalf of a spy for whom he seemed to have had contempt, describing him, in Yiddish, as "a schmuck," although an internal FBI postmortem suggested there had been a series of systemic failures, one of which had been a reluctance to plan the initial interview at which Bloch had made his only admissions. It had been thought that, psychologically, men of Bloch's background, erudition, fitness, and almost Prussian bearing would be more likely to respond positively to someone of similar background and class, but nobody in the FBI had been willing to replace the Hispanic special agent who happened to "have the [interview] ticket," for fear of being accused of racism. In those circumstances, Bloch had been able to recover his composure and maintain his silence.

BLUNT, ANTHONY. Recruited by the NKVD at the end of 1936 on the recommendation of **Guy Burgess** and while still working as a tutor at Trinity College, Anthony Blunt did not have any direct access to classified information until he was commissioned into the Intelligence Corps in 1940. When he attended a military intelligence training course at Mytchett Place and Minley Manor in Aldershot, he took notes of everything he saw and passed them to his contact, Anatoli Gorsky, codenamed VADIM, who worked at the Soviet embassy in London under diplomatic cover under the alias "Gromov." In 1942,

Gorsky was replaced by Boris Kreshin, codenamed MAX. Codenamed TONY, Blunt never joined the **Communist Party of Great Britain** (CPGB), although he nearly accepted an invitation to do so. During his five years inside MI5, Blunt proved adept at running men and women as agents, among them his boyfriend **Jack Hewit**, whom he deployed against a **homosexual** Roman Catholic priest, Father Clement Russell, formerly a member of the **British Union of Fascists** and a suspected by MI5 of being a subversive. Among Blunt's other agents were Susan Maxwell, an MP's widow whose boyfriend, Knut Wijk, worked in the Swedish embassy; Lady Dalrymple-Champneys, who was close to the Egyptian ambassador; and Miss Foster Hall, who was the Turkish military attaché's secretary. He also deployed another homosexual friend, Peter Pollock, against suspect Hungarians, and recommended Brian Howard as an MI5 officer.

In April 1964, when he confessed to MI5 that he had been a Soviet mole, Blunt acknowledged that he had acted as a "talent-spotter" to recommend suitable recruits, had used his homosexual contacts to acquire secrets, and that one of his sources had been Tom Wylie, a civil servant who was the resident clerk at the War Office. Wylie had supplied Blunt with material useful to his Russian contacts but had probably been unaware that his lover was passing it on. The breadth of Blunt's homosexual contacts, many of whom had been employed in intelligence units during World War II and subsequently went on to important posts in Whitehall and elsewhere, led MI5 to conduct lengthy investigations into his relationships dating back to his schooldays. One affair at Cambridge, with **Michael Straight**, resulted in Straight's claim that he had been recruited as a Soviet spy by Blunt. This assertion, combined with the threat to confront him with Straight, persuaded Blunt to confess in return for an immunity from prosecution offered by the attorney general.

Blunt's MI5 interrogators were never entirely convinced that he had honored his commitment to make a full confession and cooperate in return for immunity from prosecution, and gained the impression that he had never incriminated anyone MI5 had not already suspected. He only admitted to having talent-spotted Straight and two other card-carrying CPGB members, Leo Long and John Cairncross, although the latter was actually approached by Burgess, leaving

Cairncross unaware of Blunt's role. Few others knew of Blunt's espionage, apart from **Litzi Friedman** and **Kim Philby**, **Edith Suschitsky**, Bob Stewart of the CPGB, Brian Simon, and the academic Goronwy Rees, although some of Blunt's acquaintances, such as Dennis Proctor, unwittingly assisted him by providing references of his good character.

In his lengthy but friendly interrogations conducted by MI5's Peter Wright, Blunt admitted having passed hundreds of MI5 documents to the NKVD; betrayed the identity of a Secret Intelligence Service mole, **Tom Driberg**, in the Kremlin as an MI5 informant inside the CPGB; and compromised every clandestine operation he ever gained access to.

Exposed in a Parliamentary statement made by Prime Minister Margaret Thatcher in November 1979, Blunt was stripped of his knighthood and died in March 1983. The beneficiary of his will, his long-term boyfriend John Gaskin, committed suicide in Dundee in July 1998 by throwing himself in front of a train.

BOBAREV, EVGENNI. A KGB officer based at the *rezidentura* in Ottawa, Evgenni Bobarev was the target of a **honeytrap** operation planned by the Royal Canadian Mounted Police (RCMP), who "dangled" a beautiful model who had been fully briefed at cocktail parties held on the embassy circuit. Bobarev appeared to fall for the woman and for three months conducted an illicit affair with her. However, just as the RCMP intended to close the trap and threaten to expose Bobarev's philandering to his wife, Bobarev unexpectedly returned to Moscow. Although a leak was suspected, the RCMP later established that the KGB had been tipped off by a mole, Gilles Brunet, who would be dismissed, still undetected, in December 1973.

BOND, JAMES. Sexual entrapment is a constant theme in Ian Fleming's books, and in his first Bond novel, *Casino Royale*, 007 is betrayed by a subordinate, Vesper Lynd, who had been coerced into spying for the Soviets because of her love for a Polish pilot who has been imprisoned while on a mission. A similar plot appears in *The Property of a Lady*, in which an SIS clerk is compromised in "some unattractive sexual business" and forced into becoming a Soviet spy.

In *Live and Let Die*, Bond rescues Solitaire, a beautiful white Haitian who had been a nightclub telepathy act before she joined Mr. Big, an important Soviet spy. In *From Russia with Love*, Bond is given an assignment to travel to Istanbul to receive a glamorous defector who is to steal a Spektor cipher machine from the local Soviet consulate's code room. When Bond and the defector begin an affair, they are filmed in his hotel bedroom by a hidden camera, a classic **honeytrap** technique prevalent during the Cold War when the book was written and the movie was made.

In *Goldfinger*, Bond encounters Jill Masterton helping her employer, SMERSH's treasurer, to cheat at cards, and he then helps her sister revenge her murder. In *Thunderball*, it is Dominetta Vitali who conspires against her lover, Emilio Largo, who has stolen a pair of nuclear weapons, and in *On Her Majesty's Secret Service* 007 marries Teresa di Vicenzo, the daughter of the chief of the Union Corse. In *The Spy Who Loved Me*, 007 encounters a student working as a motel manager terrorized by thugs, and in *Diamonds Are Forever* a glamorous smuggler has become involved with a ruthless criminal gang. Thus in most, but not all, of the Bond books, there is a significant female interest, thereby ensuring that 007's name would forever be closely associated with beautiful women, often with unusual, suggestive names, such as Honeychile Ryder, Pussy Galore, Kissy Suzuki, and Mary Goodnight. In fact, the only stories in which there is not a girl for Bond are *A Quantum of Solace*, a tale of marital infidelity in Bermuda, and *Octopussy*, where the plot centers on a corrupt former British intelligence officer.

Ian Fleming wrote a total of 12 books and nine short stories describing 007's adventures. As a former wartime naval intelligence officer and well-connected journalist, he filled the pages with information that was not always fiction, and certainly contained considerable sexual material, some of which was considered controversial at the time of publication. For example, in *Casino Royale* he referred to "the sweet tang of rape," and in most of his stories Fleming inextricably linked sex and espionage. He also took the opportunity to discuss **homosexuality** in *From Russia with Love*, and refers to various contemporary cases of sexual blackmail, making oblique references to **John Vassall** and **George Blake**.

Fleming died in August 1964 before the genre achieved unequalled box-office success as a movie series, beginning with *Doctor No* in 1962, but the film series served to enhance Bond's reputation as the epitome of dashing English style and cold ruthlessness mixed with a degree of misogyny and some sadomasochism.

BOSSARD, FRANK. Betrayed in 1965 to the Federal Bureau of Investigation (FBI) by Nikolai Chertov, a Soviet GRU officer based in New York, Frank Bossard was a British expert on guided missiles who was arrested and sentenced in May 1965 to 21 years' imprisonment.

Born in 1912, Bossard's career in the Royal Air Force prospered during World War II in the Middle East, despite a conviction for embezzlement in 1934. He was commissioned and developed an expertise in radar, taking up a teaching post at the Air Service College on the Hamble in 1946.

Confronted in the Ivanhoe Hotel in London in March 1965 with evidence of his lunchtime espionage, photographing documents he had removed temporarily from his office in the Ministry of Civil Aviation, Bossard confessed that he had found himself in financial difficulties while in Germany as an intelligence officer interviewing Eastern bloc refugees for the Joint Intelligence Bureau. He had been given a large entertainment allowance to assist his work but he had spent much of it on prostitutes. Married to a woman half his age, Bossard had fallen into debt; when he was approached by the Soviets in London, after he had been transferred to the Ministry of Civil Aviation in 1961, he began selling classified information. According to his confession, Bossard would listen to Radio Moscow for coded instructions on which of three dead drops in rural Surrey to fill, and would be paid for each delivery. His hobby, as a collector of rare coins, provided a cover for his illicit income, but his espionage was brought to a halt by the FBI source codenamed NICNAC, and he died in prison in 1978.

BOURNONVILLE, EVA DE. In November 1915, the Postal Censorship Department (PCD) in London detected letters containing secret writing, addressed overseas, and the correspondence was traced to a hotel in Upper Bedford Row. The author was traced by placing a supposedly indiscreet military officer in the premises and waiting for information he had mentioned to various residents to appear in the letters. This led to the identification of a Swedish visitor, Eva de Bournonville. She was arrested when her handwriting was found to match the suspect mail and was interviewed by **Basil Thomson**, to whom she gave a confession, admitting that after her arrival in England in October 1915 she had applied, unsuccessfully, for a job in the PCD but had been turned down because her referees had hardly known her. She was tried at the Old Bailey in January 1916 and sentenced to death, but was reprieved and then deported to Sweden in February 1922.

Nine years later, a former German spy, Jules Silber, revealed in his 1931 memoirs, *Invisible Weapons*, that he had penetrated the Postal Censorship Department, where he had been employed between October 1914 and June 1919. Significantly, Silber described how he had volunteered his services to the Germans by writing to one of the addresses on the PCD's Suspects Index and had begun to send them highly secret information. The German intelligence service, initially cautious of this unknown source, had decided to send an agent, Eva de Bournonville, to London to join the PCD and establish the self-appointed spy's bona fides. When the PCD intercepted her letters, Silber learned about them and attempted to warn the Germans, but his message arrived too late to save the woman. Fortunately for him, she never mentioned the true purpose of her mission when she was interrogated by Thomson.

BOURSICOT, BERNARD. A French diplomatic service officer, Bernard Boursicot was identified by a Chinese defector, Yu Zhensan, as the victim of a bizarre **honeytrap** in Beijing, where he had been posted to the French embassy in 1964 at the age of 20 as an accountant. Boursicot had formed a relationship with an actor, Shi Pei Pu, a male impersonator who later claimed to have borne him a child. Shi Pei Pu said the baby boy, Bertrand, had been sent to live with relatives in the north so as to avoid persecution during the Cultural Revolution. To maintain the illicit relationship, Boursicot was persuaded to bring embassy papers to Shi Pei Pu's home, where they were copied by Ministry of State Security officials. He was eventually introduced to the child in 1973 while on a visit to China, having resigned from the Foreign Service the previous year.

In 1975, Boursicot rejoined the Foreign Service and was posted to the consulate in New Orleans, and then was transferred to the French embassy in Ulan Bator, where he resumed his espionage so he could continue his affair with Shi Pei Pu. Eventually he brought both his lover and child to Paris in 1983 and Shi Pei Pu found work as an opera singer.

When Zhensan identified Boursicot, he was placed under observation by the Direction de la Surveillance du Territoire, and found to be living with his son and the actress who actually turned out to be a man. Under interrogation he admitted that the child had been bought from a family of Uighurs, a tribe from northeast China with Caucasian features. Boursicot, whose strange story was to become the subject of the book *Liaison*, a play *M. Butterfly*, and a movie, was sentenced in May 1986 to six years' imprisonment, but was released after having served four years.

BOWEN, ANN-CHRISTINE. In 1968, a secretary in the British Ministry of Defense, Ann-Christine Bowen, the daughter of an army officer, was posted to NATO headquarters in Brussels where, two years later, she met **Rainer Rupp**, a Hauptverwaltung Aufkrarung (HVA) agent. Rupp revealed his true role, indoctrinated her into his politics, and persuaded her to remove classified documents from her office and bring them home overnight so he could photograph them. The couple was married in 1972 and within five years Rupp had joined NATO's International Economics Division and had gained further access to secret material. After their third child was born, Ann-Christine became disenchanted with espionage and, following the Soviet invasion of Afghanistan in December 1979, thought she had convinced her husband to break contact with his HVA controllers, but in fact he continued to spy, in return for $1,500 a month.

The Rupps were arrested in July 1993 after researchers working in the old East German HVA archives, using a cryptographic key bought by the Central Intelligence Agency from General Rolf-Peter Devaux, discovered clues to two spies codenamed TOPAZ and TURQUOISE. In 1993, Rupp was sentenced to 12 years' imprisonment for treason, and his wife to 22 months, suspended.

BOYD, BELLE. A spy for the confederacy, Belle Boyd collected information about Union troops based in and near her home in Martinsburg, West Virginia, in July 1861 and passed it to General T. J. "Stonewall" Jackson. When she was 19 years old, she was captured aboard a rebel ship and escorted to Boston by a Union officer, Lieutenant Hardinge, who promptly fell in love with her and arranged for her release. They were married in London in August 1864 but two years later he died, and Boyd returned to the United States as an actress. She later recalled her adventures in her autobiography, *Belle Boyd in Camp and Prison*. She would marry again twice, and succumbed to a heart attack in Wisconsin Dells, Wisconsin, in 1900.

BRA CAMERA. Among the more ingenious surveillance equipment created during the Cold War was a silent, miniature camera concealed inside a specially designed East German brassiere, and used by Staatsicherheit (Stasi) personnel to take clandestine photographs. The bra contained a Soviet-made F-21 Ammer spring-driven camera that was cradled in the bottom of the bra while the lens was positioned centrally, between the cups. Almost completely undetectable, the device could take up to 20 pictures and be worn with a summer dress with the shutter controlled by a remote release held in a pocket. Codenamed WEISE ("meadow"), the bra was perfected by a group of four Stasi women in the province of Suhl, fabricated by some of the Stasi's 42 disguise experts at the Operativ-Technischer Sektor, and then distributed to other surveillance units.

BRANDT, HILDA. According to Kurt Singer, the author of *Women Spies*, there was a mysterious German Communist named Hilda Brandt who had been a member of his underground cell at Kiel University and had played a key role in persuading Klaus Fuchs to become a Soviet spy, passing atomic secrets to the NKVD. When persecuted by the Nazis they spent three months together in the same room, with only Hilda occasionally venturing out for groceries, before they made their escape to England as refugees. She would later return to Europe to act first as a courier for the Comintern in France and Denmark, and then as an espionage organizer in Poland, Czechoslovakia, Germany, and Scandinavia, while her lover remained in England, working in the Physics Department of Bristol University before joining Birmingham University and then the Manhattan Project.

At the end of World War II, Hilda apparently met Fuchs again in London for a single night together, but after his arrest on espionage charges in 1950 he made no mention of her in his confession. Despite Kurt Singer's detailed account of Hilda Brandt's participation in Fuchs's espionage, there is no evidence that she ever existed.

BREWER, ELEANOR. The wife of Sam Pope Brewer, the *New York Times* correspondent in Lebanon, Eleanor had an affair with **Kim Philby**, whom she met and fell for in September 1956 while he was living at his father's house in Ajaltouin, a mountain village outside Beirut. According to her memoirs, *The Spy I Loved*, "by the summer of 1957 we were deeply in love," and they planned to marry as soon as she could obtain a divorce in Mexico, which she achieved in July 1958. Coincidentally, Philby's wife Aileen, the mother of five of his six children, died suddenly at their home in Sussex in December 1957. This left Eleanor and Kim free to marry, and they did so in London in January 1959.

Born in Seattle and a graduate of Washington University, Eleanor was working for the advertising agency J. Walter Thompson in San Francisco when the war broke out. She was posted to Istanbul for the Office of War Information and married her first husband in Rome in 1948 before accompanying him to posts in Madrid, New York, and Rio de Janeiro before his assignment to Beirut in 1956.

Unaware that Philby was a Soviet spy, Eleanor was taken by surprise when he suddenly disappeared one evening in January 1963 from their fifth-floor apartment on rue Kantara. She heard from him 10 days later, on 4 February, and then again a week later she received a letter postmarked in Syria. Finally, at the end of May, she flew to London, and when in September she was instructed to visit the Soviet embassy she learned of the arrangements for her flight to Moscow at the end of the month, where she was reunited with Philby.

Eleanor remained in Moscow with Kim for the next nine months, but in May 1964 she returned to the United States to see her daughter and renew her passport. However, when in November she was able to rejoin him, she suspected he was having an affair with

Melinda Maclean, and once he eventually admitted this, she left Moscow, in May 1965, for the last time.

BRIK, YEVGENNI. Codenamed HARP by the KGB and GIDEON by the Royal Canadian Mounted Police (RCMP) Security Service, Yevgenni Brik was born in New York, the son of an Amtorg employee. Trained as a KGB illegal, Brik was sent to Canada under the alias David Soboloff and opened a photographic shop in Montreal. However, he fell in love with the wife of a Canadian soldier, and she persuaded him to surrender to the RCMP in Ottawa. Reluctantly he agreed to become a double agent and the very same evening held a rendezvous with his KGB contact, Ostrovsky. In fact, Brik was never an enthusiastic double agent and simply wanted to live quietly with his girlfriend and her two children.

When betrayed by Gilles Brunet, a Soviet mole inside the RCMP, Brik was recalled to Moscow, where arrangements were made for him to be handled by British Secret Intelligence Service (SIS) case officers. A rendezvous was arranged, but when Brik turned up accompanied by a woman, contrary to instructions, it was presumed he had come under KGB control. He was not seen again until 1992 when, having been released from prison, he had reached Riga and made contact with the RCMP. SIS then arranged for Brik's exfiltration and resettlement in Ottawa.

BRISCOE, NORA. A lifelong fascist who had been widowed in 1932 and had sent her son to be brought up and educated in Germany in 1936, Nora Briscoe was arrested in March 1941 with **Mollie Hiscox** while she was working as a temporary typist in the Ministry of Supply. A member of the Right Club, she was convicted in June 1941 at the Old Bailey of having removed official documents from her office, and was sentenced to five years' imprisonment.

BRITISH UNION OF FASCISTS (BUF). Created in October 1932 under the leadership of a former Labour Member of Parliament Sir Oswald ("Tom") Mosley, the BUF mimicked the German Nazis and was strongly suspected of acting as a Fifth Column, advocating a National Socialist coup in Great Britain. The British government ordered MI5 and the Metropolitan Police Special Branch to keep a watch on the movement in December 1933, and after April 1934 penetration operations were mounted to ascertain the organization's membership and its links to Italy and Germany. The BUF's own director of intelligence, the publisher W. E. D. ("Bill") Allen, was one of several high-level sources supplying information to MI5's **Max Knight**, who also received reports from Mosley's long-serving assistant, Margaret Monk.

An estimated 25 percent of the BUF's membership was women, and MI5 employed both genders to identify its plans, leadership, and local branches. The BUF never revealed its full strength, and was estimated in 1936 to have a following of around 4,000, although Mosley claimed half a million. His almost hypnotic charm attracted many women supporters, and after his wife Cynthia died in May 1933, he was free to conduct affairs with her younger sister Alexandra ("Baba"), then married to Major "Fruity" Metcalfe; his stepmother-in-law, Grace Curzon; and then in 1939 to marry his mistress, Diana Mitford, who, until her divorce in 1933, had been married to Lord Moyne's son Bryan Guinness. Mitford's younger sister Unity became a friend of Adolf Hitler's and, having moved to Munich, stayed with him at the Berghof in May 1939.

The complexities of the family and sexual connections between members of the BUF, with the Mitfords being Winston Churchill's cousins, made the task of monitoring its activities and its involvement in espionage politically sensitive. After his detention in 1940, Mosley denied any connection with Hitler or Benito Mussolini although MI5 had secret evidence suggesting the BUF had been funded by both. He also called for the BUF to remain loyal to the Crown after the declaration of war, yet some of his followers, including **Nora Briscoe** and **Mollie Hiscox**, subsequently were convicted of breaches of the Defence Regulations. Other fascist sympathizers, such as **Anna Wolkoff**, were also imprisoned, suspected of having passed information to the enemy. However, although BUF membership was sufficient to disqualify individuals from joining the armed services, many did succeed in fighting the enemy with great distinction and gallantry.

BRONX. The MI5 codename for Elvira de la Fuentes, the daughter of the Peruvian ambassador in Vichy who briefly had been married to a man named Chaudoir. Because of her father's diplomatic status, de la Fuentes was able to travel widely across France during the first half of World War II and acted as a courier for the Secret Intelligence Service. However, in 1942 she was recruited while on vacation in the South of France by an Abwehr officer, and when she reported this in London in October 1942 she was transferred to MI5's care. Her case officer, Christopher Harmer, assigned her the codename BRONX after the gin-based cocktail she invariably drank at their meetings in the Hyde Park Hotel. Although BRONX was actually a lesbian, she reported in letters containing secret writing that she had developed some top-level contacts by playing bridge—among them Lord Louis Mountbatten and Lady Diana Cooper—and that she was often pursued by inebriated, indiscreet staff officers. In fact, the text of her letters was prepared by her handler, Hugh Astor, and she remained in contact with the Abwehr until May 1945, having participated in the deception scheme intended to promote the area around Bordeaux as a likely target for the D-Day assault.

BUCAR, ANNABELLE. Employed at General Walter Bedell-Smith's U.S. embassy in Moscow in 1947, Annabelle Bucar fell for Konstantin Lapshin, a singer at the Moscow Operetta, unaware that he was working for Colonel Gleb Strokov, of the NKVD's **Second Chief Directorate** (SCD). When offered the opportunity for a secret marriage, sponsored by Lapshin's uncle, Bucar accepted and subsequently refused to return to the United States. In 1952, she was persuaded by the NKVD to write a book, *The Truth about American Diplomats*, critical of American foreign policy, that gave an account of what she claimed was life at the embassy. According to Bedell-Smith, who recalled the episode in his 1950 memoirs *My Three Years in Moscow*, Lapshin "courted almost every unattached young foreign woman in Moscow."

Coincidentally, the prewar NKVD defector Alexander Orlov wrote a play, *American Girl*, in 1960 about a successful KGB operation against a woman employee of the U.S. embassy in Moscow who refused to return to the United States and stayed on in Moscow. In the play, the American girl was named Helen Lee and her lover, Yermolov, was described as a singer from the Bolshoi Theater, and the operation against Lee had been run by two NKVD colonels and one

NKVD general. One of the KGB colonels was named in the play as Nikolai Ivanov. Actually, one of the NKVD officers who really had participated in the operation was Colonel Boris Ivanov of the SCD's American Department, who had been supervised by Generals Raykhman and Pitovranov.

The parallel between Orlov's play and the real incident was extremely close, even extending to the last name of Ivanov. In reality, Boris Ivanov was later appointed *rezident* in New York. No explanation was ever obtained from Orlov before his death in 1973 about the parallel between his play and Annabelle Bucar's experience.

BUDBERG, MOURA. Born in the Ukraine, the third and youngest daughter of Count Ignary Platonovich Zakrevski, and married for the second time to Baron Budberg, a czarist diplomat who would be assassinated at his palatial home, Yendel, in Estonia, Moura became the mistress of Robert Bruce Lockhart and then Maxim Gorky, for whom he worked as his secretary. When Bruce Lockhart, the British government's official British agent, was arrested and held as a hostage by the Bolsheviks, rumors abounded that he had been betrayed by Moura.

Educated privately in St. Petersburg and Newnham College, Cambridge, Moura married Count Johann Benckendorff, a junior diplomat at the Russian embassy in Berlin in 1911. When war broke out, her husband joined the army while she returned to St. Petersburg to become a hospital nurse. There she met Bruce Lockhart in 1918, as he described in his memoirs, *British Agent*. An accomplished linguist, she was also a talented musician and played the accordion.

After the 1917 revolution in Moscow, Moura attempted to reach Estonia but instead was arrested and, accused of espionage, was imprisoned but was saved by Gorky's intervention. She later settled in London, where she became H. G. Wells's mistress, and she returned to Estonia and the Soviet Union regularly. As she was able to travel to Moscow without a visa, her access raised many suspicions about her, and she was rumored to have visited Josef Stalin and to have accompanied him to Gorky's funeral. She worked as a translator for authors, also as a literary agent, and was employed by film producer Alexander Korda. As a hostess in prewar London, she entertained writers and politicians, among them George Bernard Shaw, Duff

Cooper, and Anthony Eden. However, her apparent contact with the Soviet Union and with the ambassador in London, Ivan Masiky, made her suspect, and her friend Klop Ustinov submitted reports to MI5 concerning her activities. In 1951, following the defection of her friend **Guy Burgess**, she identified Anthony Blunt to Klop as a member of the **Communist Party of Great Britain**. Her precise role and her relationship with Moscow remained a mystery when she died in November 1974.

Her MI5 file reveals that she had been the subject of surveillance almost continuously since 1922, although Ernest Boyce of the Secret Intelligence Service (SIS) had occasionally vouched for her when she had encountered difficulties in traveling to England. MI5 found her friendships with such known Soviet agents as the publisher James MacGibbon and the scientist J. B. S. Haldane hard to understand, but concluded that she was merely an adventuress and a natural intriguer. Indeed, when in 1940 she was dismissed from the Joint Broadcasting Committee, an SIS front organization, she joined another Soviet spy, André Labarthe, as an assistant on his journal, *La France Libré*, and meddled in Free French politics. Her mischief in undermining General Charles de Gaulle in favor of Admiral Emile Muselier prompted Desmond Morton, Winston Churchill's intelligence adviser, to ask Sir David Petrie, MI5's director-general, whether she should not be warned about her behavior. Despite numerous investigations, MI5 concluded that she was probably not a Soviet spy, although plenty were willing to believe she was, including Rebecca West, who had also been H. G. Wells's mistress and had submitted several reports to MI5 about her.

BURGESS, GUY. A Soviet spy recruited at the end of 1934 to spy for the NKVD by his friend **Kim Philby**, Guy Burgess was a predatory, promiscuous **homosexual** who exploited a network of contacts originally cultivated at Cambridge to acquire sensitive political information for the Soviets. Employed as a BBC radio producer for *The Week at Westminster* and other programs, Burgess, codenamed MADCHEN ("maiden"), was ideally placed to introduce himself to a wide range of possible sources, and at least two were his lovers. One, Edouard Pfeiffer, whom Burgess traveled to Paris to see, was close to the French premier Edouard Daladier, and the other was a Swiss journalist, **Eric Kessler**, whom he would recruit for MI5 when he was appointed to a diplomatic post in the Swiss embassy in London upon the outbreak of war. Among those Burgess recommended to the BBC as good interviewees were J. B. S. Haldane, later identified as a GRU spy, the Marxist historian Christopher Hill, **Tom Driberg**, and **Anthony Blunt**.

Burgess, whose younger brother Nigel was a career MI5 officer, never concealed his sexual preferences and when in May 1951 he defected to Moscow, accompanied by Donald Maclean, he had not come under suspicion as a spy. However, after he fled to Russia, a lengthy MI5 investigation revealed an extensive gallery of homosexuals whose careers were compromised, and among them was the diplomat Sir Fred Warner, a future ambassador to Tokyo. According to Blunt, Burgess propositioned anyone he met whom he admired, either for sex or espionage, leaving the molehunters with much to research. One suspect, Sir Dennis Proctor, remarked while being interviewed by MI5's Peter Wright that there had been no need for Burgess to recruit him as he had kept no secrets from him.

In 1950, Burgess, having served as private secretary to the Foreign Office minister of state, Hector McNeil, was transferred to Washington, D.C., under a final warning for his erratic behavior about which there had been numerous complaints. In Washington, he lodged in Kim Philby's basement at 4100 Nebraska Avenue, but when in 1951 he learned that MI5 was closing in on Donald Maclean, he engineered his recall to London at the end of April by being stopped three times in one day for driving offenses in Virginia while driving, accompanied by a hitchhiker, to a conference in South Carolina. His withdrawal to London, arriving on the *Queen Mary* on 7 May, was an ideal pretext for a meeting with Maclean, at which they arranged his escape.

According to Peter Wright, Anthony Blunt told him that Guy Burgess had been asked by his KGB controllers to conduct an affair with Clarissa Churchill, who was later to marry Anthony Eden. Apparently Burgess found this was one Soviet request with which he could not comply.

Burgess led a melancholy life in Russia, mainly because of Soviet disapproval of homosexuality, although he did acquire a boyfriend, Tolya, but reportedly he did travel to Beijing to participate in the entrapment of a Western diplomat in a **honeytrap**. He died in 1963 and had his ashes scattered at his mother's home in Hampshire.

BURTON, RICHARD. Famous for having used his astonishing linguistic skills to translate the *Kama Sutra of Vatsyayana* and the equally erotic *The Perfumed Garden*, Richard Burton was a British intelligence officer and Oxford graduate. Born in Torquay in 1821, his father was an army officer in poor health who traveled widely to find an ideal environment for his retirement. Thus by the time Burton went up to university to read classics, he was already fluent in French, German, Spanish, Italian, Portuguese, and Greek. Later he would master 35 languages and have a knowledge of a further 60 dialects.

Employed by the East India Company in Sind, Burton was fluent in many languages and explored the subcontinent, often in disguise, and collected information about rebel tribes and dissident natives. His report, compiled for General Sir Charles Napier, on the use of **homosexual** brothels by British troops in Karachi caused a scandal, and he later joined the consular service, serving in Damascus, but his account in 1858 of having posed as a Muslim pilgrim to penetrate the holy cities of Mecca and Medina established his reputation as an adventurer. Knighted in 1887, he died in 1890, whereupon his widow destroyed his diaries and manuscripts.

– C –

CADET, MADAME. A married secretary working for the financial attaché at the Vichy French consulate in New York in 1941, Madame Cadet fell in love with an agent employed by British Security Coordination (BSC) and was persuaded to pass him copies of confidential telegrams. When she was transferred to the Vichy French embassy in Washington, D.C., her lover went too, as did one of her friends who was appointed secretary to the ambassador, Gaston Henry-Haye, who also agreed to supply BSC with documents from her office.

CAMBRIDGE FIVE. While **Kim Philby**, Donald Maclean, and John Cairncross were emphatically heterosexual, **Anthony Blunt** and **Guy**

Burgess were active and predatory **homosexuals**, and both exploited the weakness of individuals in their circle who shared their proclivities. While a lecturer at Cambridge, Blunt engaged in an affair with **Michael Straight** and later recruited him as a spy for the Soviets. He also used his lover **Jack Hewit** as an agent provocateur against homosexual security suspects, and as a lure to distract diplomatic couriers while their dispatch cases were opened and the contents copied. Similarly, Guy Burgess became involved with **Eric Kessler**, the prewar press attaché at the Swiss embassy in London, and although he believed he was supplying information to MI5, much of it was also being passed to the NKVD. *See also* BREWER, ELEANOR.

CARRÉ, MATHILDE. Formerly a French Army nurse, Mathilde Carré became the mistress in 1940 in Paris of a Polish Air Force officer, Roman Garby-Czerniawski, who headed a resistance organization codenamed INTERALLIÉ. In October 1940, Garby-Czerniawski was invited to London to confer with the British Secret Intelligence Service (SIS) and the Polish commander-in-chief, General Wladislaw Sikorski, but in his absence Carré had quarreled with the network's chief radio operator, Gane. Cutting short his visit, Garby-Czerniawski parachuted back "blind" into the Loire Valley and, upon his return to Paris learned that on 3 November the Abwehr in Cherbourg had arrested Raoul Kiffer, one of INTERALLIÉ's principal subagents. Under duress, the former French Air Force NCO had implicated one of Garby-Czerniawski's assistants, Bernard Krutki. When both men were left alone in an interrogation room in the Abwehr's headquarters in the Hotel Edouard VII on the Avenue de l'Opera, their conversation was recorded and Krutki unwittingly disclosed Garby-Czerniawski's address in St. Germain-en-Laye.

Within three days of arresting Garby-Czerniawski, on 17 November 1941, his entire network had been rounded up and Mathilde Carré swiftly transferred her allegiances to the Abwehr and became the mistress of Sergeant Hugo Bleicher, one of the Abwehr's most successful and imaginative investigators. It was his idea, now in the possession of four of INTERALLIÉ's transmitters, to resume contact with London to report the arrest of Garby-Czerniawski and Carré's intention to take over the network. None of the Polish wireless operators would collaborate, but Carré told her captors of a Frenchman,

Henri Tabet, who had previously left INTERALLIÉ after a disagreement. Under duress, Tabet agreed to send a signal, carefully enciphered by Carré. The transmission was duly acknowledged and there then followed three months of a sophisticated radio game that gave the Abwehr a unique insight into SIS's activities. Unfortunately, it also led to the elimination of the main circuit, AUTOGIRO, run by **Special Operations Executive** (SOE).

On 24 October AUTOGIRO experienced the loss of its wireless operator, Georges Begué, who was arrested when he called at a compromised address in Marseilles. This left the circuit with only one operator, Georges Bloch, who had been dropped on 6–7 September. He too was arrested, by police equipped with direction-finders in Le Mans on about 13 November, which meant that Pierre de Vomecourt was without any means of communicating with London. Undeterred, he searched Paris for another radio and just after Christmas was introduced to Mathilde Carré, who revealed her link with London and offered to service AUTOGIRO.

Fatally, SIS in London agreed to accept AUTOGIRO's messages via INTERALLIÉ, and thereby doubled the Germans' knowledge of the resistance structure. The message was sent via the Canadian Legation in Vichy, and this persuaded de Vomecourt that Carré could be trusted. Accordingly he channeled all his communications through her, which meant that her Abwehr lover, Hugo Bleicher, was reading every item.

After nearly two months of working with Mathilde Carré, de Vomecourt eventually realized that all was not well and challenged her with being in contact with the enemy. He had noticed a strange delay in her transmissions and had been suspicious about the arrest of a courier. Also, she had seemed to be able to obtain German travel stamps for documents without much difficulty. Upon being confronted, Carré admitted her liaison with the Abwehr, which placed de Vomecourt in considerable difficulty. He had no other method of warning London that both AUTOGIRO and INTERALLIÉ had been compromised, and he could neither simply disappear nor take any overt steps to warn the rest of his circuit. Indeed, he had just been sent another agent, Jack Fincken, as an assistant. Nor did he explain to London that INTERALLIÉ's link was being used by the Abwehr to supply misleading information, including some false intelligence about the *Scharnhorst*, *Gneisenau*, and the *Prinz Eugen*, which were able to escape from Brest and return up the channel to Germany unscathed. Instead, de Vomecourt persuaded Carré to switch sides again and operate as a triple agent. It was an extraordinary gamble, but it did lead the Germans to endorse a bold plan: de Vomecourt would be allowed to return to London with Carré, where she proposed to work for the Abwehr; he would later return to France with a British general. Thus, on 12–13 February, an SIS fast motor gunboat attempted to collect Carré and de Vomecourt from a beach in Brittany. It failed to pick up the two agents but it did deliver another F-Section pair, Claude Redding and his wireless operator, G. W. Abbott. Both were quickly arrested, together with their Royal Navy escort, Sublieutenant Ivan Black.

A more successful pickup was fixed for 26–27 February and on this occasion de Vomecourt and Carré were taken to Dartmouth, where de Vomecourt promptly revealed Carré's duplicity and the fate of INTERALLIÉ. He was given a warm welcome in London and was received by General Sir Alan Brooke, Anthony Eden, and Lord Selborne, but Carré was interrogated by MI5, SIS, and SOE before being imprisoned, first at Holloway and then Aylesbury.

De Vomecourt's intention had been to return to France with Carré, but once his version of events had been confirmed he was allowed to parachute back alone on 1 April. He landed on his brother's estate near Limoges and proceeded to Paris where Roger Cottin had been running AUTOGIRO in his absence. And in order to buy time from Bleicher, who had been expecting Carré accompanied by a notional British general, the Abwehr was told via its INTERALLIÉ wireless that de Vomecourt had been delayed in London but would be back by the next full moon. Isolated from this dangerous radio link and without a wireless operator, de Vomecourt was obliged to communicate with F Section by courier via Virginia Hall, an American journalist working for the *New York Post* who ran a safe house in Lyons. Despite the handicap of having a wooden leg, Virginia Hall was a highly successful F-Section agent and later a senior officer in the CIA's Latin America division.

Authorizing de Vomecourt, who was himself thoroughly compromised and known to the Abwehr, to work with Virginia Hall seems an extraordinary risk to have taken. Once her courier was caught and

Bleicher realized that de Vomecourt had slipped back into France, AUTOGIRO was doomed. Cottin, who had been kept under constant German surveillance, was arrested immediately and soon afterward Leon Walters, the Belgian in whose flat de Vomecourt was staying, was taken in for questioning. On 25 April, Bleicher caught up with de Vomecourt in a café while he was meeting Jack Fincken; Noel Burdeyron, who had represented AUTOGIRO in Normandy since the previous July, was next, and then the Comte du Puy. Last of all was Christopher Burney, another F-Section agent who was dropped near Le Mans on 31 May with instructions to contact AUTOGIRO's man in Caen and then work for Burdeyron. He was eventually arrested on 1 August, by which time Virginia Hall had learned of the roundup and alerted London.

The AUTOGIRO debacle led to the arrest of Abbott, Redding, Black, Cotten, Burdeyron, Wolters, Fincken, and de Vomecourt. Altogether 15 members of AUTOGIRO were arrested, as well as de Vomecourt's brothers Philippe and Jean. Only the latter did not survive the war. Seven of its members, including Pierre de Vomecourt, were liberated from Colditz at the end of the war, together with the "prominente" hostages. When Hugo Bleicher was interrogated by MI5 after the war, he claimed that de Vomecourt had betrayed his entire network in return for favorable treatment. In the meantime, Carré, known as La Chatte, was deported to Paris, sentenced to death for collaboration, and then reprieved.

CASEMENT, SIR ROGER. Born in Dublin of Ulster parents, Casement joined the British Consular Service and in August 1902, after five years in West Africa, was dispatched to the Congo to investigate reports of atrocious conditions there. Casement found that slavery, mutilation, and torture were daily events in the landlocked Belgian colony and in January 1906 he presented the Foreign Secretary, Lord Lansdowne, with a comprehensive dossier of institutionalized abuse of the 20 million native inhabitants tolerated by the Belgian authorities. The eyewitness report caused a political furor in Europe; Casement took some well-earned leave and was then appointed British consul in the Brazilian port of Para.

While based in Para, Casement was sent on a second mission, this time to the Putumayo district of the Amazon basin where, according to allegations made in Barbados, British subjects recruited to work on the rubber plantations had been ill treated. According to Casement's report, which he submitted to Lord Lansdowne's successor, Sir Edward Grey, the claims made about conditions in Putumayo were entirely accurate, and in June 1911 the author was rewarded with a knighthood.

The following year Casement retired in poor health to Ireland and became active in the nationalist cause, encouraging the Irish Volunteers and distributing anti-British propaganda in America, where he was reported to have held meetings with the German ambassador. When war broke out, he traveled to Berlin in an attempt to negotiate German help to raise a nationalist army to drive the British from Ireland, and arrangements were made in London for his arrest on a charge of treason.

Casement's effort to raise an Irish army from the prisoner-of-war camps in Germany failed, so he returned to Ireland with the intention of starting a rebellion himself. However, the movements of the submarine that carried him across the North Sea from Wilhelmshaven were monitored by British Naval Intelligence and preparations were made for his arrival with two companions in County Kerry, in April 1916. Casement was arrested and at his trial the following month he was found guilty of treason and sentenced to hang. There was a considerable outcry against the death penalty, but the protests were silenced by publication of Casement's very explicit diaries that showed him to be an active **homosexual**. Although some who regarded Casement as a martyr denounced the document as a politically inspired forgery, forensic tests conducted on pages held by the National Library in Dublin and the Home Office in London as recently as 1993 indicate that the five notorious *Black Diaries* were authentic, a fact never disputed by Casement himself, who was led to the scaffold at Pentonville on 3 August 1916. In April 1994, all the documents were released to the Public Record Office at Kew, and their authenticity was confirmed.

The extent to which Casement's homosexuality influenced his political judgment and his actions remains debatable, but it may be that what was perceived as a private vice may have given him a sense of social exclusion that encouraged him to take an almost self-destructive path. Certainly the way in which his sexual proclivities were exploited helped ensure that the death sentence was not commuted, but it may also be the case that his treason was borne out of a resentment toward a British establishment and government that made his preferences unlawful.

CAVELL, EDITH. During the retreat to the Marne after the battle of Mons in August 1914, many Allied troops were cut off by the Germans and made their way to Brussels where an English nurse, Edith Cavell, hid them before arranging an escape route to neutral Holland. One French evader, Gaston Quien, returned to Cavell's hospital in 1915, claiming to have been sent on a secret mission. At the time the nurse, by now a Red Cross matron, was sheltering 35 Allied soldiers with the help of a colleague, Phillipe Baucq, at the Berkendael Institute and she confided in Quien. Soon afterward, at the end of July 1915, Baucq and his sister Elizabeth Wilkins were arrested by the German *feldgendarmerie*, and Cavell was taken into custody six days later, on 5 August, by Captain Otto Mayer, who persuaded her to confess to a charge of espionage in return for guaranteeing the lives of the Allied soldiers. Although she was interrogated in French, the document she signed as a confession was a translation, written in German, and implicated a Belgian, Herman Capiau. She and Baucq were executed on 12 October 1915, creating worldwide revulsion and protests and a great propaganda opportunity for the British, which was exploited fully.

Cavell's execution outraged international public opinion because although she had admitted to espionage, her profession was portrayed as placing her above such considerations, and her gender should also have given her a measure of protection. The German cause suffered lasting damage from what was perceived as an atrocity and an affront to civilized behavior, and the British naturally took full advantage of the incident. However, by doing so the British effectively put women into a unique category, ensuring they would receive very different treatment in the future. Thereafter, no woman convicted of espionage in Britain would suffer the death penalty, and there would be great unease when, after World War II, it would be revealed that women had been sent on clandestine missions into enemy-occupied territory.

CENTRAL INTELLIGENCE AGENCY (CIA). Although a presidential decision directive, made by President Gerald Ford, prohibits the Central Intelligence Agency from planning the assassination of foreign leaders, and the CIA has made a public commitment not to recruit current members of the Peace Corps, the clergy, or American journalists, there are no restrictions on how the agency recruits its human sources, leaving sexual entrapment an option. However, during the course of the Cold War there were no examples of Soviet personnel being coerced into espionage by the CIA, and Burton Gerber, who served as the Soviet/Eastern European Division's chief, has declared that if the issue had arisen he would have vetoed any attempt to achieve recruitment through coercion. In fact, the CIA occasionally assisted Soviet personnel who had found themselves financially embarrassed as a result of a sexual indiscretion, as happened in the cases of **Aleksandr Ogorodnik** and **Yuri Nosenko**. In both examples, the CIA was able to provide funds to assist the individual out of his predicament, thereby earning his gratitude.

CHAMBERS, WHITTAKER. The defection of Soviet spy Whittaker Chambers from the Communist Party of the United States of America (CPUSA) in 1937 went virtually unnoticed for two years until he began to make allegations of espionage against his former contacts and named them. Then working as a *Time* journalist, Chambers denounced Harry Dexter White, Victor Perlo, and **Alger Hiss** in evidence given to Congress in August 1948 as active Soviet agents, and when Hiss denied the assertion under oath he was later prosecuted and convicted of perjury. At his trial in May 1949, Hiss claimed only to have known Chambers as a freelance journalist under the alias "George Crossley" and insisted he had not seen him since July 1935. However, Chambers was able to recover 65 State Department documents entrusted to him by Hiss in 1938, and three rolls of exposed film containing copies of more official papers bearing notes in Hiss's handwriting, which proved that Hiss had lied.

Under cross-examination, and in an attempt to destroy Chambers's credibility, Hiss's defense lawyers accused the defector as being a liar, a thief with a history of stealing from the New York Public Library, a pornographer, and a predatory **homosexual**. The issue of Chambers's sexual proclivities became central to the case, and the jury failed to reach a verdict in July 1949. At a retrial in January 1950, Hiss was convicted of perjury and sentenced to five years' imprisonment.

Chambers died in July 1961, unaware that his allegations of espionage against Alger Hiss and his wife Priscilla had been substantiated by a VENONA decrypt that identified Hiss as a GRU source codenamed ALES. Independent support for Chambers also came from another defector, **Elizabeth Bentley**, and from a former CPUSA activist Nathaniel Weyl. Eventually the Federal Bureau of Investigation would receive more evidence in an anonymous letter from a well-informed source who turned out to be Victor Perlo's ex-wife Katherine.

CHATEAU-THIERRY, DUCHESSE DE. Shortly before World War II, Sonia, the Duchesse de Chateau-Thierry, a Dutch lady of Jewish extraction, established a fashionable salon in London and began holding soirees for prominent members of society. MI5 would learn that the duchess had been assisted by a maid, My Erikson, and a Danish adventurer, **Vera Schalburg**. The latter left England before the outbreak of war but returned in September 1940 to reestablish contact with the duchess.

Under interrogation, Vera Schalburg revealed that the duchess's activities in London had been sponsored by a certain Dr. Rantzau of Hamburg, later identified as an Abwehr officer, Nikolaus Ritter. She had been assisted by a Dr. Henry, or Dr. Heinrich, and gradually the entire network was placed under surveillance by MI5. Among those questioned were a squadron leader, Philip de Froberville, and a man named Mackenzie who had been Schalburg's lover. One suspect, named Karlinski, was never traced, but MI5 concluded that the salon had been intended as a cover for a major German espionage organization in London but had not been activated because of a shortage of funds. There was also some evidence that the Abwehr intended to launch a similar operation in the United States, although that plan was abandoned.

CHAVEZ, JUDY. Following the defection of Arkadi Shevchenko in April 1978, the Federal Bureau of Investigation (FBI) supervised his resettlement in Alexandria, Virginia, but was unprepared for his need for female companionship. The FBI special agents responsible for his care resorted to looking in the telephone directory for an escort service, and hired a 22-year-old Georgetown call girl, Judy Chavez, to act as Shevchenko's companion. At the time, having abandoned his wife, son, and daughter, the defector was at a low ebb and he developed a close bond with Chavez, who became his partner and confidante, traveling with him to Hawaii on vacation and meeting his obvious emotional and physical needs, both of which reached a crisis point when he learned that his wife had died in mysterious circumstances following her recall to Moscow. Ultimately his relationship with Chavez faltered, and she then published an account of her experience in *Defector's Mistress*. In 1978, Shevchenko married his lawyer, Elaine, and they remained together until his death in 1998.

CHULKOV, PAVEL. The deputy chief of the British section of the KGB **Second Chief Directorate**'s Tourist Department, Pavel Chulkov was subordinate to the notorious General **Oleg Gribanov**, who hatched a plot to ensnare a British businessman staying at the Hotel Metropole in Moscow in a classic **honeytrap** involving a local prostitute. A video camera had been installed in a room to record the encounter but the Briton failed to show up. In his absence, Chulkov got drunk and, forgetting about the special equipment, spent the night with the woman. The next morning, realizing that his indiscretion had been recorded, he shot himself.

CISSEY, GENERAL DE. Having been taken prisoner during the Franco-Prussian War in 1871, General de Cissey was confined in a comfortable villa in Hamburg, where he was befriended by the beautiful Baroness de Kaulla. Four years after his release, when he was appointed the French minister for war, General de Cissey was reacquainted with the baroness in Paris, unaware that she was employed by the famous Prussian spymaster **Wilhelm Stieber**. When it was explained to him that his mistress was an enemy agent, de Cissey discreetly withdrew from the relationship and a scandal was avoided.

COHEN, LEONTINA. Of Polish origin and brought up in New York as a Roman Catholic, Lona Petka was an enthusiastic member of the **Communist Party of the United States of America** (CPUSA) when in July 1937, aged 24, she met a fellow radical, Morris Cohen, at a Madison Square Garden rally shortly before he traveled to fight with the Abraham Lincoln Battalion in the Spanish Civil War.

Morris, who had won an athletics scholarship to Mississippi State College to play football and whose immigrant parents had run a grocery store in the Bronx, graduated from the University of Illinois in social studies. After working as a substitute teacher, he had taken a temporary job at the Soviet pavilion of the 1939 World's Fair held in New York and had moved from there to Amtorg to work in the staff canteen.

When Petka met Cohen again, in early 1940, he had returned home as a wounded veteran and a graduate of the NKVD espionage training school in Barcelona. She was then working as a nanny in Manhattan, looking after Alan Winston, a member of the wealthy diamond family. Cohen was attracted to her and saw her each week on her day off, but he omitted to disclose what he did when he was not working in the Amtorg cafeteria, which was undertaking secret missions for his Soviet contacts. Much to his family's disapproval, she quickly moved in with Cohen, and his family came to believe that she had virtually entrapped him with her sex appeal. However, soon after their marriage in July 1941, which his family refused to attend, he revealed his role as a Soviet spy and explained that his NKVD contacts wanted her to participate too. Initially reluctant to get involved, accusing her new husband of treason, Lona overcame her scruples when he insisted he had betrayed nobody, and certainly not his political beliefs, and reportedly persuaded a sympathizer to steal a new cannon from an aircraft factory and pass it on to the Soviets. During World War II, while her husband served abroad for two years as a cook with the Quartermaster Corps in Europe, Lona worked in a munitions plant and acted as a courier for NKVD, codenamed LESLIE, collecting information from contacts in Santa Fe, New Mexico. At the NKVD's request she gave up being a union activist in her factory, a sacrifice she was willing to make for the cause.

At the end of hostilities, Morris trained to become a teacher in New York assigned to a secondary school in Manhattan and received instructions from the illegal *rezident*, **Willie Fisher**. Both Cohens subsequently became part of the spy ring codenamed VOLUNTEERS organized by Julius and **Ethel Rosenberg**, but as the Federal Bureau of Investigation (FBI) closed in on the network in July 1950 they fled abroad, telling their friends they were moving to California. As one of their last duties, they attended a rendezvous with Ted and **Joan Hall** in New York to give them instructions.

Following their sudden disappearance, supposedly to take a job as a scriptwriter in Hollywood, the cashing of a $1,000 savings bond, and the closure of their bank account, Morris's father told friends that his son and daughter-in-law had left the States forever. According to the defector Vasili Mitrokhin, they were sheltered in Mexico by two members of the local Communist Party, codenamed FISH and OREL.

Unburdened by children, the Cohens were devoted to each other and eventually surfaced in London, posing as Peter and Helen Kroger, a pair of antiquarian book dealers from New Zealand. The FBI later speculated that the couple had fled to Australia before making their way to Europe, and the evidence of American Express travelers checks purchased in Vienna and redeemed in Paris on 8 February, in Hong Kong on 18 February, and then Tokyo, suggested the couple had taken a roundabout route to Geneva and Zurich, where bank accounts were opened in their names, and eventually to London.

When they were arrested in January 1961, having been compromised during MI5's investigation of **Harry Houghton**, the Cohens refused to disclose their true identities, which were eventually established by a fingerprint check with the FBI. *See also* COSTELLO, PADDY.

COMMUNIST PARTY OF GREAT BRITAIN (CPGB). As a prewar branch of the Communist International, and effectively a clandestine instrument of the NKVD, the CPGB employed women in a covert role because of their ideological commitment, their discretion, and apparently in the mistaken belief that they would escape the scrutiny of the authorities who would be concentrating on the male membership. Accordingly, although few women reached senior posts within the Party or were elected to the Central Executive, several played key positions within the network of underground cells, acting as couriers. Because Bob Stewart, who maintained the NKVD's link between the Soviet embassy's *rezidentura* and the CPGB's covert cadres, feared hostile surveillance, he relied upon his wife Margaret, his daughter Annie, and his assistant Agnes Aitken to make contacts on his behalf and deliver secret messages to his sources. Although ostensibly only secretary to the CPGB's Control

Committee, which exercised discipline over the branches, Stewart traveled abroad extensively and was identified to MI5 in February 1940 by the defector Walter Krivitsky as the CPGB's principal spymaster. This information filtered back to Stewart from **Anthony Blunt**, who read his MI5 file in late 1940 and warned him that he had been compromised. Stewart then effectively dropped from sight and was appointed to the CPGB's school for organizers, but in reality left his operational activities to the three women in his life.

Proof that the CPGB relied upon women agents and took full advantage of them was supplied by the MI5 mole **Olga Gray**, who undertook several missions for Bob Stewart, including one to Bombay in June 1934 and another to Moscow in March 1936.

During MI5's investigation into the CPGB's spy ring at the Woolwich Arsenal, evidence emerged that although Percy Glading initially had been thought to be the main culprit, the real organizer had been Albert Williams and his wife **Nellie Williams**.

COMMUNIST PARTY OF THE UNITED STATES OF AMERICA (CPUSA). Although ostensibly an independent political party, the CPUSA also acted as a branch of the NKVD, talent-spotting candidates suitable for recruitment, passing information to Moscow, and using local chapters as cover for espionage. The CPUSA provided the NKVD with a pool of committed, ideologically reliable personnel and instant access to union activists who worked in sensitive government posts. Some of the senior CPUSA positions were filled by NKVD personnel, and the secretary-general, Earl Browder, took secret instructions from the Kremlin and received messages addressed to him by the codename HELMSMAN. Significantly, his common-law wife, **Kitty Harris**, was an NKVD spy, codenamed ADA; his sister Marguerite had worked for years in Europe and the Far East as an illegal; and his niece Helen Lowry was married to Iskhak Akhmerov, the NKVD illegal *rezident*. In 1940, Browder was imprisoned on passport fraud charges relating to the use of false travel documents issued to volunteers seeking to fight during the Spanish Civil War for the republicans in the International Brigade, and his conviction implicated World Tourists Inc., a company controlled since its creation in 1929 by the CPUSA and run by Akhmerov's predecessor as NKVD *rezident*, Jacob Golos. Akhmerov's principal assistant was **Elizabeth Bentley**, a CPUSA member since 1935 who was known to Browder and who acted as a courier, maintaining a link between the New York *rezidentura* and the NKVD's networks in Washington, D.C.

Study of the VENONA decrypts revealed much of Browder's involvement with Soviet espionage and his reliance on women, but evidently he feared being contaminated by his sister's illicit activities and begged Moscow to release her from her clandestine missions so she would not embarrass him or the CPUSA. Accordingly, Marguerite was recalled and transferred to administrative duties at the CPUSA's headquarters in New York.

Although a policy decision to insulate the CPUSA and other Communist parties from direct involvement in espionage had been taken in Moscow in 1938 following the Woolwich Arsenal case in London, the precautions taken were soon abandoned because of the pressing need to exploit CPUSA connections within the Manhattan Project. Some NKVD *rezidentutra* staff, such as Olga Khlopkova, codenamed JULIA, and Olga Pravdina, codenamed MARGARET, acted as intermediaries to distance individual sources from the CPUSA, but the priority given to the urgent acquisition of atomic secrets led Moscow to abandon the strict compartmentalization rule by allowing GRU spy rings to work with NKVD networks and authorizing both organizations to tap CPUSA contacts. Ultimately, these breaches in tradecraft led to most of the Soviet *apparat* being uncovered by the Federal Bureau of Investigation (FBI) and implicated Julius and **Ethel Rosenberg**, Ruth Greenglass, codenamed WASP, and Klaus Fuch's sister Krystel. The consequences for all of them were appalling. The Rosenbergs were executed, Krystel committed suicide, and only Ruth Greenglass, who had been 21 at the time of her recruitment, escaped imprisonment, due to her husband's cooperation with the FBI that resulted in him negotiating her freedom and a sentence for him that had him released in December 1960.

COPLON, JUDITH. A Soviet spy identified by VENONA texts as a spy codenamed SIMA, Judith Coplon was employed as a clerk by the U.S. Department of Justice, handling requests from the Federal Bureau of Investigation (FBI) for surveillance warrants, giving her access to the most sensitive counterespionage operations.

Coplon came under suspicion because on 31 December 1944 the NKVD *rezident* in New York, Stepan Apresyan, reported to Moscow that "SIMA has got work in the Registration of Foreign Agents Branch of the War Office Division of the Department of Justice." On 8 January 1945, he gave a further update to Moscow, and this was the first telegram in the series that the FBI broke sufficiently to show that the Justice Department had been penetrated by a spy who had been moved down to Washington, D.C., early in 1945. Evidently she had been looked over by one of the *rezident*'s subordinates, Vladimir S. Pravdin, the TASS press agency editor in New York:

> SERGEI's [Vladimir Pravdin] conversation with SIMA took place on 4 January. SIMA gives the impression of being a serious person who is politically well developed and there is no doubt of her sincere desire to help us. She had no doubts about whom she is working for and said that the nature of the materials in which we are interested pointed to the fact that it was our country that was in question. She was very satisfied that she was dealing with us and said that she deeply appreciated the confidence shown in her and understood the importance of our work.
>
> SIMA's transfer to a new job was made at the insistence of her superiors [64 groups unrecoverable] generalizing materials from all departments. SIMA will probably start work on 15 February.
>
> On the basis of this preliminary information there is reason to assume that in her new job SIMA will be able to carry out very important work for us throwing light on the activities of the HUT [FBI]. The fruitfulness of her work will to a considerable extent depend upon our ability to organize correct and constant direction. It should be remembered that SIMA from an operational point of view is quite undeveloped and she will need time to learn conspiracy and to correctly gain an understanding of the questions which interest us.
>
> A final decision on the question of direction and liaison can be taken only after she has moved to CARTHAGE [Washington, D.C.] when it will be ascertained specifically what her new job consists of.

Another VENONA text, dated 26 June 1945, showed that SIMA had taken up her new position with the Justice Department in Washington but was still being run by the New York *rezidentura*, and evidently had already supplied her Soviet contact with an analysis of her division's work:

Your No. 4195. After SIMA's transfer to CARTHAGE [Washington, D.C.], she was instructed to refrain from removing documents until she was quite sure that she was trusted. As you were advised earlier, on the advice of her superiors, SIMA is studying the Russian language with the aim of [1 group unrecovered] a post in the department of the CLUB [Department of Justice] which is investigating the actions of the USSR and the Communists. SIMA was given the task of studying the CLUB, its methods of work, the way in which documents are kept. On this matter, SIMA compiled [121 groups unrecoverable].

Further VENONA texts suggested that Coplon had written numerous memoranda for her NKVD contacts about her highly sensitive work and also proved that the Soviets had realized that some parts of their most secret communications had been compromised, and that the code words BANK, CABARET, HOUSE, and CLUB were known to the Americans, even if there was little Moscow could do to rectify retrospectively the breach in the security of their communications.

A total of eight VENONA intercepts were more than enough to make the FBI realize in 1948, as the first text of January 1945 indicated, that a spy had penetrated the Justice Department. As soon as FBI Special Agent Bob Lamphere extracted the vital date of the spy's commencement in her new post, 15 February 1945, on an internal transfer from New York, Judith Coplon was confirmed by Inspector Leo Lauchlin in consultation with the assistant attorney general as SIMA, for she was the only person to have switched from the Justice Department's Economic Warfare section to Washington, D.C. Preliminary enquiries into her background showed that her parents were living in Brooklyn, and she had graduated in 1943 from Barnard College, where she had been involved briefly with the Young Communist League.

Coplon's access had allowed the NKVD to remain one step ahead of the FBI, tipping off the Soviets each time a new suspect came under the FBI's scrutiny, so the only action to be taken was to remove the suspects from their jobs. Coplon was placed under discreet surveillance that revealed she was having an illicit affair with Harold Shapiro, a Justice Department attorney, and that she made two trips a month to New York to visit her parents. When she was followed to

Manhattan on 14 January 1949 she was seen to meet a man for dinner who subsequently was identified as Valentin A. Gubitchev, an employee of the United Nations secretariat, and they were watched at two further meetings, on 18 February and 4 March. At this latter rendezvous both were arrested; Gubitchev was found to be carrying an envelope containing $125, while Coplon's handbag revealed a wealth of classified data, including some documents that had been prepared by the FBI as a "barium meal" to test whether Coplon gave them to her Soviet contacts.

At her trial the FBI concealed the exact nature of the "confidential informant" that had led to the investigation of Coplon and she deployed the defense that her relationship with Gubitchev was entirely romantic, and that the information she was carrying was nothing more than notes she had prepared while writing a novel. The prosecution neatly destroyed the "innocent liaison" ploy by disclosing details of her affair with Harold Shapiro, and she was convicted and received a sentence of between 40 months' and 10 years' imprisonment for conspiring to pass classified secrets to Gubitchev, who was also convicted.

Coplon's conviction was later overturned on appeal, on the technicality that the FBI's telephone intercept had been unlawful; the clear impression had been left that the FBI had begun its investigation as a consequence of a wiretap on Coplon's office line, so all the evidence that flowed from that source was deemed inadmissible. The alternative was to reveal that the FBI had been led to Coplon by VENONA, but that expedient was considered too high a price to pay, so she was freed to marry one of her lawyers, Albert H. Socolov, and settle in Brooklyn, where she opened several restaurants.

COSTELLO, PADDY. Born in 1912 in Auckland, New Zealand, the fourth of eight children of an Irish immigration, Desmond Patrick ("Paddy") Costello graduated from Auckland University College and won a scholarship in April 1932 to Trinity College, Cambridge. In October 1936, he was appointed an assistant lecturer in classics at Exeter University where his wife, Bella Lerner, who was of Ukrainian Jewish extraction but born in London, was elected secretary of the local branch of the Communist Party of Great Britain. Known as "Bil," she had married Costello in 1935 and, according to a report written by the

New Zealand Security Intelligence Service (NZSIS), he had competed to match her as "a dedicated and ruthless communist."

In November 1940, Costello joined the New Zealand Army and was posted to the Middle East, where he soon won promotion and was appointed an intelligence officer on General Bernard Freyberg's staff. In July 1944, he was discharged from the army and sent to Moscow to work at the newly opened New Zealand legation. Fluent in Russian, Costello remained at the legation until it was closed in June 1950, when he was transferred to the legation in Paris. He was asked to resign on security grounds in July 1954 and the following year was appointed professor of Russian at Manchester University, where he died in 1964.

An investigation conducted by MI5 and the NZSIS after his death revealed that Costello, codenamed LONG, had been a Soviet spy since his recruitment at Cambridge and had been responsible in May 1953 for issuing New Zealand passports in the names of "Peter and Helen Kroger" to Morris and **Lona Cohen**, both KGB illegals who would be arrested in London in January 1961.

COURTNEY, ANTHONY. A naval officer who had retired from the Royal Navy in 1953 at the age of 48 to set up an export consultancy business, Anthony Courtney two years later contested the Hayes and Harlington constituency in the 1955 general election. Fluent in Russian and German, with long experience in the Admiralty's postwar Naval Intelligence Division, Courtney had been sent to the Soviet Union as deputy to Admiral Geoffrey Miles, head of the naval mission in January 1942, and after his election to the Commons returned to act as an adviser for British firms. In Moscow, he befriended Zinaida Volkova, an Intourist official at the Hotel Ukrainia, and on a further visit in June 1961, following the death of his wife from a heart attack in March, he had spent the night with her in his hotel room. Unknown to Courtney, this encounter had been filmed by the KGB but he was not blackmailed immediately.

Evidently, the KGB waited a further four years, when Courtney mounted a campaign from the Opposition benches to draw attention to the increasing Soviet abuse of their immunity. During the debate of his Diplomatic Privileges Bill in January 1966, he protested the employment of 20 chauffeurs by the embassy who, he claimed, were professional intelligence officers. This led to the distribution of six photographs of himself, of which three were of him with Zinaida on a bed, to his constituency agent, to Parliamentary colleagues, to Chief Whip Willie Whitelaw, and to the *News of the World*, but Courtney was unmoved. He knew the pictures had been taken in June 1961, three months after the death of his first wife in March, and before his marriage in March 1962 to his second wife. Indeed, he had declared his affair to his new wife and had even introduced her to Zinaida during a trip they had taken together to Moscow. On another visit to Moscow, in August 1964, when his second marriage was in trouble, Courtney conducted a long-distance telephone conversation with his wife to persuade her not to file for divorce, and evidently this call was monitored by the KGB. News of the existence of the photos circulated, and Zinaida was cited in Elizabeth Courtney's divorce petition on the grounds of his adultery.

Upon receipt of the photos, Courtney went to 10 Downing Street twice, once to brief Harold Wilson, and on a second occasion two days later, to see George Wigg. He also contacted an old friend, Sir Roger Hollis, then the director-general of the Security Service, who had assigned an MI5 Soviet expert to investigate the photographs.

In fact, MI5 had been suspicious of Courtney for some years, dating back to 1954 when he had made a call to Kamensky, the head of the Soviet Trade Delegation in London. What made the call unusual was that Kamensky's first instinct had been to telephone the KGB's deputy *rezident*, Sergei Kondrashev.

MI5 suspected that while Courtney's relationship with Zinaida may have begun in June 1961, it might have continued on some of his subsequent trips to Moscow, perhaps in June 1962 or twice in 1963, when he had been unaccompanied by his new wife. Not mentioning the doubts that had arisen about his version of events, Whitelaw counseled Courtney to remain silent on the entire business, but when Elizabeth petitioned for divorce, citing Zinaida, the matter became public in October. Courtney subsequently lost his Parliamentary constituency at the October 1966 general election. Two years later he published his memoirs, *Sailor in a Russian Frame*.

CUSHMAN, PAULENE. An actress of great beauty during the American Civil War, Paulene Cushman, born Harriet Wood in New Orleans in June 1833, was recruited into the Union Army's intelligence service, then headed by Allan Pinkerton, and was employed as an agent provocateur to identify Confederate sympathizers. She also undertook missions behind enemy lines, claiming to be searching for a wounded brother while collecting military information from unsuspecting rebel soldiers. She was arrested by General John Hunt Morgan, who also succumbed to her blandishments, but she was condemned to death anyway. However, she was freed when the Confederate forces holding her were overrun by the Union.

After the war she returned to the stage but, failing to achieve any success, she died of an overdose in San Francisco in June 1893.

– D –

DEEP ROOT. A Royal Canadian Mounted Police (RCMP) Security Service code name for an operation in mid-1968 intended to entrap Natasha Makhotina, the very attractive, vivacious wife of a Soviet diplomat based in Ottawa. She was spotted conducting an affair with her French Canadian driving instructor, a good-looking cab driver whom the RCMP recruited as JOKER. Codenamed DAMSEL, Natasha was a target only as a means of reaching her husband, Vladminir A. Kakhtoin, who was known to have been co-opted by the KGB *rezidentura*. JOKER and Natasha continued to have a passionate affair, some of which was filmed by the RCMP. Eventually, in June 1969, Makhotina was approached by an RCMP case officer and offered the opportunity to hold a longer conversation about defection, but soon afterward she and her husband were ordered back to Moscow. Declaring herself to be in love with JOKER, Makhotina was placed under house arrest and the ambassador's wife was seen comforting her before she was escorted aboard an Aeroflot plane home.

Soon afterward JOKER and his wife received an invitation to meet the Makhotins in Moscow, and they accepted despite the RCMP's objections. However, no attempt was made by the KGB to subvert, compromise, or recruit JOKER, and he returned to Canada safely. Later the RCMP concluded that DEEP ROOT had been betrayed by a Soviet mole, Gilles Brunet.

DEJEAN, MAURICE. Formerly the French ambassador in Moscow for eight years, Maurice Dejean was named by the defector **Yuri Krotkov** as having been compromised in a **honeytrap** in which he had fallen for the charms of a beautiful Russian ballerina, Larissa Kronberg-Sobolevskaya, in 1958, a classic **swallow**. According to Krotkov, Dejean had been seduced initially by a voluptuous interpreter, Lydia Khovanskaya, while he had distracted Dejean's wife, Marie-Claire. The entire operation had been supervised by the KGB's General **Oleg Gribanov**.

As part of the charade, Dejean had been assaulted by a KGB officer posing as her outraged husband, and she was recalled to Paris in February 1964, interrogated by Marcel Chalet of the Direction de la Surveillance du Territoire (DST), and dismissed, although he denied ever having betrayed any secrets. The DST was inclined to believe his story, although there was a possibility he had been recruited by the Soviets while serving in Berlin in 1938 when the French diplomatic codes were known to have been compromised there. Alternatively, Dejean might have been recruited either in wartime London when he was serving with General Charles de Gaulle and was in official contact with Soviets, or while he was ambassador to Czechoslovakia from 1945 to 1949.

DELILAH. According to the Book of Judges in the Old Testament, Delilah used her considerable sensual powers, in about 1161 B.C.E., to extract information from enemies of the Philistines, and to seduce a wise Judean judge, **Samson**, who possessed extraordinary strength. Having been promised 1,100 pieces of silver, the beautiful Delilah sought to discover the source of her lover's strength, and eventually he confided in her that, as a member of the Nazarite sect whose members did not cut their hair, he derived his strength from his hair. Delilah then waited until her lover was asleep in a drunken stupor and used a pair of scissors before beckoning the Philistines to arrest him. Unable to resist, he was blinded and placed on display in the temple, but she was killed when he dislodged a pair of columns, causing the temple to collapse.

DENNING REPORT, THE. The resignation of **John Profumo** on 5 June 1963 led Prime Minister Harold Macmillan to appoint Lord

Denning a fortnight later to conduct an investigation into the circumstances of the scandal, and he completed his enquiries in a couple of months. He then wrote the entire document in manuscript, and it was published at half past midnight on 26 September. The first printing of 30,000 was sold almost instantly by Her Majesty's Stationery Office in Kingsway, with 4,000 sold in the first hour. Years later, Denning recalled that he had not been paid for his task and had received no royalties, even though the *Daily Telegraph* had bought the rights to publish the entire document as a newspaper supplement, and had not even been thanked by Macmillan. As well as dealing with the central issues—of the nature of the relationships between **Stephen Ward**, Jack Profumo, **Eugene Ivanov**, and **Christine Keeler**, and the security implications—Denning extended his research to cover what he termed various other "rumours affecting the honour and integrity of public life" and investigated allegations relating to Douglas Fairbanks Jr., Duncan Sandys, Ernest Marpes, and John Hare. None of these had any potential security implications, but Denning described orgies at which the guests were served by a near-naked man wearing a mask, and he also pursued the various candidates for the man photographed with the Duchess of Argylle, pictures that had been presented in evidence at the duke's divorce proceedings. Denning's report traduced the hapless Stephen Ward, without ever indicating that the osteopath had acted as an MI5 agent in an attempt to **honeytrap** the Soviet naval attaché. Nevertheless, the judge regarded the deeply flawed document as his greatest contribution to English jurisprudence and maintained to his death that Ward had been a deeply wicked and immoral criminal.

D'EON, CHARLES. Born in 1728, Charles D'Eon was a lawyer and a skilled swordsman when his thesis on the finances of King Louis XIV of France attracted the attention of the king's successor, Louis XV, who recruited him into the King's Secret, a group of agents employed by the French Crown. D'Eon's reputation was enhanced by his transvestism; habitually dressed as a woman, he frequently undertook missions using the alias Lia de Beaumont. His female role was so convincing that many believed he had been born a girl or a hermaphrodite, but when he died in England in 1810 a postmortem examination proved his male gender.

Among D'Eon's exploits were a mission to St. Petersburg to persuade the Empress Elizabeth to enter into a secret alliance with France, and one to England in 1763 to establish whether a settlement of the Seven Years' War could be negotiated. Dressed as a woman, he stole documents from an officer working for the Duke of Bedford, and established the British government's wish for peace. Appointed a chevalier, D'Eon remained in England until ordered back to Paris by Louis XVI; when he was subsequently required to wear women's clothes for the remainder of his life, he returned to London, where he worked as a fencing instructor.

DERIABIN, PIOTR. A senior NKVD officer based at the *rezidentura* in Vienna, Piotr Deriabin defected in February 1954 after he discovered that his wife had slept with the head of his department, Vladimir Pribytkov.

On 15 February 1954, Deriabin, a 33-year-old Siberian from Lolot, walked into the American military headquarters in Vienna and asked for political asylum. He identified himself as a case officer in charge of security at the local NKVD *rezidentura* and described his background as a career intelligence officer with experience as a member of Josef Stalin's personal bodyguard, as a veteran of the siege of Stalingrad, and as a graduate of the Red Army's Higher School of Counterintelligence.

Wounded four times and decorated five times during World War II in which he served as an infantry officer, Deriabin had been recruited by the NKVD as a security officer in Barnaul before he joined the elite Guard Directorate of the Kremlin in 1947. To his credit was his long membership of the Komsomol and his prewar career as a teacher, as well as his surveillance work in the Altai Kray province of his native Siberia, but these assets did not prepare him for what he learned about the Soviet hierarchy. "Neither the betrayal of Party principles, as he thought he had learned them years before, nor even the unjust condemnation of the innocent revolted him so much as the gross moral double standard of his leaders. The Soviet leaders' dedicated obsession with pleasure and power illustrates as nothing else could how completely the early ideals of the Revolution have vanished," he said in his autobiography, written in the third person.

After six years in Moscow, during which his first wife died and he married for a second time, Deriabin attended the Marxism-Leninism Institute and in May 1952 was transferred to the Austro-German section of the **Second Chief Directorate**. Here, in July 1952, he supervised the abduction of Dr. Walter Linse, the anti-Communist lawyer based in West Berlin. A refugee who had fled from East Germany in 1947 to head the Association of Free German Jurists, Linse was tried in secret for treason and sentenced to 25 years in the labor camps. In September 1953, Deriabin was posted to Vienna, accompanied by his wife and daughter, to concentrate on the West German Security Service, the Bundesamt für Verfassungsschutz, headed by Otto John. However, in February of the following year, he was implicated in the defection of a visitor, Anatoli I. Skachkov of the Soviet Petroleum Administration. Skachkov's defection to the Americans, while under Deriabin's jurisdiction, would have led to a reprimand or perhaps a worse punishment. He had a row with his wife and, apparently on impulse, took a taxi to the American Kommandantura.

Deriabin was the only Soviet defector to become an established **Central Intelligence Agency** (CIA) officer, and at the time of his death in September 1992, aged 72, after a long battle against cancer, he was still making regular visits to Langley from his home in nearby northern Virginia. He testified before congressional committees four times, taught at the Defense Intelligence College after his retirement from the CIA in 1981, and completed graduate studies at the University of Michigan and the University of Virginia. He married for a third time in the United States and had a son, Peter Junior.

Five years after his defection, Deriabin teamed up with an experienced *Time* and *Newsweek* journalist, Frank Gibney, to write *The Secret World*, which was based upon two *Life* articles published in March 1959. Although only Gibney was credited with having edited *The Penkovsky Papers*, Deriabin also played a major role in the book's preparation. In this extract from his memoirs, written characteristically in the third person, he gives a glimpse of life in the Kremlin under Stalin and **Beria**.

DEUTSCH, ARNOLD. Born in Austria in August 1904, Arnold Genrikhovich Deutsch spent five years at primary school, eight in a gymnasium, followed by five in Vienna University's chemistry faculty.

He joined the Communist Party of the Soviet Union in 1931, having been a member of the Austrian Communist Youth Organization since 1922, and the Austrian Communist Party since 1924. He had been employed by the Comintern in Vienna from December 1928 to December 1931, as an NKVD officer since August 1932, and had been posted to Paris, Vienna, and London. Deutsch could write in German, French, and English fluently, and could read and write Italian and Spanish. Between 1928 and 1932, he operated for the Comintern in Greece, Romania, Palestine, Syria, Germany, and Czechoslovakia. His 28-year-old wife, Fini Pavlovna, worked from 1931 to 1935 as "Liza Kramer" under illegal cover and was by profession a teacher.

Deutsch's parents were Jewish; his father was a country schoolteacher who moved to Vienna, where he worked for a merchant. In 1916, he served in the Austrian Army as an ordinary soldier until he opened a clothes shop. Deutsch left his parents in 1929, having studied physics, chemistry, and philosophy at Vienna University and obtained a degree of doctor of philosophy. He then went to Moscow as part of an Austrian Communist Party delegation and was recommended for clandestine work, which he began with a mission in May 1932 to Greece, Palestine, and Syria. In January 1933, he was assigned to Paris to work for Karin and carried out technical tasks for him, including photographic work, and set up crossing points across the French frontier to Belgium, Holland, and Germany.

In February 1934, Deutsch went to London alone to recruit **Edith Suschitsky**, whom he knew from Vienna. In London, he worked for the illegal *rezident*, Ignaty Reif, from April to June 1934, and from June to July 1935 with Alexander Orlov. In August 1935, he returned to Moscow on leave but was back in London in November 1935, as acting *resident*. In April 1936, Theodore Maly was appointed the illegal *resident*, but Deutsch resumed the role again at the end of August. Maly returned briefly and was again in charge between January 1937 and June 1937, when Deutsch resumed until November 1937. While in London Deutsch studied psychology at London University, building on his work with the controversial Viennese Marxist sex therapist **Wilhelm Reich**, but did not take finals and instead went to work for his uncle, Oscar Deutsch, the Hungarian immigrant who founded the Odeon cinema chain in Birmingham. His cover for 10 months was a job in the advertising department, at £20 a month, but because he only had a student visa he was forced to leave the country in September 1937 with his wife Sylvia, who was his radio operator, and daughter, who had been born in London in February 1936, returning only for 10 days in November to secure his network's future before departing for Moscow.

During his period in London, Deutsch was responsible for the recruitment of Edith Suschitsky, **Kim Philby**, HEIR, and ATTILA. He also arranged to meet **Guy Burgess**, Donald Maclean, and John Cairncross separately in Paris. Deutsch had always intended to return to London but Walter Krivitsky's defection in the summer of 1937 made this impossible. Krivitsky had known his mother-in-law in Vienna, and he had been introduced to him by Maly in Paris in June 1936

In March 1939, languishing in Moscow, Deutsch was asked to write a number of essays on Britain, beginning with one on the country's political structure, and an account of the former illegal *rezidentura* in London, and compile psychological portraits of Philby, Maclean, Burgess, **Anthony Blunt**, and Cairncross. These profiles drew on Deutsch's psychosexual experience and training with Reich, the therapist who advocated free love and placed great store by the orgasm.

At the end of December 1940, Pavel Fitin recommended that Deutsch go to the United States as the illegal *rezident* with Boris Kreshin as his assistant, to renew contact with **Michael Straight** and the sources codenamed 19TH and MORRIS, and to recruit new agents in the defense industry and ministries, as well as recruiting agents for work in Europe. Fitin suggested that Deutsch and Kreshin should travel disguised as Jewish refugees from the Baltic and in 1941 Deutsch embarked on the SS *Kayak* to cross the Indian Ocean. When war broke out in the Far East, he was stuck in Bombay and was forced to return to Moscow via Teheran, arriving in April 1942. His second attempt to reach the United States ended tragically on 7 November 1942 when the SS *Donbass* was sunk by a U-boat in the Atlantic.

Curiously, Moscow's decision to deploy Deutsch overseas as an illegal was taken after Anthony Blunt had passed Anatoli Gorsky the contents of his MI5 dossier in March 1941. Blunt's report revealed MI5's certainty that Deutsch was a Soviet intelligence agent and contained several details, including the dates that he had traveled to Britain. Although the file contained no information on any of Deutsch's contacts, it did note that he had been vouched for by his uncle, who had been investigated together with his immediate circle on suspicion that they might be linked to Soviet or German intelligence.

DEUTSCH, JOHN. Appointed director of central intelligence (DCI) by President Bill Clinton in 1995, John M. Deutsch was an abrasive academic with a reputation for arrogance from his former role as provost of the Massachusetts Institute of Technology, with ambitions to become the secretary of defense. When asked by the president to become DCI, Deutsch demurred and recommended another candidate, Air Force General Michael Carns, but Carns was forced to withdraw from the nomination, having employed an illegal immigrant as a housekeeper. In these circumstances, reluctantly, Deutsch accepted the post.

Deutsch lasted just 17 months as DCI before being replaced by his deputy, George Tenet, the fifth DCI in six years, but his departure in December 1996 proved embarrassing when he asked to retain his **Central Intelligence Agency**–supplied laptop because he intended to remain as a consultant. However, a routine inspection of it at his home revealed that the hard drive contained unauthorized classified information, that it had not been isolated from the Internet or from other members of the Deutsch household, and that it had been used to access pornography. A CIA security investigation was initiated, and Deutsch declared that his son had been responsible for downloading pornography from the Internet. A report was submitted to his successor, and Tenet accepted a recommendation that Deutsch should lose his consultancy contract and his security clearances. Two years after his resignation, the attorney general, Janet Reno, declined to bring criminal charges against him, and on President Clinton's last day in office Deutsch was granted a pardon.

DIAZ, VIVIANA. In March 1943, Viviana Diaz and her husband, Jose Francisco Xavier Pacheco e Cuesta, were arrested by MI5's defense security officer in Trinidad and transferred to Camp 020, the interrogation center in west London. When questioned, the two professional dancers confessed that they had been sent by the Abwehr on a mission to Havana, where they had been instructed to seduce Allied seamen and send shipping information back to Germany in reports written in secret ink concealed in the ordinary mail.

Both had performed at the Winter Garden in Berlin and the Piccadilly Hotel in London and had gained an international reputation for erotic dancing when in March 1942 they were interned in Brussels by the Germans. There, Diaz had negotiated their release with an Abwehr official named Karsten, and they had agreed to undertake a mission to Havana. They were given further instructions by the Abwehr in Madrid and then had boarded a ship for the transatlantic voyage to Cuba.

According to Diaz's MI5 file, she was treated for syphilis at Holloway prison, and then deported to Cuba at the conclusion of hostilities.

DISCREDIT OPERATIONS. The KGB term for operations conducted by the **Second Chief Directorate** to ennsare targets in **honeytrap** operations, mainly in Moscow hotel rooms that had been wired for sound and video. *See also* ALSOP, KENNETH; COURTNEY, ANTHONY; DEJEAN, MAURICE; DURANTY, WALTER; GUIBAUD, LOUIS; HAAVIK, GUNVOR; HARRISON, GEOFFREY; KROTKOV, YURI; LOUISA; RHODES, ROY; SAARDEMICHEL, FRANCOIS; SMITH, EDWARD ELLIS; VASSALL, JOHN; WATKINS, JOHN.

DOBROVA, MARIA. A GRU illegal established in New York as a beautician, Maria Dobrova was identified to the Federal Bureau of Investigation (FBI) by Dmitri Polyakov in 1962. After a period of surveillance she was abducted by FBI agents and kept in isolation so she could be interrogated. According to the FBI's Bill Sullivan, she initially agreed to cooperate with her captors but subsequently changed her mind and committed suicide.

DODD, MARTHA. The daughter of William Dodd, appointed the American ambassador in Berlin in 1933, Martha Dodd had an affair with a Soviet diplomat and was recruited by him as a spy. She became a committed Communist codenamed JULIET 2 and under his guidance was directed to sleep with Nazi officials to obtain information. She then acquired another Soviet lover, and when she returned to New York in December 1937 she was placed under the control of the NKVD's illegal *rezident*, Iskhak Akhmerov, and codenamed LIZA. Her file in Moscow described her as a "sexually decayed woman ready to sleep with a handsome man."

In June 1938 she married a millionaire and fellow Communist, Alfred Stern, a wealthy Soviet sympathizer from a Fargo, North Dakota, banking family. Educated at Harvard, Stern had first married the daughter of the Chicago merchant baron Julius Rosenwald, and reputedly had been paid $1 million to divorce her. Stern used his wealth to support the **Communist Party of the United States of America**'s publishing ventures and also financed Boris Morros, a Hollywood film producer and Soviet spy. Morros, however, became an informer for the Federal Bureau of Investigation (FBI), and he implicated his partner, Jack Soble, who was interrogated. Soble admitted his espionage; as well as providing evidence against his brother Robert, he claimed that Martha Stern had spied as a Soviet agent in her father's embassy before the war. Soble was sentenced to seven years' imprisonment in September 1957, and later tried to commit suicide in the Lewisburg Federal Penitentiary. When the Sterns were indicted on charges of espionage, they fled the country and took up residence in Prague, remaining there until 1979 when they made a successful application to have their indictment quashed. After the principal prosecution witness, Boris Morros, succumbed to cancer in January 1961 in New York, all charges against them in the United States were dropped.

DRIBERG, TOM. A graduate of Christ Church, Oxford, and born in 1905 to the retired chief of police for Assam, Tom Driberg was recruited as a source by MI5's **Max Knight** in 1921 and instructed to join the Young Communist League. He was a predatory **homosexual** and he used his many social connections to further his career in politics and journalism. In 1942, while working for Lord Beaverbrook's *Daily Express*, he was elected to the House of Commons, having been expelled by the **Communist Party of Great Britain** (CPGB) on the grounds that he was an MI5 mole, a charge he had denied.

While Driberg never had access to classified information, his role as author of the William Hickey column gave him an entrée into London society and ensured he was extremely well connected, even if his several arrests on charges of indecent assault (on which he was acquitted after a trial at the Old Bailey) and gross indecency made him a notorious figure, with a reputation that he reveled in, according to his 1977 autobiography, *Ruling Passions*.

Driberg's usefulness as a source inside the CPGB had come to an end when his identity was discovered by **Anthony Blunt**, who had promptly tipped off the NKVD. Thereafter Driberg remained in contact with Max Knight but was suspected of having established a relationship with the Czech Intelligence Service, the **Statni Bezpecnost**. In 1956, soon after **Guy Burgess** and Donald Maclean had emerged from hiding and given a press conference at the National Hotel in Moscow, Driberg arranged to meet Burgess and interview him for a short biography, a project endorsed by MI5. He was able to visit Burgess and his Russian boyfriend Tolya at their apartment in Moscow and spent a weekend with him at his country dacha. The result was *Guy Burgess: A Portrait with Background*, a best seller that filled in some of the gaps in MI5's investigation of the defecting diplomats. While staying in Moscow, Driberg visited a public urinal behind the Metropole Hotel that was notorious as a haunt for homosexuals and was photographed by the KGB engaged in oral sex. When shown the resulting pictures, Driberg quickly agreed to work for the KGB and, according to the defector Vasili Mitrokhin, was codenamed LEPAGE.

Ennobled as Lord Bradwell after he had retired as chairman of the Labour Party, Driberg died in August 1976.

DUCIMETIERE, ROSE. Having fallen for a waiter in St. Martin, Paris, who claimed to be Swiss, Rose Ducimetiere agreed to pass him military information she acquired during her work as a nurse at the Val de Grace Hospital so he could sell it to the editor of a Swiss military journal. In October 1916, a routine postal censorship inspection revealed secret writing in one of her letters and she was charged with espionage and condemned to death. Her sentence was later commuted to life imprisonment by President Raymond Poncaré.

DUNCAN, ANDREW. Formerly the commanding officer of the Gordon Highlanders and the 52nd Lowland Division and a former deputy inspector-general of the Territorial Army, Brigadier Andrew Duncan was withdrawn from his post as defense attaché at the British High Commission in Islamabad in August 2005 when it became known that he had developed an ostensibly platonic relationship with a beautiful academic suspected of being an Pakistani Inter-Services Intelligence (ISI) agent. Aged 56 and married, Duncan was not accused of any impropriety with the woman, a research fellow at the Institute of Strategic Studies for the previous two years, but, according to the Ministry of Defense in London, had been returned home because he "had lost the confidence of his High Commissioner."

At the time, Anglo-Pakistani relations were particularly tense because of the recent suicide bombings in London on 7 July by young men of Pakistani origin who had visited the country to attend religious schools. Liaison between the ISI and its British counterparts had been jeopardized by the discovery of covert listening devices inside the High Commission, and there was suspicion that elements within the ISI had targeted British personnel to monitor locally conducted counterterrorist investigations.

DURANTY, WALTER. The veteran *New York Times* correspondent in Moscow for 12 years until 1934, who was granted a rare exclusive interview with Josef Stalin in 1929, was a victim of an NKVD **honeytrap** that caught him in a compromising situation with his **homosexual** lover. Thereafter, Duranty was threatened that unless his reports from Moscow conformed to the Communist Party line, he would be exposed and ruined. Accordingly, Duranty was one of several foreign correspondents who sent dispatches home that glossed over the truth about Stalin's regime and omitted to mention the famine caused by his policy of agricultural collectivization that had resulted in starvation across the Ukraine. The one journalist to write stories on the subject for the *Manchester Guardian*, Malcolm Muggeridge, was vilified for his eyewitness accounts of chronic food shortages and the persecution of the Kulak farmers, and the truth would only emerge when Robert Conquest revealed the pressure Duranty had submitted to.

Duranty, who had been born in Liverpool in 1884 and had lost a leg in a rail accident in France in 1924, was awarded a Pulitzer Prize in 1932 for his reporting from Russia, and subsequent attempts to have the prize withdrawn have proved unsuccessful. Duranty died in Florida in 1957.

– E –

EDMONDS, EMMA. During the American Civil War, Emma Edmonds, who had been born in Canada in 1842, volunteered to spy against the Confederacy. She did so disguised as a man and as a freed black slave, and was able to cross the lines at Yorktown, Virginia, to sketch the local defenses. She would undertake a further 11 secret missions for the Union, often masquerading as a black laborer or an Irish peddler as she described in her 1865 autobiography, *Nurse and Spy in the Union Army*.

Having fled from Canada in 1856 to escape a marriage arranged by her father, Edmonds had settled in Rhode Island as Franklin Thompson and worked as a traveler selling Bibles. She then joined the Second Michigan Infantry and in 1862 was employed by General George McClellan to reconnoiter Yorktown. When she learned that many of the fortifications included "Quaker guns"—wooden logs painted to look like cannons—her information allowed the Union forces to prevail.

In 1867 Edmonds returned to Canada where she married Linus Seelye and bore him three children. She eventually succumbed to malaria in September 1898 in La Porte, Texas, having been granted a pension of $12 a month by a special Act of Congress in July 1884.

EDWARDS, MENA. In 1915, Mena Edwards, a beautiful model employed by Eastman Kodak in New York, approached the U.S. Justice Department and alleged that she and her equally attractive roommate, Martha Heldt, had been befriended by two German diplomats, Franz von Papen and Karl Boy-Ed. The government was interested in the pair as they were, respectively, the military and naval attachés, and Edwards volunteered to collect information from the suitors while they entertained the women across Manhattan. However, in August 1915 von Papen and Boy-Ed were asked to return home, and rumors circulated that their removal had been the result of reports submitted by Edwards, although in his 1952 memoirs von Papen protested that her stories of wild parties had been fabrications. Nevertheless, both men's careers were damaged by the tales and they received a poor welcome upon their return home.

ENERO. The KGB **Second Chief Directorate** (SCD) codename for an Italian diplomat at the embassy in Moscow who was spotted conducting an affair with a secretary working at the French embassy. With this evidence of ENERO's philandering, a **swallow**, codenamed SUKHOVA, was installed as his maid and he was promptly **honeytrapped**. ENERO was then honeytrapped a second time while on a trip to Tashkent by another swallow, Diana Kazachenko.

The KGB's pitch to ENERO was two-pronged. A Russian friend of his warned him that the militia had had just rounded up a criminal gang that had been blackmailing foreigners, and they had found a set of compromising photographs with him and his maid. While ENERO was digesting this news, he was also the subject of an official complaint from Kazchenko's family, who claimed that he had raped the woman and that subsequently she had become an invalid when her abortion was mishandled. Reeling from the shock, he agreed to supply the SCD with information in return for no public scandal. I. I. Kuznetsov was sent to Rome when he returned home to introduce him to a case officer from the *rezidentura*. However, after an initial meeting, and a payment of $500, ENERO dropped from view and by the time he was traced he had gone into retirement, pleading ill health. Accepting that he was no longer of any value, the KGB dropped ENERO.

EXNER, JUDITH CAMPBELL. One of President John F. Kennedy's many lovers, Judith Exner, later to be married to MGM and Warner Bros. contract actor William Campbell and then the golf professional Dan Exner, distinguished herself from the rest because of her simultaneous relationship with Sam Giancana, the notorious Chicago Mafia boss. She came from a wealthy background—her father, Joseph Immoor, was a prominent architect with a home in Pacific Palisades and a large Roman Catholic family, and her older sister Jacqueline was an actress, having adopted the stage name Susan Morrow. In contrast, Giancana had been one of Al Capone's henchmen. By the age of 20, in

1928, he had been arrested three times for murder but had never been convicted. Thirty years later, he was the undisputed mobster leader and partner in Las Vegas and Havana casinos, exercising secret control over numerous corrupt businesses and unions.

Originally picked up by the gangster-turned-movie-producer Johnny Rosselli when she was 17 while "hanging around the studios" in 1951 in Los Angeles, Exner was introduced to Giancana at a party held at the French Room of Miami's Fontainebleau Hotel in March 1960 by Frank Sinatra, who had himself dated her since late 1959. Giancana was smitten by the beautiful brunette but soon afterward she met actor Peter Lawford, who passed her on to Jack Kennedy at a party held at the Sands Hotel in Las Vegas. Exner's relationship with Kennedy would be manipulated by both Giancana, who was anxious to exploit his links to the administration, and by J. Edgar Hoover, the aging director of the Federal Bureau of Investigation (FBI) who tapped the talkative Exner's telephone and recorded several of her more embarrassing calls to the Oval Office. The White House switchboard logs would later show more than 80 calls, and the transcripts were so compromising that some believed the more sensitive conversations had been orchestrated deliberately by Rosselli, who maintained contact with Exner for his own motives. He had been approached by Robert Maheu, a former FBI special agent and then an intermediary representing the **Central Intelligence Agency** (CIA), to find a hit man capable of assassinating Fidel Castro. This scheme, codenamed ZR/RIFLE, was authorized by the White House and financed with a budget of $150,000 supplied by the CIA's deputy director for plans, Richard Bissell, and was intended to eliminate Castro on the eve of the Bay of Pigs invasion. Its failure would provide Rosselli and Giancana with what they thought would be lasting leverage with the CIA against future FBI interference.

At Maheu's request, Giancana agreed to solve the problem of Castro although actually the Mafia simply did not have the gunmen in Cuba that the CIA thought it had, and realized that the assassination could not be achieved with a shooting. Nevertheless, Giancana and Rosselli knew from Maheu that the CIA was behind the plot, and actually they were quite willing to participate without the lure of Bissell's offer of financial reward. They relied upon the mob boss in Florida, Santos Trafficante, to provide the assassins with access to

Castro, and he recruited Juan Orta, the Cuban leader's secretary, who was supplied with some lethal pills with which to complete his task. Orta failed in his mission and instead took refuge in the Venezuelan embassy shortly before the Bay of Pigs invasion. Trafficante's backup assassin, Tony Varona, was also unable to complete his assignment, although he would become the mob's link with Bill Harvey, the experienced CIA officer placed in charge of Task Force W, the Miami-based team ordered to carry out the White House's bidding.

To complicate the issue, and unknown to Maheu, Giancana had developed a covert relationship with the Kennedy brothers, who believed the mobster could influence the 1960 election and deliver the union votes, especially from the Teamsters he controlled. Accordingly, Exner passed large sums of cash from Kennedy to Giancana and, having been present at two of their meetings, she also knew of the scheme to eliminate Castro.

Exner's affair with Kennedy and his friendship with Sinatra were suspended while the FBI's organized crime division went in pursuit of Giancana, but ultimately the administration failed to provide any protection for Rosselli, who would be deported to Italy as an illegal immigrant. As for Hoover, he would circulate a memorandum dated 27 February 1962 to Robert Kennedy's Department of Justice regarding the transcripts of Exner's indiscreet telephone conversations whenever the topic of his retirement was raised by the administration. Doubtless unaware of her own significance, Exner's role was exploited by Hoover, Giancana, and Rosselli for their own purposes. Hoover was invited to a private lunch with the president in March 1962, only his second such encounter, although no record was kept of their exchanges. That same afternoon, Kennedy called Exner to warn her that her home telephone was tapped, although Hoover may not have revealed to him the extent of the technical and physical surveillance she was under. On one occasion in August 1962, two technicians, the sons of the director of security at General Dynamics Corporation, were spotted breaking into Exner's apartment on Fontaine Avenue in west Los Angeles, apparently to install listening devices, but the incident was not reported by the FBI to the local police because of the sensitivity of the operation. Although the FBI traced the pair back to General Dynamics, no further action was taken, and the episode suggests that others knew of, and were interested in, Exner, who remained unaware of the break-in until she acquired a copy of her own FBI file decades later.

Exner's affair with the president was the subject of evidence she gave to Frank Church's Senate Select Committee on Intelligence Activities in 1975, in which she disclosed much but denied having conducted a simultaneous relationship with Giancana, but two years later, she admitted in her autobiography, *My Story*, ghosted by David Demaris, that some of her earlier testimony had been misleading, and she had not been pressed to be more candid. She also revealed that she had acted as a courier to pass documents and money from her lover John Kennedy to Giancana and Rosselli. Although many of the details about Exner's affair would be corroborated by White House records and FBI surveillance files, the veracity of her claim to have been made pregnant by Kennedy was never confirmed, and she eventually succumbed to cancer at her home in Newport Beach, California.

– F –

FALK, ELKE. A vulnerable young secretary, Elke Falk was recruited by a **Romeo spy** after she advertised in the lonely hearts column of a newspaper. Gerhard Thieme responded, but he was a KGB illegal, Kurt Simon, codenamed GEORG, and he quickly recruited her under a false flag. He encouraged her to apply for a post in the civil service and in 1974 she was given a job in the Federal chancellor's private office. Codenamed LENA by the KGB, Falk was replaced by another illegal, using the alias Peter Muller, and another codenamed ADAM. In 1977, she was switched to the Transport Ministry and in 1979 she was moved to the Economics Ministry, but she was arrested in 1989 and sentenced to six and a half years' imprisonment. A few months later, she was exchanged in a spy swap with East Germany.

FEUCHTINGER, EDGAR. Born in Metz in 1894, Edgar Feuchtinger joined the Kaiser's army as soon as World War I started, in August 1914, and served in an artillery regiment. After the war, he joined the Reichwehr as a career soldier and in August 1939 was promoted to the rank of lieutenant colonel to command the 227th Artillery Regiment. By April 1943, he had been appointed the commanding officer of the Schnellen Division West's motorized troops, and in March 1944 he was transferred to the Russian front to be the deputy leader of the 8th Panzer Division.

Up to this moment, Feuchtinger's career had been exemplary, but when he was switched to command the 21st Panzer Division in France, he absented himself briefly to be with his girlfriend in Paris and was not at his post on D-Day. He quickly returned to his unit and fought bravely with his troops, winning the Knight's Cross in August for gallantry, but his dereliction of duty on the day of the Allied invasion led to his arrest in January 1945. He was arrested, charged with corruption and desertion, and incarcerated at Torgau prison, where he was sentenced to death. However, his sentence was commuted to service at the front as a gunner, and, in March 1945, he deserted and then gave himself up in Hamburg to the British, who sent him to London for interrogation. From the end of May 1945 until July 1945, Lieutenant General Feuchtinger was held at Trent Park, Cockfosters, where he was accommodated with a group of other senior German officers, including General Gerd von Massow, with whom he held a private conversation that was recorded by MI19. In their exchange, Feuchtinger was heard to confide to von Massow that when he had been in Pinsk, he had heard from a nurse working at the officers' hostel where he had been accommodated that the previous year the town's entire Jewish population of 25,000 had been shot and buried in mass graves.

Because he was never personally implicated in any war crimes, Feuchtinger was repatriated in August 1947. Sometime in 1953, he was recruited as a spy by the Soviet GRU. He subsequently went to live in East Berlin, where he died in mysterious circumstances in January 1960.

FIELD, NOEL. Born in London to American parents living in Zurich, where his father was a psychiatrist, Field graduated from Harvard and in 1926 joined the State Department, where he became friends with **Alger Hiss** and Laurence Duggan. Both were already active Soviet agents and, according to his former Soviet controller, Field too worked as a spy during this period. After 10 years in the State Department and against the wishes of his controller, Field moved to Geneva to work for the League of Nations, and while there he in some way became implicated in the plot to murder **Ignace Reiss**, a senior Soviet illegal.

Like numerous other important Soviet intelligence organizers, Reiss fell victim to Stalin's purges, but instead of obeying his recall to Moscow he went into hiding in Switzerland. He was lured to Lausanne in September 1937 but a murder attempt was unsuccessful. It was at this point, following an intensive Swiss police investigation, that Field lost his usefulness to the NKVD and he was cast adrift. However, as a committed ideologue, Field never lost his faith and even traveled, as a tourist, to Moscow the following year.

Upon his return from the Soviet Union, Field was posted to undertake refugee relief work in Perpignan, then crowded with survivors of the Spanish Civil War, and in October 1940 left the League of Nations to continue his work for the Unitarian Service Committee in Marseilles. He was obliged to flee to Switzerland in October 1942, when the Nazis extended their grip of France to take over the Vichy unoccupied zone, but by then Field had established contact with remnants of an underground Kommunist Partei Deutschland (KPD) cell, and with Allen Dulles, the Office of Strategic Services (OSS) representative in Berne. Whatever the precise nature of his covert courier activities for OSS and the KPD, Field during this period was to contaminate virtually every Communist he came into contact with, and when he traveled to Prague early in May 1949 to look for a post at the Charles University, he was arrested and taken to Budapest for interrogation.

Field himself was to remain in solitary confinement in an Allami Vedélmi Hatosag (AVH) prison, without charge but subject to frequent interrogation, until November 1954 when he was released without explanation. In the meantime, the Hungarian foreign minister, Laszlo Rajk, had been arrested, accused of having been a Soviet spy, convicted at a show trial, and hanged. The same fate befell Traicho Kostov, Bulgaria's deputy prime minister, and even the Polish Communist Party first secretary, Wladyslaw Gomulka, was thrown into prison, but the thread connecting the three was the allegation, contained in their separate indictments, that each had been recruited and run on behalf of OSS by Field, described as "one of the leaders of the American espionage service" headed by Allen Dulles. Even Rudolf Slansky, who himself as the powerful secretary of the Czech

Communist Party had overseen the purge in Czechoslovakia, was arrested, charged with espionage, and executed. In fact, of course, Slansky, like Rajk and Gomulka, had shown too much independence from Moscow and had fallen victim to Stalin's paranoia, and it is likely that Field only survived, to be released 20 months after Stalin's death in March 1953, because, like his wife Herta and his brother Hermann, he held an American passport. Field had indeed aided Rajk's return to Hungary in 1943, having arranged his escape from an internment camp in France, doubtless with OSS's help, but his route through Yugoslavia served to compromise him when, four years later, Tito distanced himself from Stalin and the combination of links to OSS, Field, and the Yugoslavs were considered highly incriminating. Dozens of other Communists in Czechoslovakia, East Germany, and Poland to whom Field had given assistance in the war found themselves contaminated and purged. Some survived years of imprisonment and the Gulag, but many others were less fortunate.

Three months after Noel Field disappeared in Prague, his brother Hermann, then living in Warsaw, started on a journey to find him, but he only reached Okecie Airport, where he was taken into custody by the Urzab Bezpieczenstwa (UB). Noel's wife Herta, who awaited Hermann's arrival in Prague, was baffled by his failure to catch his flight, and later in August 1949 she too was arrested by the Czech police and sent to Budapest, where she was imprisoned, isolated from her husband. Hermann would not be released from his confinement in a basement cell at Miedzyszyn, a secret UB facility outside Warsaw, until November 1954, only days before his brother and sister-in-law were freed in Budapest. Hermann promptly flew to Zurich, but Noel and Herta chose to seek political asylum in Hungary, apparently undaunted by their experience. One influence over their decision to make their permanent home on the Sashegy Hill, overlooking Budapest, may have been the eagerness of the Federal Bureau of Investigation (FBI) to question them about their links to the **Communist Party of the United States of America** (CPUSA). Since the end of the war, his friend Alger Hiss had been convicted of perjury for having lied about his espionage, Lawrence Duggan had committed suicide by throwing himself out of his Madison Avenue office window in December 1948 while under investigation by the FBI, and numerous former CPUSA members had denounced Noel Field as a spy who had betrayed secrets from inside the State Department. Field knew that he was of intense interest to the FBI because when he had sought to renew his American passport in 1949 he had been granted a short extension, and informed that the document was only good for travel back to the United States. Field must have known that a former CPUSA courier, J. B. Matthews, had named Field as a fellow Communist in testimony before the Dies Committee in November 1938, and perhaps that another FBI informant, **Whittaker Chambers**, had also denounced him, but what he did not know was that he had also been identified positively as a Soviet spy by a defector, **Hede Massing**, in 1947, and she had been in a position to know a great deal about his espionage because she had recruited him in the first place. She and her husband Paul had acted as Soviet illegals before the war but, disillusioned by Stalin's excesses, had broken with the Party and agreed to cooperate with the FBI to whom she had identified Field as one of her top sources. However, as the Fields had remained abroad, out of jurisdiction, the FBI had been powerless to pursue them.

During his imprisonment in Budapest, Field had been cross-examined by numerous interrogators, but one of the most brutal had been Colonel Josef Swiatlo, the UB officer who had arrested his brother Hermann at Warsaw Airport, and who had traveled to Hungary to question him. Even by the UB's standards Swiatlo was a ruthless individual with a terrifying reputation, and as deputy director of the feared 10th Department he had arrested the Party's general secretary, Wladyslaw Gomulka. None of this might have become public knowledge but in early December 1953, while on an official visit to East Berlin, Swiatlo had seized the opportunity to defect to the **Central Intelligence Agency** (CIA), and late in September 1954 he announced at a press conference in Washington, D.C., that he intended to expose the true, political nature of the show trials that had been held across Eastern Europe. Unaware that Swiatlo's nickname was "the butcher," the CIA had sponsored him to broadcast to Poland over Radio Liberty, and his very detailed disclosures were considered to be extremely effective in that the Polish regime had been stunned to learn of the UB's malign activities. Swiatlo's 10th Department had been responsible for maintaining Party discipline, and this had given him the right to spy on the most senior officials of the land. Not surprisingly, Swiatlo's broadcasts had proved devastating, as all his listeners recognized the authenticity of his remarks.

Whatever else the broadcasts achieved, Noel and Herta Field were to be released and paid compensation within weeks of Swiatlo's revelation confirming that he had interrogated them personally in Budapest where they had been incarcerated. Hitherto the Czech, Polish, and Hungarian authorities had claimed complete ignorance of what might have happened to the three members of the Field family. However, once Swiatlo exposed the truth, all three governments were forced to admit at least that the trio had been imprisoned. Field, whose health never fully recovered from his incarceration, died in 1972.

FISHER, WILLIE. Appointed the NKVD's illegal *rezident* in New York in November 1948, Willie Fisher was living as an artist under the alias Emil R. Goldfus when he was arrested at the Latham Hotel, Brooklyn, in May 1957 by the Federal Bureau of Investigation (FBI), having been identified by a defector, **Reino Hayhanen**.

The FBI's investigation of Goldfus revealed, from a hotel bill found in his room, that he had recently returned from Daytona Beach, Florida, whence he had fled following Hayhanen's defection. His original entry into the United States had been from Canada in November 1948, and his arrival in Quebec from Cuxhaven aboard the SS *Scythia* in the middle of the month had been accomplished with an authentic American passport identifying him as Andrew Kayotis, a naturalized American citizen living in Detroit. The real Kayotis, who was Lithuanian in origin, had returned in poor health to Kaunas in July 1947 where he had died soon afterward.

In early 1950 Fisher rented a furnished apartment in New York in the name of Goldfus. The birth certificate he carried was genuine, but it belonged to a child born in Manhattan to a German immigrant family in 1902, who had died just after his first birthday, in October 1903. The identity of Martin Collins, the name under which he was registered at the Latham Hotel, was entirely false and supported only by a forged birth certificate. A bankbook issued by the East River Savings Bank in June 1950 showed a balance of $1,386, with the most recent entry dated 5 April 1957. A further $15,000 was recovered from a safe-deposit box held at the Manufacturers Trust Company in the name of an acquaintance. In his hotel room, FBI special agents found a coded message written in five-figure groups on a slip of graph paper, and a piece of wood covered with sandpaper was split open to reveal a 250-page one-time pad printed in red and blue, together with a signal schedule. Close examination of an ostensibly ordinary pencil produced 18 microfilms, some of them containing letters from his wife and daughter in Moscow. They also found a box of condoms, suggesting that Fisher had been in the habit of using prostitutes.

Arrested on immigration charges, Fisher was flown to an immigration holding center at McAllen, Texas, where the FBI attempted to break the prisoner's silence by offering him resettlement and a handsome pension in return for his cooperation.

Under interrogation, Fisher quickly declared himself to be Rudolph I. Abel, supposedly a Russian refugee who had bought a false American passport in Denmark. He named his parents, claimed he once had been a teacher of English in Moscow, and accepted that he was eligible for deportation but denied any involvement with espionage. Nor was there much evidence to implicate him. A detailed forensic analysis of Fisher's activities during his eight years in the field failed to disclose any significant espionage. Although there was plenty of incriminating paraphernalia found in his apartment, including a Hallicrafter shortwave wireless receiver, a radio schedule, microdot equipment, and large sums of cash, there was no evidence of any significant intelligence gathering. When translated, a copy of his most recent signal home proved to contain an innocuous message to his mother, details of the chemical composition of a soft film laminate, and an acknowledgment from his wife of some gift packages. Apart from some cryptic messages concerning signals to be used in Mexico City, presumably part of an escape plan, the only secret messages found proved to be seven letters from Fisher's wife Ilya and their newly married daughter Evelyn, containing mainly trivial domestic news about their apartment and dog. Having analyzed the information contained in the correspondence, the FBI concluded that Fisher had left New York for Moscow on 10 June 1955, and had traveled via Paris and Vienna. Although of minor intelligence value, the letters give some insight into Fisher's home circumstances, and a letter dated 20 February 1956 from his daughter suggested Fisher had left Moscow the previous November:

It is almost three months since you went away. Although it's not so much to compare with eternity, still it is a long time and the more so as there is a great quantity of news to tell you. First of all, I am going to marry. Please don't be astounded. I am much surprised myself, and still it is a fact to be taken for granted. My future husband seems to be a good guy. He is thirty-four and a radio engineer. Mother likes him very much. We met at the birthday of our friend who lives in the bungalow. On Feb. 25 we shall celebrate our wedding. I hope you will like him when you get back. I think you will have much to talk about. News number two—We are to get a new flat of two rooms—it is not what we're supposed to get but it is a flat for ourselves and much better than what we have now. News number three—I found a job, engineer referent in aviation, so now I shall be somewhat closer to you. The job seems to be a decent one. They promised to pay me well and my future boss seems to be an intellectual and polite guy. I did some odd jobs there and received a pretty sum of money. My future husband and I are both deeply interested in photography, especially in color photography. He has an Olympia car and we both enjoy meddling with it. We received both your letters and the key from the suitcase, but the latter is still wandering somewhere. Our childhood friend writes regularly and sends you his and his family's best regards and wishes. All our friends wish you health and happiness and a happy and quick way home. Well, this is all I have to say. Yours, Evelyn.

Fisher's wife also experienced difficulty in reconciling herself to her husband's absence and one of his possessions, probably his guitar, is a reminder of his departure. In an undated note, she wrote:

After your departure, I certainly was ill. There was a hardening of the arteries of the heart. I sleep poorly and I do not go out on the street. I walk on the balcony. Sometimes I approach your instrument and look at it and want to again hear you play and I become sad. For the remaining money I asked them basically to have them send it all to you. Evelyn has married (in late February) and she, after getting married, always says there are no such men as her papa and therefore she is not too much in love with her husband. You are the best of all for us And don't frown, everyone says this who knows you. If you look at things with a philosophical point of view, then taking hair from your head doesn't pay. I kiss you firmly and congratulate you. Try to arrange everything so that you do not delay the period of our meeting. Years and age will not wait for us. How are you there? How is your stomach? Take care of yourself—I want to live together with you for ourselves.

A further, undated letter from Evelyn appeared to be birthday greetings, which would suggest it was written shortly before Fisher's true birthday, 2 July 1956, a deduction confirmed by the reference to her wedding, which had been scheduled for 25 February.

> Many happy returns. Daddy dear, I am missing you so much. You just cannot imagine how much I need you. It is about four months now since I have married and to me it seems like an eternity, so dull it sometimes is. In general, he is a good chap, but he isn't you. I have got a job. My boss . . . is a bit like you though not so broadminded and not a very great erudite. Though very clever. I am in a great hurry now as I have to go to work.

The next in the sequence is from Fisher's wife, dated 6 April, in which she indicates that she has not received a reply to her earlier note:

> I am writing a second letter—up till now I only heard from you from the trip. I want very much to find out how you are. How is your health? I am gradually beginning to come to myself. I could go for a rest but I am afraid to travel alone, so that I have not yet decided, although I passed the medical board. How necessary you could be to me now. And how good it is that you do not feel the need of being with us. Evelyn works part time and on her free time from her husband and work she took me to the doctor and at the same time she herself had a check-up. Spring here will again be late. Up till now, it has been cold, damp and snow. The winter was simply horrible. And I am worried about my flowers. Evelyn says the plum trees froze and it's hard to get the plums. Your father-in-law . . . is awaiting your earliest return, and I, although I know it is silly, am counting off the days of the known period. I have not received your package yet. . . . A childhood friend visited us . . . we talked a lot, reminisced, and most all day, dreamed. Don't let us down. In general, our whole life, constant waiting. That's the way it is, dear. Write as often as possible. The children, there are two now, send greetings. Son is very disturbed what kind of an impression he will make on you. He might not appeal to you at once. I kiss you firmly. I wish you luck, health, and most of all a speedy return.

By 21 June, the date of the next letter from Abel's wife, she has heard from her husband. A reference to Fisher gathering the last apple harvest was helpful in pinning down the period he spent in the Soviet Union the previous year, and the comment about a dacha and servant prove he is a privileged member of Soviet society:

At last we received your small package. Everything pleased us very much, and as usual, whatever you do, with care and attention. We were glad to receive a letter from you and to learn that everything is fine with you. It is a pity you have not had letters from us—such a long time. I sent you several. Congratulations on your birthday. We drink a toast to your well-being and your early promised return. We are at the summer place. In many respects our garden has suffered. On the best apple trees, from which last year you culled a plentiful harvest, only now have the leaves started to appear. I am still fighting with the house servant and do not have a new one. . . . The television works but I seldom look at it. The dog behaves very well—she too awaits her master, and I also wait. It is desirable to have a husband at home; at the present time I feel your absence more, especially since I have been with you and remember what you promised me before your departure. Our new chef is wonderful, attentive and tactful.

The last letter from Fisher's wife, dated 20 August, acknowledges receipt of her husband's gift:

How glad I was to learn you have received one of my letters. We received the package in May. It is a shame the hyacinths traveled long and two of them perished altogether. The rest are planted and already have rooted. This is a live greeting from you. Next year they will bloom. We count every month that passes and you remember this.

The day after her mother had written, Evelyn wrote a third letter to her father, dated 21 August, evidently in response to one from him:

We liked your presents very much—we planted the hyacinths that survived and by now three of them have sprouted. You say you want more particulars about my husband. I shall try to give you a better picture of him. He is short, green-eyed, rather handsome. He is rather gay and talkative when the conversation considers cars or football. He works as an engineer—he is capable though rather lazy. . . . You ask me whether I am happy with him. As one of our greatest poets once said, there is no happiness in life but there is peace and free will. The only thing that troubles me is that I find him boring sometimes. Now about my in-laws. They are awful. I do wish you were with us. Everything would be much easier for us then. I am missing you very much. I thought at first that my husband could substitute you in some respects, but now I see that I was mistaken. Now about my work. I like it fine. I have a splendid boss. He is a very interesting man, clever, talented, tolerant and handsome. We like each other and spend much time talking about various things. He is 44, single and rather unhappy. I wish you could see him and talk to him. My health is OK. PS I have started writing poetry in this language. Next time I shall send you a sample.

Having heard his characteristically northern English accent, his interrogators suspected "Abel" to have used yet another identity, that of a British businessman called "Mr. Milton" for whom Morris and **Lona Cohen** were known to have given a dinner party at their East 71st Street home in February 1950, and there was a belief that Morris Cohen, an electrical engineer by trade, might have worked briefly as Fisher's wireless operator, but no supporting evidence was found apart from passport photos of the two Cohens recovered from Fisher's briefcase, attached to a large quantity of dollar bills.

Even if it appeared that Fisher had not achieved much of operational importance, he clearly was valued by the Soviets, and in February 1962 he was freed from a 30-year prison sentence and swapped for the U-2 pilot Gary Powers, who had been shot down near Sverdlovsk in May the previous year. While in the federal penitentiary, Fisher improved his very considerable artistic skills and, after his departure for Berlin, left behind several noteworthy pictures that were to become much sought-after collectors' items. According to some of those who knew him upon his return to Moscow, Fisher was never trusted entirely again by the KGB, not because his mission had been a failure, but just because he had spent so long in the West. Fisher became something of a celebrity, but his popularity within the KGB suffered when he took up the cause of two former colleagues, Pavel Sudoplatov and Leonid Eitingon, both close associates of **Beria**, who had been imprisoned and purged after Stalin's death. Fisher himself died in November 1971 and it was only much later that his much-publicized background was revealed to be as false as the name Abel. His parents were Russian émigrés of German background named Fisher and he was born in Benwell, Newcastle upon Tyne, in July 1903. His father, Genrykh M. Fisher, a radical revolutionary and a friend of Lenin's, had immigrated to England two years earlier, and had worked in the Armstrong shipyard as an engine fitter. During the Russian revolution of 1905, Genrykh had practiced his political agitation on the crews of two Russian ships that had docked in the Tyne for repairs. After the failure of the rising, Genrykh had been implicated in a plot to send arms and subversive literature to Russia. The scheme had failed and various participants were prosecuted for their part in it; although Genrykh escaped being charged, it apparently jeopardized his chances of obtaining British nationality. During World War I, he continued his political activities among visiting Russian crews but returned to Russia in 1921, taking his son—who had evidently come to share his Bolshevik ideology—with him. According to one report, Genrykh renewed his friendship with Lenin and became his close confidant, and was assigned an apartment in the Kremlin. The following year Genrykh adopted the name A. Fisher to publish his memoirs, *In Russia and England: Observations and Recollections of a Petersburg Worker, 1891–1921*, and he died in 1935, but there is some evidence that his son later returned to London on his British passport, and may have fought in the Spanish Civil War.

FLETCHER, HAROLD. A mathematician employed by the Government Code and Cypher School on highly secret cryptographic work, Harold Fletcher was denounced as a spy in 1939 in an anonymous letter addressed to the Foreign Office. A check on his personnel file revealed that in 1935 Fletcher had traveled to Germany with his mistress, Gula Pfeffer, and upon his return had reported having been introduced to one of her relations, a Captain von Pfeffer who was an intelligence officer. When Fletcher was interviewed, he denied having passed any classified information to Gula and insisted he had terminated the relationship. However, when she was interned as an enemy alien, Fletcher recommended her release, claiming alternatively that she was harmless or that she could be used as a double agent. MI5 conducted a lengthy investigation into Fletcher, suspecting he had passed information to von Pfeffer, who was employed by Kurt Jahnke's intelligence bureau, but no evidence was found to support a prosecution.

FOGGO, KYLE. In 2006, Kyle ("Dusty") Foggo, the executive director of the **Central Intelligence Agency** (CIA), was arrested by the Federal Bureau of Investigation (FBI) after allegations of corruption were made concerning contracts granted to his friend Brent Wilkes, who had been accused of bribing a Congressman, Randy Cunningham, with cash and prostitutes. The FBI heard that Foggo, who had gained a reputation for being fond of casinos and hookers while he was stationed at Tegucigalpa, Honduras, had performed oral sex on a prostitute at a party, and had used his CIA credentials to enter a strip club. Foggo resigned his post, the agency's third-most senior position, soon after his home and office had been raided by the FBI. In November 2005, Cunningham was sentenced to eight years' imprisonment after having pleaded guilty to accepting $2.4 million in bribes. In May 2007, additional charges of fraud, conspiracy, and money laundering were brought against Foggo and Wilkes.

FRANCILLARD, MARGUERITE. Executed by a firing squad at St. Lazare prison in Paris in January 1917, Marguerite Francillard was an 18-year-old French dressmaker when she was recruited by a German who described himself as a silk salesman. She agreed to act as his courier, carrying documents from his agents in France to him in Switzerland, but in 1916 she was arrested when a search at the frontier revealed her true role.

FRIEDMAN, LITZI. The daughter of a Viennese bookseller, Israel Kohlman, Litzi married **Kim Philby** in February 1934, at the age of 23. A divorcée, who had wed Katl Friedman when she was 18, she was closely connected to the NKVD through her friend **Edith Suschitsky**. When she was investigated following Philby's defection in January 1963, MI5 learned that she had conducted several affairs before she had left the country to live in East Germany. Among those compromised by her were a Secret Intelligence Service officer, Tony Milne, and a senior Foreign Office diplomat, Michael Stewart, who was later appointed the British ambassador in Athens. Both acknowledged having conducted affairs with Litzi, unaware that she was a Soviet spy, and denied ever having compromised any classified information.

– G –

GAERTNER, FRIEDLE. Codenamed GELATINE by her admiring MI5 case officer, Friedle Gaertner was a beautiful cabaret artist who, like her equally glamorous sister Lisel, had come to London from Austria. Lisel had married Ian Menzies, whose elder brother Stewart would be appointed chief of the Secret Intelligence Service in November 1939, but Friedle worked in nightclubs and before the outbreak of World War II acted as an informer for MI5's **Max Knight**, attending gatherings at the local Ausland Organization headquarters in London, and identifying Nazi sympathizers. Immediately after Anschluss in March 1938, she asked to change her passport at the embassy, thereby ensuring she would be registered as pro-Nazi. Ostensibly employed by the novelist Dennis Wheatley as his secretary, Friedle Gaertner was introduced to **Dusan Popov** soon after his arrival in England in December 1940, and she supplied both him and the Abwehr with political gossip, picked up from indiscreet friends, until May 1945.

GERHARDSEN, VARNA. In 1954, while staying in an Intourist hotel in Yerevan during a student delegation, Varna Gerhardsen was seduced by a KGB **raven**, Evgenni Belyakov, who subsequently blackmailed her, claiming that their relationship had been filmed. Her husband was Einar Gerhardsen, a former mayor of Oslo who had been elected Norway's prime minister in 1945. Belyakov was subsequently posted to the KGB *rezidentura* in Oslo to maintain contact with Varna, who cooperated because she wanted to avoid embarrassing her husband, who was 15 years her senior. She continued to supply information about NATO, Norwegian political personalities, and policy toward the United Nations for three years until Belyakov was withdrawn following a domestic dispute with his wife. Gerhardsen died in 1970 and her husband died in 1987, apparently unaware that she had tried to protect his reputation by passing secrets to the KGB.

GOBIN, MATHILDE. Part of a German husband-and-wife stay-behind team in Brussels, Mathilde Gobin and her husband Josef were arrested at their home in Brussels in October 1944, having been betrayed by ISOS intercepts that suggested they had been recruited and run by an Abwehr officer, Moritz Köchling. Neither of the Gobins would admit to espionage and, in the absence of any other evidence, they were transferred to Camp 020 at the end of December 1944 for intensive interrogation. Of particular concern to MI5 was the identification of SOPHIE and BERTHA who had appeared in the ISOS traffic as members of their network.

Mathilde was lodged at night at Holloway prison, and driven each day to Ham Common for her interviews, but neither made any admission until Josef was informed that he had been sentenced to death and would be moved to what was described to him as the condemned cell. Here, under pressure from other Belgian prisoners, he finally admitted his role and revealed that as well as engaging in espionage for Köchling, he had also supplied him with black-market goods, and that SOPHIE was their codename for butter, and BERTHA was bacon. In his confession, which was countersigned reluctantly by his wife, Gobin also revealed the ingenious hiding place for his radio transmitter that hitherto had escaped discovery despite the most rigorous of searches, concealed inside a specially constructed desk. Both prisoners were returned to Belgium for prosecution at the end of hostilities

GOERTZ, HERMAN. In November 1935, Dr. Herman Goertz was arrested at Harwich upon his return to England and charged with breaches of the Official Secrets Act. He had been the tenant of a bungalow in Stanley Road, Broadstairs, which he had rented the previous September but had left without paying the rent to his landlady, Mrs. Florence Johnson. Accordingly, she called the police and a search of the house revealed that her tenant had left a mass of incriminating espionage paraphernalia and sketches of local airfields, including the nearby RAF station at Manston. Local residents were equally scandalized to learn that Dr. Goertz's attractive young companion, Marianne Emig, was not his niece at all. Unaware of the excitement he had caused, Goertz returned in November from a trip to the Continent and was arrested as he landed at Harwich. At his Old Bailey trial in March the following year, he was sentenced to four years' imprisonment at Maidstone.

After his release and deportation, Goertz undertook a further mission for the Abwehr, this time alone and by parachute to Ireland to establish contact with the Irish Republican Army. He remained at liberty for 19 months before he was arrested and interned for the remainder of the war. Due to be deported at the end of hostilities, Goertz remained in Dublin but committed suicide in May 1947 when he learned he was to be returned to Germany. Soon afterward, Marianne Emig was spotted in Germany and underwent an interrogation conducted by the Security Service, but she coyly refused to answer any questions about the precise nature of her relationship with Goertz.

GOLENIEWSKI, MICHAL. Prior to his unexpected defection in Berlin in December 1960, Michal Goleniewski was a senior officer in the Polish Sluzba Bezpiecezenstwa (SB) who had sent several anonymous letters to the **Central Intelligence Agency** (CIA) identifying various SB and KGB assets. Although his motives were unclear, the source who called himself SNIPER and typed his messages in good German eventually revealed that his decision to start a new life in the West had been prompted by a love affair, and his girlfriend accompanied him to the United States for resettlement. Not all the information Goleniewski provided could be acted on by the CIA as it was received, because to do so might compromise the source who, unusually, was not only an SB officer but also reported to the KGB's *rezidentura* in Warsaw, and therefore heard plenty of gossip about hot cases run by the First Chief Directorate. In particular, Goleniewski was able to supply the first clues that led MI5 to **Harry Houghton**, **Irwin Scarbeck**, and **George Blake**, among several others.

GOULD, MAUD. In December 1913, the new landlord of the Queen Charlotte public house in Rochester discovered a cache of documents hidden in the building, and among them was a portfolio of British Admiralty maps, a rental agreement on a house in Wandsworth, and the copy of a letter dated 8 October 1903, signed by "F. A. Gould Schroeder," in which the author described having won the Iron Cross in the Franco-German War of 1870, and having subsequently worked for the German Secret Service across much of Europe.

Instead of being passed to the pub's previous landlord, the collection of papers was handed in to the police and an investigation was started that revealed that Frederick Gould, now a cigar merchant in Winterton Road, Wandsworth, was actually Adolph Schroder who had immigrated to England in 1858 at the age of four. Other correspondence recovered from Rochester suggested that Gould had been a badly paid German spy working for a man referred to simply as "St," most likely the Kaiser's chief intelligence officer, Gustav Steinauer. Accordingly, Gould's mail was intercepted and in February 1914 a series of telegrams revealed that he had negotiated the sale of some unknown item in Belgium for £30. Special Branch detectives then followed his wife, Maud Gould, to Charing Cross station, where she was seen to buy a return ticket to Ostend, but she was arrested on the train when three envelopes were spotted concealed in a traveling rug. She was escorted to Bow Street police station but on the way she attempted to discard the envelopes, which were found to contain two Admiralty charts of Saphead and Bergen, a gunnery book, and a blueprint detailing the engine room of a Royal Navy cruiser. When her house was raided, more incriminating documents were discovered in Gould's desk, including an intelligence questionnaire listing 36 items of interest about British warships.

Both Goulds were charged with breaches of the Official Secrets Act and in April 1914 Frederick pleaded guilty at the Old Bailey and was sentenced to six years' imprisonment, but Maud was acquitted because her husband insisted she had no knowledge of what had been inside the envelopes.

GRAY, OLGA. The daughter of a *Daily Mail* journalist who had been killed in the trenches during World War I, and calling herself Ann, Gray was recruited at a Conservative Party garden fete by MI5's **Maxwell Knight** at Edgbaston and paid £2.50 a week. Over seven years of operational work, initially at the Friends of the Soviet Union and then at King Street as John Strachey's secretary, she proved to be an exceptionally talented agent. After she gained the trust of Percy Glading, the **Communist Party of Great Britain**'s (CPGB) national organizer, he used her as a courier to deliver secret information to Party contacts in India. She reported to MI5 on the long-suspected overlap between the CPGB and Soviet espionage, and revealed to Max Knight the existence of a covert wireless link with Moscow run by the secretary-general, Harry Pollitt, and explained how the cipher system was based on a book, information that enabled the Government Code and Cypher School cryptographers to break the traffic codenamed MASK.

Prolonged surveillance and information from Olga showed that Glading had renewed contact with some of his old colleagues at the Woolwich Arsenal and was copying blueprints supplied by them of armaments manufactured at the plant. Also implicated was Paddy Ayriss, the wife of George Hardy, a CPGB activist in the seamen's unions, based in London but originally from Merseyside. Both Hardy and his wife would appear in the MASK traffic, but although Ayriss was suspected of having acted as a courier, moving between Glading, the illegal "Paul Hardt," and the Soviet embassy, there was never any evidence to justify her arrest. Accordingly, she was one of the members of the spy ring who escaped any criminal charge when the police rounded up the network in January 1938.

Born in 1906, Olga's MI5 work began as a typist in the Anglo-Soviet Friendship Society, where she was talent-spotted by the CPGB as a potential courier. Her first mission, to Paris in June 1934, carrying a wad of sterling notes concealed in a sanitary towel, led to her voyage to India to deliver cash to an address in Bombay. This was considered an important mission by Knight because it demonstrated that she had succeeded in gaining the trust of the CPGB leadership, was being initiated into the Party's clandestine organization, and was likely to increase MI5's knowledge of subversion in India, where the Communist Party of India (CPI) had been outlawed. Olga's visit to Bombay was an opportunity to assess the damage sustained by the CPI, assist the local security apparatus, the highly efficient Indian Political Intelligence Bureau, and gauge the strength of the CPI's links to the outside world, if not the Comintern.

Olga's role as a penetration agent came to an end in 1938 when she appeared as a witness for the prosecution at Glading's Old Bailey trial, at which he was convicted of breaches of the Official Secrets Act and imprisoned. Olga subsequently married a Canadian serviceman and emmigrated to Ontario. *See also* WILLIAMS, NELLIE.

GRAYEVSKY, VICTOR. In February 1956, a Polish journalist, Victor Grayevsky, borrowed a secret file from the office of his mistress, Lucia Baranowski, who was married to the deputy prime minister and was also secretary to Edward Ochals, the Polish Communist Party leader, and took it to the Israeli embassy in Warsaw to be copied. The file contained one of four advance texts of the speech to be delivered to the 20th Congress of the Communist Party of the Soviet Union on 25 February by Nikita Khrushchev, in which he denounced the crimes of Josef Stalin.

Born Victor Spielman in Krakow in 1925, Grayevsky changed his name after he fled Poland following the Nazi invasion in September

1939. Educated in Kazakhstan, he returned to Warsaw in 1946 to attend the Academy of Political Science before joining the PAP news agency. His parents and sister immigrated to Israel in 1949, and in 1955 he visited them when his father fell gravely ill and was converted to Zionism. Upon his return to Warsaw, his mistress, unaware of its significance, allowed him to temporarily remove Khrushchev's speech; it was delivered to Mossad, which in turn passed it on to the U.S. **Central Intelligence Agency** (CIA).

In 1957 Grayevsky, having agreed to be recruited by the KGB, immigrated to Israel and was appointed to the Foreign Ministry's Eastern European division, and director of radio broadcasts in Polish to the immigrant population. Four years later, he resigned from the Foreign Ministry to take up the post of director of Russian language broadcasting, and in 1965 he was placed in charge of all Israeli foreign broadcasts. Throughout this period, he was in touch with the KGB through embassy personnel, but after diplomatic relations were severed in 1967, he communicated mainly through Soviet émigrés and Russian Orthodox priests, and was run by Mossad as a double agent. According to his KGB handler, who never suspected Grayevsky had supplied Khrushchev's secret speech to the CIA even before it had been delivered, Moscow awarded him a special Soviet decoration for his loyalty to the Soviet cause. Grayevsky died in October 2007, aged 82.

GREENHOW, ROSIE. Born in Montgomery County, Maryland, in 1817, Rosie Greenhow was a prominent Washington socialite and the widow of a respected physician. She was also a Confederate sympathizer recruited in 1857 by Captain Thomas Jordan as a spy to collect political and military information from her popular salon and pass it through couriers to Richmond, Virginia. Arrested in August 1861 after a lengthy investigation conducted by Allan Pinkerton, Greenhow was imprisoned until May 1862 with her nine-year-old daughter, and then released to Richmond.

In July 1862, Greenhow was sent to Europe by President Jefferson Davis to gather support for the rebels, but upon her return in September 1864, as she attempted to breach the blockade at Cape Fear, North Carolina, she was drowned, apparently weighed down by $2,000 in gold stitched into the hem of her dress as she tried to swim for the shore.

GREIBL, IGNATZ. Born and educated in Munich, Ignatz Greibl graduated from Long Island Medical College and Fordham University and was working as a physician in the émigré community concentrated in Yorkville, Manhattan, when he wrote to Josef Goebbels volunteering to spy for the Abwehr. Ignatz's offer was accepted and he became an agent even though he was acquiring prominence as a pro-Nazi, taking a prominent role in the Friends of New Germany, and organizing a swastika-decorated rally at Madison Square Garden in 1934. Greibl's wife, Maria, whom he had met while serving in the German Army, was also an enthusiastic Nazi and a spy, and she acted in a supporting role as her husband recruited other agents from among the expatriates and passed on information through a network of couriers working on transatlantic liners. Their sources included Christien Danielsen, who supplied naval blueprints stolen from the Bath Iron Works at Bangor, and Willy Lonkowski, employed as an engineer at the Ireland Aircraft Corporation on Long Island. A Federal Bureau of Investigation (FBI) special agent, Leon Turrou, later established that the Greibls used the Norddeutsche-Lloyd shipping company's private telegraph system to communicate directly with the Abwehr in Bremen.

In February 1938, the Greibls were implicated in espionage by Gunther Rumrich and under interrogation by Turrou; the doctor eventually admitted that he had been involved with the Abwehr since January 1937 when he and his mistress, **Kay Moog**, had traveled to Germany aboard the *Europa* and been recruited by members of the crew. They had suggested that Moog move to Washington, D.C., and make herself useful by entertaining administration officials. After he completely incriminated himself, Greibl agreed to work as a double agent and entrap Karl Herman, whom he described as the Gestapo's chief in New York. A search of Herman's home revealed a mass of evidence; Herman quickly revealed the extent of his network and claimed to have been working under duress.

Turrou's investigation identified 18 conspirators, and the 14 of those still at liberty were subpoenaed to attend a grand jury in May 1938, but none turned up. Like Ignatz Greibl, who returned to Germany on the SS *Bremen*, they had fled the country. The FBI arrested Greibl's wife but after her protests of innocence had been taken up by the *America Review* she was released on $50,000 bail, and promptly slipped aboard a ship bound for Europe. The fiasco proved to be a huge embarrassment for the FBI's director, J. Edgar Hoover, who fired Turrou but was unable to prevent him from publishing his version of events. Of the entire spy ring, only Rumrich and three others were convicted and imprisoned, and charges against the remainder were eventually dismissed in March 1950.

GRIBANOV, OLEG M. A senior KGB officer and ultimately chief of the **Second Chief Directorate** (SCD) in the 1950s, General Oleg Gribanov acquired a reputation as a skilled manipulator of targeted Western diplomatic personnel, exploiting their weaknesses and achieving considerable success in acquiring their cooperation through coercion. His adversaries granted him grudging respect as telltale signs of his handiwork emerged during the painful debriefings of his hapless victims, many of whom failed to fully grasp the extent to which he had orchestrated their predicament. In particular, Gribanov's characteristic fingerprints were found all over the cases of **John Vassall**, **Louis Guibaud**, **Maurice Dejean**, and a French businessman, **Francois Saar-Demichel**, and had directed the activities of **Yuri Krotkov**. According to various defectors who had encountered him, Gribanov had created the 14th Department, a unit specializing in elaborate counterintelligence deception campaigns intended to protect valuable KGB assets and mislead hostile foreign agencies.

Gribanov's KGB career came to an end in 1964 following the defection of one of his SCD subordinates, **Yuri Nosenko**. Supposedly, Gribanov was dismissed for having failed to exercise proper supervision over Nosenko, who first approached the **Central Intelligence Agency** in Geneva in June 1962 before he finally switched sides in February 1964. However, some Western counterintelligence experts were skeptical of Nosenko's authenticity and suspected that he was part of one of Gribanov's elaborate deception schemes.

GRIGOVIN. Identified by Peter Wright as a member of the KGB *rezidentura* in London who had been seduced by one of the high-class call girls occasionally employed by MI5, Grigovin resisted an attempt to pressure him into recruitment. According to Wright's account in *SpyCatcher*, the KGB officer refused to cooperate when he was caught with his lover, and simply put on his clothes and returned to his embassy, presumably to report the incident. Whether Wright recalled Grigovin's name correctly is open to doubt, as there is no official record of any Soviet with this name serving in London.

GROW, ROBERT. In 1952, the KGB's Vladimir Kotov mounted an operation against the U.S. military attaché in Moscow, Major General Robert W. Grow, whose diary had been photographed with the help of his maid, an agent codenamed SMOLENSKAYA. Kotov filmed Grow in several compromising situations with SMOLENSKAYA in the hope of blackmailing him but Kotov was uncertain of success because Grow was very anti-Soviet. The alternative strategy adopted was the publication of *On the Warpath*, purportedly written by a British Army defector, Major Richard Squires, who claimed he had acquired a copy of Grow's diary from a journalist in Frankfurt. Actually the book had been ghosted by Ernst Henri, a journalist who had worked at the Soviet Embassy in London during the war.

By taking selected extracts from the diary and quoting them out of context, the KGB intended to discredit Grow, who was immediately withdrawn to face court-martial charges, and to that extent the operation succeeded. However, Grow was certain his dairy could not have been copied in Germany, and he was acquitted.

The KGB also collected a lot of compromising material about Grow's assistant, but the assistant left Moscow in 1951.

GUERRERO, ANTONIO. In September 1998, 42-year-old Antonio Guerrero was arrested by the Federal Bureau of Investigation (FBI) and charged with collecting intelligence about the Boca Chica Naval Air Station at Key West for the Cuban Dirección General de Inteligencia (DGI). Guerrero's girlfriend was a masseuse, Maggie Becker, whom he met while teaching salsa, although he was employed as a janitor at the airfield. According to a computer file recovered by the FBI, Guerrero, codenamed LORIENT, and his coconspirators—Geraldo Hernández, Ramón Labanino, René González, and Fernando González—were members of a network known as the **RED AVISTA** (Red Wasp) and his relationship with the 50-year-old Becker was simply a convenient cover approved by the DGI. Despite the evidence, Becker remained loyal to Guerrero, "a total person of peace, a total person of love," who wrote more than 175 love poems from his prison cell.

GUIBAUD, LOUIS. In 1962, Colonel Louis Guibaud, the air attaché at the French embassy in Moscow, shot himself after he had been caught in a KGB **honeytrap**. Surveillance on his apartment suggested he was experiencing marital problems with his wife so a **swallow** was deployed to entrap him. Guibaud's suicide had such an impact on **Yuri Krotkov** that it prompted his subsequent defection in London.

GUINDON, ROY. Codenamed BROKEN ARROW by the Royal Canadian Mounted Police (RCMP) Security Service, Roy Guindon was working at the Canadian embassy in Tel Aviv in 1966 as a security guard when he was spotted by a Shin Beth surveillance team as he held a clandestine rendezvous with a suspected KGB officer. The Canadian authorities were informed and Guindon was recalled on a pretext to London where he was met by RCMP officers and escorted home to Ottawa for questioning. When challenged by his interrogators, Guindon admitted that while he had been posted in Moscow, he had been seduced by a beautiful woman, Larissa Dubanova, he had met at the Bolshoi Ballet. She had claimed to be an interpreter and spoke perfect English, and after she became pregnant, they underwent what he believed had been a marriage ceremony. When he was transferred to Warsaw, she followed him, supposedly having suffered a miscarriage, and persuaded him to let her have cipher material from the embassy code room, where he acted as night guard. He also admitted having installed listening devices in some of the embassy conference rooms, but because of his cooperation with the RCMP, he was never prosecuted. As a result of the BROKEN ARROW case, the RCMP instituted a major survey of vulnerable personnel who had served in Moscow and uncovered a series of similar examples where support staff, especially those with access to communications equipment and crypto materials, had been targeted deliberately by the KGB.

GUNDAREV, VIKTOR. In February 1986, Colonel Viktor Gundarev defected from the KGB *rezidentura* in Athens with his seven-year-old son Maxim and his Russian mistress, Galina Gromova, and was granted asylum in the United States. Gundarev later used the press to complain about his post-defection living conditions in the United States, and thereby to apply pressure to improve the generosity of his **Central Intelligence Agency** (CIA) protectors.

Born in Siberia, Gundarev had served previously in India and Portugal and had been in Athens for three years. His defection was prompted by months of disagreements with his *rezident*, Nikolai Krestnikov, and he had also learned that his wife Tatiana had been to the *rezident* to complain about his affair. Fearing an imminent recall, Gundarev contacted the CIA's David Forden and was exfiltrated. His principal meal ticket turned out to be the identification of a former U.S. Navy submarine commander, John Bothwell, as a spy, although he turned out to have been acting as a double agent.

– H –

HAAVIK, GUNVOR. Arrested in January 1977 on charges of espionage as she met her KGB contact in Oslo, Gunvor Haavik was convicted and imprisoned. In her confession, she stated that she had been caught in a classic **honeytrap** while working as a secretary at the Norwegian embassy in Moscow. During interrogation, several parallels emerged in her story with that of **Ingeborg Lygren**, another secretary employed by Norwegian intelligence, who had been the target of a lengthy molehunt. According to KGB defector Mikhail Butkov, Haavik was one of two very successful moles run by the KGB's Third Department of the First Chief Directorate, the other being a Foreign Ministry official, Arne Treholt, who apparently produced some of the same documents as Haavik.

The daughter of a doctor from Odda, near Bergen, Haavik never married and died in prison.

HALL, JOAN. Born to parents of Russian-Jewish extraction, Joan Krakover was an undergraduate at the University of Chicago when, aged 17 in 1946, she met Ted Hall, then working on a master's degree in physics after spending two years working on the Manhattan Project at Los Alamos and Oak Ridge. He had also been a Soviet spy since October 1944 when he and a Harvard friend, Saville Sax, offered to supply atomic bomb secrets to the New York *rezidentura*. Hall, who had Anglicized his surname from Holtzberg in 1936 at the age of 11 with his older brother, had gone to work at Los Alamos in January 1944 as a Harvard graduate and was one of the most brilliant physicists of his generation. Also, like his mother Bluma, a Communist sympathizer but not a member of the Party, he used Sax as an intermediary to deliver classified material to his NKVD contact, Sergei Kurnakow, then working under journalistic cover and codenamed CAVALRYMAN. When he was based at Los Alamos, Hall relied on Sax and an unknown woman he knew as "Helen," who later turned out to be **Lona Cohen**, to act as his couriers. According to the VENONA decrypts, the NKVD codenamed Hall MLAD ("youngster") and Sax STAR ("old").

Hall, then aged 21, married Joan Krakover in June 1947 and he then revealed to her his past secret life as a Soviet spy. He had by then fallen out of contact with the Soviets but when he and Joan decided to resume their political activism and join the **Communist Party of the United States of America** (CPUSA), he asked Sax to relay a message to the NKVD to alert them of his decision. The reply from the *rezidentura* raised no objection but wanted to maintain contact. However, the Halls were keen to abandon espionage and there followed a meeting in a New York park, at the end of 1949, between the Halls and the Cohens at which Joan, then four months pregnant, and Ted were persuaded to rejoin the network and at this point recommended two sources, ADEN and SERB, for recruitment. Although Hall had not had a security clearance since his departure from Los Alamos in June 1946, evidently the Soviets felt he still had potential. Thus contact was reestablished, but in March 1951 Hall and Sax were picked up by the Federal Bureau of Investigation (FBI) to undergo separate but simultaneous interrogations based on suspicions raised by some VENONA fragments. Both men denied any involvement in espionage and in June 1952 the Halls moved to New York, where he took up a cancer research post at the Sloan-Kettering biophysics laboratory. Established in New York, they resumed meetings with the Soviets, this time with a case officer working at the United Nations, but a year later, with Joan pregnant again, they told him they intended to break contact permanently and move to Greenwich, Connecticut.

Following an offer of a more challenging research post at Cavendish Laboratory, the Halls moved with their three daughters to Cambridge in July 1962 and would remain there until Ted's death in 1999.

HANSSEN, ROBERT P. A senior Federal Bureau of Investigation (FBI) official who spied for the GRU and KGB and was estimated to have caused damage costing $44 billion to the U.S. government, Robert Hanssen volunteered to spy for the GRU in New York in November 1979 by walking into the Amtorg office and making the offer to the GRU officer he had been assigned to watch. He sold a collection of classified information, including the identity of TOP HAT, for $20,000, but gave up the following year after he confessed to his wife and promised his local priest to stop passing classified information to the Soviets. He remained inactive until 1984 when he reestablished contact with the Soviets in Washington, D.C.

In 1990, Hanssen met Priscilla Galey, a 33-year-old stripper working at Joanna's, a club on M Street, and sent her a $10 tip and a note expressing his admiration for her "grace and beauty." Soon he gave her his official business card, they became regular lunch companions, and at a further meeting he paid for her to have some much-needed dental work costing $2,000, and then gave her an expensive diamond and sapphire necklace, claiming it was from a recent inheritance.

Hanssen also took her on a trip to Hong Kong, where they registered in separate rooms in the same hotel for two and a half weeks while he conducted a routine inspection of the local legal attaché's office. The FBI later speculated that although both later denied having had a sexual relationship, apparently for the sake of his family, she admitted having given him oral sex. One possible motive for his developing the relationship may have been his wish to recruit her to undertake minor tasks on his behalf in support of his espionage.

In 1991, Hanssen gave Galey an American Express card on his account, a secondhand Mercedes, and a laptop computer, but when in 1992 she used the card to pay for some Easter presents for her nieces in Columbus, Ohio, he turned up to recover the card. Thereafter, Galey succumbed to a crack cocaine habit, wrecked her uninsured car, spent a year in prison on drug-dealing charges, and became a street prostitute, cut off from all contact with her benefactor. Later, she would recall that she usually earned $200 a night as a stripper, but when she delighted Japanese tourists by attaching flaming matches to her nipples, she could make up to $800. Memorably, she also remarked "stripping isn't so bad, especially when you get over being naked."

Hanssen formed friendships with other strippers, including Dep Mullinas, a Vietnamese who danced under the professional name "Brooke." She, too, was investigated by the FBI, but there was no evidence of her complicity in his activities.

Hanssen was arrested in February 2001. In July 2001, he pleaded guilty to 13 counts of espionage and was sentenced to life imprisonment without parole. During his extensive debriefing, a condition of avoiding the death penalty, Hanssen revealed an astonishing life of bizarre sexual fantasy, some of which he had shared with his lifelong friend, army officer Jack Hoschouer. He concealed a video camera in his bedroom so Hoschouer could watch tapes of Hanssen in bed with his wife Bonnie on a closed-circuit television system when he visited, and posted explicit descriptions of their lovemaking on an Internet adult bulletin board using their real names. He also sent pornographic pictures to Hoschouer, including many of his wife, a habit he had begun when his friend had been serving in Vietnam.

Although many of Hanssen's colleagues were mystified by motivation, and wondered how an apparently devout churchgoing Roman Catholic, Republican-voting conservative and father of six could have led such a tangled double life over so long a period, others recalled some of his strange behavior and antisocial attitudes. He was considered by most as a slightly creepy oddball, but undoubtedly a man of considerable intellect and talent, especially in the field of computers, which also made him unusual at FBI headquarters. None suspected his duplicity and were appalled when the scale of his betrayal eventually emerged.

Bonnie Hanssen remained loyal to her husband despite his conviction, and his plea bargain with prosecutors enabled her to receive his $50,000 annual pension, to which she would have been entitled if he had died. He remains in solitary confinement for life at Florence, Colorado.

HARNACK, MILDRED. Originally from Milwaukee, Wisconsin, Mildred Fish met her husband, Arvid Harnack, at the University of

Wisconsin. They married in 1925 when she was 24, and she accompanied him when he returned home to Germany in 1929 to work at the University of Jena. He was forced to leave by the Nazis in 1929 and moved to Humboldt University in Berlin before joining the Ministry of Economics. While they were in prewar Berlin, Mildred became a friend of **Martha Dodd**, the American ambassador's daughter who was also a Soviet spy.

Although Arvid became a member of the Nazi Party in 1937, he was by then a committed Communist and involved in the Soviet espionage network later known as the Red Orchestra. His wife also played a significant role in the organization and recruited an Abwehr cryptographer, Horst Heilmann, to acquire sensitive information about German progress on breaking Soviet cipher traffic from his Funkabwehr office in the Mattäikirchplatz. Mildred also took one of her language students, 31-year-old Luftwaffe Lieutenant Herbert Gollnow, as her lover; at Arvid's direction, Gollnow transferred in October 1941 from his studies at Berlin University's Auslandswissenschaftliche Fäkiltat to the Abwehr, where he was assigned to the supervision of sabotage operations on the Eastern Front. Under interrogation at the Lehrterstrasse military prison, Gollnow would later describe Mildred as "the ideal perfection of womanhood" and claimed that his affair with her was "one of sexual bondage." During their relationship, Gollnow, who had once been a Nazi, supplied Mildred and Arvid with valuable military reports concerning the Russian campaign and was accused of having betrayed details of operations that led to the deaths of three dozen German parachutists who had been dropped behind the Red Army's lines.

In July 1942, the Harnacks were arrested and Arvid was garroted in December while Mildred was given four years' imprisonment. Her sentenced was appealed and, in February 1943, she was beheaded. Altogether an estimated 159 members of the Rote Kapelle were arrested, and most members of the network were executed, including Gollnow, who was shot in Tegel prison also in February 1943, and Arvid's nephew, Lieutenant Wolfgang Havemann of naval intelligence. Codenamed ITALIAN, Havemann was arrested in September 1942 at his base at Flensburg and accused of having compromised U-boat operations off Murmansk and Archangel.

Mildred Harnack is the only American woman known to have been executed by the Nazis in the Third Reich.

HARRIMAN, AVERELL. Formerly President Franklin D. Roosevelt's special envoy to Great Britain during World War II and then the U.S. ambassador in Moscow, Averell Harriman enjoyed the confidence of President **John F. Kennedy** and was an adviser to the White House during several administrations. According to KGB defector Anatoli Golitsyn, he was also a Soviet spy who had been recruited after he had fathered a child while on a visit to Georgia in 1927.

After Golitsyn's defection in Helsinki in December 1961, he revealed that he had been told by a colleague about a prewar NKVD recruit codenamed MAGNATE who had achieved considerable success in the financial world, and whose career seemed to coincide with that of the hugely successful investment banker who married Randolph Churchill's ex-wife, Pamela Digby. Harriman died in 1986.

HARRIS, KITTY. The NKVD agent who had handled Donald Maclean in London and Paris before World War II, Kitty Harris had been Earl Browder's common-law wife. Born in London, she had immigrated to Canada with her parents as a child and subsequently became active in the **Communist Party of the United States of America** (CPUSA) in Chicago, together with her sisters Jennie and Tilly. Thereafter she operated under her own name as an illegal in China, working with Browder, whose NKVD codename was HELMSMAN. As he rose to prominence in the CPUSA, Browder attempted to distance himself from potentially embarrassing links with other NKVD agents, to the extent that he asked Moscow to release his sister Marguerite from her clandestine activities in Europe because her arrest and exposure would be bound to attract unfavorable publicity.

Harris returned to the United States during the war to participate in a network that succeeded in penetrating Los Alamos. She appeared as ADA in the VENONA traffic from Mexico City, and upon her recall to the Soviet Union, she was detained at a psychiatric institution. After her release, she was confined in a mental institution and died at home in Gorky in October 1966.

HARRISON, GEOFFREY. The British ambassador in Moscow, Sir Geoffrey Harrison was recalled to London in 1968 when he admitted that he had been **honeytrapped** by his maid, Galyna. Educated at Winchester and King's College, Cambridge, he had joined the Foreign Office in 1932 and served in Tokyo and Berlin before World War II. After the war, he held senior appointments in London and was ambassador in Brazil and Iran before being sent to Moscow in 1965. Galya had bumped into him, apparently unexpectedly, in Leningrad while he was on a visit there and had suggested a romantic tryst at her brother's apartment close by. Harrison succumbed and later confessed the blackmail attempt to a senior colleague in the Foreign Office.

HAYHANEN, REINO. A KGB officer from a village near Leningrad who had served as an interpreter in the Karelia Peninsula during the Soviet-Finnish War, Reino Hayhanen was later transferred to Estonia, where he was taught English, and in 1948 he was sent to Tallin for intensive training as an illegal codenamed VIK. A year later he was smuggled into Helsinki by a TASS correspondent and spent the next two years establishing his "legend" as Eugene Maki, the son of a naturalized American citizen. He was to be staged through Finland and his cover was to include marriage to a local girl, Hanna Kurikka, despite the fact that he already had a wife and son in Russia, and another son by a mistress, M. M. Gridina.

In 1951, he had turned up at the American embassy in Helsinki and, upon production of an authentic birth certificate showing him to be Eugene N. Maki, born in Enaville, Idaho, and his signature on a formal statement confirming that he had not served in the Finnish Army or voted in Finnish elections, both constitutional requirements for the retention of American citizenship, he was issued with a passport. Once his application for a U.S. passport was accepted, Hayhanen was recalled to Moscow to hear details of his main assignment: to travel to New York, where he would be joined by Hanna after six months. Using this genuine document, he traveled to England the following year and caught the *Queen Mary* in Southampton for a transatlantic voyage to New York, where he acclimatized himself. Soon after the arrival of his wife, the Hayhanens rented an apartment in Brooklyn, but in March 1953 they bought a house in Peekskill,

New York. Once established, Hayhanen operated independently as an illegal and held only one clandestine meeting, on a subway train, with a KGB officer, Mikhail N. Svirin, whom he had encountered previously in Moscow, at the very beginning of his mission. He would not meet his *rezident* until August 1954, at a prearranged rendezvous outside a cinema in Flushing. Under the *rezident*'s supervision, Hayhanen opened a photographic shop in Newark, New Jersey, as a cover for his activities but, upon his return from six months' leave in Moscow in late 1955, the *rezident* submitted an adverse report about his subordinate's competence. Aware of the likely reception awaiting him, Hayhanen broke his journey in Paris to defect to the **Central Intelligence Agency** (CIA) in an alcoholic haze. During his five years at liberty as an illegal in the United States, he told the CIA that he had sent about 30 messages to Moscow and had received 25. By a remarkable coincidence, his first, concealed in a hollow coin, was already in the possession of the Federal Bureau of Investigation (FBI), having been handed in to the New York police in Brooklyn in the summer of 1953, but the FBI had failed to decrypt the message contained in a tiny microfilm. Hayhanen disclosed his personal code and demonstrated how the five-figure groups had to be substituted by being subtracted from four separate key numbers: the numbers represented by the seven letters of the Russian word *Snegopa*, or "snowfall"; the date 3 August 1945, which was the end of the war with Japan; the first 20 words of a traditional Russian folksong; and finally his own personal number, 13. Once this procedure was completed, the message in Hayhanen's coin, which evidently had been mislaid by his *rezident*, was transformed into a note of welcome, some instructions regarding financial support for his business cover, a caution that it was premature to take receipt of a radio transmitter, and some security advice, dated six weeks after his arrival in the United States:

> We congratulate you on a safe arrival. We confirm the receipt of your letter, to the address V repeat V and the reading of the letter no. 1. For organisation, we gave instructions to transmit to you $3,000 in local currency. Consult with us prior to investing it in any kind of business, advising the character of the business. According to your request, we will transmit the formula for the preparation of soft film, together with your mother's letter. It is too early to send you the Gammas. Encipher

short letters, but the longer ones make with insertions. All the data about yourself, place of work, address, etc. must not be transmitted in one cipher message. Transmit insertions separately. The package was delivered to your wife personally. Everything is all right with the family. We wish you success. Greetings from the comrades. December 3.

Hayhanen's meal ticket comprised three separate items of solid information: enough circumstantial information for the FBI to trace Hayhanen's *rezident* to the Latham Hotel in New York and arrest "Mark Collins" on 21 June 1957; to disclose sufficient data for the FBI to trace Master Sergeant **Roy A. Rhodes** of the U.S. Army Signal Corps and convict him as a Soviet spy codenamed QUEBEC; and to reveal details of a dead drop in the Bear Mountain State Park used to supply financial support to Morton Sobell's wife, Helen.

Hayhanen completed a 37-page confession in May 1957 for the FBI in which he gave an account of the various tasks he had undertaken. He recalled early in 1953 having met a courier in Hoboken, a Finnish seaman codenamed ASKO, whom he had paid for the delivery of several messages. He also claimed that one *rezident*, Abel, had been entrusted with just three tasks, only one of which proved to be of special interest to the FBI. Hayhanen recalled requests from Moscow to trace the whereabouts of three people: a Swedish ship's engineer named Olaf Carlson believed to be living in Boston; a possible recruit in Arleigh, New Jersey; and Master Sergeant Roy Rhodes of the U.S. Signal Corps. Only in the last case had he achieved a degree of success, having traced Rhodes's sister to Salida, Colorado, who had disclosed her brother's current address. The subsequent investigation revealed that Rhodes, who had been posted to the U.S. embassy in Moscow between 1951 and 1953 as a mechanic and chauffeur, had been blackmailed into cooperating with the KGB. A case summary found at Hayhanen's home in Peekskill, concealed inside a hollow steel bolt, offered damning evidence of what had happened to Rhodes:

> Roy A. Rhodes (Codename QUEBEC) Born in 1917 in Oiltown, Okh. A senior sergeant in the War Ministry, former employee of the US military attaché staff in our country. He was a chief of the garage of the U.S. embassy. He was recruited to our service in January 1952 in our country. He left in June 1953. He was recruited on the basis of compromising materials, but he is tied to us with his receipts and the infor-

mation he had given in his own handwriting. He had been trained in code work at the ministry before he went to work at the Embassy but as a code worker he was not used by the Embassy. After he left our country he was sent to the School of Communications of the Army CI services at the city of San Luis, Calif. He was to be trained as a mechanic of the coding machines. He fully agreed to cooperate with us in the States or in any other country. It was agreed that he was to have written to our embassy here special letters but we have received none during the last year. It has been recently learned that he is in Red Bank N.J., where he owns three garages. The garage work is being done by his wife. His father, Mr. W.A. Rhodes, resides in the United States. His brother works as an engineer at an atomic plant in Camp Georgia.

Of crucial interest to the FBI was Hayhanen's evidence concerning the illegal *rezident*. Although he knew the man by sight, he had never learned his cover name, but he recalled that on one occasion he had visited a storeroom in Fulton Street, Brooklyn, used by the illegal. The FBI found the address, which was a fifth-floor studio and storeroom rented to a commercial artist named Emil Goldfus, and kept them under surveillance. On 23 May 1957, a man answering the *rezident*'s description, as supplied by Hayhanen, was spotted but on that occasion the suspect effortlessly shook off the FBI special agents attempting to keep him under observation. Three weeks later, Goldfus reappeared and was traced to the Latham Hotel in Manhattan, where he was registered under the name "Martin Collins." Under interrogation, he would admit to being Colonel Rudolf Abel, but many years later, long after Hayhanen's death in 1961, the illegal *rezident* would be positively identified as **Willie Fisher**, a veteran NKVD officer born to a Russian émigré family in England.

Hayhanen was resettled at Keene, New Hampshire, but was reported to have died of cirrhosis of the liver in 1961.

HELFMANN, HEINZ. Heinz Helfmann was 60 years old when he was recruited by the Hauptverwaltung Aufkrarung (HVA) while attending the Leipzig Trade Fair in 1953 in an attempt to promote his wine business. He was initially paid to collect apparently innocuous information in the Federal Republic. He was then asked to persuade his girlfriend, 44-year-old Irmgard Roemer, a Foreign Ministry secretary, to let him copy telegrams from the German embassy in the Vatican.

When Helfmann was arrested by the Bundesamt für Verfassungsschutz (BfV), he admitted to having been paid $25,000 and was sentenced to five years' imprisonment, and Roemer received three years' hard labor. His other girlfriend, Elfriede Buechner, served nine months.

HERNANDEZ, LINDA. The 43-year-old wife of Nilo Hernandez, Linda Hernandez was sentenced in Miami to seven years' imprisonment in February 2000 after the couple had been convicted of having spied for the Cuban government. They pleaded guilty in 2007 to being unregistered agents of a foreign government, counting airplanes at Homestead Air Reserve Base, tracking troop movements at Fort Bragg in North Carolina, monitoring boat movements on the Miami River, and trying to infiltrate an exile group.

Born in New York City, Linda Hernandez was a child when she moved to Cuba, where she met Nilo. Both joined the Cuban Army and held the rank of sublieutenant when they returned to the United States in 1983 to join an espionage network known as the **RED AVISTA**.

HERZOG, GISELA. Recruited by the KGB in 1954, with the codename MARLENE, Gisela Herzog was employed in the Personnel Department of the Federal German Foreign Ministry in Bonn until she married a French diplomat and moved to Paris in 1958. During the two years she remained in her post, Herzog identified numerous potentially vulnerable Foreign Ministry employees, among them her friend Leonore Heinz, who would be seduced by **Heinz Sutterlin**. When she learned of Leonore's intention to marry Sutterlin, she begged her KGB contacts to break up the relationship because of the damage it would do to her friend when she discovered the truth, but her intervention failed.

HEWIT, JACK. Born in Gateshead in 1917, Jackie Hewit avoided work in the local shipyard, where his mother and father were employed, and moved to London to become a dancer. In 1936, he was picked up in a pub and taken to a party hosted by Tom Wylie at the War Office where he met **Guy Burgess**. He moved into Burgess's flat in Chester Square, which was also shared with **Anthony Blunt**, with whom Burgess would share the remainder of his life.

Although ostensibly serving in the army during World War II, Hewit acted as an agent provocateur for MI5, developing friendships with **homosexuals** suspected of subversion. He also performed the role of decoy when escorting foreign couriers carrying diplomatic pouches to ports and airfields in northern England. These trips often involved overnight stays in hotels, during which Hewit distracted the couriers and separated them from their briefcases, the contents of which were copied in a long-standing operation codenamed TRIPLEX.

Hewit, who in 1938 lived briefly with Christopher Isherwood in Belgium, and was E. M. Forster's lover, died in December 1997.

HILL, GEORGE A. In 1942, George Hill, a legendary anti-Bolshevik, was sent to Moscow to liaise with the Soviet intelligence authorities on behalf of **Special Operations Executive** (SOE). His acceptance by the Soviets was surprising considering the publicity given to his two volumes of memoirs, *Go Spy the Land: The Adventures of I. K. 8 of the British Secret Service* in 1932 and *Dreaded Hour* four years later. Known to his friends as Peter, Hill won the Distinguished Service Order (DSO) for rescuing the Romanian crown jewels from Bucharest only hours before the Red Army began its occupation.

Born in Estonia to a timber merchant who traveled constantly in the Near East, and educated by French and German governesses, Hill could speak half a dozen languages and was a natural recruit for intelligence duties when he reached the Western Front at Ypres in April 1915 with a battalion of Canadian infantry attached to the Manchester Regiment. Initially an interpreter, Hill was soon undertaking dangerous missions into No Man's Land, where he was badly wounded. A transfer to the War Office followed, and this in turn led to an assignment in Greece where he learned to fly and, based in Salonica, took his plane behind enemy lines to land and drop off Allied agents. In 1916, Hill traveled to Egypt for a new assignment and en route met Compton Mackenzie whom, he recalled, "was running a brilliant secret intelligence department against the Germans."

In July 1917, when Hill was back in England on leave, he was ordered to Russia to join the Royal Flying Corps mission at Petrograd but by the time he arrived the revolution had taken place and the intrepid airman found himself caught up in the strife. His main adventure began when he accepted a commission from the Romanian ambassador to rescue the Romanian crown jewels, which had been deposited in the Kremlin for safekeeping, together with most of Bucharest's treasury, and return them to Jassy, the temporary seat of government in war-torn Romania. Thus, Hill found himself escorting a train of treasure across the newly declared Soviet republic and over five or six battlefronts to the Romanian frontier. The epic journey lasted nine days and, after receiving the thanks of the Romanian prime minister, Hill returned to Moscow to help organize **Leon Trotsky**'s intelligence apparatus along the German front. During this period of chaos, Hill teamed up with the notorious Sidney Reilly, the Secret Intelligence Service (SIS) agent who later would be lured back to the Soviet Union and executed.

The Allied occupation of Archangel in August 1918 abruptly ended Hill's relationship with the revolutionaries and he went into hiding just before the Cheka arrived with warrants to arrest him and Reilly. By discarding his uniform and growing a beard, Hill successfully evaded the Cheka and was evacuated with the rest of the Lockhart mission to Finland in October 1918. Hill undertook one further, brief undercover assignment back into Soviet Russia, lasting three weeks, and was back in London by Armistice Day, 11 November 1918. Upon his return, Hill was welcomed by his chief and Colonel Freddie Browning of SIS. In the coming months, he was to be decorated with the Military Cross and Member of the Order of the British Empire (MBE), and was mentioned in dispatches three times. In 1919, he was awarded the coveted Distinguished Service Order, appropriate recognition for an intelligence officer who survived astonishing adventures at a turbulent moment in history, and was to spend a further three years in the Near East either operating for SIS or, briefly, on Sir Halford Mackinder's staff.

Upon his return to London, Hill found that SIS was no longer in a position to finance his escapades, so he took his wife Dorothy to live in a caravan parked in a farmer's field in Colemans Hatch, Sussex. There, he managed to survive, as a technical adviser to film companies making movies about Russia, and by living off the generosity of his friends. It was while he was acting in this capacity on *The Forbidden Territory*, Dennis Wheatley's first novel, that he met the author and became the basis of *The Eunuch of Stamboul*. In 1930, he found a job as manager of the Globe Theatre, and for a short time was deputy general manager to the impresario Charles B. Cochran. During this period, he wrote two plays, *It is the Law* and *Release*. **Kim Philby** recalled that while the jolly Hill was in the Soviet Union for SOE, "a very belated security check of his conference room revealed a fearsome number of sources of leakage."

While MI5 was curious that the Soviets should have been willing to allow such a well-known figure to take up residence in Moscow, it vetoed an attempt by Hill to extend his remit and represent MI5 and SIS as well as SOE. MI5 was also concerned that the NKVD had allowed Hill's former mistress to join him in Moscow from Siberia, and Guy Liddell expressed the view that the liaison channel resulted in Hill passing on rather more information than he received.

After the war, Hill was appointed the manager of the Apollinaris Mineral Water Company in Germany, and for the last 10 years of his life experienced a degree of comfort that had hitherto eluded him.

HISCOX, MOLLIE. Born Gertrud Blount in 1911 and convicted in March 1941 of possessing official documents without authority, Mollie Hiscox was part of the **British Union of Fascists** (BUF) anxious to pass information about the location of factories, shortage of materials, and the establishment of submarine bases in Northern Ireland to Germany through **Nora Briscoe**. Hiscox was the German-born mistress of Jock Houston, once a leading BUF member until his expulsion in 1936 when he joined the Nordic League. By May 1940, he had abandoned his wife and three children to live with Hiscox in Chisqick High Road, using the alias "Mr. and Mrs. Hudson," and thereby he evaded his internment order until he was arrested in December 1940.

Initially all three—Hiscox, Houston, and Briscoe—had come under MI5's surveillance after an agent reported suspicions about Briscoe, who worked in the Ministry of Supply and later was detained for the remainder of the war. Briscoe's son, who spent the war in Germany, was repatriated at the end of hostilities and in 2007 wrote a book based on his mother's notes for an autobiography.

Hiscox had been employed as a travel agent for German holidays and traveled to Germany frequently. She was also a founder member of the Link in 1937 and her letter, dated 31 August 1939 and addressed to Adolf Hitler in which she had pledged her support, was returned by the censorship authorities. Convicted at the Old Bailey in

June 1941 of breaches of the Defence Regulations, she was sentenced to five years' imprisonment, and in 1944 announced her engagement to Jock Houston.

HISS, ALGER. A graduate of Johns Hopkins University and the Harvard Law School, Alger Hiss in June 1929 was appointed secretary to Oliver Wendell Holmes, the Supreme Court Justice. He then practiced law in Boston and New York before joining the government in May 1933 as assistant counsel to the newly created Agricultural Adjustment Administration. In August 1935, after a period of secondment to the Nye Committee, which was conducting a congressional investigation into the international arms industry, Hiss joined the Department of Justice. Six months later he transferred to the State Department where he acted as secretary to the American delegation to the Dumbarton Oaks Conference, and accompanied the secretary of state, Edward Stettinius, to Yalta in February 1945 before making a brief visit to Moscow, where he was received by the deputy Soviet foreign minister, Andrei Vyshinsky. Upon his return he was appointed secretary-general of the United Nations conference at San Francisco, and in January 1946 attended the first meeting of the U.N. General Assembly in London as a senior adviser to the American delegation. In 1947, he left public service for the prestigious post of president of the Carnegie Endowment for International Peace, but in August 1948 he was named by **Whittaker Chambers** as a Soviet agent and one of his underground Communist contacts.

Hiss denied the allegation and sued Chambers for libel but lost the case when Chambers produced State Department cables, dated 1938, and four memoranda written in Hiss's hand that he insisted had been given to him by the spy. Hiss was charged with perjury but the jury was unable to agree on a verdict, so a second trial was held in November 1949 at which Hiss was convicted and sentenced to five years' imprisonment. After his release in December 1954, Hiss wrote his autobiography, *In the Court of Public Opinion*, protesting his innocence, and in 1988 produced a second volume, *Recollections of a Life*. After his release from prison, Hiss divorced Priscilla and worked first for a manufacturer of women's hair accessories, and later as a salesman for a New York printing business. He later remarried and was living in retirement on Long Island when the VENONA decrypts were declassified, one of which indicated that, together with his wife and his brother Donald, he had worked as a GRU spy since his recruitment in 1935. The text, sent from Moscow to Anatoli Gorsky in Washington, dated 30 March 1945:

> Further to our telegram No. 283. As a result of A's chat with ALES the following has been ascertained:
>
> 1. ALES has been working with the NEIGHBOURS [GRU] continuously since 1935.
> 2. For some years past he has been the leader of a small group of the NEIGHBOURS PROBATIONERS [GRU agents], for the most part consisting of his relations.
> 3. The group and ALES himself work on obtaining military information only. Material on the BANK [US State Department] allegedly interest the NEIGHBOURS very little and he does not produce them regularly.
> 4. All the last few years ALES has been working with PAUL who also meets other members of the group occasionally.
> 5. Recently ALES and his whole group were awarded Soviet decorations.
> 6. After the YALTA conference, when he had gone on to Moscow, a Soviet personage in a very responsible position (ALES gave to understand that it was Comrade VYSHINSKY) allegedly got in touch with ALES and at the behest of the Military NEIGHBOURS passed on to him their gratitude and so on.

As the assistant secretary of state who had attended the Yalta Conference as part of the U.S. delegation, Hiss was the only person who fit Gromov's profile, and the message thereby ended the long-standing controversy concerning his espionage.

HOFER, HELDRUN. A secretary employed by the Bundesnachrichtendienst (BND) station in Paris, Heldrun Hofer was seduced by an illegal codenamed ROLAND who claimed to be in touch with a neo-Nazi organization. In February 1973, he introduced Hofer to VLADIMIR in Innsbruck, who said his father had been an Abwehr officer who had known Admiral Wilhelm Canaris. In fact, VLADIMIR was another KGB illegal, Ivan D. Unrau, and he maintained contact with Hofer until she was transferred back to the BND's headquarters at Pullach. However, soon after her return she became engaged to a colleague and broke off her relationship with ROLAND. The KGB responded by producing a new illegal, codenamed FRANK, who was introduced by MAZER who claimed to be ROLAND's father. They asserted that her value to the neo-Nazis was so important that FRANK would act as her courier.

Hofer was arrested in December 1977 as she drove to a rendezvous with FRANK in Austria after a tip from the French Service de Documentation Exterieure et de Contre-Espionage (SDECE) and quickly confessed. The following day she attempted suicide by throwing herself out of a sixth-floor window, and was seriously injured.

HOFFMANN, JOANNA. Ostensibly a hairdresser employed aboard the Hamburg-America Line *Europa*, Joanna Hoffmann was identified to the Federal Bureau of Investigation (FBI) as an Abwehr courier by Gunther Rumrich in February 1938. Rumrich was an espionage suspect and U.S. Army deserter implicated by an MI5 investigation into letters sent to Mrs. Jesse Jordan in Dundee. MI5 concluded that Mrs. Jodon had been acting as a mail drop for the Abwehr, and some of her correspondence had come from a mysterious source codenamed CROWN that the FBI traced to Rumrich, then living in New York. Coincidentally, Rumrich was arrested by the police for his involvement in a rather amateurish scheme to obtain 35 blank U.S. passports, so when he was confronted with evidence of his espionage he had quickly confessed and named Hoffmann as his link to Germany.

Hoffmann's confession to the FBI's veteran special agent Leon Turrou named a doctor, **Ignatz Greibl**, as one of her contacts, and a letter found in her possessions incriminated Otto Voss. Turrou questioned Voss, then working for the Sikorsky Airplane Company in Farmingdale, and he in turn identified Willy Lonkowsky and Carl Eitel, both Abwehr agents who had already returned to Germany.

Hoffmann went on trial in Manhattan in October 1938 with Otto Voss and Eric Glaser, a German immigrant who had served in the U.S. Army in Panama with Rumrich and, at the time of his arrest, was in the Air Corps. Rumrich gave evidence against all three defendants and after a trial lasting six weeks they were convicted; Hoffmann was sentenced to four years' imprisonment.

HÖHENLOE, PRINCESS STEPHANIE VON. Often thought to have been Adolf Hitler's favorite actress, Princess Stephanie von Höhenloe was a rabid Nazi who moved in the highest social circles on the Continent and in London. Born to a Jewish father in Vienna and trained as a ballerina, Stephanie Richter had an affair with Emperor Franz Joseph's son-in-law and in May 1914 married Prince Friedrich von Höhenloe in London.

Occasionally Hitler's escort, she was rewarded with the Schloss Leopoldskron, near Salzburg, and was close to Joachim von Ribbentrop, Herman Göring, and Heinrich Himmler. She eventually left England in 1940, having lost a High Court action against the newspaper magnate Lord Rothermere, who stopped paying her a promised retainer. She then joined her longtime companion, Fritz Widemann, recently appointed the German consul-general in San Francisco, and formerly Adolf Hitler's commanding officer on the Western front in World War I. She eventually left him, and when she was detained briefly by the U.S. Immigration Service, she had an affair with its director. During World War II, she was consulted about Hitler's character by the Office of Strategic Services, and she died in June 1972 in Geneva.

HÖKE, MARGARETE. In 1981, 51-year-old Margarete Höke, codenamed DORIS, was charged with having spied for the KGB for the past 11 years. She had been employed in the Federal German president's private office in Bonn since 1959 and had served five presidents. During that time, she used a camera concealed in a lipstick to copy more than 1,700 classified documents for her Hauptverwaltung Aufkrarung lover. According to her confession, she had been seduced in 1968 by Hans-Jurgen Henze, alias Franz Becker, codenamed HAGEN, and he had persuaded her to pass him information by claiming to be a postgraduate student working on a research project. He then admitted that he was working for a right-wing organization of German patriots, based in Brazil, and Höke agreed to continue her espionage in return for 500 deutsche marks (DM) a month. When Becker returned to East Germany in 1976, he continued to maintain contact with her by attending regular rendezvous in Cologne and Zurich.

In 1979, Höke was instructed to suspend her activities while the Bundesamt für Verfassungsschutz conducted a security review, but a year later she was assigned a new codename, VERA, and put in touch with a KGB illegal, RENATA, to act as her courier. However, in August 1985 Höke was arrested, and in 1987 sentenced to eight years' imprisonment and a fine of 33,000 DM.

HOLM, RICHARD L. One of the most admired members of the clandestine service found his career in jeopardy after an operation he inherited upon his appointment as the **Central Intelligence Agency**'s (CIA) station chief in Paris in 1993. The operation, which had been authorized by his predecessor, Jay Gruner, involved the recruitment of a source inside the Elysée Palace by a woman subordinate who subsequently failed to disclose that she had begun an affair with her source. At some unknown point, her agent revealed to the French authorities that he had become romantically involved with an undeclared CIA officer based at the U.S. embassy, and he was run as a double agent, both to identify other members of the station and to feed the agency with false information. Holm had not been consulted on the ongoing operation when he was posted to France, having recently recovered from appalling burns inflicted during a plane crash while on duty in the Congo, but was expelled from Paris in 1995 when the French authorities chose to make the affair public; he was replaced by Michael McBride. Holm was subsequently censured by a report issued by the CIA's inspector-general, but was then awarded a medal, and after his retirement was recalled to Langley as a counterterrorism expert and contractor.

HOMINTERN. A term first mentioned and perhaps invented by the poet W. H. Auden in a 1940 issue of the *Partisan Review*, homintern was intended to describe the clique of left-wing homosexual intellectuals who were sympathetic to Moscow, of whom some were thought to be likely candidates for espionage. The term was adopted by author Richard Deacon, who saw a pattern in the malign influence exercised by Soviet spies such as **Guy Burgess** and **Anthony Blunt**, and their coterie of friends whom he believed were intent on changing the West's culture, or at least subverting the tradition of liberal democracies, to proselytize **homosexuality**. Deacon, formerly foreign manager of *The Sunday Times*, took considerable comfort from the rather illiberal Soviet attitudes toward homosexuality.

HOMOSEXUALITY. In countries where homosexual behavior was considered a vice and outlawed, one consequence was to make the practitioners vulnerable to pressure and blackmail. Exploiting what many societies regarded as deviancy provided the unscrupulous with a lever to extract the reluctant cooperation of an otherwise law-abiding individual. Indeed, the greater the social status of the victim or the sensitivity of the position of trust held, the worse the likely repercussions if resistance was exercised. Accordingly, homosexuality was long viewed as a potential source of coercion, and security clearances were routinely withheld from anyone honestly acknowledging his or her sexual preferences, with a formal policy declaring homosexuals to be security risks made in 1954. This attitude of course encouraged concealment and inevitably made the practice more difficult to admit, and in effect played into the hands of those seeking to gain an advantage. However, during Senate hearings conducted in 1985, the Federal Bureau of Investigation asserted that of 50 espionage convictions since the end of World War II, only two had concerned homosexuals, and neither had been blackmailed.

This cycle was only broken at the end of the 20th century when formal announcements were made in the United States and Great Britain, hitherto two of the more intolerant environments for sexual liberality, that henceforth active homosexuality would no longer be an automatic bar to a clearance. Indeed, the **Central Intelligence Agency** established with official sponsorship a gay and lesbian group, and in February 1999 the British Secret Intelligence Service (SIS) took the unprecedented step of declaring the posting of an officer, Christopher Hurran, to Prague with his Venezuelan homosexual lover. This was a remarkable change in attitude, considering that only a few years earlier a former SIS chief, **Maurice Oldfield**, had lost his security clearance when he admitted that he had for years been a homosexual.

Behind the issue of relative vulnerability and the decriminalization of sexual relations between consenting adults of the same gender, there remains an intriguing confluence of homosexuality and espionage devoid of the threat of public exposure. For instance, the notorious Cambridge spies are often cited as examples of a homosexual clique, headed by **Guy Burgess** and **Anthony Blunt**, who engaged in both treason and moral turpitude. Of course, their network was not exclusively homosexual, as demonstrated by the manifest heterosexuality of the other principal members of the ring, **Kim Philby** and John Cairncross, even if rumors have circulated about the possibility that Donald Maclean perhaps was bisexual. Philby married **Litzi Friedman**, Aileen Furse, **Eleanor Brewer**, and Rufina Ivanova, fathered five children with his second wife and one with a mistress, and conducted numerous affairs throughout his life. Although John Cairncross was childless, he married twice and was mildly homophobic, detesting Anthony Blunt who, unknown to him, had talent-spotted him, and mildly disapproving of Guy Burgess who had sounded him out for eventual recruitment by James Klugmann.

Philby, as the first of the "Ring of Five," was introduced into espionage by women, **Edith Suschitsky** and Litzi Friedman, and his actual recruiter into the NKVD was **Arnold Deutsch**, a noted psychologist who had made a study of human sexual behavior. Nevertheless, it is true that Blunt and Burgess moved in a louche *galere*, and both were flamboyant in parading their sexual preference, even if it made them vulnerable to arrest. Indeed, this particular shared illegality may even have served to make the rest of their illicit activities easier to indulge in, for together they recruited Tom Wylie and Brian Simon as sources.

Anthony Blunt certainly engaged in a homosexual relationship with **Michael Straight** when the latter was his student at Trinity College, Cambridge, in 1937, and later employed **Jack Hewit** as an MI5 informant. As Straight later acknowledged in his confession to the Federal Bureau of Investigation and MI5, and in his autobiography, he was recruited as a Soviet spy, actively engaged in espionage upon his return to Washington, D.C., where he found a job in the State Department, and remained silent long after he had abandoned the cause. At any time, he could have denounced his former lover to the authorities, but he chose not to do so out of loyalty.

The covert nature of these sexual relationships undoubtedly provided useful cover for other clandestine activities, as MI5 eventually learned when molehunters trawled through the social debris of the 1930s to forensically reconstruct the precise nature of each friendship developed by the spies. The complexity of the university contacts, the promiscuity of the participants, and their employment by often secret agencies meant the task of building a wiring diagram of the various links between the suspects proved exceptionally hard, and revealed some curious loyalties characterized by Wystan Auden's remark that he hoped he would have the courage to betray his country before a friendship. Burgess was described as having propositioned everyone he admired, but was that as a potential sexual partner or as a likely spy? Burgess and Blunt undoubtedly exploited their homosexual connections, and they left Brian Simon in place in Cambridge to identify other potential recruits. For MI5's molehunters, attempting years later to establish who knew whom and to reconstruct the chronology of introductions, the task of exploring these covert links was difficult.

HONEYTRAP. The term applied to a staged encounter in which one of the participants is sexually compromised, usually by an intelligence agency in the hope of exercising influence over him or her through blackmail. *See also* DEJEAN, MAURICE; GRIBANOV, OLEG; GUIBAUD, LOUIS; HARRISON, GEOFFREY; KROTKOV, YURI; LYALIN, OLEG; RAVEN; SMITH, EDWARD ELLIS; SWALLOW; VASSALL, JOHN.

HOUGHTON, HARRY. A civilian employee of the British embassy in Warsaw, Harry Houghton was disciplined for trading on the black market while on a secondment in a clerical capacity to the embassy for a period of 15 months between July 1951 and October 1952. He had left the Royal Navy in 1945 with an honorable discharge and a small pension after 24 years' service, and having achieved the non-commissioned rank of master at arms, he was found a civilian post in the naval dockyards at Gosport. He lived in a small, four-room cottage at 8 Meadow View Road, Broadwey, and after his return from Warsaw, worked as a clerk at what had then been the Underwater Detection Establishment at Portland in Dorset. In January 1957, he was transferred to the Port Auxiliary Repair Unit at the same base, which had been renamed the Admiralty Underwater Weapons Establishment. Before the war, he had married Peggy, a widow in his hometown of Lincoln, but their childless marriage ended in divorce in 1958 after 23 years.

In 1960, a Polish source, **Michal Goleniewski**, tipped off the **Central Intelligence Agency** (CIA) that the KGB had recruited a source in the British embassy in Warsaw with a name like "Horton," and MI5 quickly traced the best candidate, who was codenamed LAVINIA. The 56-year-old Houghton was placed under surveillance and MI5 watchers moved into Broadwey, close to his home just outside Weymouth, but no attempt was made to isolate him from classified papers at the Portland base as, theoretically, his job in the repair unit gave him no access to secrets. Nevertheless, when he traveled to London by train on a Saturday morning, he was observed to exchange envelopes with a stocky, middle-aged man who carried a shopping bag. While some of the watchers stuck to Houghton and trailed him back to Dorset, another group peeled off and kept their contact under observation as he made his way to his hotel in Bayswater.

Discreet enquiries at the hotel revealed Houghton's link to be a Canadian guest, a bachelor named Gordon A. Lonsdale, who had only recently moved in. Further surveillance and an overheard conversation produced a pattern of meetings between Houghton and Lonsdale, usually on the first Saturday of the month, as happened the following 6 August. At the first meeting, which had taken place in a small public park opposite the Old Vic theater near Waterloo Station and had lasted an hour, Houghton had been accompanied by Ethel Gee, a colleague from Portland with whom he spent the weekend at the Cumberland Hotel, Marble Arch. Both had driven up to London in Houghton's new car, an inexpensive Renault Dauphine, and later had attended a performance of the Bolshoi Ballet at the Royal Albert Hall with tickets supplied by Lonsdale. Whereas Houghton's job did not give him access to secrets, Gee's position in an adjoining building that housed the Drawing Office records section most certainly did. She had worked at the base since October 1950 and had moved from the Stores Department in 1955, two years before she had been accepted as an established civil servant. Although she spent much of her spare time with Houghton, Gee, who was known as Bunty, lived with her elderly mother, uncle, and disabled aunt in a small terraced house at 23 Hambro Road, Portland. She too was placed under surveillance, as was Lonsdale, who drove away from the rendezvous in a Vauxhall Vanguard. At the second meeting, on 6 August, two MI5 watchers kept Houghton and Lonsdale under observation as they met outside the Old Vic, and later sat so close to them in Steve's Restaurant, Lower Marsh, that they were able to eavesdrop on some of their conversation, which centered on a newspaper report of the recent defection of two American National Security Agency analysts, **Bernon Mitchell** and William Martin.

MI5's watchers learned that Lonsdale, who was referred to within the Security Service by his codename LAST ACT, ran an amusement machine and jukebox leasing business from a small office at 19 Wardour Street, so a permanent observation post was established in the Falcon, a public house directly opposite Lonsdale's building. On Friday 26 August, the watchers followed Lonsdale to his branch of the Midland Bank in Great Portland Street where he had held an account since April 1957. There he was seen to deposit a tin box and an attaché case, and then flew to the Continent on the following Sunday, having told friends he was visiting Canada. Later, when the case was removed from the bank and examined by the Security Service over the next weekend, it was found to contain a roll of film for a miniature Minox camera, an apparently innocuous Ronson table lighter, and a zip bag for developing film with a Praktina camera inside fitted with a special lens and attachment for photographing documents. There was also a single sheet of paper on which was typed a list of London street names, followed by some meaningless figures. Under X-ray examination, the lighter could be seen to contain a small hollow, and when MI5's technicians unscrewed the mechanism they found a one-time pad and a tiny radio schedule that indicated a signal watch on the first and third Sunday of the month. If any further evidence was needed, this was proof positive that MI5 had at last found a genuine illegal. All the paraphernalia was replaced in the case and returned to the bank but toward the end of the month the operation was repeated with the intention of copying the coding material. In the meantime, MI5's technicians had developed a method of taking the 250 pages of the one-time pad apart, photographing them, and then reassembling the sheets so it could not be spotted that they had been disturbed. The plan worked perfectly and a complete replica of Lonsdale's one-time pad was passed to cryptographers at Government Communications Headquarters (GCHQ) who thereafter intercepted and decrypted all of Moscow's bimonthly shortwave traffic destined for Lonsdale. When the Minox film was copied and printed, it was discovered to be a series of holiday snaps of Lonsdale and a good-looking woman, probably taken in Prague. From correspondence recovered much later, it was deduced that the subject probably had been his wife.

On 24 October 1960, Lonsdale returned to the bank for his briefcase and, having been alerted by an obliging bank manager, MI5's watchers followed him to his office in Soho and then, by tube from Piccadilly, to Ruislip Manor station, West London, where he disappeared from view. However, after a meeting with Houghton at the Maypole public house in Ditton Road, Surbiton, on the evening of 5 November, Lonsdale—in his new car, a distinctive white American Studebaker Farina—led MI5's watchers to Willow Gardens, Ruislip, and once again dropped from sight. However, the following morning, he was spotted emerging from a nearby house, at 45 Cranley Drive. This address led to the identification of two further KGB illegals and provided strong evidence that Lonsdale had not realized that the contents of his case had been examined.

Lonsdale's destination that Saturday evening had been a bungalow at the end of a cul-de-sac but the watchers were able to establish an observation post in a nearby house, at the corner of Courtfield Gardens, with a view of the rear of the suspect property. Research into the occupants showed them to be an apparently respectable middle-aged couple who for three years had run an antiquarian book business from premises in the Strand, in central London, having been in the country since December 1954 when they had rented a furnished house at 18 Penderry Rise in Catford, southeast London, and a secondhand bookshop nearby, at 190 The Drive.

As well as leading MI5 to the occupants of the bungalow in Cranley Drive on 24 October, who now fell under suspicion for the first time, Lonsdale inadvertently revealed his new address in London, a ninth-floor, one-bedroom flat in the White House, an apartment block in Albany Street, just north of Regents Park. This, too, became the subject of technical surveillance, from the flat neighboring number 634, where Arthur Spencer from GCHQ and his monitoring equipment were secretly installed, and from the one directly above Lonsdale's. According to the building's management, Lonsdale had been accepted as a tenant with written references from two officials of the Royal Overseas League, a club in Park Place, just off St. James's Street, catering to foreign visitors to London. Apparently, this was where Lonsdale had stayed soon after he had first arrived in London, between March and April 1955, before moving in May 1955 to the White House in Regent's Park, where he had remained until June

1958, It contained few furnishings, but there was a single possession of significance, a large Bush Radiogram capable of tuning into Moscow's shortwave broadcasts.

Elaborate arrangements were made to conceal the combined MI5 and GCHQ project launched next door to Lonsdale. A woman MI5 officer pretended to be a new tenant and went off to work every morning, apparently leaving her flat empty. In reality, Spencer remained there for two months, moving about silently and never going outdoors. In addition, a listening device was placed through the wall that was linked by a secure landline to equipment at MI5's headquarters, where every gasp of Lonsdale's very active love life was recorded. Spencer monitored RAFTER apparatus, which determined the exact frequency of Lonsdale's wireless signals, and wore an earpiece connected to Lonsdale's Radiogram, so as to alert him every time the illegal listened in to Moscow. Although the first attempt to decrypt one of his messages was unsuccessful, because GCHQ had failed to spot the correct starting point in the one-time pad, a further illicit inspection of the contents of the Ronson lighter was made and the relevant page was identified. Thereafter, every message received by Lonsdale from "the Centre" was intercepted and read in full. To the surprise of MI5, none contained any clue as to the existence of any other agent, apart from SHAH, the Soviet cryptonym for Houghton who evidently was Lonsdale's sole preoccupation, although as the *rezident* it was almost certain he would have been supporting others. Years later, one such agent, Mrs. Melita Norwood, was identified as having been in regular contact with him.

Continued surveillance on Lonsdale over the following fortnight brought Lonsdale to a rendezvous with Houghton and Gee on the first Saturday in December, held outside the Old Vic. On the following afternoon, Lonsdale led MI5's watchers back to Ruislip, where the watchers linked up with their colleagues who had established a static observation post close to Cranley Drive. For legal reasons, MI5 was later to pretend that little had been known about the Krogers until after their arrest, but in fact a good deal of research had been undertaken already, and several issues worthy of further investigation had become apparent. Kroger was well liked in the book trade, but was regarded as something of a novice, for he often paid substantially over the odds to build his stock of titles, and his knowledge of the business was noticeably superficial. Nevertheless, he was popular among his trade rivals and had experienced no difficulty in being elected to the trade's two associations.

MI5 discovered that the couple had entered Great Britain on New Zealand passports, but they both spoke with American accents, hers being a particularly strong Brooklyn twang. However, according to the New Zealand authorities, their passports were authentic and had been issued in Paris by the New Zealand consulate, on an application accompanied by the required birth and marriage certificates, which had been mailed from what was subsequently discovered to be an accommodation address in Vienna. The genuine Peter Kroger had indeed been born in Gisborne, New Zealand, but he had not married "Helen Hale" in New York in 1943. He was dead, and the official in the consulate responsible for authorizing the application issuing the passports had been **Paddy Costello**, a Russian-speaking academic with a long history of leftist politics who was later to be appointed professor of Russian at Manchester University.

An illicit search of Lonsdale's flat in November revealed his onetime pad and a signal plan, and his communications with Moscow over a period of two months were monitored and decrypted. These had disclosed operational instructions relevant to Houghton, codenamed SHAH by the KGB, together with some messages from his wife, but nothing to indicate he was running other agents.

The opportunity to arrest the network occurred on the first Saturday of January 1961 when Houghton and Lonsdale held their regular rendezvous close to Waterloo Station, and when the CIA announced that its Polish source codenamed SNIPER had escaped to West Berlin. On that morning, Lonsdale received and decrypted a message from Moscow and, before leaving his flat, he wrote a letter to his wife in which he omitted to mention the girl who had spent the previous night with him, and emphasized his feeling of isolation by quoting a line from a melancholy Russian poem:

> For the last 20 minutes I have been pacing my room and I simply cannot continue the letter. This is literally a case of "I am weary, I am sad, and there is no one to shake hands with." I am not complaining. But even you cannot imagine how saddened I feel in general and especially at this moment.... I celebrated New Year's with a fellow baptized and punctually at midnight Moscow time we drank Stolichnaya to all

friends in the Union. We drank separate toasts to you and the children. I personally felt very sad this was the 8th New Year since 1954 which I celebrated without you. Some wise man said in the long ago "such is life." . . . I'll be thirty-nine shortly. . . . Is there much left?

Throughout their journey, by car to Salisbury and thence by train to London, Houghton and Gee were monitored by MI5 watchers operating from a series of inconspicuous vehicles and from a small aircraft equipped with receivers tuned to a homing device surreptitiously fitted to Houghton's Renault. Ethel Gee had chosen to accompany Houghton so as to do some shopping in London and was present when Houghton met Lonsdale in Waterloo Road. Led by Superintendent George Smith, Special Branch detectives closed in as the pair greeted the Russian. When Lonsdale was searched, he was found to be carrying two sealed brown envelopes, one containing £125, the other 15 $20 bills. In Gee's shopping straw bag were four Admiralty files and a sealed tin containing a roll of undeveloped film. When processed, the film was found to have 310 exposures, all from a classified book, and 42 negatives of drawings relating to the construction of the submarine HMS *Dreadnought*.

Synchronized raids were mounted on the Krogers in Ruislip and the homes of Houghton and Gee in Dorset. When confronted later the same evening by Superintendent Smith and Detective Chief Inspector Ferguson Smith of the Special Branch, the Krogers innocently denied any knowledge of Lonsdale, the man who habitually had stayed with them overnight on the first Saturday of each month. However, a search of Mrs. Kroger's handbag, snatched by an alert policewoman, revealed a white envelope containing a six-page letter, handwritten in Russian, a glass slide holding three microdots, and a sheet of paper bearing a typed list of London street names. This latter item was recognized by Smith as the same piece of paper that he had seen in Lonsdale's bank deposit. The Krogers were taken into custody and a longer, more intensive search of the bungalow yielded five passports, including two British passport blanks and two New Zealand passports hidden behind a bookcase. Four cameras, including Lonsdale's Praktina, and various large sums in cash and travelers checks, were also recovered from the loft, which was festooned with a 74-foot radio antenna connected to a specially adapted radiogram and tape recorder. Among the Krogers' possessions were glass slides and a microscope for handling microdots, handwritten signal plans referring to dates in November and December 1960, and an Olympia typewriter with a print face matching notes found in Lonsdale's flat. Beside Kroger's bed was a hip flask containing whiskey and three hidden compartments, one of which was full of a black powder, magnetic iron oxide, a substance used for making Morse symbols recorded on magnetic tape easy to read; a family Bible had sheets of light-sensitive cellophane paper treated with silver bromide in between its leaves. Some of the material was similar to that found at the White House, such as a torch with hollow batteries, a tin of talc with a microdot reader and a set of radio call signs inside, and a Ronson table lighter bearing two sets of one-time pads and signal plans printed onto a tiny photographic negative. The pads were typical KGB, printed on highly flammable cellulose nitrate, impregnated with zinc oxide, making them easy to destroy. The search continued for nine days, at the end of which a large cavity was discovered in the foundations under the kitchen floorboards and there, below a heavy concrete slab, was a sophisticated high-speed shortwave transmitter complete with a tape-keying apparatus, control charts, and various other accessories. Eventually the investigation was concluded, but some years later a second transmitter was accidentally uncovered in the garden by the new owners. Nor was that quite the end of the story, for two further items were found by a nominee acting for Lonsdale who was given access to the house: two forged Canadian passports, allegedly issued in June 1956 to James T. Wilson and Jane M. Smith, complete with exit stamps from Holland and Belgium, sewn into a leather writing case, and a pair of wooden bookends with $4,500 sealed inside.

At Houghton's cottage, detectives found three Admiralty files that had been removed by Gee from Portland the previous day, hidden in a radiogram. In the bedroom was an Exakta camera and three Admiralty charts in a suitcase; in addition, there was a plan of the naval base with HMS *Osprey*, the Royal Navy's school of submarine warfare, where the very newest sonar technology was tested, highlighted in pencil. A Swan Vesta matchbox produced coded instructions for a rendezvous in London, and the garden shed yielded an old paint tin containing £650. At Gee's home, her bedroom provided a handwritten, 12-point questionnaire on the subject of the latest developments in British antisubmarine detection equipment. Recovered from three separate handbags was a list of 18 Admiralty files, a piece of paper bearing the serial number of a classified file concerning sonar, another list detailing the four files handed to Lonsdale by Houghton, and the three files found at his home. In custody, Houghton and Gee had quickly confessed, while Lonsdale and the Krogers stubbornly refused all cooperation. When the police eventually obtained the Krogers' fingerprints and discovered their previous career from Charles Bates, the FBI's legal attaché in London, they were incriminated further. Peter and Helen Kroger were revealed by Bates as Morris and **Lona Cohen** from New York, both known to the FBI as suspects in the **Rosenberg** case who had vanished in 1950.

None of this background data emerged during the eight-day trial in London, during which Houghton admitted his guilt, Gee pretended she had been an innocent dupe, Lonsdale took the blame upon himself, and the Cohens, who were charged as "Kroger," maintained their complete innocence. Lonsdale received the longest sentence of 25 years' imprisonment, with the Krogers receiving 20, and Houghton and Gee receiving 15 each. Because the other three defendants were eventually exchanged in a spy swap, Houghton and Gee ended up serving the longest.

Under interrogation, Houghton admitted that he had been selling secrets from Portland since 1953 when he had met a Soviet known to him only as "Nikki" outside the Dulwich Art Gallery. From MI5 photographs, Houghton had identified Nikki as Nikolai Korovin, the current KGB *rezident* at the embassy, who promptly returned to Moscow accompanied by an attaché, one of his subordinates, Vasili A. Dozhdalev.

After his trial, at which he had alleged that he had been coerced into cooperation by threats against his family and his girlfriend in Warsaw, Houghton made a more candid statement in which he identified Vasili Dozdalev, a KGB officer under diplomatic cover, as the case officer who had succeeded "Nikki."

HOWARD, EDWARD LEE. A **Central Intelligence Agency** (CIA) officer destined for an extremely sensitive posting to Moscow as a case officer, where he was to handle some important assets, Ed Howard was dismissed in June 1983 after a **polygraph** revealed some past drug use and his admission that he had stolen money from a fellow passenger. Embittered by his experience, Howard approached the KGB and offered to sell information he had learned while being briefed for his Soviet mission. He met the KGB in Vienna, but his relationship was compromised in August 1985 when **Vitali Yurchenko** defected and gave a detailed description of a disaffected CIA officer who had sold details of Adolf Tolkachev's espionage and had compromised two technical sources.

Adept in countersurveillance techniques, Howard spotted that the Federal Bureau of Investigation had placed his home under observation, so he persuaded his wife Mary, who had also been trained as a CIA officer, to assist in his escape. In September 1985, Howard was able to use his CIA training to evade his watchers and fly to Moscow, where he died in an alcohol-related accident in June 2003.

HOWARD OF EFFINGHAM, LADY. In February 1941, Lady Howard of Effingham, who had arrived in London from Poland in November 1935 as a Hungarian refugee Malwina Gertier, was detained in Holloway prison as a suspected Nazi spy but was released five months later. In 1938, she married an impoverished peer, the 6th Earl of Effingham, even though she had established a relationship with a wealthy arms dealer, Edward Weisblatt, and had come under surveillance by Special Branch and MI5. One MI5 officer, the Earl of Cottenham, described her as a "not unattractive gipsy gamin' type, highly-sexed I should say." No evidence was ever found to substantiate the widespread suspicion that she had been collecting sensitive information from young soldiers, diplomats, and War Office personnel.

Formerly a member of the **British Union of Fascists**, Lady Howard was released from Holloway in July 1941 and her marriage was dissolved in 1946.

HUNLOKE, HENRY. The Defense Security Officer in Palestine, Henry Hunloke came under suspicion in 1944 because three of his colleagues had reported to London that he had acquired a Jewish mistress and was believed to be leaking sensitive information to her about British measures taken against gangs of Jewish terrorists. An investigation was conducted by Security Intelligence Middle East, but no evidence was found to indicate that he had been indiscreet, and accordingly his security clearance was restored and he was given access to ISPAL, decrypts of intercepted wireless traffic exchanged between various suspect groups and organizations in the region.

In June 1935, Hunloke was elected to the House of Commons as the Member of Parliament for Derbyshire West at a by-election following the ennoblement of Edward Cavendish, Lord Hartington, to the Duke of Devonshire. His daughter Philippa would later become the third Viscount Astor's second wife.

– I –

IKAR. The KGB **Second Chief Directorate** codename for an Italian attaché at the embassy in Moscow who was **honeytrapped** and told the woman was pregnant and had obtained an abortion. He was blackmailed by a KGB officer masquerading as an enraged husband and signed an agreement in which he undertook to supply information to avoid public exposure. He also supplied a copy of the cipher in which he communicated with Rome, and the combination to his office safe but later wrote to his contact begging him to destroy the incriminating document. Instead of complying with his wishes, the KGB gave IKAR a skillful facsimile of the agreement and allowed him to tear it up, unaware that the original had been retained in archives, perhaps for future use.

ILLEGALS DIRECTORATE. The KGB's Directorate S, designated Line N of the First Chief Directorate, was the organization responsible for the deployment of illegal agents to the West, usually transiting through third countries to develop a false "legend" or background before being established in a target city, either to remain dormant until activation or to undertake operations away from the hostile surveillance that often handicapped the legal *rezidentura*.

Unlike their counterparts who enjoyed the protection of the Vienna Convention afforded to diplomats, including immunity from arrest, illegals are extremely vulnerable and, if caught, face imprisonment and maybe execution. Although some Western agencies deploy intelligence professionals under nonofficial cover, they usually work in the international commercial sector and the nature of the totalitarian regimes they seek to penetrate precludes opportunities to insert long-term moles in the way adopted by the Soviet and Eastern bloc. The selection and training of suitable candidates willing to resist the temptations of the decadent West and endure perhaps years of isolation was highly specialized and only a handful of successful volunteers would be sent on missions.

Such limited information that has become available about the secret activities of Line N suggests that individual agents dispatched to Canada and the United States were often accompanied by women who either were, or acted as, their wives. Among examples of husband-and-wife teams deployed in the West include Morris and **Lona Cohen**, arrested in London in January 1961; Lise-Lotte and **Alexandre Sokolov**, deported from the United States in October 1964; and Margarete and **Igor Tairov**.

There is some evidence to suggest that illegals were dispatched alone on their missions if they had a wife remaining in the Soviet Union, and this certainly happened in the cases of **Willie Fisher** and **Konon Molody**, the only two *rezidents* ever captured in the West, although **Yevgenni Brik**'s vulnerability seems to have stemmed from his loneliness in Canada where he acquired a girlfriend. Fisher's wife Ilya remained in Moscow with their daughter, and the Federal Bureau of Investigation recovered a half-empty box of Sheik condoms, evidence to suggest he habitually used prostitutes, in contrast to Molody, who was adept at picking up girlfriends, a detail of his clandestine life he did not confide to his wife Galyusha in Moscow.

The role of women in the lonely life of an illegal was central to their performance, and **Valeri Makayev**'s failure in 1951 was partly caused by a relationship he had formed with a ballerina in Manhattan.

ILONA. KGB codename for a British woman working in the Censorship Department of the Control Commission for Austria in 1949. An unmarried spinster, she conducted an illicit affair with a Soviet officer, Lieutenant Metkov, who was acting under the supervision of Nikolai Skortskov, an aggressive member of the NKVD's Vienna *rezidentura*. One evening, while Metkov was entertaining ILONA, Skortskov burst in on the couple and attempted to threaten her with blackmail, but she dismissed him with contempt, put on her clothes, and left, calling Skortskov, "a fucking Kommissar."

IVANOV, EUGENE. The assistant naval attaché in London since March 1960, Captain Eugene Ivanov was identified in April 1961 as a potential defector by **Oleg Penkovsky**, his GRU colleague with whom he had attended the same military academy. Ivanov was therefore targeted by MI5, with considerable political consequences when it was learned that he was in contact with **Christine Keeler**, who was also having an affair with a senior British politician, **John Profumo**. Having graduated in 1953, Ivanov married later the same year to Maya Gorkina, daughter of Aleksandr Gorkin, chairman of the Supreme Soviet Court, and he was thought to be vulnerable because he was a womanizer. In December, he was posted to the GRU *rezidentura* in Oslo, where he remained for five years without a vacation. An MI5 operation to **honeytrap** him that employed his friend **Stephen Ward** was abandoned, and Ivanov was recalled to Moscow in January 1963. He later became an alcoholic and, with journalist Gennadi Sokolov, wrote his memoirs, *The Naked Spy*, before his death in January 1994. *See also* DENNING REPORT, THE.

– J –

JARDINE, THERESA. In June 1944, MI5's star double agent Juan Pujol reported to his Abwehr controller that one of his subagents, Theresa Jardine, designated 7(3), was to be transferred to the South-East Asia Command's (SEAC) headquarters in Kandy, Ceylon. Codenamed GLEAM by MI5, she was a notional member of the ARABEL network and lover of DICK, an Indian poet and head of his own political movement, the Brotherhood of the World Aryan Order. Supposedly employed as secretary of the Aryan World Order until her call-up by the Women's Royal Naval Service in February 1944, and known to the Abwehr as JAVELINE, she later recruited a series of equally notional sources—including ANDRIES, a Dutch liaison officer; Dave Close of the U.S. Navy; JACK, a Royal Air Force wing commander; a Royal Navy officer codenamed EDWARD; and BILL, supposedly a colonel on Lord Louis Mountbatten's staff—but ceased writing her letters in February 1945 following a road accident. In reality, she existed only in the mind of Pujol, known to MI5 as GARBO, and to the Abwehr as ALARIC.

Jardine's lover, known as Rags, lived in Swansea but after he was recruited by GARBO he moved to the Brighton area, where his reports on Allied troop movements were considered more relevant to the anticipated cross-channel offensive. A political fanatic, Rags was disappointed by the Welsh Nationalists he encountered because he regarded their perspective as too narrow. He believed in the superiority of the Aryan race; his organization, the Aryan World Order, collected lists of Jews and Communists who would be disposed of at the appropriate moment, and circulated propaganda broadcast from German radio stations. On his own description, the Aryan World Order consisted of a dozen activists, some of whom had been imprisoned as subversives, while others had been called up for military service. Three remained in contact and joined GARBO: David, designated 7(2) and codenamed DONNY, who was a retired seaman living in Swansea and the founder of the Aryan World Order; 7(5), codenamed DRAKE, the employee of a commercial firm in Swansea who was arrested in May 1944 when he attempted to follow instructions and establish himself in the Exeter or Plymouth area, charged with entering a restricted area, and imprisoned for a month; and 7(6), a Welsh fascist also from Swansea, who proved reluctant to travel and was put on half-pay in January 1945 before being paid off in March.

Rags taught his mistress Hindustani but no sooner had she been recruited into his spy ring than she was sent to London to attend a Wren induction course at Mill Hill, where she was given secretarial training. Shortly before she left for the Far East, while she enjoyed some embarkation leave in London with Rags, he showed her how to use secret ink and gave her questionnaires and a cover address in London, where she could send mail to GARBO.

MI5's decision to send Jardine to Ceylon had been prompted by a request from the local deception staff, headed by Peter Fleming, for a reliable channel to the enemy, and as she had been the mistress of an Indian and had developed an understanding of Indians, it had seemed appropriate that she should volunteer. Accordingly, she underwent a special course at a Wren training camp near Newbury, Berkshire, to improve her language skills and then embarked for Colombo.

Jardine's objective was to supply the Japanese with information, but the route to Tokyo, via air mail to London and then forwarded by

GARBO to Lisbon and Madrid where it was transmitted by radio to Berlin for assessment before being handed to the Japanese embassy for inclusion in a signal to Tokyo, was necessarily very time-consuming. Two of Jardine's letters, dated 1 October and 17 October 1944, reached GARBO in London in early November, and he sent them to his cover address in Lisbon on 12 November. There, they were collected by the Germans and carried in the diplomatic bag to Madrid, whence they were sent by radio to Berlin on 1 December. The Abwehr then took three weeks to consider the content before they appeared on the Japanese embassy's link to Tokyo on 23 December, designated "K INTELLIGENCE (Secret Agent's report)."

MI5 regarded this delay as an advantage because it meant that the messages could contain a high degree of authentic intelligence. Her first letter was relayed by GARBO in September 1944 but analysis of the subsequent Abwehr wireless traffic revealed that the content had coincided rather too closely with reports from other agents in the region, and this had raised the Abwehr's suspicions. Alarmed, MI5 had asked SEAC what had gone wrong, only to be told that Fleming routinely sent the same deception material by several different routes in the hope that at least one eventually reached the enemy, but this was wholly contrary to the procedures followed in London, where separate channels were compartmentalized. Fortunately, when Berlin queried the Abwehr in Madrid about the similarities in the messages, the reply was quite plausible, that doubtless Jardine had supplied the same information to some of the Indian nationalists to whom she had been introduced by Rags, without being aware that they, too, were reporting to the Axis. This explanation was accepted by Berlin but MI5, unable to control or coordinate the deception campaign in Kandy, decided that the risk to the rest of GARBO's network was too great, and accordingly Jardine was put out of action by a car accident in which her bottle of secret ink was broken. She then wrote to GARBO explaining that she would not be able to return to work at SEAC until she had been declared fit by a medical board, which might equally order her repatriation. This, and her lack of any secret ink, prevented her from sending any further messages until the end of hostilities in Europe.

JOHNSON, ROBERT. In February 1953, Sergeant Robert Johnson attempted to defect to East Berlin but was persuaded by the Soviets, to whom he had been introduced by his Austrian mistress, to return to his post and spy. He subsequently married his mistress, by whom he had a son, and also recruited another friend serving in G-2, Sergeant **James Mintkenbaugh**, to help him copy classified documents. When he was discharged from the U.S. Army in 1956, he reenlisted the following year. In March 1961, he was posted to the Armed Forces Courier Center at Orly, near Paris, where he supplied vast quantities of information to his Soviet contacts for $300 a month. Later, after he had been posted to Washington, D.C., in May 1964, Johnson was reluctant to maintain contact with the Soviets and, fearing exposure by his wife, deserted. Finally, in November 1965, he volunteered a confession to the Federal Bureau of Investigation in Reno in which he admitted having spied for the KGB since 1953, and implicated Mintkenbaugh. He said that during his hours alone in the top security document storage bunker he had copied thousands of highly secret papers that were routinely exchanged between the Pentagon and NATO headquarters, carried by official escorts. Sentenced to 25 years' imprisonment, Johnson died at Lewisburg Federal Penitentiary in May 1972 after he had been stabbed by his son who had just returned from Vietnam.

JUDD, ALAN. The pseudonym adopted by Alan Petty, a Secret Intelligence Service (SIS) officer, "Alan Judd" published a novel, *Legacy*, in which he described the case of a married British Army officer who was sexually compromised with his girlfriend by the NKVD in Berlin immediately after the war, and ostensibly was blackmailed into passing classified documents to his Soviet contacts for many years thereafter. In fact, Petty's plot was drawn from an authentic double-agent case in which the officer had immediately reported the attempt to coerce him and had been instructed by SIS to pretend to succumb and cooperate.

– K –

KABAN. Soviet codename for a spy, previously known as KIRILL, who worked as an academic in the Canadian Centre for Arms Control and Disarmament in Ottawa, recruited by the KGB's Sergei

Tretyakov in 1990. When Colonel Tretyakov defected in October 1999 from the KGB *rezidentura* in New York, he identified KABAN to the Federal Bureau of Investigation, which passed on the information to the Canadian Security Intelligence Service (CSIS).

According to Tretyakov, KABAN was one of the three Canadians he recruited while in Ottawa, and had worked for Prime Minister Pierre Trudeau as a political adviser. He had passed classified information regarding Canada's plans to buy diesel-electric submarines and also sensitive RAND Corporation reports. After he left the Canadian government, KABAN retained his links to the Liberal Party and later was granted a lucrative permit, financed by the World Bank, to develop housing in Tver, a town 100 miles from Moscow. While in Russia, KABAN, who was married but lonely, was handled by the Russian Federation's Foreign Intelligence Service, the Sluzhba Vnezhney Razvedki (SVR), which ensured his loyalty by introducing him to a beautiful interpreter whose affair with him was videotaped. Tretyakov later recalled, "I was later given transcripts of these sex sessions and I remember reading several pages and thinking the best thing you can do when you are making love to a woman is not to talk at all because you sound rather stupid."

Although CSIS identified KABAN and learned he had acquired a large housing renewal contract in Moscow and was still engaged in promoting various business partnerships in the former Soviet republics, no action was taken against him.

KAHLE, WILHELM. A GRU illegal codenamed WERNER adopted the identity of a genuine West German and worked as a laboratory assistant at universities in Cologne and Bonn before moving to Paris as a language teacher. His objective as a **Romeo** was to cultivate and seduce suitable women with access to classified information, and he concentrated on German embassy secretaries, a U.S. embassy clerk, and a British secretary working for NATO. He also targeted BELLA, a West German secretary based at the embassy in Tehran who in 1975 was transferred to London, and MONA who was employed by a Swedish paper manufacturer in Paris. However, the KGB was unimpressed by Kahle's performance and in 1978 he was recalled to Moscow to undergo a **polygraph** examination on the pretext that his new posting might involve a similar experience. In fact, Kahle had fallen under suspicion and he confided to ANITA, a KGB **swallow**, that he had grown accustomed to living in France and had lost the will to complete his missions. Shocked by his admission, ANITA had recommended that he attend some ideological training, but according to defector Vasili Mitrokhin, Kahle was removed from the **Illegals Directorate** in 1982.

KAHLIG-SCHEFFLER, DAGMAR. A 27-year-old blonde divorcée who had worked in Chancellor Helmut Schmidt's private office since December 1975, Dagmar Kahlig-Scheffler was seduced by Herbert Schröter, a **Romeo spy** working for the East German Hauptverwaltung Aufkrarung (HVA) but posing as an engineer. She was arrested a couple of years later when her HVA controller, Peter Goslar, came under surveillance by the Bundesamt für Verfassungsschutz. When Goslar's home was searched, various confidential papers were found, including Schmidt's notes of a conversation with James Callaghan about his recent discussions with President Jimmy Carter. Goslar was then watched as he collected more information from Kahlig-Scheffler and, under interrogation, she revealed she had fallen for Schröter while on holiday at the Bulgarian resort of Varna with her seven-year-old daughter, and she was sentenced to four years and five months' imprisonment for espionage.

Codenamed INGE by the HVA, Kahlig-Scheffler had been duped into a "Potemkin wedding" to her lover. She believed that her marriage in East Berlin to Schröter had been valid, but in fact the entire ceremony had been staged by the HVA, complete with a bogus pastor. Her commitment to Schröter, whom she had believed was an East German engineer named Herbert Richter, was so complete that she had even agreed to send her daughter to a boarding school in Switzerland so she could devote more time to him and to espionage. In reality, Schröter was already married and was also involved with another spy, Gerda Osterrieder, a secretary in the Federal German Ministry of Foreign Affairs.

KAPP, NELLIE. A secretary employed by the Sicherheitsdienst in Ankara, Nellie Kapp defected to the American Office of Strategic Services (OSS) in 1944. The daughter of the prewar German consul in Cleveland, Ohio, Nellie Kapp had fallen in love with an OSS officer and was able to supply information concerning CICERO.

KAREV. The KGB codename for a 30-year-old married British diplomat compromised by his family's maid. She was codenamed CD by the **Second Chief Directorate** (SCD) and she told her lover that she had undergone an abortion arranged by a friend, one of the militia responsible for guarding the embassy. Grateful for his discreet intervention, KAREV repaid the favor by identifying the Secret Intelligence Service personnel in the embassy. To ensnare him further, CH claimed to have become pregnant for a second time, and then announced that she had been arrested on currency changes for possession of the money he had given her. KAREV responded by contacting a Soviet whom he probably knew to be a KGB officer and begged for his help in obtaining an abortion and having the currency charges dropped. The KGB agreed to do so, but only on condition that he agreed to contact with the KGB during his next posting. Although he accepted these terms, KAREV did not respond when the KGB tried to reach him, and on the advice of **Kim Philby**, the SCD decided not to expose him publicly.

KEELER, CHRISTINE. A 19-year-old dancer at Murray's Cabaret Club in London's West End, Christine Keeler was introduced during a weekend party at Lord Astor's home Cliveden in July 1961 to **John Profumo**, then the secretary of state for war in Harold Macmillan's government. They conducted a brief affair that lasted until August when the cabinet secretary, Sir Norman Brook, asked Profumo whether he would be willing to participate in an entrapment operation planned by MI5 against a Soviet diplomat, **Eugene Ivanov**. Mistakenly convinced that MI5 had discovered his relationship with the dancer, Profumo wrote to Keeler, telling her he was unable to see her again.

At the time, Keeler was lodging at 17 Wimpole Mews with a society osteopath, **Stephen Ward**, who was working as a source for MI5, and she was also seeing Ivanov. When she subsequently received publicity as a witness in the prosecution of her Jamaican boyfriend, Lucky Gordon, who had threatened to kill her, Keeler disclosed details of her affair with the politician, and sold Profumo's letter to a newspaper. Initially, Profumo denied there had been "any impropriety" in his relationship with Keeler, but in June 1963 he admitted the truth and resigned his Parliamentary seat, devoting the remainder of his life to charitable works.

Keeler would be imprisoned for nine months at Holloway, having been convicted of giving perjured evidence at Lucky Gordon's trial, and Ward committed suicide in July 1963 while facing charges of living off the income of prostitutes. After her release, she declined into alcoholism, contributed to three inaccurate ghostwritten autobiographies, and went to live quietly in Westcliff-on-Sea in Kent. In her final book, *The Truth at Last*, published in 2001, Keeler claimed to have had an affair with Eugene Ivanov, to have undergone an abortion to avoid having Profumo's baby, and to have seen MI5 Director-General Sir Roger Hollis and Anthony Blunt conspiring with Stephen Ward to pass nuclear secrets to the Soviets. Her assertions contradicted the evidence she had given previously to Lord Denning, who had conducted the official enquiry into the Profumo affair, and they were disbelieved. *See also* DENNING REPORT, THE.

KEKKONEN, URHO. Elected the president of Finland in 1956, Urho Kekkonen was a Soviet spy who had been recruited in 1947 while minister of justice through the influence of his mistress, Anne-Marie Snellman, the Associated Press correspondent in Helsinki, codenamed AILR. An ambitious politician, Kekkonen served as his country's prime minister between 1950 and 1956, while simultaneously holding the interior and foreign affairs portfolios. Codenamed TIMO, he was recruited by a member of the NKVD *rezidentura*, Ivan Pakkanen, and later handled by Yuri Voronin and the local *rezident*, Mikhail Kotov. As a reward for her assistance, Snellman was given diamonds and a lengthy vacation in the Crimea.

KENNEDY, JOHN F. Soon after joining the U.S. Navy in October 1941, Ensign Jack Kennedy was posted to the Office of Naval Intelligence (ONI) in Washington, D.C., through the influence of his father, Joe Kennedy, who knew the director of naval intelligence, Captain Alan G. Kirk, formerly the naval attaché at his embassy in London. However, Jack's affair with a suspected Nazi spy, **Inga Arvad**, led in January 1942 to his transfer to the Charleston Navy Yard in South Carolina.

Both before and during his presidency, John F. Kennedy had a succession of girlfriends, three of whom had strong intelligence connections. **Judith Exner** was also Sam Giancana's mistress, and she had also been involved with another Mafiosi, Johnny Rosselli. Both had potentially embarrassing links to the **Central Intelligence Agency** (CIA), although it would seem that the Federal Bureau of Investigation was monitoring the relationship rather more closely than the CIA. Certainly J. Edgar Hoover let the president's brother, Robert F. Kennedy, know in February 1963 that he was aware of the indiscreet telephone calls Exner made to the Oval Office. During the 11 months following May 1961, Exner made 20 visits to the White House. Once elected to the White House, Kennedy used the services of an East German call girl, **Ellen Rometsch**, at least 10 times and maintained a lengthy affair with **Mary Meyer**, the wife of a senior CIA officer, Cord Meyer. The extent to which any of the three influenced Kennedy, or extracted information from him, if any, is unknown but their illicit trysts and his reckless, insatiable womanizing certainly made him vulnerable to pressure, if not blackmail. His risk taking extended to having affairs with his wife's press secretary, Pamela Turnure; at least three White House aides, Diana de Vegh, Priscilla Wear, and Jill Cowan (the latter pair known as "Fiddle and Faddle"); Jackie's friend Helen Husted, married to David Chavchavadze; and at least one 19-year-old intern, Mimi Beardsley, who worked for Pierre Salinger in the press room. He also constantly propositioned a 26-year-old blonde Hungarian émigré, Enüd Sztanko, who taught languages at Georgetown University, whispering to her at an intimate White House dinner, "I hope you are not a spy." She replied, "If you must know, there is a microphone under the table."

Kennedy's relationship with the notoriously unstable Marilyn Monroe prompted considerable speculation, especially after her provocatively sensual rendition of "Happy Birthday, Mr. President" so publicly at the Madison Square Garden party held to celebrate his 45th birthday in May 1962. She died, of an apparently self-administered drug overdose, in August 1962, having been disconnected from contact with Robert and John Kennedy amid rumors of her brief affair with the president, supposedly consummated over a weekend at Bing Crosby's Palm Springs ranch in March 1962.

Kennedy, who boasted he had lost his virginity to a white prostitute in a Harlem brothel at 17, made himself vulnerable by having affairs overseas and at the end of June 1963 arranged to stay overnight at the Villa Serbelloni at Bellagio on Lake Como to entertain Marella Agnelli, the wife of the chairman of Fiat, during an official visit to Italy. The 17th-century property, surrounded by 50 acres of gardens, was owned by the Rockefeller Foundation, then headed by the puritanical Dean Rusk who was especially embarrassed and offended when he learned the true reason for Kennedy's request to borrow the property.

Kennedy's philandering and the details of his relationship with Sam Giancana would eventually become public, although considerable efforts were made to protect his reputation, including the editing of four of the recording tapes made by him in the White House. Altogether 260 hours of cabinet deliberations, private conversations in the Oval Office, and numerous telephone calls were recorded by Kennedy on equipment secretly installed by the Secret Service at his request, but at least two of the tapes show evidence of having been cut and spliced, and some others were destroyed, of which the only surviving material consists of the transcripts of four, and they remain sealed.

Declassified FBI and CIA files show that in June 1963 Jack Kennedy expressed concern about the implications of the **Profumo** scandal in London following allegations made by a prostitute, **Mariella Novotny**, that the president had been one of her clients. The local FBI legal attaché, Charlie Bates, and the CIA station chief, Archie Roosevelt, were instructed to monitor MI5's investigation of Novotny, and Roosevelt's deputy, Cleveland Cram, was assigned the task of liaising directly between the ambassador, David Bruce, and the Security Service. The FBI's dossier, codenamed BOWTIE, revealed that one of Bruce's friends, American businessman Tom Corbally, had played a central role in hosting parties attended by Novotny at his rented flat in Duke Street, Mayfair, and he had been one of the first to tip off the embassy to the danger of the White House becoming embroiled in the Profumo debacle.

Kennedy's long-term medical problems, dating back to a childhood of serious illness, including colitis, aggravated by a school sports injury to his spine, led to a life of pain and dependency on pills and frequent injections of amphetamines. He was also diagnosed in 1947 as suffering from Addison's disease, a disorder affecting the adrenal gland that enhanced his libido. This combination contributed to his extraordinary promiscuity, which left him, probably more than any other American president, susceptible to coercion.

KENT, TYLER. A 29-year-old American embassy clerk arrested in May 1940 in London and convicted of unauthorized possession of classified information at his apartment, Tyler Kent was imprisoned for seven years. Also convicted with him was his coconspirator, **Anna Wolkoff**, who received 10 years. Until his arrival in London in September 1939, Kent had served for five and a half years in Moscow where he had acquired a beautiful mistress, Tanya Ilovaiskaya, who had links to the NKVD.

When MI5 received a tip from Kurt Jahnke that some of Ambassador Joseph Kennedy's telegrams were reaching Berlin, the news was passed to the State Department but the investigation uncovered no leaks until October 1939 when Kent was seen visiting a suspected Nazi agent, Ludwig Ernst Matthias, at a hotel in London. Matthias was a naturalized Swede of German origin, and he had been kept under surveillance by MI5 all the time he was in London. Soon afterward Kent applied for a transfer to the American embassy in Berlin, a request that was under consideration when he was taken into custody.

Kent was also placed under surveillance and watched while he associated with members of the Right Club, a pro-Nazi group of political activists that included Anna Wolkoff. His Moscow-born mistress, meanwhile, was Irene Danischewsky, the wife of an army officer who was away from home.

Kennedy waived Kent's diplomatic status for a search to be made of his flat on 20 May, and it was found to contain copies of some 1,900 confidential embassy cables, among them secret messages passed between Winston Churchill and Franklin D. Roosevelt, and other material including duplicate keys to the embassy's code room. Under interrogation, Kent admitted that he had photographed some documents using a camera left to him by a colleague, another cipher clerk who had since been posted to the U.S. embassy in Madrid. This disclosure prompted a massive operation conducted by the Federal

Bureau of Investigation's Louis Beck, who quickly discovered that the vice consul, Donald Nichols, had been having an affair with Tanya Ilovaiskaya who, if she was not herself an NKVD officer, possessed a driver's license issued by the NKVD and had permission to travel abroad. Beck uncovered numerous other security lapses, including a **homosexual** relationship between a cipher clerk, Robert Hall, and the ambassador's secretary, George Filton.

Much of the material Kent had removed from the embassy suggested he had been in league with the Soviets, not the Nazis, because some of the letters referred to MI5's interest in current FBI cases, including Evelyn Strand, a Comintern agent trained in Moscow as a radio operator but then working at the New York headquarters of the **Communist Party of the United States of America**, and Terence E. Stephens, a veteran of the International Brigade in Spain. Another purloined telegram was a request from MI5's Guy Liddell for FBI surveillance on two suspects, Armand Feldman and Willie Brandes, both implicated in the 1938 Woolwich Arsenal case in which Soviet spies had stolen secret blueprints of Royal Navy weaponry. Kent was deported at the end of the war and until his death in 1988 always denied having spied for the Soviets.

KESSLER, ERIC. Codenamed ORANGE by MI5, Eric Kessler was a Swiss journalist in London before the war and who was anti-Nazi and considered by the Secret Intelligence Service as a possible intermediary for a scheme to establish a clandestine radio station in Europe for broadcasting propaganda into Germany.

Appointed the Swiss press attaché when World War II began, he was recruited by his **homosexual** lover, **Guy Burgess**, and supplied information from inside the Swiss embassy until he was appointed editor of the *Neue Zürcher Zeitung* in 1944.

KEYSER, DONALD. The 59-year-old deputy chief of the U.S. State Department's East Asia bureau was arrested in 2004 when he admitted having become infatuated with 37-year-old Isabelle Cheng, a Taiwanese intelligence officer based at Taiwan's de facto embassy in Washington, D.C. A total of 3,659 classified documents were recovered from his home, and at his trial in October 2007 Keyser pleaded guilty to three felony charges and was sentenced to a year and a day's imprisonment in a federal penitentiary, and a $25,000 fine.

The couple had become intimate in 2002 when President Jiang of the People's Republic of China visited the United States, and Cheng asked his lover for information. He had replied in an e-mail, "Your wish is my command." Later, in a tapped telephone conversation, after the pair had been watched by a Federal Bureau of Investigation special surveillance unit making love in a car, he had remarked, "The food was good. The wine was good. The champagne was good, and you were good." When Keyser was arrested, Cheng promptly returned to Taiwan.

Fluent in Mandarin, with his fourth wife working at the **Central Intelligence Agency**, Keyser had been educated at the University of Maryland and had spent two years at the Stanford Interuniversity Center in Taiwan.

KHOKHLOV, NIKOLAI. During World War II, Nikolai Khokhlov operated behind enemy lines as a partisan and played a role in the assassination of Wilhelm Kube, the Nazi *gauleiter* of Minsk. In 1952, he married Yania Timashkevits, who came from a strong Christian Uniats family, and fell under her influence. After a period of four years in Romania, where he was sent to perfect his cover, he was ordered to travel to Frankfurt to murder Georgi S. Okolovich, the leader of the exiled NTS Ukrainian nationalists. However, inspired by his wife, he gave himself up to his intended victim at Okolovich's apartment in February 1954.

Okolovich persuaded Khokhlov to surrender to the **Central Intelligence Agency** (CIA) but he was reluctant to do anything that would jeopardize his chances of smuggling Yania and their young son Alushka to the West. Nevertheless, he gave the name to the CIA of Nikita Khorunsky, the Soviet mole inside the NTS organization, and helped his contacts entrap two of his colleagues, Kurt Weber and Hans Kurkovich. Both men also agreed to defect, but an attempt to ensnare their handler, Colonel Oleg Okun, failed. Khokhlov was overcome with remorse when, instead of joining Weber and Kurkovich in the West, Okun fled to Moscow. Khokhlov's wife and son were arrested soon afterward, and when this news filtered to the defector in April, he called a press conference in Bonn, at which he displayed a silenced gun, loaded with cyanide-tipped bullets, disguised as an innocent-looking packet of cigarettes, in the hope that publicity might give his family some protection. Whether the ploy succeeded is doubtful, but Khokhlov moved to Switzerland, where he wrote his melancholy memoirs, *In the Name of Conscience*. In 1954 and again in 1956, he gave evidence to the Senate Judiciary Committee.

In September 1957, while attending a conference in Germany, he was injected with a tiny but highly toxic quantity of radioactive thallium, but he survived the attempt on his life and, after his recovery, moved to the United States under yet another identity. According to another First Chief Directorate defector, Oleg Gordievsky, the KGB did trace Khokhlov to his new home in New York in 1977 but failed to obtain permission to have him liquidated. He later moved to San Bernardino, California, and died in September 2007.

KIM, SUIM. On 18 June 1950, Kim Suim was executed in Seoul after being convicted of espionage. She had been recruited as a spy by her Communist lover, Lee Kung Kook, in 1942, and after the war she had been employed as a receptionist at the Banto Hotel, which was used by the U.S. Army as a military headquarters. While working on the switchboard, Kim listened in to many of the telephone calls and relayed this intelligence, and other information she picked up from lonely soldiers, to the North Koreans. Later, she was transferred to a secretarial post in the U.S. Provost Marshal's office, where she had access to counterintelligence material. By the time the ceasefire had been agreed, Kim had proved very successful and had established a photographic studio in the basement of her home so that she could process the secrets she had stolen. Her arrest came when she turned her attention to spying on the government headed by President Syngman Rhee, who was elected in August 1948.

KING, MARTIN LUTHER. The American black civil rights leader and future Nobel Peace Prize winner was placed under intensive surveillance by the Federal Bureau of Investigation (FBI) in March 1962, on the authority of President John F. Kennedy and his brother, the attorney general, after it was learned that one of Dr. Martin Luther King Jr.'s senior advisers, Stanley Levison, had been a leading member of the **Communist Party of the United States of America** (CPUSA) until 1957.

Levison, qualified as a lawyer, was subpoenaed to appear before the Senate Internal Security Subcommittee in April 1962. Although the FBI reported that he was no longer formally a CPUSA member, it had access to the Party's internal activities though SOLO, a long-term penetration achieved through two brothers, Jack and Morris Childs, which indicated that the CPUSA regarded King as a priority and an asset, and that at least until 1963 Bayard Rustin, one of his closest black aides, was a Party activist, and that King knew it. Rustin had been a veteran Young Communist League campaigner but his **homosexuality** had kept him on the fringes of the many protests, demonstrations, and boycotts he organized.

A lengthy, intrusive investigation was initiated, and later authorized by President Lyndon B. Johnson, that revealed King to be a regular client of prostitutes, leading Johnson to call him a "hypocrite preacher." Wiretaps and listening devices recorded King's many extramarital affairs, and a secret plan was drawn up by the FBI's director, J. Edgar Hoover, in December 1963, part of a wider project codenamed COINTELPRO to disrupt political extremists, to leak details of the political campaigner's private life to the media and others. Hoover called King publicly "the most notorious liar in the country" and in a speech to Loyola University referred to "sexual degenerates in pressure groups" and was determined to discredit him, break up his marriage, and ultimately intended to intimidate him into passing on his leadership to a more suitable candidate. Hoover called King "a tomcat with obsessive degenerate sexual urges" while one of the FBI surveillance team, Charles D. Brennan, was a witness to "orgiastic and adulterous escapades, some of which indicated that King could be bestial in his sexual abuse of women."

The campaign of harassment, which included surreptitious entries into his offices, the mailing of anonymous letters, and the dissemination of embarrassing transcripts of his encounters with prostitutes in sleazy hotels, the White House, and elsewhere continued for four years. An internal FBI enquiry conducted in 1977 recommended that the illegal tape recordings of King's private conversations, including 19 reels made at the Willard Hotel over two days in February 1963 that were particularly controversial, should be sealed and entrusted to the U.S. National Archives.

King was murdered in April 1968 in Memphis, Tennessee, but his lone assassin, James Earl Ray, was traced to London, arrested, convicted in March 1969, and imprisoned for 99 years. He died in prison in April 1998, age 70, of liver failure.

KNIGHT, MAXWELL. A brilliantly intuitive MI5 case officer, Max Knight headed a subsection of the counterespionage B Division that recruited and ran penetration agents against target organizations, principally the **Communist Party of Great Britain** (CPGB), the **British Union of Fascists**, the Link, and the Right Club. Knight's most successful agent was **Olga Gray**, recruited in 1931 and codenamed M-21, to gain the trust of the Party's national organizer, Percy Glading. Gray would report for the next seven years, and eventually gave evidence at the espionage trial in 1938 that convicted Glading of espionage.

Knight also recruited women agents to join fascist groups, and he ran Helene Munck, Marjorie Mackie, and Joan Miller, all agents who succeeded in befriending senior figures who were suspected of being Nazi sympathizers. All three gave evidence during the trial of **Anna Wolkoff**, who was convicted of espionage in 1940.

Knight was also the MI5 case officer who recruited and ran **Tom Driberg**.

KOECHER, KARL F. After they arrived in New York from Austria in December 1965 as refugees from Czechoslovakia, 31-year-old Karl Koecher and his attractive 19-year-old wife Hana were granted American citizenship in 1971. Fluent in Russian, English, French, and Czech, Koecher found a job as a freelance translator for Radio Free Europe while Hana worked as a grader in the diamond business. He also earned a master's degree at Indiana University and a PhD at Columbia before accepting an academic appointment as a lecturer in philosophy at Wagner College, Staten Island.

In April 1972, Koecher applied for a post as a **Central Intelligence Agency** translator and in February the following year he received a security clearance as an interpreter in the Soviet Division, located in Rosslyn, Virginia. His main function was to translate and analyze tapes of conversations that had been recorded by clandestine means, and among the transcripts he made were several from TRIGON, who was Soviet diplomat **Aleksandr D. Ogorodnik**, material that Koecher gave to Vesek Krelik, his contact at the Czech embassy in Washington, D.C. When confronted by the KGB, Ogorodnik committed suicide by slipping a cyanide capsule into his mouth.

Koecher continued to work full-time for the CIA until February 1975 when he moved to New York and became a contract employee, preparing political analyses of Soviet events and personalities, while also teaching at the State University of New York in Long Island. During this period, the Koechers visited various sex clubs in New York, including Hellfire and the notorious Plato's Retreat, and hosted wife-swapping parties in their apartment, to which they invited colleagues.

In 1979, as his work for the CIA diminished, he made an unsuccessful job application to the National Security Agency, and soon afterward he came under surveillance by the Federal Bureau of Investigation (FBI). He was arrested with his wife on 27 November 1984 as they prepared to fly to Switzerland, and later admitted that they had operated as Czech spies for the previous 19 years.

Koecher had originally encountered the FBI back in November 1970, apparently in an attempt to ingratiate himself, with a report that without any warning he had been approached at his home by a Czech intelligence officer. Koecher claimed to the FBI that he had dismissed the incident as a clumsy attempt to recruit him, and he had no doubt calculated that the episode would reflect to his credit. However, the investigation conducted by the FBI in 1983, following information supplied by a Czech defector, satisfied them that Koecher and his wife were highly competent illegals.

Charged with passing CIA secrets to the Czechs between February 1973 and August 1983, the Koechers were swapped in Berlin in February 1986 as part of a deal brokered by Wolfgang Vogel, the East German lawyer. In return for the Koechers, the Russian dissident Anatoli Shcharansky was released from a 13-year prison sentence, and two agents and a Czech convicted of helping refugees flee to the West were also given their freedom.

The damage assessment in the Koechers' case drew attention to the Koechers' lifestyle, and in particular to the danger that they might have ensnared colleagues during their wife-swapping parties, or identified individuals who might have been vulnerable to blackmail because of their attendance at orgies.

KOEDEL, MARIE. The daughter of Simon E. Koedel, a German from Bavaria who settled in the United States in 1903 at the age of 22, Marie Koedel collected shipping information from the New York waterfront for her father, a long-term Abwehr spy. She was eventually denounced to the Federal Bureau of Investigation by her former fiancé in October 1944, and the Koedels were arrested, detained, and eventually deported to Germany at the end of the war.

KONENKOVA, MARGARITA. Married to New York sculptor Sergei Konenkov, Margarita was a Soviet spy codenamed LUKAS who in 1941 conducted a love affair with physicist Albert Einstein. A former lawyer who spoke five languages, Margarita was introduced to Einstein by his stepdaughter Margot who was also a sculptor, and in 1941 was a frequent weekend visitor to the 66-year-old widower's home at Princeton and his rented cottage on Long Island. Her husband was commissioned to make a bust of Einstein at his Greenwich Village studio that later was exhibited at the Institute for Advanced Studies.

The precise nature of Margarita's mission remains unknown although NKVD officer Pavel Sudoplatov revealed she had been a spy, and her love letters, disclosed in 1998, proved the intensity of the relationship at a time when Einstein was seeking to persuade the Roosevelt administration of the dangers of Nazi research into atomic weapons. In 1945, Margarita, aged 51, returned to Moscow and was not seen in the West again.

KONRAD. The Romanian Departamentual de Informatii Externe (DIE) codename for a "skirt-chasing" U.S. Air Force serviceman working at an airbase at Wiesbaden in 1958 who was compromised by MIMI, a DIE officer who routinely trawled the local bars for potential recruits. According to Ion Pacepa, then the DIE *rezident* in charge of Romanian operations in West Germany, he had "recorded most of their amorous encounters," but MIMI "had no luck in building any serious relationship with KONRAD, who flitted from one girl to the next, so I proposed blackmailing him with the videotapes we had." However, this suggestion was turned down and the tapes were sent to Moscow where they were studied in an attempt "to draw a psychological portrait of KONRAD's sexual appetites." The Soviets then prepared "a female agent who would be capable of keeping KONRAD between her legs, as the saying went, and might even become his wife." Pacepa defected to the United States in July 1978, whereupon the KONRAD case was terminated.

KROTKOV, YURI. A well-known writer and filmmaker in the Soviet Union, Yuri Krotkov defected while on a visit to London in September 1963. Although he was not a KGB officer, Krotkov revealed that he had had occasionally acted as a KGB co-optee, and recalled that he had participated in a **honeytrap** to compromise the French ambassador in Moscow, **Maurice Dejean**. He also revealed that **John Watkins**, formerly the Canadian ambassador in Moscow, was a **homosexual** who had also fallen victim to entrapment

A Georgian by birth, Krotkov's parents were an actress and an artist. After university in Tbilisi, he moved to Moscow in 1938 and joined the Literary Foundation of the Union of Soviet Writers. He served in the Red Army during the war and as a TASS correspondent. In 1959, as a favored intellectual, he made a journey by car across Poland, Czechoslovakia, and East Germany. In 1962, he visited Japan and India, and the following year defected in London while on an approved visit, accompanied by the usual contingent of KGB escorts. He arrived on 4 September and while staying at a hotel in Bayswater he alerted an English acquaintance of his decision not to return home, who in turn contacted MI5, which kept him under discreet surveillance and ensured his plan to elude the KGB went off uninterrupted.

After his defection in London, Krotkov continued to write and in 1967 published *The Angry Exile*, a critique of postwar social conditions in Moscow. Two years later he gave evidence to the Senate Committee on Judiciary under the name "George Karlin" and in 1979 published *Red Monarch*, a semisatirical biography of Josef Stalin. Krotkov was allowed to settle in the United States but he was never accepted as an authentic defector, and he eventually died in Spain.

KUCZYNSKI, URSULA. Codenamed SONIA by the GRU, Ursula Kuczynski was an experienced German Communist of Polish extraction who settled in Switzerland in 1939 to manage a cosmopolitan spy ring consisting mainly of expatriates. Her husband, Paul Hamburger, had been imprisoned in China while on a GRU mission in Shanghai, so Kuczynski and her two children, accompanied by a loyal old governess, Lisa Boeckel, found accommodation in a chalet at Caux-sur-Montreaux where a radio link was established with Moscow. Among Kuczynski's agents were two British Communists, Len Beurton and Allan Foote, who coincidentally had known each other while working for the International Brigade during the Spanish Civil War, and in 1940 Moscow ordered her back to England for a new assignment. However, possessing only a German passport Kuczynski agreed to obtain a divorce from her husband in China and marry Beurton so she could qualify for British citizenship. Beurton agreed to the scheme but, unexpectedly, the couple fell in love and began a passionate affair that would last for 50 years. This unexpected turn of events dismayed the children's nurse, Lisa Boeckel, who, though not entirely sure of the role played by Kuczynski, telephoned the local British consul in an attempt to denounce her as a spy.

Once she had recovered from her anger and been filled with remorse, Boeckel confessed to Kuczynski and agreed to return to her native Germany. As Allan Foote later recalled, "as long as she remained in Switzerland—or SONIA and [Len] remained in love—she would be a perpetual danger to us all. . . . She was a faithful old thing and I was fond of and sorry for her. Had sex not reared its ugly head she would have been with us to the end, but it was too dangerous to have a weak link in the chain. It was bad enough to have the head of the network and your fellow-operative behaving like a honeymoon couple, without the thought that at any moment the faithful retainer might try yet another denunciation—and perhaps with success this time."

Kuczynski was able to return to England in July 1940 and find a house near Oxford where she was eventually joined by Beurton to build a new network, one that would survive until it was endangered by the arrest of Klaus Fuchs in 1949. In Foote's memoirs, *Handbook for Spies*, the author concealed the identities of Beurton, Hamburger, and SONIA, referring to her husbands as "Bill Phillips" and

"Schultz" respectively, because at the time of publication Beurton and Kuczynski were still married and living in Oxfordshire, and under investigation by MI5. However, as soon as Fuchs was arrested Kuczynski fled to East Germany where she was joined soon afterward by her husband and children.

KÜHN, RUTH. In August 1935, Ruth Kühn arrived in Honolulu accompanied by her mother Friedl and stepfather, Dr. Bernard Kühn, an anthropologist embarking on a project to study Japanese influence on Polynesia. While the German scholar, who had connections with the Brazilian coffee industry, busied himself with his academic work, financed by payments made from the Rotterdamsche Bank in Holland, his wife and his beautiful stepdaughter opened a hairdressing salon that developed a clientele among the wives of U.S. Navy personnel based at Pearl Harbor. According to one report, the two women acquired useful information about warship movements from their customers, and Ruth apparently accepted a proposal of marriage from one officer.

In October 1940, the Federal Bureau of Investigation (FBI) began an investigation of the Kühn family after receiving a tip that suggested Ruth was making regular visits to Japan and returning with large amounts of cash that she laundered through a doctor on the *Lurline*, a Matson Line ship sailing between Honolulu and the West Coast. No evidence of espionage was discovered then, although the Kühn's bank transactions were monitored, but shortly after the surprise attack on Pearl Harbor in December 1941 Bernard Kühn was arrested and charged with espionage, a wireless transmitter having been discovered during a search of his substantial villa.

In an agreement reached with his FBI interrogators to save him from the death penalty, Kühn admitted that he had been recruited by the Sicherheitsdienst and had been sent on his mission to spy for the Japanese, and had reported to the local Japanese vice consul Otojira Okuda. To facilitate their observations and communications, Ruth bought a beach house at Kalama on Lanakai Bay and used a prearranged system of lights in certain rooms at particular times to signal to Japanese submarines offshore the number of Pacific Fleet ships in the anchorage. The FBI special agent in charge, Robert L. Shivers, was able to obtain Kühn's cooperation because of incriminating documents and messages found in the incinerator at the Japanese Consulate-General on Nuuana Avenue that the consul-general, Nagao Kita, had failed to destroy entirely. They clearly implicated the Kühn family, and when questioned Bernard confirmed that he had taken his instructions from Ruth. At his trial in February 1942 his son gave evidence as a witness for the prosecution, and then went on to serve in the U.S. Army.

Dr. Kühn's death sentence was commuted to 50 years' hard labor, but Ruth and Friedl were interned at Crystal City, Texas. At the end of the war, the women were deported to Germany but upon his release from Fort Leavenworth Penitentiary Bernard was accommodated on Ellis Island, New York, until December 1948 when he was given permission to emigrate to Argentina.

– L –

LAIS, ALBERTO. The Italian naval attaché in Washington, D.C., during World War II, and the former director of naval intelligence, Admiral Alberto Lais conducted an affair with **Elizabeth (Betty) Pack**, an agent working for British Security Coordination (BSC). According to BSC's official history, he not only allowed his cipher clerk to provide her with a copy of the Italian naval codebook, but he also disclosed details of a sabotage plot intended to disable Italian merchantmen in American harbors. This evidence of his involvement in the sabotage resulted in his expulsion and return to Rome.

LAPPAS, SIMON. In July 2002, 27-year-old analyst Simon Lappas, working for the Australian Defence Intelligence Organisation (DIO), passed classified documents to a prostitute, Sherryll Ellen Dowling, and instructed her to sell them to a foreign embassy. Although he claimed the material might be worth $5,000, they were never sold; Lappas was arrested and, in December 2002, convicted after a trial lasting 10 days in December 2002 at which Lappas did not deny the offense but claimed an impaired mental state. He pleaded guilty to two charges of communicating three proscribed documents to an unauthorized person, and Dowling, aged 26, pleaded not guilty to receiving them. According to the prosecution, Lappas had started working at the DIO in November 1999 and arranged for Dowling to visit him at his Narrabundah home in July 2000, where she stayed for three days. Soon afterward Lappas admitted to a work colleague what he had done, and he was then interviewed by a DIO security officer.

LATY, AMIR. In December 2004, Amir Laty, a suspected Mossad officer working under diplomatic cover at the Israeli consulate in Sydney, was withdrawn after only 18 months in the post following an investigation conducted by the Australian Security Intelligence Organisation (ASIO) that revealed he had acquired several admirers, among them Caitlin Ruddock, the 26-year-old daughter of the Australian attorney general, Philip Ruddock. According to ASIO, Laty had met the accounting lecturer at the University of New South Wales when they had both studied in Beijing seven years earlier, and after his arrival in Australia he had attempted to cultivate a woman employed by the Defense Department, and another working in the Department of Prime Minister and Cabinet.

LECOUTRE, ALTA. An experienced Soviet spy codenamed MARTHA, Alta Lecoutre had been the mistress of Pierre Cot, codenamed DAEDALUS, France's prewar minister of air in Edouard Daladier's government. After the German occupation, she moved to London with her husband, Stanislas Seymoniczky, a suspected Soviet spy. In England, she acquired a job in the offices of General Charles de Gaulle as secretary to André Labarthe, another Soviet agent who had worked for the French Ministry of Air until 1938. Until 1940 Labarthe, codenamed JEROME, was de Gaulle's director-general of French armament and scientific research. The identities of MARTHA and JEROME would not become known to Western security agencies until 1964, when some of the GRU's VENONA traffic with London was decrypted.

LENZKOW, MARIANNE. A 31-year-old divorced teletype operator employed by the Federal German Ministry of the Interior in Berlin, Marianne Lenzkow was introduced to two men, Kalle Schramm and Kai Petersen, in 1960 by a friend, the Danish-born fiancé of a barmaid in a Bonn nightclub. Schramm and Petersen claimed to be members of the Danish Military Mission and Lenzkow accepted an invitation to join Schramm for a weekend at the military mission's guest house at Plauen, near Chemnitz. Once there, she was seduced by Schramm, who recruited her under a false flag, asserting that her information was needed by the Danish Intelligence Service, which suspected that Denmark was not being treated as an equal partner by its NATO partners. Lenzkow agreed to the arrangement and began passing copies of teletype messages from her office to her friend Anita Brünger, the Bonn barmaid, and her fiancé, Eric Michaelson.

In 1961, Lenzkow suggested that her younger sister, 25-year-old **Margarethe Lubig**, who was a secretary in the Ministry of Defense, should meet Kai Petersen, and a rendezvous was agreed in Vienna. The two sisters spent a week with Schramm and Petersen, and soon afterward Lubig was engaged to Petersen and agreed to pass him secrets for the Danes.

The sisters were exposed in 1990 when a senior Hauptverwaltung Aufkrarung (HVA) officer, Colonel Heinz Busch, defected to the Federal German Bundesnachrichtendienst (BND) and revealed that an East German actor, Roland Gandt, codenamed VENSKE, had been recruited by one of his subordinates, **Karl-Heinz Schneider**, to seduce and run an agent whom he had run for more than 25 years. Furthermore, the agent's sister, codenamed ROSE, had fallen for Gandt, and both women been run under a false flag. BND molehunters quickly identified ROSE as Margarethe Lubig, who confessed and implicated her sister, who died before she could be brought to trial in Düsseldorf.

LESSER, DR. ANNAMARIE. Subsequently better known as "Fraulein Doktor," Annamarie Lesser was a German spy in France during World War I. Her talent was for making senior officers commit indiscretions, one of which resulted in the capture of a French fortress by the enemy.

LINTON, FREDA. Born Fritzie Lipchitz in Montreal of Polish parents, Freda Linton worked for the Film Board of Canada at the end of World War II and was the mistress of **Fred Rose**, a Member of the Canadian Parliament since 1932 and an important GRU agent. Codenamed VERA, she also acted as a go-between for Professor Raymond Boyer, an academic from McGill University who researched the development of high explosives. Rose and Linton were identified by the defector Igor Gouzenko in September 1945 as members of a GRU spy ring in Ottawa. Although a total of 21 suspects were charged, only 15 were prosecuted, and charges against Linton were dropped.

LJUSKOVA, NATALIA. In May 1992, two espionage suspects were arrested in Finland carrying British passports in the names of James Peatfield and Anna Marie Nemeth. Both were really Russians, identified as Igor and Natalia Ljuskova, apparently undertaking a preliminary training assignment, an essential and characteristic feature of illegal operations known as *stazhirovka* or "staging," used to establish the credentials and documentation of agents before their deployment on their main mission as illegals. The real Peatfield and Nemeth, living in England, were astonished and mystified by the use of their names by the Russian Foreign Intelligence Service.

LONETREE, CLAYTON. In December 1986, a U.S. Marine, Sergeant Clayton J. Lonetree, approached Jim Olson, the **Central Intelligence Agency** (CIA) station chief in Vienna, and confessed to having allowed KGB personnel into the classified areas of the embassy in Moscow at night. Lonetree had been the victim of a classic **honeytrap** conducted by a KGB agent, Violette Seina, while he had been posted to Moscow between September 1984 and March 1986. Seina previously had worked at the embassy as a locally employed telephone operator and translator, but her genial "Uncle Sasha" was actually a skilled KGB officer, Aleksei G. Yefimov, who manipulated the young Native American and persuaded him to compromise classified information.

Lonetree's confession resulted in the detention of six other Marines, including Corporal Arnold Bracey, who was suspected of having had several affairs with various Soviet women. In the end, the charges against all except Lonetree were dropped, and he was convicted in August 1987 in a military court on 12 counts of espionage and collaborating with the Soviets to supply floor plans of the embassies in Moscow and Vienna, and identifying U.S. intelligence personnel.

Lonetree was sentenced to 30 years' imprisonment, but following a further detailed enquiry by the Naval Investigative Service, it was concluded that the KGB never did gain access to the embassy, and his sentence was cut in May 1988 to 25 years, in 1992 to 20 years, and then to 15 years. Finally, he was released in February 1996. Another suspect implicated, Sergeant Robert Stufflebeam, escaped without charge altogether.

Initially, Lonetree's confession was regarded as exceptionally important at Langley where an analysis of the documents that might have been compromised at the CIA station in Moscow showed that they had included details of almost all of the CIA's 1985 losses. Such losses included the list of assets that had been "wrapped up with almost reckless abandon," according to Paul Redmond, the South-East Europe Division's counterintelligence chief who had created the RIVER CITY file, highlighting the extent of the KGB arrests. It would take five years and many false trails before Sandy Grimes and Jeanne Vertefeille identified their colleague **Aldrich Ames** as one of the sources responsible for the CIA's hemorrhage of secrets. However, although Lonetree's confession appeared at first glance to offer a solution to the problem that had befallen the agency, he never admitted to having allowed KGB personnel into the CIA station in the embassy. Indeed, his denials, videotaped after his conviction, seemed very convincing, and the only evidence to support the allegation came from Bracey, who retracted the claim the day after he had made it. Something that struck the counterintelligence investigators as odd at the time was Lonetree's recollection of having been asked by the KGB to defect in Vienna. This was strange behavior because the Marine would have been infinitely more valuable while at liberty in the West and with continuing access, than as a wasted resource languishing unproductively in Moscow. Why had the KGB pressed him to defect? Only years later did it become obvious that Lonetree's defection would have served to confirm to the CIA that he alone had been responsible for the RIVER CITY losses. It also became clear, much later, that the KGB had been in a position to monitor Lonetree's confession in Vienna because the deputy chief of mission, **Felix Bloch**, had been briefed twice a week by the CIA on the station's activities.

LOPOKOVA, LYDIA. A prima ballerina with the Diaghalev troupe and the daughter of a Russian impresario who ran a ballet company in St. Petersburg, Lydia Lopokova seduced John Maynard Keynes, then aged 42, and became his wife in 1925, a marriage that was controversial because the Eton and King's College, Cambridge–educated economist was a well-known **homosexual** who had been living openly with a man for many years. Formerly the editor of the *Economic Journal*, Keynes wrote for the *Economist* and was the author of numerous books, including *The General Theory of Employment, Interest and Money* in 1936. Universally recognized as one of the most brilliant economic geniuses of the era, researchers would be puzzled by his apparent dramatic change of opinion, often advocating Socialist approaches and policies favorable to Moscow after his marriage. Throughout their relationship, Keynes continued to move in homosexual circles in Cambridge, regularly hosting dinner parties for members of the Apostles secret society while his wife lived in Gordon Square, London, becoming a prominent member of the Bloomsbury set and frequently hosting Ivan Maisky, the Soviet ambassador.

In 1922 Keynes had attended the Genoa Conference as a *Manchester Guardian* correspondent and met Soviet foreign minister Georgi Chicherin, and in 1941 negotiated terms for Lend-Lease with the Treasury's assistant secretary, Harry Dexter White. Although White was not suspected of espionage at the time, his 1933 book *The International Payments of France, 1880–1913*, included acknowledgments to two other Soviet spies, Lauchlin Currie and George Silverman. Keynes would later encounter White when they planned the creation of the World Bank and the International Monetary Fund.

Among Keynes's friends there was a strong suspicion that, having fallen under Lydia's influence, he had become an agent of influence for the Soviets, as he collaborated with Harry Dexter White to forge the Bretton Woods monetary agreement in New Hampshire, which proved advantageous to Moscow. White died suddenly of cardiac arrest in July 1948 after he had been accused of espionage by **Elizabeth Bentley**, and Keynes succumbed to a heart attack in London in April 1946 after having returned to England on the *Queen Mary*.

LORENZEN, URSEL. In March 1979, Ursel Lorenzen disappeared from her apartment in Brussels, where she worked as a secretary to

NATO's British director of operations. A security investigation revealed that Lorenzen's lover, Dieter Will, the manager of the Hilton Hotel at Brussels Airport, had also fled the country. When she appeared soon afterward in an East German television propaganda broadcast claiming to have been forced by her conscience to seek political asylum, it was realized that she had been a long-term mole for Hauptverwaltung Aufkrarung (HVA), codenamed MOSEL. Having fallen for an HVA **Romeo**, codenamed BORDEAUX, Lorenzen's defection had been prompted by the arrest of another spy, Ingrid Garbe, who was a secretary at the Federal German mission to NATO and in a position to compromise the couple.

LOUISA. The KGB **Second Chief Directorate** codename for a diplomat at the French embassy in Paris who was seduced by a **Romeo** directed by **Oleg Gribanov**. When confronted with photographs of her encounter, she agreed to cooperate but after she returned to Paris she broke off contact, and her identity did not become known for 30 years, until 1992 when Vasili Mitrokhin defected to the British Secret Intelligence Service.

LOWRY, HELEN. The niece of Earl Browder, secretary-general of the **Communist Party of the United States of America**, Helen Lowry acted as an assistant to Iskhak Akhmerov, the NKVD illegal *rezident* in New York between 1942 and 1945, and after a passionate affair they applied to Moscow for permission to marry. Codenamed ALBERT and from a poor Tartar family, Akhmerov had been posted to the United States after having served since 1937 as deputy to Boris Bazarov, formerly the illegal *rezident* in Berlin and codenamed KIN. Before that, he had been in Turkey, where he learned to speak the language fluently, and in Beijing, where he had attended American College posing as a Turkish student.

After having obtained Moscow's consent to their marriage, Helen, codenamed ELZA, and her husband moved to Baltimore in March 1942 to run a growing number of Soviet agents in Washington, D.C. His cover in Baltimore, under the alias Bill Grenyke, was that of a furrier, a trade he had learned from his stepfather, and the premises were supplied by a local NKVD asset codenamed KHOSYAIN.

Elizabeth Bentley had known Helen simply as "Catherine," who had visited her a couple of times after the death of Jacob Golos and during her deteriorating relationship with "Bill," whom she suspected wanted to take control of her network, but she never guessed that he was Helen's husband. In early 1946, following the news of Bentley's defection, Helen and Iskhak were ordered back to Moscow as a precaution, along with their legal counterparts in New York, Roland Abbiate, alias Vladimir Pravdin, and in Washington, Anatoli Gorsky. Once back in the Soviet Union, Iskhak and Helen moved to Leningrad under Intourist cover and were put to work by the KGB attempting to entrap American scientists visiting the city as tourists.

LUBIG, MARGARETHE. The younger sister of **Marianne Lenzkow**, Margarethe Lubig was a secretary in the Federal German Ministry of Defense in 1961 when she was introduced in Vienna to Kai Petersen, a Hauptverwaltung Aufkrarung (HVA) officer posing as a Dane. The couple was soon engaged and Lubig was persuaded to give him classified material on the pretext that NATO was excluding Denmark from information that it was entitled to. Over the next 26 years, she would continue to spy from her various postings, to NATO headquarters at Fontainebleau and to the German military attaché's office in Rome. However, as a devout Roman Catholic, her conscience troubled her and she confided in Petersen that she wanted to make a full confession to a priest. Accordingly, he made elaborate arrangements for a trip to his mother in Denmark so she could visit a local church and receive absolution. This she did, and was also introduced to Petersen's superior in the Danish Intelligence Service, who thanked her for her cooperation.

The charade was eventually exposed in 1990 when a senior HVA officer, Colonel Heinz Busch, defected to the Federal German Bundesnachrichtendienst (BND) and revealed that an East German actor, Roland Gandt, codenamed VENSKE, had been recruited by one of his subordinates, **Karl-Heinz Schneider**, to seduce and run an agent whom he had run for more than 25 years. Furthermore, the agent's sister, codenamed ROSE, had fallen for Gandt, and both women been run under a false flag. BND molehunters quickly identified ROSE as Margarethe Lubig, then aged 60, and she quickly confessed, received a 19-month suspended sentence, and implicated her sister Marianne, who died before she could be brought to trial in Düsseldorf.

The BND subsequently established that Lubig's "confession" to a Danish priest had been a charade, with HVA agent Heinz Hüppe playing the role of her forgiving confessor. Another HVA agent, an East German based in Sweden, had play-acted Petersen's mother, while a member of the Communist Party of Denmark had adopted the role of the senior Danish intelligence officer.

LUMMER, HEINRICH. A senior Christian Democrat politician and formerly a member of the West Berlin Senate, Heinrich Lummer was caught in a **honeytrap** in a hotel room in bed with a Hauptverwaltung Aufkrarung (HVA) **swallow**, Suzanne Rau. When confronted with photographs of himself naked, in bed with Rau, Lummer rejected the attempt to blackmail him and informed the Bundesamt fur Verfassungsschutz

LUTSKY, E. P. In November 1956, E. P. Lutsky, a married KGB officer operating under diplomatic cover in New Zealand, turned his attention to an attractive single woman, a clerk who worked in the Passport Department of the Australian High Commission in Wellington. She did not encourage his advances, but when in July 1958 he appeared unexpectedly at her home with a box of chocolates, she informed the High Commission's security officer who contacted the New Zealand Security Service (NZSS), the local security organization headed by Brigadier Hubert ("Bill") Gilbert. He advised that the woman should simply tell Lutsky to leave her alone, and he did not make further contact until October 1960 when he visited her home to announce that he was returning to Moscow. However, two months later, his replacement, Nikolai Shtykov, telephoned for a meeting and suggested, when they sat chatting in his car, that when she returned to Canberra another of Lutsky's friends might contact her.

Shtykov remained under NZSS surveillance until he was declared persona non grata in July 1962, along with his *rezident*, Vladislav Andreev.

Eventually, KGB officer **Ivan Skripov** did hold a rendezvous with her, but it was monitored by the Australian Security Intelligence Organization, and he was expelled in February 1963.

LUTZ, RENATE. A secretary in the German Federal Republic's Ministry of Defense, Renate Lutz married her **Romeo**, Lothar, in September 1972, knowing he worked for the East German Hauptverwaltung Aufkrarung (HVA). She was arrested with him at their Bonn apartment in June 1976 and, charged with espionage, she was sentenced to six years' imprisonment. He received 12 years, but they were later freed in an exchange of spies negotiated by the HVA chief **Markus Wolf**.

LYALIN, OLEG. A KGB defector from the *rezidentura* in London who was persuaded, while conducting an illicit affair with his secretary, Irinaa Templyakova, to cooperate with a joint MI5–Secret Intelligence Service team of case officers six months before he took political asylum, in August 1972. Confronted with his compromising behavior, Lyalin agreed to trade information in return for eventual resettlement in England, and he soon supplied a complete order-of-battle for the KGB in London. He also revealed his own mission, reconnoitered while posing as a textiles buyer across the Midlands, to select targets for attack by Special Forces in the event of war, including the Fylingdales early warning radar installation in Yorkshire, V-bomber bases, and the London tube, scheduled for flooding by the River Thames after strategically placed bombs had detonated. Chillingly, the defector also described a plan to infiltrate agents disguised as official messengers into Whitehall's system of underground tunnels to distribute poison gas capsules. He also identified other members of the London *rezidenturas* who were expelled in operation FOOT. Codenamed GOLDFINCH, Lyalin's debriefing covered five volumes and was circulated widely among Western intelligence agencies. In Ottawa, it was copied by Gilles Brunet and passed to his KGB handlers.

Lyalin's recruitment was accomplished by Tony Brooks of SIS and Harry Wharton of MI5, but his defection was unplanned, having been prompted by his arrest on drunk driving charges by a Metropolitan Police traffic patrol. When detained, Lyalin arranged for his handlers to be contacted, and MI5 dispatched a team, equipped with the antidotes to various poisons, to extract him from the police station and supervise his asylum. Lyalin and his girlfriend were resettled. While living in Great Britain with a new identity, Lyalin was the target of a sustained effort by the KGB to trace him, and **John Symonds** was approached to use his police contacts to establish his whereabouts. He died in February 1995.

LYGREN, INGEBORG. An unmarried member of the Norwegian Military Intelligence Service headed by Colonel Wilhelm Evang, Ingeborg Lygren worked, prior to 1956, as a Russian translator. Evang chose her to go to Moscow under cover as the ambassador's secretary and to operate there on the **Central Intelligence Agency**'s (CIA) behalf, locating and filling agency dead drops, a task for which she had received specialist training by the CIA in Norway before her departure in February 1956.

In Moscow, Lygren replaced another unmarried secretary, **Gunvor Haavik**, who had served there for the previous nine years. Lygren wanted to learn to drive in Moscow and applied for a driving instructor from *Burobin*, which supplied services to embassies. At first, they were unable to help her, but in March 1957 a former commander of a tank regiment, Aleksei Vasilyevich Filipov, was appointed her instructor. Lygren continued her association with Filipov after she obtained her driver's permit in June 1957 because she felt she was not yet a good driver. He even accompanied her on some of her searches for potential dead-drop sites. In October 1957, she reported that Filipov had made advances to her and that he was probably working for the KGB, but she said that she could handle the situation. In August 1959, Lygren returned to Oslo.

In November 1964, Inspector Asbjørn Bryhn, the head of the Norwegian Security Service, learned that during her service in Moscow Lygren had become Filatov's lover and had slept with him in her bedroom, which was connected directly through an unlocked door with the room housing the embassy's archives and the safe containing the ambassador's ciphers. Lygren had full access to this safe as well as to the other safes in the embassy. She had the keys and knew the combinations. Bryhn learned that she often declined to accompany her embassy colleagues on Sunday outings, preferring to stay in the embassy, where she would have been the sole occupant, so her access was therefore often total. Lygren had remained in Moscow until August 1959.

Bryhn's investigation revealed that Lygren had mailed 13 letters to 10 different CIA agents in the Soviet Union who probably had been compromised. On 14 September 1965, Lygren was arrested and on 18 September she was formally charged with espionage. She then made a partial confession to having handed over a key and safe combination to her KGB lover, but then retracted it. Two months later, on 14 December, the prosecutor ordered Lygren's immediate release for lack of evidence.

– M –

MACDERMOT, NIALL. A MI5 officer during World War II, Niall Macdermot had been a member of the New Britain movement while an undergraduate at Oxford, and had fought with another member of the audience at a meeting. The other died of cardiac failure, and Macdermot was charged with manslaughter but was acquitted because the dead man had a medical history of heart weakness.

Having qualified as a barrister, Macdermot was elected to the House of Commons in February 1957 as the Labour Member of Parliament for Lewisham and served as financial secretary to the Treasury in Harold Wilson's first government in 1964. He was considered subsequently for an appointment as a law officer when MI5 noted that he kept a Russian mistress, Ludmilla Benvenuto, in Italy who had links to Italian Communists and the Soviets. Macdermot admitted the relationship and was excluded from a ministerial appointment. In 1970, having divorced his wife, he left the Commons to take up a post with the International Commission of Jurists in Geneva.

MACLEAN, MELINDA. Born into a wealthy American East Coast family, Melinda Marling was a student at the Sorbonne in 1940 when she met Donald Maclean, then a junior diplomat at the British embassy in Paris. She initially rejected his proposal of marriage, on the grounds that he would be too boring a husband, but changed her mind when he revealed that he was actually a Soviet mole working for the NKVD. Attracted to the excitement of a life of espionage, she married him at the embassy in June shortly before they were evacuated to England. While her husband worked at the Foreign Office, Melinda returned to New York, where she lost her first baby. She then returned to London but in 1944 accompanied her husband to Washington, D.C., and in July 1946 bore him a son, Donald.

When finally on 25 May 1951 MI5's net closed in on Maclean and he was forced to flee the country, a heavily pregnant Melinda played a crucial role in deceiving the MI5 surveillance on her husband, and for the benefit of the microphones installed in her home at Tatsfield, Kent, pretended that she had never met their dinner guest, Roger Styles. In realty, Styles was the alias adopted by her husband's Foreign Office colleague and fellow spy **Guy Burgess**, who was supposed to escort Maclean across the Channel to France and was certainly known to her as an old friend. However, in order to conceal the existence of the technical surveillance in the house and to avoid criticism that might follow the hostile interrogation of a woman close to birth, she was never confronted by MI5.

Maclean's last-minute, midnight Friday night escape, hastily orchestrated to prevent an imminent interview with molehunters scheduled for Monday 28 May, ensured he escaped charges of espionage and seriously handicapped MI5's investigation into leaks from the British embassy in Washington, D.C., disclosed by VENONA texts dating back to 1944. It also meant that other members of his spy ring, though under suspicion, would never face criminal sanctions.

Although Melinda Maclean never enjoyed direct access to classified information, she was certainly a willing coconspirator and made every effort to conceal the circumstances of her husband's flight. Despite his alcoholism and a violent incident that occurred in Cairo in 1949, she remained loyal and would eventually follow him to Moscow in September 1953, eluding the surveillance placed on her while on a trip with her three children to Switzerland.

Once in Moscow, Melinda conducted an affair with **Kim Philby** in 1964, and left her husband to live with Philby in 1966. In 1979, she returned to the United States, where she now lives. Her lawyer in New York City refused requests from the Federal Bureau of Investigation for an interview. A widow since 1983, she lives in quiet seclusion in upstate New York, remaining silent on the precise contribution she made to the notorious Cambridge spies.

MAKAYEV, VALERI M. Appointed the KGB's illegal *rezident* in New York in 1950, Valeri Makayev had spent the previous two years in Warsaw preparing for the assignment and establishing himself as Ivan M. Kovalik, a man of the same age born in Chicago to Ukrainian parents and who had been taken to Poland as a child. Equipped with an authentic passport issued by the American embassy in Warsaw, after pressure had been applied to a corrupt clerk, Makayev arrived in New York on the SS *Batory* in March 1950 and found a temporary job as a furrier before exploiting his considerable musical abilities by obtaining a teaching post at New York University.

Makayev's arrival in New York coincided with the posting of **Guy Burgess** to Washington, D.C., and one of his tasks was to use him as a courier for **Kim Philby**, who had been out of contact since he had been appointed the Secret Intelligence Service station commander the previous September. Personal contact was established at the end of November 1950, but Makayev's performance as an illegal was adversely affected by his love affair with a Polish ballerina, codenamed ALICE, who ran her own ballet studio in Manhattan. Distracted by ALICE, Makayev failed to recover a dead drop that included $2,000 and a crucial message intended for Philby in the vital days after Burgess had returned to London on Monday, 7 May 1951, and his defection three weeks later, on Friday, 25 May.

Makayev was recalled to Moscow to explain his negligence and was allowed to return to New York to work under **Willie Fisher**, but he even bungled that mission by losing a Swiss coin containing instructions for the *rezidentura*. When recalled again to Moscow, he was dismissed from the **Illegals Directorate**.

MASSING, HEDE. Austrian by birth and married at 17 to Gerhardt Eisler, one of the Kommunist Partei Deutschland's (KPD) leading figures and a friend of the legendary Soviet illegal **Richard Sorge**, Hede Massing traveled to the United States in 1923 and stayed, working in an orphanage in Pleasantville, New York, until she acquired her citizenship in December 1927. Later she would claim to have "married into the Party at a time when she did not understand politics, and simply wanted a better life for all."

According to the statement she made to the Federal Bureau of Investigation (FBI) in late 1947, she had returned to Europe in January

1928 and, while studying in Berlin, had met and had been recruited by Sorge. A year in Moscow followed, where she was indoctrinated into the Comintern, ready for new role as an illegal based in Berlin, and had married another NKVD agent, Paul Massing. Supervised by **Ignace Reiss**, Hede Massing worked openly for the KDP, on one occasion traveling to London to audit the accounts of the **Communist Party of Great Britain** but also undertaking clandestine work for the Soviets. She operated a mail drop for Ignace Reiss and in 1932 was introduced to Walter Krivitsky, who apparently rejected her as unsuitable for a particular mission he had in mind for her.

In October 1933, Hede returned to New York aboard the *Deutschland* as a correspondent for the *Weltbuehne* and moved in with Helen Black, the representative of the Soviet Photo Agency. She took her orders from Valentine Markin, whose cover was that of a director of a small cosmetics company owned by a **Communist Party of the United States of America** member named Hart. During this period, Hede acted as a courier, taking microfilms to Paris, and as a recruiter, successfully persuading **Noel Field** and his wife Herta to join her network but failing to acquire his State Department friend **Alger Hiss** who, Hede discovered, was already involved with a separate spy ring in Washington, D.C. After a single, preliminary encounter with Hiss, Hede was warned to keep away from him. "Never see him again. Stay away from him and forget him," she was told by her controller.

> I understood, of course. There had apparently been a reprimand and these were urgent, emphatic instructions. I had met a member of another apparatus. I had had a conversation with him in which I had disclosed that I was working in a parallel apparatus. That was strictly taboo, and disliked by the big boss here and by the bigger bosses in Moscow.

Following the murder of Ignace Reiss, Hede expressed doubts about her own commitment to her new controller, whom she subsequently learned was **Elizaveta Zarubina**, the wife of Vasili, the *rezident* in New York, and was summoned to Moscow. Hede arrived in November 1937 and underwent months of interrogation by Peter Zubelin to confirm her continued loyalty, but she was too disillusioned to continue. The following year she returned to New York and broke off contact with Helen Gold and the Zarubinas. When the FBI approached her after the war in regard to its investigation of Gerhardt Eisler, she agreed to give evidence against Alger Hiss; her testimony secured his conviction on a charge of perjury, following his denial on oath of charges made by another defector, **Whittaker Chambers**.

Massing died in New York in March 1981 of emphysema. Her autobiography, *This Deception*, was published in 1951 and was largely a compilation of an 18-part story, *I Spied for the Soviet Union* that had been carried by many newspapers. However, just before she died she gave her only television interview to the Canadian Broadcasting Corporation and described how invariably she had relied on sex to recruit her sources. Although she would not name any of her spies, apart from **Noel Field** and Larry Duggan, she recalled that she had depended on good-looking men and women to cultivate and manage members of her network, saying, "with women it was mostly done with sex. I would always send someone who was handsome. They generally went to bed with whoever it was. And it worked."

MATA HARI. Codenamed H-21 by the Germans, Mata Hari was the exotic Indonesian stage name (in Hindi, "Eye of the Dawn") adopted by Margaretha MacLeod, the wife of a Dutch Army officer stationed in Java, in the East Indies. She was arrested in February 1917, convicted of espionage, and executed by firing squad at Vincennes on 15 October.

Born of mixed race to Adam Zelle, the Dutch owner of a hat shop, and his Javanese wife in 1876, she was married in 1894 but fled to Paris in 1904 following the death of her son, and thereafter established a reputation in Europe and Egypt as an erotic, flimsily clad dancer purporting to demonstrate native Oriental performances. Her first appearance, aged 29 at the Musée Guimet in 1905, proved a great success, and she supplemented her income by taking wealthy lovers, among them a rich German, Alfred Kieper, and a French financier, Xavier Rousseau. By 1906, she had acquired the same manager as the composer Stravinsky and the dancer Nijinsky, and she would perform in Vienna and Amsterdam, but was in Berlin in August 1914 when World War I broke out. Short of money after her accounts had been frozen, she traveled to Amsterdam where she was invited by the local German consul to collect information and correspond with him in secret writing. Having agreed to do so, and now with sufficient funds to return to Paris, she later insisted she had discarded her supplies of secret ink and abandoned the offer of espionage.

One of her lovers was a Russian pilot, Captain Vadim Maroff, who was wounded while flying over the German frontlines. She was given permission to visit him in hospital at Vittel by Captain Georges Ledoux of the Deuxième Bureau, who seems to have recruited her to act as an agent on a mission to Belgium. However, when she tried to travel to Rotterdam from Vigo on the SS *Hollandia* in December 1916 she was arrested in Falmouth, escorted to Holloway prison by Detective Inspector George Grant, and interrogated at Scotland Yard because she had been mistakenly identified as the German spy Clara Benedict. Once the confusion had been sorted out in London by Assistant Commissioner **Basil Thomson**, she was warned not to attempt to continue her journey to Germany. She returned to the Palace Hotel in Madrid where she befriended Major Kalle of the German embassy who indiscreetly told her about plans for a U-boat to land troops in Morocco. She attempted to deliver this news to Captain Ledoux but when she reached Paris in January 1917 she was accused by the Sureté of having supplied information to the Germans in Madrid. She was arrested in February 1917 with evidence acquired by a wireless station on the Eiffel Tower from 13 December 1916, interrogated by the relentless Pierre Bouchardon, and charged with having been recruited by her German lover, von Kalle, who had apparently paid her 3,500 pesetas.

MacLeod's defense was that although she admitted she had been recruited by Major Kalle in Madrid, she had only made herself available because she had been instructed to do so by Captain Ledoux of the Deuxième Bureau who had interviewed her in Paris in August 1916 and allegedly had urged her act as a double agent against the Germans.

Convicted in July of espionage by a court-martial on the basis of an incriminating German intercept that identified her as an agent codenamed H-21, and without any exculpatory testimony from Captain Ledoux, she was shot three months later on 15 October.

The story of Mata Hari inspired three films, one starring Greta Garbo, and several books, although declassified files of the French investigation cast considerable doubt on whether she ever truly engaged in espionage for anyone.

MAUGHAM, WILLIE SOMERSET. Maugham was already a well-known and successful writer, the author of *Of Human Bondage*, when, in September 1915, he was approached to join the British Secret Intelligence Service (SIS).

Aged 41 and handicapped by a clubfoot, Maugham was too old for military service and had already served on the Western front in a Red Cross ambulance unit, and was anxious to leave London where his mistress's impending divorce from her husband on the grounds of her adultery was set to create a scandal. Ostensibly Maugham went to Switzerland, presumably to complete his play *Caroline*, but actually to reestablish contact with some of SIS's agents, and his first assignment was to watch an Englishman with a German wife who was living in Lucerne. He took a room in the Hotel Beau Rivage in Geneva and filed his weekly reports by taking the ferry across the lake to the French side. Maugham was back in London early in the New Year to see *Caroline* open in the West End, and then in March he resumed his duties in Switzerland, accompanied by his newly divorced mistress, Syrie Wellcome, who was also the mistress of SIS's Major John Wallinger. Syrie and Willie stayed in Switzerland until June when they moved to the French spa of Brides-les-Bains for a brief holiday, and then he returned to London to resign from SIS.

Maugham did not write about his melancholy experiences in Switzerland until 1928 when he released *Ashenden*, which gave a fictionalized version of his intelligence missions during the war.

In *Ashenden*, the hero travels to Lucerne to investigate an English expatriate who is married to a suspected enemy agent and he lures him onto French territory so he can be arrested, a tale that is very close to the first assignment Maugham undertook in Switzerland for SIS. Maugham conceded that his stories were "on the whole a very truthful account of my experiences."

The *Ashenden* stories were sufficiently authentic to alarm Winston Churchill, who declared that they were a breach of the Official Secrets Acts. Accordingly Maugham burned 14 of the remaining unpublished *Ashenden* manuscripts. All his stories were based on fact, although in his preface Maugham claimed "this book is a work of fiction, though

I should say not much more so than several of the books on the same subject that have appeared during the last few years and that purport to be truthful memoirs."

In August 1916, almost as soon as he returned to London, Maugham set off on a long voyage to the Pacific, but as he made his way back through New York in June 1917 he received another request from SIS, this time through Sir William Wiseman, SIS's representative in the United States. Wiseman's proposal was that Maugham should travel to Petrograd and deliver a large sum of cash to the Mensheviks in the hope of keeping Russia in the war. Reluctantly Maugham agreed to the mission and in July arrived in Vladivostok by steamer from Tokyo and embarked on the Trans-Siberian Express bound for the Russian capital. Once again, his cover was that of a writer, which proved convenient as Maugham spent much of the day learning Russian, and most of the night enciphering reports to London. In his coded messages, Maugham referred to himself as "Somerville," the name adopted by Ashenden while in Switzerland.

In October 1917, Maugham was invited to meet Prime Minister Alexander Kerensky, who asked him to travel immediately to Lloyd George in London with a secret plea for political support and, more importantly, for weapons and ammunition. Maugham promptly left for Oslo where he was met by a destroyer that took him to Scotland. The following day, he was in Downing Street but the prime minister was unwilling to help Kerensky. As Maugham contemplated how he should break the news to Kerensky, the Bolsheviks seized power and the issue became academic. SIS asked Maugham to go to Romania instead, but he declined, pleading poor health.

Having recovered from his tuberculosis, Maugham continued his literary success and scoured the world for tales to entertain. His *Ashenden* stories also included some based on Maugham's work in Petrograd.

Soon after the outbreak of World War II, Maugham returned to London from his home on the French Riviera and volunteered his services to an intelligence contact, Ian Hay, in the hope of working for SIS again. Aged nearly 70, Maugham's offer was politely declined but he did travel to the United States at the request of the Ministry of Information to improve Britain's propaganda. After the war, he returned with his longtime companion, Gerald Haxton, to his home in

Cap Ferrat where he died in December 1965. His greatest literary success, *Of Human Bondage*, was thought to have been partly autobiographical, and concerned a doctor's preoccupation with a scheming French prostitute.

MAY, ALLAN NUNN. Having obtained his doctorate in experimental physics at Trinity Hall, Cambridge, Allan Nunn May traveled to Leningrad in September 1936 to continue his studies. Upon his return to Great Britain, he joined the board of *Scientific Worker*, the journal of the Communist Party–dominated union, the National Association of Scientific Workers. He was appointed to a teaching post at London University but was evacuated to Bristol with his department when war broke out, and in April 1942 joined the Tube Alloys project at Cavendish Laboratories in Cambridge to work on the development of an atomic bomb.

In January 1943, May was posted to Montreal to participate in the Manhattan Project, where he remained until September 1945 when he returned to London University. However, less than a fortnight before his departure, a GRU cipher clerk at the Soviet embassy in Ottawa, Igor Gouzenko, defected with 109 documents he had removed from his code room. Among them were copies of nine telegrams implicating May as a spy codenamed ALEK that provided details of a rendezvous to be held the following month in London. MI5 hoped to catch May as he met his Soviet contacts, but he failed to attend the meetings, apparently having been tipped off that he was under suspicion. He was eventually arrested on 4 March 1946 and on 1 May was sentenced to 10 years' imprisonment. Although he admitted having held some 10 meetings with his handlers in Montreal, he refused to name the person responsible for his recruitment, which apparently had occurred shortly before his departure for Canada. When interviewed in Wakefield Prison by MI5's Jim Skardon in March 1949, he would say only that his recruiter "was no longer within reach" but in August 1953, soon after his release, he married Hildegarde Broda, formerly the wife of his former Cavendish colleague Engelbert Broda, an Austrian physicist who had left the country in April 1948 after their divorce.

Engelbert Broda, known as a Communist, had come to England in 1938, and his close association with May led MI5's Ronnie Reed to conclude that he had probably played a part in May's recruitment. May's subsequent marriage to Mrs. Broda also attracted his organization's attention. Reed noted that within a fortnight of his return to England in 1945, May had traveled to Cambridge to meet Russian-born physicist Lev Kowarski and Engelbert Broda.

May remained reluctant to reveal anything about his involvement in espionage at Cambridge, although a statement released when he died in January 2003 suggested that he had made the initial approach to the Soviets. Another potential candidate was Yakov Chernyak who, according to the KGB's archives, had worked at Cavendish before the war, before moving to Canada, and had succeeded in recruiting May. Chernyak's possible role was never discovered by MI5, and May's wife, later appointed Cambridge's chief medical officer, remained implicated in her husband's espionage.

MCAFEE, MARILYN. In 1994, Dan Donahue, the **Central Intelligence Agency (CIA)** station chief in Guatemala City, called on his ambassador, Marilyn McAfee, and revealed to her that the Guatemalan Intelligence Service was bugging her bedroom and, on the basis of the transcripts of her surreptitiously recorded conversations, had concluded that she was a lesbian conducting an illicit affair with her secretary, Carol Murphy. Mrs. McAfee revealed that her two-year-old black standard dog was named "Murphy," and the eavesdroppers had listened in to her petting the animal. When news of this encounter circulated in Washington, D.C., the CIA was accused of having smeared the ambassador.

MEYER, MARY. Married to the senior, Yale-educated **Central Intelligence Agency** (CIA) officer Cord Meyer, who wore an eye patch after having been wounded in the Pacific in World War II, Mary Pinchot was a blue-eyed, blonde Vassar graduate and artist from a wealthy background. Her sister Antoinette was married to Ben Bradlee, editor of the *Washington Post*. She had a lengthy affair with **John F. Kennedy** and from October 1961 was a regular, late-night visitor to the White House when the president's wife was out of town. According to the official White House log, over the next two years she was signed in 13 times by Kennedy's secretary, Evelyn Lincoln, and a further unknown number of occasions as the anonymous companion of presidential aide Dave Powers. Meyer confided in few about her affair, but did tell Cicely Angleton, wife of the CIA counterintelligence chief, James Jesus Angleton.

According to the socialite's own story, she even smoked marijuana with the president. Their relationship only became public knowledge following her murder years later when, aged 43, her body was found on 12 October 1964 beside the Chesapeake & Ohio Canal towpath in Georgetown, apparently the randomly selected victim of a homeless black schizophrenic, Ray Crump, who was accused of shooting her twice in the head but acquitted of her first-degree murder. The gun was never found.

Mary's husband Cord served as the CIA station chief in London between 1972 and 1975, and in 1982 published his memoirs, *Facing Reality: From World Federalism to the CIA*.

MIDNIGHT CLIMAX. The codename of a **Central Intelligence Agency** (CIA) operation conducted at 225 Chestnut Street on Telegraph Hill in San Francisco to test the effect of drugs and sex on unsuspecting businessmen, until it was terminated in 1965. Visitors to the CIA-sponsored brothel were secretly administered LSD in an effort to establish whether the victims would lose their inhibitions and become loquacious under the influence of alcohol, sex, and psychedelic substances. They were watched through two-way mirrors by behavioral researchers supervised by Dr. Sidney Gottlieb as part of MK/ULTRA, a program run from April 1953 in Marin and New York City to develop countermeasures for techniques thought to be the subject of Soviet experiments. During the 11 years of its existence, MK/ULTRA encompassed some 140 different experiments with the codenames ARTICHOKE, DELTA, NAOMI, CHICKWIT, THIRD CHANCE, and DERBY HAT conducted at numerous facilities ranging from federal prisons to mental health institutions. The CIA's inspector-general, John Earman, recommended the project should be closed in 1962, and the New York facility was abandoned in 1965, only to be investigated in 1973 by congressional committees pursuing allegations of CIA misconduct.

The MK/ULTRA program was conducted at several universities, including the Stanford Research Institute, with volunteer participants, but when LSD was declared illegal in 1965 the plug was pulled on the whole project. In January 1973, the director of central intelligence, Richard Helms, ordered the destruction of all the remaining MK/ULTRA files.

MILNER, IAN. Born in 1911 in New Zealand, the son of a well-known educationalist and rector of Waitaki Boys' High School, Ian Milner graduated from Canterbury College, Christchurch, in 1933 and then traveled to the Soviet Union before going up to New College, Oxford, in 1934, where the confirmed Marxist joined the **Communist Party of Great Britain** (CPGB). After graduating in June 1937, Milner studied at Berkeley, California, and then Columbia University in New York. In August 1939, he returned to New Zealand, where he campaigned against his country's participation in the war, and then the next year took up an academic post at the University of Melbourne, where he became active in the Communist Party of Australia (CPA). In November 1944, he joined the Australian Department of External Affairs and in January 1947 was appointed to the United Nations Security Council's secretariat in New York. There he remained, with the rank of first secretary, under intermittent surveillance by the Federal Bureau of Investigation, and apart from one visit home in late 1949, when the Australian Security Intelligence Organization kept a watch on him, and a temporary secondment to UN duty in Seoul, he remained in the United States until his annual vacation in June 1950. Then he and his wife Margot took their leave in Switzerland, but unexpectedly traveled to Vienna, and early in July slipped over the Czech border, never to venture to the West again. Instead, he took up a post teaching English literature at Charles University, and he remained in Prague until his death in 1991. Four years later, when the VENONA material was declassified, Milner was identified as having been a Soviet spy.

Milner's sudden decision to live behind the Iron Curtain was connected with what had happened very recently to his External Affairs colleague, Jim Hill, who had been run by Semen Makarov, an NKVD officer based at the Canberra *rezidentura*. Whereas Milner was only mentioned in two VENONA texts, Hill's name appeared in several others and subsequently was ascribed the codename TOURIST.

The VENONA texts showed Hill to have been one of Makarov's key sources, but he remained an official in the Department of External Affairs, first in the Post Hostilities Division working alongside Milner, and then in London after his transfer to the Australian High Commission with the rank of first secretary late in December 1949. Although his brother Ted, a leading barrister, was a well-known Communist, Jim Hill's CPA membership, which dated back to 1938, had lapsed, but he realized his connections had been investigated in the middle of June 1950 when he was visited at his office in the Aldwych by MI5's Jim Skardon, who gently invited him to follow the example of **Allan Nunn May** and Klaus Fuchs and confess to having passed secrets to the Russians. Hill declined the offer and spluttered denials, but Skardon had succeeded in conveying the impression that the ubiquitous Security Service had accumulated a large file on the diplomat's illicit activities. That same evening Hill, thoroughly shaken by his alarming and unheralded encounter with MI5, recounted his experience to a group gathered at the home of scientist Dr. Eric Burhop, and among those present were Rojani Palme Dutt of the CPGB, and the Australian journalist and CPA activist Rupert Lockwood, who happened to be in London on his way back from a World Council of Peace meeting in Stockholm. It was very soon thereafter that Ian Milner sought permission in New York to go on his annual leave to Switzerland, and by the time he and his wife had fled into Czechoslovakia, Hill had been denied access to classified data and had been recalled to Canberra. In January 1951, Hill was transferred to the Legal Services Bureau of the Attorney-General's Department, and when it was made clear to him that his career would go no further, he retired into private practice in June 1953.

Milner had been tipped off to Hill's confrontation with MI5's famed interrogator and had drawn the necessary conclusions prompting his flight. He would later leave his wife and live with Jarmila Fruhailová, a Czech diplomat whom he had met while working at the United Nations. When his **Statni Bezpecnost** (StB) file, no. 9006, was released, Milner was identified as an StB source codenamed DVORAK and known by the alias "A. Jänsky."

MINCEMEAT. In an effort to add some verisimilitude to a deception operation intended to convey the impression in 1943 that the Allies would launch an invasion of Sardinia, in preference to the real objective of Sicily, a girlfriend was found for a British officer who was dumped off the coast of Spain near Huelva carrying supposedly secret documents. The Royal Marines courier, Major William Martin, was actually the corpse of a homeless Welshman, Gwyndr Michael, who had died in London. However, with the consent of his family, his body had been used to enhance the ploy, and an Admiralty secretary, Paddy Bennett, volunteered to play the role of his fiancé, supplying a photograph of herself at the seaside wearing a swimsuit for her lover's wallet. Later married to a Member of Parliament, Sir Julian Redesdale, Paddy Bennett was sworn to secrecy but was recognized when the operation was documented in 1953 by Ewen Montagu in *The Man Who Never Was*. The detail of Major Martin's fiancé, together with other authentic pocket litter, such as a theater ticket stub and some private correspondence, was designed to support the courier's existence, and although the Germans gained access to the contents of the briefcase chained to his wrist, it is unclear that the enemy believed them.

MINTKENBAUGH, JAMES. In July 1965, James Mintkenbaugh was arrested and sentenced to 25 years' imprisonment, having been identified as a KGB spy by his former army friend, Sergeant **Robert Johnson**. Sergeant Mintkenbaugh had been discharged from the U.S. Army in 1956 and subsequently undertook various assignments for his Soviet contacts while working as a real estate agent in northern Virginia. A **homosexual**, he had agreed to supply documents to Johnson and admitted that he had been tasked by the Soviets to identify other homosexuals in the army based in Berlin.

According to Mintkenbaugh's confession, for a year from the spring of 1957 he had acted as link to Johnson, who was then based at a U.S. Army missile site in California. Mintkenbaugh's KGB case officer in Washington, to whom he delivered intelligence from Johnson, was identified as Petr Yeliseyev.

In July 1959 Yeliseyev briefed Mintkenbaugh to expect a message summoning him to a meeting in Berlin and told him to prepare himself for a four-month absence from the United States. The letter arrived in September 1959 and Mintkenbaugh flew to Berlin where he was met by Gennadi Skvortsov, who escorted him to Moscow where he was given several weeks' training in tradecraft and communications. During that period, according to his subsequent confession, he was entertained several times by Aleksandr Feklisov.

Knowing that Mintkenbaugh was homosexual, the KGB asked him if he would agree to marry an illegal and live with her in the United States, and he was introduced to a woman known only as Irene. They spent a short holiday together in Leningrad and shortly before his departure Feklisov told him he would receive instructions to meet and marry her in New Jersey. Then they were to live in Washington where he should find some sort of business.

Accordingly, Mintkenbaugh renewed contact with Yeliseyev in Washington in January 1960 and rented and furnished an apartment in Arlington, Virginia. However, Yeliseyev told him that Irene had contracted tuberculosis and would not be joining him in the United States.

MITCHELL, BERNON S. A National Security Agency (NSA) cryptographer since July 1957, Bernon Mitchell and his mathematician friend William H. Martin disappeared while visiting Cuba in June 1960. Both men were **homosexuals** and had been assigned to the NSA's intercept site at Kamiseya in Japan when they had served together in the Navy Security Group. They had visited Cuba in December 1959 together, where it was presumed that they had made contact with the Soviets, but the statement they left, in a bank in Laurel, Maryland, did not address the issue. In December 1960, the pair held a press conference in Moscow to denounce the NSA publicly, claiming that the organization was reading the wireless traffic of more than 40 countries.

The two were considered brilliant cryptographers, but as civilian employees they were scheduled to undergo "lifesyle" **polygraphs** as part of a new security screening procedure, and they feared their homosexuality would cause them to lose their security clearances. Once in the Soviet Union, they revealed details of a highly secret NSA intercept program based in California that monitored Soviet high-frequency missile test reports from radar stations transmitted to Moscow. Although the NSA had not yet solved the four-part messages, the Soviets quickly encrypted the traffic but chose an insecure system that was quickly broken by the NSA.

Embarrassed by the defections, the NSA conducted a review of personnel policy and identified 26 homosexual employees, who had their security clearances revoked for "indications of sexual deviation" and were summarily dismissed.

Mitchell, who came from a staunchly Republican family in Eureka, northern California, married Galya, a university professor who taught piano, and remained in Russia until his death in 2005 in St. Petersburg. Enquiries made on his behalf by his brothers Emory and Cliff, whom he met occasionally in Eastern Europe and Egypt to receive small sums of money, confirmed that he would be prosecuted if he returned to the United States.

MOLNAR, ADRIENNE. Following the defection of Erich Vermehren and his wife to the Secret Intelligence Service in Ankara in December 1943, other Abwehr officers in Turkey were recalled to Berlin to undergo interrogation by the Gestapo. Reluctant to submit to such an ordeal, Dr. Willi Hamburger was persuaded by his lover, a glamorous Hungarian, Adrienne Molnar, to defect to the local representative of the American Office of Strategic Services. His defection, coming so soon after the Vermehrens switched sides, would have a lasting impact on the Abwehr, which soon would be absorbed into the Reichssicherheitshauptamt, the Reich Security Agency.

MOLODY, KONON. A KGB illegal *rezident* in London who took up his post in 1955, Konon Molody was arrested in January 1961 when he was compromised by one of his agents, **Harry Houghton**. He had been operating under the alias of "Gordon Lonsdale" but MI5's research demonstrated that this identity had been fabricated with considerable care. His birth certificate, issued in Ontario on 7 December 1954 in respect of a birth registered at Cobalt, Temiskaming, on 7 August 1924, was genuine, as was his passport issued on 21 January 1955. However, when the Royal Canadian Mounted Police (RCMP) traced the two referees who had acted as sponsors for the application, neither had heard of Lonsdale, and both disowned what had purported to be their signatures. An RCMP investigation showed that the earliest trace of "Lonsdale" under arrest in London was at lodging houses in Picksmill Street, and later Pendrell Street, Vancouver, in November 1954. According to U.S. records, he had crossed the Canadian border by train at Niagara Falls on 22 February 1955. British immigration records indicated that he had arrived in England at Southampton from New York aboard the liner *America* on 3 March 1955. The other stamps in his passport showed that since his arrival Lonsdale had been abroad, sometimes for up to 10 weeks at a time. Indeed, just four months after his arrival in London he had visited Scandinavia for a fortnight with a coach party of tourists, and at its conclusion a fortnight later, had joined a similar group for a two-week tour of Italy. There were other trips abroad in 1957, 1959, and finally August 1960. However, it was the FBI that finally established the truth. Enquiries made later in Canada revealed the father of the real Gordon Lonsdale to be Jack E. Lonsdale, a lumberjack of mixed race who had been separated from his Finnish wife, Alga Bousu, a year after his son's birth at their home in Lang Street in the remote gold mining settlement of Kirkland Lake, 55 miles northeast of Cobalt. He explained that his wife, whom he had married in January 1924, had left him for a Finn named Hjalmar Philaja. When her son enrolled in the local infants school, he did so under the name Arnold Philaja. Alga and Hjalmar had remained in Canada until 1932, when they had returned together to Karelia, Finland, with the eight-year-old child. It was only when his mother attempted to obtain a passport for Gordon in September 1931 that she registered his birth, six years late. Not long after their arrival, probably in about 1934, Gordon had died. This would have made "Lonsdale" 37 years old at the time of his arrest, yet in his letter to his wife he let slip that he was approaching his 39th birthday, a discrepancy of two years. The physician who had treated the Lonsdale family, Dr. W. E. Mitchell, and who had also delivered Gordon, was traced to Toronto and when he checked his medical records he confirmed that the young Gordon had been circumcised within a few days of his birth. The man claiming to be "Gordon Lonsdale" in custody in London demonstrably had not. However, the illegal had obviously spent much time in North America, for his accent was certainly authentic, as was testified to by the two British intelligence officers who had unwittingly spent a considerable period with Lonsdale. Charles Elwell had attended the same full-time Chinese course at London University's School of African and Oriental Studies in October 1955, and his wife Ann Glass, who was also a skilled MI5 officer, had been photographed with Lonsdale at a party held by a Canadian diplomat, a student in the same year, in July 1956. Neither had ever suspected "Lonsdale," who had left the course in June 1957, of being a Soviet illegal. Indeed, Lonsdale was later to remark that the hardest part of his mission had been his pretence to be a novice and learn the Chinese language. In fact, he spoke it well and had coauthored the standard Russian-Chinese textbook before his departure to the West. The fact that Lonsdale, coincidentally, had been a social acquaintance of the Elwells was later to be a source of some amusement to the illegal, and some embarrassment to the MI5 officer. When Elwell, still using the cover name "Elton," was assigned to interrogate Lonsdale at Wormwood Scrubs, following his conviction, the Russian thought their previous encounter had been "clearly a painful episode in his official life." As Elwell explained to him, "Of course, I was asked to explain how it came about that my photograph was found in your flat."

In reality, Lonsdale was the son of a Ukrainian, a well-known editor of scientific journals, and had been born in Moscow on 17 January 1922. His mother Evdokia was a physician in Moscow and his paternal grandmother had come from Kamchatka, from whom Konon evidently had inherited his distinctive Mongolian features, which "Lonsdale" had plausibly described to Western friends as his "Red Indian blood." Having been duped by Lonsdale once, Elwell took some satisfaction from researching every detail of the illegal's true family background in Russia, starting with Konon's father, Trofim, who had been sent into Siberian exile in the 1880s.

Trofim left Siberia in 1908 and had studied physics at the universities of St. Petersburg and Moscow, where in due course he became one of the lecturers in physics. As a teacher and as a research worker, T. K. Molody was distinguished but it was in the field of scientific journalism that he achieved a certain modest fame. His wife, whom he married in 1914, practiced for many years as a doctor of medicine in Moscow, where her two children were born in 1917 and Konon, the future Russian intelligence officer, five years later.

After Konon's father died of a brain hemorrhage in October 1929, his mother entrusted him to the care of her ballerina sister, Tatiana, who obtained an American visa for him in November 1933 by pretending that he was not her nephew but her son. Thus Konon entered America illegally for the first time, not yet aged 12, and went to California with his aunt, where he had attended a school at Berkeley. Four years later Konon decided, against Tatiana's wishes, to return home, and in the spring of 1938 he traveled to England. In France, he was met by his other aunt, Anastasia, and together with some English friends, was driven across Europe to Tartu in Estonia where his third aunt, Serafima, lived. A year after he was reunited with his mother, Konon was drafted into the Red Army, and it is likely that at some stage he served in China, where he became proficient in Mandarin. According to his memoirs, he also operated as a partisan behind German lines.

MI5's search of Lonsdale's flat at the White House apartments produced a Royal typewriter with a print face that exactly matched some of the coded items found in the Ruislip home of Morris and **Lona Cohen**, alias Peter and Helen Kroger, and the Ronson table lighter first seen at the Midland Bank that later was the subject of a clandestine inspection. Inside a decorative Chinese scroll hanging on the wall were three bundles of dollar bills, and more U.S. currency was found in a leather money belt. Close inspection of a tin of Yardley's talcum powder in the bathroom showed it to be an ingenious microdot reader with an adjustable magnifying lens, together with a small aperture in which was concealed a signal plan for dates in 1960 and 1961. Ostensibly ordinary torch batteries had also been hollowed out as hiding places, but they were empty. Also of interest were two sales receipts from Selfridges in Oxford Street that showed the Krogers had been shopping with Lonsdale on the morning of their arrest.

When the six-page handwritten letter found in Helen Kroger's handbag was translated, it turned out to be from Lonsdale and addressed to his wife in Moscow. The three microdots proved to be correspondence to him from his mother, three letters from his wife Galyusha and one from their daughter Liza, dated 9 December 1960, and from his five-year-old son Trofim, who was clearly missing his father: "When is Daddy coming, and why has he gone away, and what a stupid job Daddy has got," he observed.

Aged 12, Liza was reported by her mother to be doing badly at school, particularly in geometry, algebra, English, and "Party training," and occasionally she played truant. Her brother had recently been trapped in the lift between the sixth and seventh floors in their apartment block, and Galyusha remarked that the children's nurse had been of little help in his rescue. From Lonsdale's private family correspondence, MI5 deduced that, despite his many girlfriends in London, he suffered from loneliness. His wife, whom he later said in his memoirs was a Pole named Halina Panfilowska, was thought probably to be of Czech origin, and she was chairman of her community's Party Cultural Commission, which looked after the welfare of the residents. She sang at social gatherings and in her letter pressed Lonsdale for more money and a white brocade dress, a tight-fitting one, and white shoes: "I beg you to forgive me but I would like to meet the New Year well. By the way, I'll be singing in two places. I beg you to carry out my request, my first and last one. I hope that you will not be angry, but I must sing and I would very much like to rise to the occasion."

Although evidently Lonsdale had been able to send Christmas presents to his children, a model car to his son and a teddy bear to Liza, he explained that the dress was quite impossible. "In respect of a white brocade dress—a very difficult matter. In other countries, brocade is not worn. It may be assumed it could be made on order, but to pass it on to you? And when? You must understand that a dress and shoes cannot be put in a pocket." However, extra cash was possible, he promised, and would be supplied by "V.M.," presumably his KGB controller. The reference in his final letter to the New Year of 1954 stated that he had not been able to celebrate the holiday with his family for the past seven years, which fit in with what MI5 had learned about his movements. He acknowledged his wife's complaint that he had missed "seven Octobers and six May Day celebrations," thereby inadvertently confirming that he had left Moscow sometime between May and October 1954. In one rather moving passage, Lonsdale wrote:

> I hope you don't think I am an entirely hard-hearted man who gives no thought to anybody. All I am going to say is I myself have only one life, a not entirely easy one at that. I want to spend my life so that later on there is no shame to look back on, if possible, whatever may be said. I do know what loneliness is. From the age of 10, during the past 29 years, I have spent only 10 years with my own people. I did not wish it and I did not seek it, but so it turned out to be. I have thought very much about it—why all this? The answer is it all started as far back as

1932 when Mother decided to dispatch me to the nether regions. At that time she could not imagine, of course, all the consequences of this step and I do not blame her.

Lonsdale's mail from his family, never released at his trial, proved that even after his return to the Soviet Union, Lonsdale's account of his activities, or of even very fundamental biographical data, could not be relied upon. For example, in one of the letters from Galyusha, she reported that his mother was unwell but his sister was unaware of the crisis: "At your Zubovsky Boulevard home all is well with the exception of mother who complains that she is not feeling well . . . she is afraid of death. But of this fear she only spoke to me, as she is afraid of upsetting Natasha. . . . You must hasten home—after all one has but one mother in the world." This short extract contains evidence that Lonsdale's mother and sister were alive, and that Lonsdale had a home on Zubovsky Boulevard, yet he was later to assert that his mother had been killed in Poland during World War II, when he was 15.

His cover was, apart from one minor medical detail, faultless, and he had fulfilled his role as a well-heeled man-about-town who had moved from Canada with his savings without difficulty. He had operated almost entirely independently of the embassy *rezident* and presumably had been briefed during the lengthy periods he had traveled abroad. All of this indicated an illegal of some stature, yet there were contradictions in his performance, quite apart from his supposed servicing of only a single source. His business, for example, was not the success he pretended it to be. Even upon his return to Moscow, after he had been swapped in April 1964 for the SIS courier Greville Wynne, Lonsdale declined to reveal his true identity, and persisted in the pretence that he was truly Gordon Lonsdale, born in Cobalt, Ontario. His subsequent memoirs, the only account of an illegal's activities ever published with the KGB's consent, were studied with interest by MI5, but they made no admission as to his true identity, Konon Tromifovich Molody, which was only discovered by SIS a year after the trial, following some discreet research in Moscow, where his mother, Madame Molodaya, was still listed in the telephone directory at 16/20 Zubovsky Boulevard. Apartments rarely change hands in Moscow, and Konon's sister was still living in the same flat in 1991. Molody may have suspected that discrepancy would be noticed, or perhaps he was anxious to make his cover story approximate as closely as possible to the truth. Whatever his motive, he explained where he had lived while undergoing the special training required to become an illegal. When he had lived in Moscow during the war, he had moved into a big block of flats near Zubovsky Boulevard: "My landlady was a member of the intelligence service, and I posed as her nephew on leave. She had no children of her own and took a great liking to me. Eventually she started calling me 'son' and I called her 'mother.'" Here, quite clearly, Lonsdale has used part of the truth, including his mother's true home address and the fact that he had been largely brought up by his aunt, to build his cover story. This is typical illegal tradecraft, but Lonsdale had not always been so meticulous. It was noted that one of his enterprises, the Automatic Merchandising Company Limited, had run into financial difficulty and had been put into liquidation by the official receiver in 1959 with liabilities of £30,000. Started in 1955 in Broadstairs by one Peter Ayres, the company had been based in the seaside resort and had been intended to sell bubblegum vending machines. After reading a newspaper advertisement, Lonsdale had backed the company by buying 500 one-pound shares and had become a director. Oleg Gordievsky, a senior KGB officer who trained as an illegal and defected to London in 1985, was to assert that "not merely did his espionage activities rapidly become self-financing: despite the large sums paid to his agents, he also produced a substantial profit for the KGB." In an interview published in a Russian magazine, Molody echoed this with the claim that "the working capital and profits from my four companies (millions of pounds sterling) which were increasing year by year," whilst the exact reverse was really true. Although at the time of his arrest Lonsdale had several large deposits in his name with the Royal Bank of Canada, both companies with which he was associated experienced cash problems. The Master Switch Company Limited of Coplestone Road, Peckham, which was one of his enterprises, possessed only one product, the Allo Switch, a motor immobilizer for cars that was exhibited in Brussels in 1960 and had won a gold medal for its inventors, but it was never a commercial success. In February 1960, Lonsdale had become a director of the company but it had fared little better than his other investment. Whether the Soviets ever knew of the financial difficulties his business ventures experienced is doubtful. Certainly his involvement with a bankrupt company was entirely contrary to the well-established principles of *konspiratsia*, and would have been vetoed by his superiors, if they had known.

That Molody had worked in London in isolation from the legal *rezidentura* had been established by MI5 when the tapes of the technical surveillance of Nikolai Korovin's home were analyzed. On the night of Lonsdale's arrest, Korovin had been watching television with his deputy, Nikolai Karpekov, yet neither made any comment when the announcement was broadcast on the news. Nor did they attempt to move to more secure premises, perhaps at the embassy, to discuss what ought to have been a crisis for the KGB. It was obvious to those who had listened in to the inconsequential conversation that had passed between the two senior intelligence officers that neither at that stage had any inkling of Lonsdale's significance to their organization. Considering the watertight compartmentalization between the **Illegals Directorate** and the remainder of the KGB, this was only to be expected.

The Lonsdale case is probably the single most documented example of an illegal and the investigation that was conducted into his background. Uniquely, after his return to Moscow, Lonsdale wrote his memoirs, *Spy*, which is believed by some to have been ghosted in part by **Kim Philby**. Whether Philby was responsible or not, there is strong internal evidence to suggest that the book had been completed by at least two authors, with little coordination. For example, Lonsdale initially refers to his Polish wife, Halina, as "a source of great happiness ever since" their marriage: "My wife has been a true friend and comrade and a wonderful mother. Her loyalty can be gauged by the fact that, despite long and painful separations, she has never once questioned the nature of my work." Although this description hardly accords with the contents of her letters, Lonsdale later in the same book, without explanation, refers to "my wife Galyusha." In fact Molody had enough relatives in the West for the FBI and MI5 to trace and determine that he had only been married once, to Galyusha, leading the investigators to the inevitable conclusion that so much of his memoirs had been invented that even the contributors had become confused.

On the British side, Peter Wright described his involvement in his notorious autobiography, *Spycatcher*, and Charles Elwell, using the familiar cover name "Elton," also published an account from MI5's perspective in the *Police Journal*. In addition, Detective Superintendent George Smith, the Special Branch officer who arrested Houghton, has also written a book, as has Houghton himself. Thus there are no fewer than five separate versions of the episode in the public domain. Despite all this material, what remains unresolved is the exact nature of Lonsdale's mission. Had it really been necessary to involve three illegals, and nine cameras, to run SHAH? Lonsdale himself insisted that he had handled other sources and, somewhat unconvincingly, asserted that all his outbound communications had been routed through another transmitter. At the moment he was taken into custody, Lonsdale claimed that he had reviewed "my activities during the recent past, wondering who else might have been caught up in the dragnet. The result of this review was, on the whole heartening. My wireless operator was safely out of the country. So were several others, who might have been severely compromised by my arrest."

Whether Lonsdale can be believed on this point is doubtful, for in his book, which was published in 1965, he was still maintaining the fiction that he had been born in Canada and that the Krogers, who were not swapped for the imprisoned British lecturer Gerald Brooke until 1970, were completely innocent of any involvement in espionage. To emphasize this patently false proposition, Lonsdale reiterated the claim of another, separate line of communication to Moscow: "Of course, I needed radio communications for service messages on operational matters, and for this purpose I had a highly-qualified signal-man operating his own transmitter. He reached the UK a few months after I did. In December 1960, I gave him orders to clear out of the country double-quick. He did."

One of Lonsdale's more plausible claims is that he had teamed up with a Soviet intelligence officer, whom he referred to only by the codename ALEC, during partisan operations in Byelorussia in September 1943. He alleged that he had first encountered ALEC, who was later to become his partner and for whom he was to work as a radio operator, while in German captivity. ALEC "was in fact a Russian intelligence officer who had penetrated the Abwehr" and he had secured Lonsdale's freedom. Later he described meeting ALEC "at the end of 1950" in New York's Central Park, a wholly likely scenario, and suggests that his "duties as Alec's Communications Officer kept me in

New York for most of my time in the United States" where he supposedly remained until the summer of 1954 when ALEC dispatched him to Canada, en route to London. Certainly Lonsdale's description of ALEC coincides with the opinions held by others who met Willie Fisher and were, without exception, impressed by him. When his IQ was tested at the federal penitentiary in Georgia, he was shown to have a near genius-level intellect. Lonsdale remarked that ALEC was

> One of the most remarkable men I have ever met in my life, who is also indeed one of the most astute intelligence officers of all time. My association with him was to be long and fruitful, and range over many countries.... He always seemed to me an exceptionally interesting and in many ways a really remarkable person. This quiet, unhurried and somewhat elderly man never attracted attention by his appearance and easily lost himself in any crowd. At a party he never attracted undue attention while at the same time impressing everyone by his attentiveness and courtesy. His intelligence and penetrating gaze never stopped for long on any particular object but always noticed everything of real interest. His self-control and tenacity always impressed me and I am sure he would be as cool as an iceberg sitting on a powder keg with a smoldering slow match in it. He would probably crack a joke at such a tense moment and discover a way of preventing the explosion!

That Lonsdale should have been trained by Fisher, and that they should have worked together during the war, was not surprising. Both were resourceful if lonely professionals who politely but firmly declined all temptations placed in their path by their adversaries. The accuracy of the remainder of Lonsdale's story is a matter of speculation. He says that at the end of World War II, which found him with the Soviet occupation forces in Berlin, he was offered the opportunity to go to university, to study international law, and then to join ALEC (Fisher) as an illegal. His first mission was to Frankfurt to track down ex-Nazis working for Reinhard Gehlen's Federal Intelligence Service, the Bundesnachrichtendienst (BND), and was then sent to the United States in 1950 to join ALEC in New York. Details of his assignment are deliberately sketchy, as the author readily concedes:

> I do not propose to describe in any detail my experiences in the United States. Any reader will understand my reason for this; some may even sympathies with it. I have very good reason to know that Mr J. Edgar

Hoover is interested in me, and I have no desire to satisfy his curiosity. I hope that many FBI man-hours will be wasted in search of the identity I used in the United States.

Lonsdale may have had good operational reasons to fictionalize his background and conceal the details of his mission in the United States; there is no explanation of how and when he learned his Mandarin, one of the few verifiable facts known about K. T. Molody, apart from the much publicized circumstances of his death, while picking mushrooms in October 1970. The Soviet press understandably omitted to mention that Molody had died a chronic alcoholic and a man bitterly disappointed by his reception in Moscow after his release from Wakefield Prison in April 1964. Evidently his KGB colleagues could not believe that anyone who had spent so long in the West could still be trustworthy.

MONTES, ANA. A senior Defense Intelligence Agency (DIA) analyst, Ana Montes was arrested in September 2001. Born in the United States of Puerto Rican parentage, she graduated from Johns Hopkins University and joined the Department of Justice, before she transferred to the DIA in 1985 as a Spanish-speaking specialist on Cuba. She made two visits to Havana for the DIA in 1993 and 1998, and at the time of arrest, in her mid-40s and unmarried, she was a senior analyst who had briefed Congress and the **Central Intelligence Agency** (CIA), was cleared for Special Access Programs and Intel-Link, the American intelligence community's internal data exchange, and had passed her polygraph tests. Her brother was a Federal Bureau of Investigation (FBI) special agent in Florida, and her sister was an FBI translator, but under interrogation she acknowledged that she had been recruited by the Cuban Dirección General de Inteligencia (DGI) before she had even joined the DIA and had been vectored into her post. She admitted having betrayed the Pentagon's war contingency plans and telling the Cubans the names of four CIA officers working under diplomatic cover at the American Interests Section of the Swiss embassy in Havana. Montes seems to have declined the opportunity of a promotion to retain her access, apparently because she wanted to continue to influence U.S. policy on Cuba, a commitment for which she showed absolutely no remorse when she cooperated with the damage assessment conducted at her prison in Fort Worth. Indeed, she asserted her hope that her conviction would help American policymakers reconsider the continuing economic blockade. The Montes penetration lasted 16 years and was sustained by over 300 meetings with Cubans operating not from the Cuban Interests Section in Washington, D.C., but by illegals. To communicate with her controllers, Montes received encrypted messages over a Cuban "numbers station" broadcasting on the shortwave that she entered on a Radio Shack laptop computer and then deciphered using a complex algorithm stored on a diskette. The discovery of the Sony radio, computer, and diskettes during a covert search of her apartment proved essential to the FBI's investigation.

The FBI's decision to arrest Montes was prompted by the terrorist attack of 11 September 2001, and the fear that her information might leak to another adversary and assist in a further atrocity, or compromise the imminent military retaliation in Afghanistan. The investigation, codenamed SCAR TISSUE, had been initiated following a tip from a DGI source to the CIA, and when eventually Montes was identified as the principal suspect she was codenamed BLUE WREN.

Montes's relationship with her Cuban contacts proved to be something of a love affair, and she would take weeks to cope with routine rotations. Her own boyfriend, another DIA analyst, remained completely unaware of her espionage. The final damage assessment concluded that she had compromised every National Security Agency source relating to Cuba and contained evidence that Fidel Castro took a personal interest in her management and welfare.

MOOG, KAY. The mistress of Nazi spy Dr. **Ignatz Greibl**, Kay was recruited by the Abwehr in January 1937 while crossing the Atlantic with him on the *Europa*. The Abwehr suggested that she move from New York to make contact with senior members of the administration in Washington, D.C., but the plan was wrecked in 1938 when Sergeant Gunther Rumrich was arrested by the Federal Bureau of Investigation and, under interrogation, implicated Greibl, who agreed to cooperate.

MOON, LOTTIE. Ginnie Moon and her equally beautiful sister Lottie were Confederate spies in their native Tennessee during the American

Civil War, and both used their considerable charms to extract information from Union soldiers, to the point that between them they became engaged to 38 soldiers simultaneously. Most would write the sister long, affectionate letters in which they inadvertently disclosed military information such as their location and the state of local morale. Lottie was also engaged to marry General Ambrose Burnside, but she failed to turn up for the ceremony and instead later married a Judge Clark.

Both women reported to General Nathan Forrest and regularly crossed the lines to deliver their reports. After the war, Lottie and her husband settled in New York where she worked as a newspaper correspondent, before moving to Europe to report on wars and then taking up acting in Hollywood.

MOORE, JOANNA. Having adopted the alias Elizabeth Farrell, Joanna Moore joined the New **Communist Party of Great Britain** in 2001 and then attended meetings of the Korean Friendship and Solidarity Campaign, a small group of Marxists sympathetic to the Democratic Peoples Republic of Korea (DPRK). In reality, she was an agent of Seoul's National Intelligence Service and was part of an operation to monitor the DPRK's activities in Serbia, Bulgaria, and London. After her exposure as a mole, Joanna Moore revealed that she had been paid £400 a week and had attended several briefings in the South Korean capital.

MORRIS, AUGUSTA. Born in Alexandria, Virginia, to a baker, Augusta married a local physician but in 1861 offered to sell a Confederate secret document to the Union for $10,000. After she was rejected, she took up espionage on behalf of the Confederacy and adopted the aliases Ada Hewitt and Mrs. Mason. When she was arrested in Washington she was found in bed with a clerk employed by the adjutant-general. When she refused to sign a loyalty oath to the Union, she was imprisoned in the Old Capitol prison but was released in June 1862 and sent to Richmond.

MUNSINGER, GERDA. Born in 1926 in Germany, Gerda Heseler married an American soldier, Michael Munsinger, and after they divorced immigrated in 1955 to Montreal where she worked as a hostess in the Gay Paree nightclub. There the beautiful blonde encountered several politicians, among them George Hees and Pierre Sévigny, the associate minister of defense. Hees was minister of trade and commerce in John Diefenbaker's government, and when his relationship with Munsinger became known to Don McCleary of the Royal Canadian Mounted Police (RCMP) Security Service, she was deported to Germany in 1961. According to her record in Germany, she had been convicted of low-level espionage on behalf of the Soviets in 1949 involving border passes and currency.

Accused of having had an affair with Munsinger for three years beginning in 1958, Sévigny initially denied the allegation but later admitted to a Royal Commission headed by Supreme Court Justice Wishart Spence that the assertion had been true.

Munsinger's relationship with Sévigny was disclosed during a Parliamentary debate in March 1966 by the minister of justice, Lucien Cardin, when dealing with the case of Victor George Spencer, a retired postal worker and Communist who had collected information for KGB Line N illegal support officers in Vancouver. Cardin had accused Diefenbaker of mishandling security lapses, and soon afterward Munsinger confirmed some of the details of her affair from her home in Munich, where she died in 1998.

Although Munsinger was never publicly identified as a spy, the scandal became Canada's first major sex and espionage case and severely undermined John Diefenbaker's authority.

MURE, DAVID. A wartime intelligence officer based in Cairo, David Mure served with "A" Force, a deception unit established to mislead the Axis about Allied plans in North Africa and the Middle East, and then chaired the XXXI Committee, a group coordinating local double agents in Beirut. While in Egypt, Mure became acquainted with Bill (later the third Viscount) Astor, then working in naval intelligence, and acquired a knowledge of MI5 and Secret Intelligence Service (SIS) operations conducted in the region. He liaised closely with **Henry Hunloke**, the Defense Security officer representing Security Intelligence Middle East in Jerusalem. After his return to London, where he founded a carpet business, Mure wrote an account of his wartime experiences in *Practise to Deceive* in which he altered the names and codenames of the many espionage cases he had handled. He followed this up with *Master of Deception* in 1980, in which he claimed that MI5's wartime director of counterespionage, Guy Liddell, had been a traitor, and then penned a novel, *The Last Temptation*, in 1984, a thinly disguised version of Liddell's life in which he referred to Astor as "Lord Asterisk."

Mure became convinced that a **homosexual** coterie within British intelligence had compromised both MI5 and SIS, and he believed that Liddell had exercised his influence to protect his old friends **Guy Burgess**, **Kim Philby**, and **Anthony Blunt**. Mure attracted much opprobrium for his allegations and for his attempts to link the Cambridge traitors to those who later became embroiled with **Stephen Ward** in the **Profumo** affair.

– N –

NATASHA. The KGB codename for a **swallow** planted on a cipher clerk named Richards who was based at the British embassy in Moscow in 1951. Richards had been identified as a potential **honeytrap** target by Colonel Grigori Pavlovsky, an experienced **Second Chief Directorate** recruiter, who had failed to cultivate him. Undeterred, the KGB planted their agent NATASHA on Richards. She worked as a telephone operator in the embassy and became Richards's mistress. She got into some sort of trouble arranged by the KGB and on their instructions she told Richards that she had an influential uncle who might be able to help her out of her difficulties if Richards would see him and persuade him to do so. Richards duly met the uncle—who was in fact Pavlovsky—and revealed that he wanted to take NATASHA home to England. Pavlovsky told him that, if he agreed to give him information from the British code room, her exit visa could be fixed, but Richards refused, saying that he could not give such information while he was in government service. When he was transferred from Moscow to Washington in 1952 the KGB made a further attempt to contact Richards, but failed, and when after his retirement he was traced by Nikolai Timofeyev of the London *rezidentura*, Richards reported his approach to MI5.

NEUMANN, WALDRAUT. Having met Wolfgang Lotz on the Orient Express, Waldraut Neumann married him in Munich, believing initially that he truly was a former Afrika Korps officer who had settled in Cairo in 1959 to run an equestrian school. After they were married, Lotz revealed to his beautiful blonde wife that actually he was an Israeli spy who had been a member of the Haganah and had fought in the British Army's Jewish Brigade during World War II. In 1964, their illicit radio transmissions were monitored, and both Wolfgang and Waldraut were arrested by the Egyptian police and convicted of espionage. She received three years' imprisonment and he was sentenced to hard labor for life, but he was freed in 1968 and exchanged for prisoners captured during the 1967 Six Days' War. In 1972, Lotz revealed in his autobiography, *The Champagne Spy*, that, while married to Waldraut, he had also kept a wife and son in Israel. Waldraut died in 1973, having converted to Judaism, and Wolfgang took up residence in Germany.

NICOSSOF, PAUL. An entirely imaginary Syrian of Slavic background, Paul Nicossof was the slightly risqué name chosen for a **nominal agent** recruited by Renato Levi, codenamed CHEESE. Levi was a colorful character who had been in contact with the Secret Intelligence Service (SIS) in Rome before the war and who was also employed by the Italian Servicio di Informazione Militar (SIM) and the Abwehr. When he turned up in Istanbul, on a mission to Cairo where he was told to receive a radio set from a Hungarian diplomat, he was arrested in October 1940 by the Turkish Sureté for dealing in counterfeit currency. Fortunately SIS was able to extract him and assist his passage to Egypt, but he traveled alone because his companion, a wireless operator, had lost his nerve in Istanbul. With SIS's help, Levi made contact with his SIM controllers in February 1941, claiming to have bought a transmitter from an Italian and to have recruited a replacement operator, Paul Nicossof. The British supplied Levi with a cipher and arranged for him to return to Italy by ship from Haifa so he could explain about Nicossof and instruct his controllers to listen for his signals on Tuesday and Thursday evenings. Thus contact was established with Nicossof, who kept the channel open until February 1945, exchanging some 432 messages, many of which contained deception material. Meanwhile, Levi himself was imprisoned in Italy, having been convicted of black marketeering, but although his SIM interrogators were suspicious of the continuing CHEESE network, they maintained the contact.

NOMINAL AGENTS. The role of sex in the collection of intelligence was so accepted by both Allied and Axis professionals during World War II, to the point that British case officers occasionally invented nonexistent sources, usually women who supposedly either supplied information to their lovers or used their charms to extract secrets from unsuspecting staff personnel. These imaginary sources were considered easier to handle than authentic double agents, such as **BRONX**, who turned out to be a lesbian, and TREASURE, who proved to be a volatile neurotic. When TATE, a Nazi parachutist of Danish parentage, needed to retain his usefulness to his Abwehr controllers, an ingenious solution was found for him, consisting of a girlfriend, Mary, who purportedly was a cipher clerk lent to the U.S. Naval Mission in London by the Admiralty.

In an effort to enhance his status, TATE, then posing as a farm laborer based in Radlett, Hertfordshire, claimed that he had given a party for some naval officers in his London flat, which he visited on weekends, and one of them had accidentally left a briefcase containing secret papers that he had copied. TATE's controllers in Hamburg had been very excited at this unexpected windfall, which included details of minefields, and he had been instructed to try and gain access to specific naval charts. Thus Mary was introduced at the end of 1942, and TATE was able to report gossip from her friends, such as the news that several convoy escorts had been switched from the Mediterranean to home waters, much to the disappointment of the crews involved, and that of the U.S. Navy which, TATE alleged, had expressed concern about the lack of protection for American merchantmen.

The Naval Intelligence Division saw great advantages in developing Mary, and MI5 consented to her transfer to Washington, D.C., as a cipher clerk. There she was in a position in 1944 to make a contribution to the D-Day deception campaign, reporting the concentration of a huge army on the Eastern Seaboard, in anticipation of the imminent invasion of Europe. On 23 May 1944, TATE claimed,

> Saw Mary for the first time in a long while. She was sent on a special mission to Washington. She says she worked on preparations for an independent expeditionary force which will leave United Sates for Europe. That is all I have found out so far.

Four days later TATE had further news:

> Saw Mary. Found out that the before mentioned expeditionary force consists of six divisions. Its commander is General Friedenhall. The objective for this army, in Mary's opinion, is South of France but I believe that Mary herself does not know much on this point.

TATE was not the only MI5 double agent to invent a love interest to enhance his status, for GARBO reported that he had recruited **Theresa Jardine**, an amorous Wren who opened a channel from the Far East.

NORMAN, HERBERT. The suicide of E. Herbert Norman, the 47-year-old Canadian ambassador to Egypt, by jumping off the roof of an eight-story apartment block on the morning of 4 April 1957 aroused suspicions that the imminent prospect of an investigation into his earlier Communist links might have led him to take his own life. His four suicide notes referred to unspecified "sins" but protested his "innocence."

Born to missionary parents in Japan and educated at the University of Toronto, Columbia University, New York, and on a scholarship to Trinity College, Cambridge, where he had been a close friend of **Anthony Blunt**, **Michael Straight**, and **Guy Burgess**, he underwent an interrogation conducted by the Royal Canadian Mounted Police (RCMP) in January 1952, but then additional evidence emerged to implicate him in Soviet espionage. There were concerns that he had been part of a university **homosexual** spy ring recruited while an undergraduate, or that his previous membership of the Communist Party of Canada (CPC) had made him vulnerable when he joined the Department of External Affairs in Ottawa in 1939.

After the war, an attempt to nominate Norman to an intelligence role in Tokyo was blocked on security grounds by General Douglas MacArthur's chief of intelligence, General Charles Willoughby, and a proposal in 1950 to appoint him to liaise between American and Canadian intelligence organizations was also vetoed. Held against him were his close association before the war with the Japanese Communist Shigeto Tsuru and his subsequent friendships with Philip Jaffe, later convicted of unlawful possession of classified documents in the 1945 *Amerasia* case, and with Israel Halperin, one of the Soviet sources compromised by the defector Igor Gouzenko.

In 1954 the U.S. Senate Subcommittee on Internal Security accumulated evidence to suggest that Norman's previous denials that he had ever been a Communist were untrue. An RCMP informant inside the CPC, Patrick Walsh, confirmed Norman's Party membership in 1935, and Tsuru, then teaching at Harvard, had just testified before the Senate subcommittee, raising the likelihood that he too had contradicted Norman. It is also possible that a **Central Intelligence Agency** officer in Cairo may have said something to Norman to alert him to the danger he was in.

When in April 1964 Anthony Blunt was asked about Norman by MI5, he had replied, "Yes, Herb was one of us."

NOSENKO, YURI. Codenamed FOXTROT by the **Central Intelligence Agency** (CIA), Yuri Nosenko was a KGB **Second Chief Directorate** (SCD) officer who approached the CIA in Geneva in June 1962 to volunteer information in the hope of defecting and acquiring medication for one of his two daughters, the asthmatic Oksana. However, his most immediate concern was the replacement of official funds for which he could not account. According to one version, this amounted to $900 stolen the previous evening by a prostitute. In another, the figure was $250, or 800 Swiss francs, spent over the past three months on women and whiskey. Whatever the truth of the two versions, he knew his KGB career would be over if he admitted what had happened, so he had turned to the CIA for help, using an American diplomat as an intermediary to make the introduction to a case officer. Tennent ("Pete") Bagley was already in Bern, and he was joined by George Kisevalter who flew in from Washington, D.C.

Attending the disarmament talks as a security expert, Major Nosenko, who had married three times, wanted to continue working in the KGB and had no intention of defecting, but in the meantime he made some significant disclosures. A former naval officer who said he had joined the KGB in Moscow in 1953, Nosenko revealed that the SCD had compromised a British official who had been caught in a **honeytrap** in Moscow while employed at the British embassy, and MI5 soon identified the suspect as an Admiralty clerk, **John Vassall**. Nosenko also named the Canadian ambassador, **John Watkins**, as having been compromised in the same way, as well as a CIA officer, **Edward Ellis Smith**. Nosenko added that he had heard MI5 had been penetrated by the KGB at a high level, and explained that he had worked in the SCD's Foreign Tourist Section before being promoted to deputy head of the U.S. embassy section. While working against American diplomats, he had employed two **homosexual** agents, codenamed SHMELOV and GRIGORI, to entrap the unwary, and recalled that he had been the case officer responsible for the recruitment of two American tourists who were homosexuals.

Nosenko returned to Moscow but defected in Geneva during a second visit in February 1964, claiming to have reviewed the KGB file on Lee Harvey Oswald. However, the Counterintelligence Staff spotted several contradictions in his debriefings, including the inflation of his rank from captain to major, and became convinced that he was a dispatched defector. The issues at stake were considerable because if Nosenko was a false defector his insistence that the KGB had played no part in the assassination of President John F. Kennedy could be considered equally bogus.

In April 1964 Nosenko was detained at a safe house for 17 months, and then was transferred to a cell-block specially constructed at Camp Peary, and he remained there, under continuous interrogation until October 1967. A year later the CIA Office of Security concluded that Nosenko was a genuine defector, and he was given an apology for his treatment, $137,062 in compensation, and a contract as a consultant. The controversy over Nosenko's bona fides was to continue for years and split the American counterintelligence community.

Sex played a significant role in Nosenko's defection, and allegedly his senior officer, General **Oleg Gribanov**, was dismissed after the defection when an internal KGB investigation showed that Nosenko, the hard-drinking son of the Soviet minister for shipping, had organized orgies for his colleagues. Nosenko's behavior in the United States after his resettlement was characterized by drunken brawls in bars and the use of prostitutes, embarrassing episodes that the CIA Office of Security had to handle.

NOVOTNY, MARIELLA. A key figure in the **Profumo** scandal of 1963, Mariella Novotny was a London prostitute with a clientele that included senior politicians and, according to her version of events,

John F. Kennedy. Thought by MI5 to be related to Antonin Novotny, the former Communist president of Czechoslovakia, Novotny claimed to have entertained Kennedy at the Hampshire House in New York with another call girl, Suzy Chang, when he had been a senator. In her unpublished memoirs, she recalled having been entertained at the 21 Club by Kennedy after she had been introduced to him by his brother-in-law, actor Peter Lawford. By October 1999, calling herself Suzy Diamond, she issued a denial from her home in Long Island, New York, that she had met Kennedy "on two occasions" and recalled, "I don't think our relationship was something you can call sleeping with someone. I don't think I had an affair with him. I never have been in a bedroom with him."

MI5 investigated Novotny in the belief she might have been a Czech agent seeking to influence or destabilize the British government, and the **Central Intelligence Agency** station in London, headed by Archie Roosevelt, took a close interest in the case on instructions from Washington, D.C. MI5 concluded that although Novotny's account of her exotic escapades in London and New York were probably true, she had not acted on behalf of the Czech **Statni Bezpecnost**. On the contrary, she had been born in Yorkshire and although she had been brought up in Czechoslovakia until the age of nine, she had fled to England after the Communist coup in 1948, her father having been a political opponent of the new regime. Supposedly he had been an airman based in Lincolnshire when he had met Novotny's part-Spanish mother. After she moved to London, Novotny worked as a nightclub stripper at the Pigale in Soho, and then at the Black Sheep Club, owned by Hod Dibben, whom she would later marry. Dibben was a close friend of **Stephen Ward** and she became part of his stable of "popsies" whom he introduced to his friends.

Novotny was arrested in March 1951 in a Manhattan apartment belonging to television producer Harry Towers and was charged with prostitution, but she skipped bail at the end of May and returned on the *Queen Mary* to London where she became well known for hosting orgies at her Hyde Park Square flat. In 1971, she published a novel, *King's Road*, and three years later contributed a series of articles for *Club* magazine in which she described her affairs with the wartime double agent Eddie Chapman, Brian Jones of the Rolling Stones, and Black Power leader Malcolm X. Then in 1978 she revealed that she had embarked on an autobiography that would describe her role as an MI5 agent codenamed HENRY, but the manuscript was never completed and she died in 1983, aged 43, in a late-night accident at home after she had taken sleeping pills.

Speculation about her involvement in espionage heightened when her immigration sponsor in New York, Harry Towers, also skipped his bail and went to live for a few months in Moscow and Eastern Europe. When he eventually returned to New York, he was convicted of bail flight and contempt of court, but the original charges linked to Novotny's prostitution were dropped.

– O –

OGORODNIK, ALEKSANDR. Codenamed TRIGON by the **Central Intelligence Agency** (CIA), Aleksandr Ogorodnik was a senior Soviet Foreign Ministry economist, specializing in Latin America, and a womanizer. While working at the embassy in Bogotá, he had an affair with a secretary, and later divorced his wife in Moscow to marry her. He then fell for a Spanish woman who was recruited by the CIA, and in 1973 she persuaded him to supply them with information. Although he had declined a request to work with the local KGB *rezidentura* as a co-optee, Ogorodnik proved very valuable because, when he returned to Moscow, he was assigned to the Ministry of Foreign Affairs' planning department and therefore had access to a large number of telegrams from embassies abroad.

Ogorodnik was trained in espionage tradecraft by George Saxe, a Russian-speaking CIA technician who held secret meetings with him at the Bogotá Hilton where TRIGON was taught to use a T-50 miniature camera concealed in a pen, and clandestine communications systems. By the time he returned to Moscow in 1975, TRIGON was proficient in the management of signal sites, microphotography, and dead drops. He was followed to Moscow by the CIA's **Martha Petersen**, although he would never hold any personal meetings with any CIA case officers because such close contact was deemed too dangerous. Instead, TRIGON received encrypted messages from a CIA "numbers station" and could request servicing through a dead drop by parking his car in a predesignated place at a particular time.

He was arrested in July 1977, as his CIA contact in Moscow, **Martha Peterson** serviced a dead drop, but he committed suicide by swallowing cyanide concealed in a pen supplied to him, at his request, by the CIA. An investigation into the loss was conducted by Leonard McCoy in an effort to establish how TRIGON had been compromised, and it was noted that translations of TRIGON's reports had been prepared by a Czech spy, **Karl Koecher**. Entirely coincidentally, Ogorodnik had been handled briefly by a CIA team of case officers that had included **Aldrich Ames**.

OGORODNIKOVA, SVETLANA. In 1970, Nikolai and Svetlana Ogorodnikov applied in Vienna for political asylum in the United States and settled in West Hollywood with their son Matvei. Because of their involvement in the local Russian émigré community and their frequent visits back to the Soviet Union and to the local consulate, the curvaceous blonde Ogorodnikova was recruited in 1982 as an informant by Special Agent John Hunt of the Federal Bureau of Investigation (FBI).

It later emerged that Ogorodnikova had an affair during the 33 meetings Hunt logged with her before his retirement in 1984, when he handed her on to Richard Miller, a colleague. He, too, became romantically involved with her, and was persuaded to pass classified information to a man introduced as her KGB controller, who was actually her husband Nikolai, but when Miller spotted the FBI's surveillance he reported in September 1984 that he was planning to entrap Ogorodnikova by acting as a double agent. His tale was disbelieved by the FBI and the following month he was arrested and charged with espionage. In a plea bargain, Ogorodnikova negotiated a sentence of 18 years' imprisonment for herself, and eight for Nikolai, in return for testimony against Miller. At his second trial, following an initial mistrial in November 1985, Miller was sentenced to two life terms plus 50 years and a fine of $50,000, but he was freed in May 1994 when his sentence was reduced on appeal.

Ogorodnikova served half her sentence and then moved to Mexico, but in 1999 she was found to be living on a ranch in Fallbrook, California, with a new husband who was the subject of a murder investigation. Once again, Ogorodnikova cooperated with the FBI and provided evidence that convicted Kimberley Bailey of murder and led in August 2002 to Bailey receiving a sentence of life imprisonment.

OLDFIELD, MAURICE. Appointed chief of the Secret Intelligence Service (SIS) in 1973, having served his two predecessors as deputy, Maurice Oldfield was an immensely bright professional who had gained a commission in Egypt while serving in Security Intelligence Middle East as a sergeant in the Intelligence Corps during World War II, and had been invited by Brigadier Douglas Roberts to transfer to SIS in London at the end of 1946.

Fluent in French and German, having traveled widely on the Continent before the war, Oldfield was the eldest son of a Derbyshire tenant farming family, with 10 younger brothers and sisters, from the village of Over Haddon. He had earned an MA in history at Manchester University on a scholarship and excelled as an organist, specializing in church music. With a first-class honors and elected to a fellowship, he had intended an academic life, but he settled for the world of intelligence and his first overseas posting was to Singapore in 1950 for three years. In 1953, he was back in London, but in 1956 he returned to Singapore as station commander, in charge of several others in the region.

Between 1960 and 1964, Oldfield undertook his last overseas posting, as SIS's station commander in Washington D.C., where he liaised with the **Central Intelligence Agency** (CIA), handling the product from Colonel **Oleg Penkovsky**, the West's star mole in Moscow. However, this was also the period when a Federal Bureau of Investigation (FBI) special surveillance group reported having observed **homosexual** activity on the part of Oldfield, but the matter was not raised in London.

Always fascinated by counterintelligence, and appointed director of counterintelligence upon his return from Washington, D.C., Oldfield was persuaded by the CIA's counterintelligence staff that the Kremlin had mounted a huge, long-term deception campaign to mislead the West about its objectives and, according to KGB defector Anatoli Golitsyn, had adopted the most Machiavellian of schemes to support their moles and labyrinthine objectives. Even Golitsyn's sternest critics could not deny that he had been responsible for tipping off the CIA to the clues that eventually led to the arrest of the NATO spy George

Paques and to the identification of Hugh Hambleton as another long-term Soviet mole inside NATO's headquarters. Whereas Paques made an abject confession and acknowledged having spied since he had been recruited by a Russian in Algiers during the war, Hambleton evaded the molehunters for a couple more decades until he was arrested in London in June 1982 and imprisoned.

Oldfield's appointment as chief in 1973 by Prime Minister Ted Heath was uncontroversial because he had served as deputy to both White and Rennie and, having been passed over once, was the obvious choice. According to Heath, he enjoyed a good relationship with Oldfield, and others had noticed the similarity between the two men. Both had attended grammar schools, were the same age, had served in the army during the war and reached the same rank, lieutenant colonel, were bachelors, and were both organists. There the similarities ended, for Oldfield had a reputation for an impish sense of humor, was a great raconteur, and was a popular member of the Atheneum, where he served on the house committee and came into contact with plenty of journalists for whom he was discreet but accessible. One of the reasons Oldfield got along with Heath was the quality of his CX, especially on the European Economic Community, one of the prime minister's preoccupations.

Oldfield was also a devout and regular churchgoer, worshipping at St. Matthew's, Westminster, where he played the organ, and claimed to read St. Augustine's *Confessions* every year. However, he would forfeit much of his privacy on 13 October 1975 when a 30-pound bomb containing antipersonnel steel bolts was found hanging on the railings outside the entrance to Marsham Court, where he lived alone. It was unknown if Oldfield himself had been the Provisional Irish Republican Army's (PIRA) target, or if the objective had been Locket's, the neighboring restaurant so popular with Members of Parliament. The chief's personal security was increased, and thereafter he was permanently accompanied by two armed bodyguards.

Oldfield's achievements as chief were recognized by his award of the Knight Commander of the Order of St. Michael and St. George in 1975, which he received at Buckingham Palace, accompanied by two of his sisters, on the same day that Charlie Chaplin was invested, and a Grand Commander three years later, making him the first and only chief to have been promoted to that coveted most senior rank of the order.

After his retirement at the end of March 1978, Oldfield moved into Brentwood House in Iffley and embarked on a research project, initially intended to be on medieval history at All Souls, Oxford, but when he discovered the amount of scholarship that had been undertaken on his chosen subject since he had left Manchester he decided to study another topic, and embarked on a study of the diaries of the first chief, Mansfield Smith-Cumming. Unfortunately this idea also had to be abandoned, partly because of the apparent disappearance of all but two volumes of the first chief's diary, but mainly because, in September 1979, he was asked by the new prime minister, Margaret Thatcher, to take up the appointment of intelligence and security coordinator in Northern Ireland where the many overlapping security and intelligence agencies seemed more adept at combating each other than the Provisional IRA. MI5, the Royal Ulster Constabulary (RUC) Special Branch, and the army all ran competing organizations in the province, and Oldfield's task was to direct their activities against the common target and restore the tense relations between the RUC and the army.

Despite a complete lack of any formal executive powers, Oldfield's formidable reputation ensured cooperation and within six months he was able to transform the intelligence environment, remaining ensconced in his quarters at Stormont Castle for weeks at a time. During his infrequent visits to London, Oldfield lived at his flat in Marsham Court, which was conveniently located directly above Locket's restaurant, and his meals were often sent up to him with a waiter. On one evening, when his waiter was delivering his dinner, an incident occurred that was the subject of a report by Oldfield's Special Branch personal protection officer. This resulted in an interview in March with the cabinet secretary, Sir Robert Armstrong, at which Oldfield was challenged about his homosexuality, and he was forced to acknowledge that over the past two decades he had lied on his positive vetting questionnaire, which specifically requested a declaration of any sexual proclivities that might leave him vulnerable to blackmail. His security clearance was revoked immediately and he resigned his post attached to the Northern Ireland office in June, to be replaced by Sir Brooks Richards, the cabinet intelligence coordinator since mid-1978. This sad episode brought to an end a very distinguished intelligence career and was the source of much dismay among his many friends who found it hard to believe that Oldfield had been a homosexual. Some preferred to believe that he had been the victim of a smear campaign orchestrated by Ulster Loyalists, and although the conspiracy theorists had a field day, the unpalatable truth was that he had been picking up young men for casual sex for some years undetected. This had been known to a very few friends, including Jimmie James, who had joined SIS in 1947 and later had served in Rangoon and Hong Kong. Finally, after a year in Berlin, James had returned to London and for a time had shared a flat with Oldfield, who suffered mild psoriasis, which made him self-conscious about his appearance. James knew many of Oldfield's secrets and was probably his closest friend in the office, but he had retired from Century House in 1972. Among those dismayed by what he termed the "shattering news" was former foreign secretary Dr. David Owen, who felt particularly betrayed:

> I was impressed by Maurice Oldfield as were most of the few politicians who dealt directly with him. Parliament was, however, now being told that we had been wrong to trust his word as Head of MI6 and that the positive vetting procedures had been totally ineffective. I enjoyed talking privately with him on world problems, often without even my Private Secretary present, and I asked myself, should I have spotted something? He had implemented the policy that had led to many people's lives being blighted, either by being dismissed from their job or having their promotion prospects blocked, because of the security doubt about homosexuals. . . . I had challenged the need to apply the policy so rigidly and had even spoken to Maurice Oldfield about it. Margaret Thatcher's announcement made me wonder not only whom I could trust but also whether I should have guessed. I had known Maurice Oldfield was a bachelor. He seemed well-adjusted, though I noticed that after a chat in the evening he was reluctant to go, leaving an impression of loneliness.

The strange circumstances of Oldfield's departure were to be complicated not only by sectarian suspicions in Northern Ireland but by a diagnosis of diverticulitis, a condition to which he succumbed in March 1981. He was buried in the Oldfield family plot at St. Anne's, Over Haddon, and his memorial service was held at the Royal Naval College at Greenwich on 12 May, conducted by a former SIS colleague, the Reverend Halsey Colchester.

Many of Oldfield's friends, who knew nothing of the circumstances in which the former chief had lost his security clearance, were appalled as details of his private life emerged and relieved that he had died just nine months after his resignation and before he had been obliged to endure any public humiliation. Even after there had been confirmation of the tragedy, some loyally refused to believe any of it and preferred to remember the donnish, shambling "Moulders," one of the most gifted intelligence officers of his generation.

OLDHAM, LUCY. The wife of Soviet spy Ernest Oldham, who had been employed by the Foreign Office as a cipher clerk since 1913, Lucy Oldham knew that her husband had been passing information to a Hungarian count, Ladislas Perelly, supposedly a banker whom he had met in Paris in 1930. Codenamed MADAM by the NKVD, Lucy wanted to leave her alcoholic husband and fell in love with the Hungarian nobleman, who was actually an experienced Russian agent, Dmitri Bystrolyotov. Oldham's motive for stealing files and telegrams from the Foreign Office was his wish to support his son who was being brought up by a German family near Bonn, a situation that gave him an excuse to travel abroad.

As Oldham succumbed to alcoholism, his wife relied increasingly on her lover, Bystrolyotov, and often threatened to leave her husband and move to France, perhaps to work as a ladies' companion or even as a prostitute. Bystrolyotov, on the other hand, was anxious to maintain the flow of information from Oldham and identify his other source in the Foreign Office, from whom he claimed to receive codes and other valuable documents.

Finally, having been sacked from the Foreign Office without a pension because of his increasingly erratic behavior, Oldham committed suicide in September 1933. An investigation was conducted into the circumstances of his death and his inexplicably large income, but it was abandoned when Lucy refused to identify her lover, who had by then fled the country. It would not be until 1940, when defector Walter Krivitsky was questioned by MI5 in London, that the scale of Oldham's betrayal became clear.

OSTERREIDER, GERDA. Seduced by Herbert Schöter, a Hauptverwaltung Aufkrarung **raven**, Gerda Osterreider was a slender 19-year-old German student on a languages course at the Alliance Française in Paris. When she returned to Bonn in 1966, she found a job as a cipher clerk in the Federal Republic's Foreign Office and gave her lover the original teletype tape on which incoming diplomatic telegrams were printed. Five years later, she was posted to Warsaw where, in Schöter's absence, she took up with a German journalist to whom she confessed her espionage. When he reported her, she was sentenced to three years' imprisonment. In his memoirs, **Markus Wolf** referred to Osterreider's lover only as "Roland G," mentioning that he had succeeded in recruiting another unnamed woman spy.

– P –

PACK, ELIZABETH. Born Amy Elizabeth Thorpe in Minneapolis in November 1916, she married a British diplomat, Captain Arthur Pack, in April 1937, and accompanied him to Warsaw when he was appointed commercial secretary at the embassy. There, while having an affair with Edward Kulikowski of the Polish Foreign Ministry, she was recruited as an agent by the local Secret Intelligence Service (SIS) station commander, Colonel Jack Shelley. In one of many moments of indiscretion, Kulikowski confided to Pack that Poland, by a secret prior arrangement with the Nazis, intended to seize part of Czechoslovakia when Germany occupied the country. This electrifying forecast, which turned out to be accurate in every respect, established Pack as a source of valuable pillow talk.

Although never described as beautiful, Pack was tall, slim, and elegant and had the ability to make herself very attractive, and available, to men, and when her affairs became too scandalous, and especially her relationship with Count Michael Lubienski, then *chef de cabinet* to the foreign minister, Colonel Joseph Beck, the ambassador asked her to leave the country, despite SIS's objections about the value of her information.

When her husband was transferred in April 1939 to Santiago, she went too, and began to write anti-Nazi articles for Chilean newspapers, adopting the pen name Elizabeth Thomas, while also asking SIS to give her more valuable war work. Finally, in 1940, she was recalled to New York and instructed by SIS to establish herself in Washington, D.C., as a journalist employed part-time by the British Information Service, a propaganda unit run from the embassy. In reality, she took her instructions from John Pepper of British Security Coordination (BSC), the SIS cover organization in the United States. Her task, established in a rented house at 3327 O Street, was to lobby the isolationists on the Senate Foreign Relations Committee, and her principal targets were Senator Connally and a friend of her mother's, **Arthur Vandenberg**. Both were committed opponents to American participation in the European war, and while Pack's efforts seemed to have little impact on Connally's views, Vandenberg inexplicably changed his position and backed President Franklin D. Roosevelt's Lend-Lease Bill.

Pack's next assignment was to be deployed against Admiral **Alberto Lais**, the Italian naval attaché and for the past three years, the director of Italian naval intelligence who, coincidentally, she had known as an acquaintance 10 years earlier, also in Washington. Her relationship with Lais, who was married to Leonora Lais with whom he had two children, resulted in him confiding in his lover in March 1941 that he had received instructions from Rome to sabotage all the Italian cargo ships in American ports. She passed on this news, too late to prevent 25 from suffering damage, but causing him to be declared persona non grata and withdrawn to Rome. According to BSC's official history, Lais also allowed his cipher clerk to sell a copy of the naval attaché codebook to her.

Betty Pack's next target was Charles Brousse, the press attaché at the Vichy French embassy. Posing as a sympathetic American journalist on the pretext of wanting an interview with Vichy's controversial ambassador, Gaston Henry-Haye, a French senator and a former mayor of Versailles, she gained the affections of Brousse who eventually went onto BSC's payroll and supplied hundreds of his embassy's documents. Among them were copies of clear-text telegrams that had been sent to France in code. However, because of his views about the British attack on the French fleet at Mers-el-Kebir in 1940, Pack's recruitment took place under a false flag, with her pretending to be working for the Americans. When, in June 1943 the Office of Strategic Services (OSS) was created, the Americans were finally indoctrinated into the BSC operation in Washington and thereafter Brousse was run as a joint agent until he was interned with his American wife Kay, along with the rest of the Vichy diplomats, at a hotel in Hershey, Pennsylvania, in November 1942. There, Betty Pack joined him, posing as his stepdaughter, and she accompanied him back to France in 1944, setting up home with him in Paris.

In 1945, Arthur Pack, who had long been separated from his wife and had been posted to Buenos Aires, shot himself when he learned he had contacted an incurable illness. Brousse then divorced his wife and married Betty, and they lived together at the Chateau de Castellnou, near Perpignan in the Pyrenees, until December 1963 when she succumbed to throat cancer. In 1966, her former BSC case officer, Harford Hyde, wrote an embroidered account of her life entitled *Cynthia*, her BSC codename. Ten years after her death, Brousse died when his home was destroyed by an accidental fire.

Some details of Betty Pack's activities had been disclosed by Harford Hyde in *The Quiet Canadian*, his 1962 biography of BSC's director, Sir William Stephenson, a version that led to litigation brought in Italy by Admiral Lais's family. Hyde had chosen not to defend the action, and in his absence was convicted of criminal libel, but his claim that Lais had compromised the Italian naval attaché code, and thereby had enabled the Royal Navy to ambush and destroy part of the Italian fleet at the battle of Cape Matapan, was unfounded. Lais may have passed useful cryptographic material to his lover, but its exploitation had not played any part in the naval engagement, and Hyde did not repeat the allegation in *Cynthia*.

Betty Pack had two children, a daughter Denise who survived her, and a son Tony who was killed in action in 1952 while serving as a subaltern with his regiment, the King's Shropshire Light Infantry in Korea, soon after he had been decorated with the Military Cross for gallantry.

PARLOR MAID. Codenamed PARLOR MAID by the Federal Bureau of Investigation (FBI), Katrina Leung allegedly in 1997 removed and copied a secret document from the briefcase of her FBI handler, "J. J." Smith, and when her home was searched in 2002 a transcript of a telephone conversation with her Chinese contact was discovered. Although neither Leung nor Smith was charged with espionage, the case demonstrated that the FBI had been active in the field over a long period.

Born Che Wen Ling in Guangzhou, Leung was brought up in Hong Kong by her aunt, Susan Chin. She met her husband Kam, who was reading for his doctorate in biochemistry, at Cornell University, where she studied engineering as a graduate before switching to economics. Apparently, her first contact with PRC officials occurred in New York in 1972 when he worked as a volunteer at the Chinese mission to the United Nations.

Leung ran her own business consulting firm in California and was a director of the Los Angeles World Affairs Council, as well as being a major Republican Party campaign contributor. She also made 71 overseas trips during the 20 years she worked as an agent for the FBI, but failed to declare 15 of them. On those trips, she is alleged to have been in contact with Ministry of State Security (MSS) officers on 2,100 occasions, and was given a gift of $100,000 by the PRC President, Yang Chankung.

Smith, who met her for trysts in London, Hawaii, and Hong Kong, is said to have found out that Leung was copying the classified material from his briefcase, and he also discovered that Leung was a double agent for the MSS, yet he apparently continued to provide Leung access to the secret information despite knowing that she was compromising it. When challenged by the FBI, Smith denied having had an affair with the attractive Leung, only to be contradicted by tapes that recorded the pair together in a hotel. Leung was also involved with another former FBI agent, William Cleveland Jr., who was the head of security at the Lawrence Livermore National Laboratory nuclear weapons research facility in California. He admitted having a sexual relationship with Leung from 1988 until he retired in 1993, and that he resumed the sexual contact in 1997 and 1999. He also continued the sexual relationship even after he discovered that Leung had unauthorized contact in 1991 with the MSS intelligence service.

Apparently, Leung worked for the MSS and China's General Ji Shengde in order to obtain political access in the United States, a manifestation of an influence operation rather than straight espionage, but she also reportedly provided information on advanced technology transfers and access to classified documents to China. Her MSS contact was codenamed MAO and Leung herself was known to the Chinese as LUO. Leung's involvement in obtaining governmental influence is mirrored by another similar operation run by Charlie Trie and Johnny Chung against the Democrats, and both clandestine operations were supervised by General Ji. One of Leung's most successful operations led to the compromise of ongoing investigations into illegal donations made to the Democratic Party. Special Agent Smith had participated in the investigation into whether China tried to funnel money into the 1996 U.S. election in an effort to gain influence inside President Bill Clinton's White House, and he also became the primary contact for Johnny Chung, allowing Smith access to the detailed account records of money passed by General Ji through Chung into the Democratic National Convention. A prolific fund-raiser, Johnny Chung cooperated with the FBI and pleaded guilty to charges stemming from his admission that he received $300,000 from Chinese intelligence officials to influence congressional campaigns.

It is likely that it was a source inside the FBI in Los Angeles who tipped off the Chinese government to a covert U.S. operation to install listening devices aboard a Boeing 767 used by the president of China while it was in the United States for refitting. The listening devices were quickly discovered, and the Chinese government disclosed the incident early in 2002, claiming to have found 27 listening devices on board, including some in the bathroom and in the headboard of the Chinese president's bed. When the FBI investigators first interrogated Special Agent Smith about his relationship with Leung, the Chinese plane was one of several issues they were keenly interested in pursuing.

Certainly Leung was well connected in Beijing, and the Indonesian Chinese tycoon Ted Sioeng, whose family was investigated by the FBI for illegal donations to the Democrats, was a friend, and she had business-related contacts with companies, such as Northern Telecom (Canada). Apparently, Smith made little effort to conceal his relationship with Leung, and she accompanied him to his retirement party, which she videotaped, and to President George W. Bush's inaugural parade in Washington, D.C. She also lectured classes at the FBI's Academy at Quantico on the management of double agents, and simultaneously carried on an affair with Cleveland. When Cleveland was challenged about this relationship, he lied, and it was not until his fourth interview that he admitted that it had lasted eight years. When questions were raised at headquarters by analysts about Leung, Smith declared, untruthfully, that she had taken a **polygraph** test and passed it. Indeed, Smith filed no fewer than 19 evaluation reports describing Leung as "reliable." In fact, he had learned in 1991 that Leung had been reporting to an MSS case officer in Beijing, and was probably a double agent, if not a triple agent.

PARROTT, GEORGE. A warrant officer in the Royal Navy responsible for supervising the rifle ranges at Sheerness, George Parrott was a gunnery expert and a former gunnery officer on HMS *Agamemmnon*. He was arrested in Chelsea in November 1912 as he collected his mail from a tobacconist's shop, and convicted of breaches of the Official Secrets Act. Parrott had been persuaded to supply information to his German mistress, the wife of a local dentist, whom he occasionally met in Ostend, and in January 1913 he was sentenced to four years' imprisonment.

The investigation into Parrott's espionage was launched in June 1912 after he had been identified as having been in contact with the German spymaster in London, Carl Gustav Ernst, who was already under police surveillance. Their incriminating correspondence was intercepted, and on one occasion Parrott was interviewed at Dover just as he was about to board a steamer for Ostend. Initially, he claimed to be a civilian but, when challenged, he admitted his rank and claimed he was visiting his mistress on the Continent. However, when Special Branch detectives followed him to Belgium he was seen only to meet a man in the Gare Maritime.

A watch was kept on Parrott, who was dismissed from the Royal Navy for having traveled overseas without official permission, and he was eventually arrested when two of his accomplices, Karl Hentschel and his wife, negotiated immunity from prosecution in return for their evidence. According to their testimony, they had acted as spies with Parrott since 1909, and they were able to prove that Parrott received regular payments from the Germans at a mail drop, a tobacconist's shop in Chelsea, addressed to a "Mr. Crough." When Parrott, then living in Battersea, turned up to collect his mail, he was arrested, and when his bank account was examined it was found that he had made 14 deposits, all money from his German controller, a man identified only as "Richard Dinger."

PAULI, LUDWIG. Imprisoned in 1992 for four years, Ludwig Pauli was a senior diplomat in the Federal German Ministry of Foreign Affairs who was **honeytrapped** by a Hauptverwaltung Aufkrarung (HVA) **swallow** while serving at the German embassy in Belgrade, having been introduced to her by an HVA officer masquerading as a journalist. Pauli succumbed to the blackmail and, after undergoing an intensive course in espionage tradecraft, was codenamed ADLER. After the collapse of East Germany, Pauli was approached by his HVA handler and asked to continue spying, and to look out for certain chalk marks as signals for a further rendezvous, but there were none, and he was arrested when he was identified as the agent codenamed ADLER.

PENKOVSKY, OLEG. A GRU officer who volunteered to supply highly classified information to the **Central Intelligence Agency** (CIA) and Britain's Secret Intelligence Service (SIS), Oleg Penkovsky told his debriefers in 1961 that he was conducting an affair with Irina Chernyavskya, the wife of a KGB **Second Chief Directorate** officer, Genrykh Chernyavsky, and that she was an English teacher in the Ministry of Foreign Trade with the opportunity to travel abroad. Penkovsky suggested that she might act as a courier to maintain contact with his CIA and SIS handlers, but the proposal was not pursued. Curiously, her name was never mentioned at Penkovsky's trial in 1963, and an entirely different woman was identified as having been his mistress.

Penkovsky described how he had met Irina, whose mother was a music teacher engaged to tutor his daughter.

PETERSON, MARTHA. Posted to Moscow under a diplomatic administrative cover in 1975 to manage contact with **Aleksandr Ogorodnik**, Martha Peterson was arrested by the KGB on 15 July 1977 as she left a concealment device for him on the Kraznoluzsky Bridge. She had spent five hours undergoing a classic countersurveillance routine to evade the KGB watchers assigned to the embassy, and she was equipped with some sophisticated radio equipment to detect local KGB transmissions.

Peterson had operated under deep cover at the embassy, keeping her distance from the CIA station and other intelligence personnel, and she wore the latest Western fashions in an effort to persuade the KGB that she was an improbable candidate for a CIA officer. When she went to service Ogorodnikov's dead drops, she carried a custom-made SRR-100 frequency scanner attached to her bra with a tiny earpiece concealed in her auditory canal, with the antenna worn as a necklace. Her established pattern of behavior, leaving work on time and only venturing out of the compound on her lunch hour, was intended to demonstrate she was a State Department regular.

When she was taken into custody, the KGB seized her concealment device, disguised as a rock, and removed her intercept receiver, but failed to spot the tiny receiver in her ear. As soon as she was released from the KGB's custody, she was escorted to the airport and put on the first aircraft out of the country. The false rock was found to contain a quantity of small denomination ruble notes, some jewelry, six T-50 camera reloads, one-time pads, a communications schedule, and a private note printed on special photographic film. Although the content would have compromised Ogorodnikov, if he had been at liberty, the fact that Peterson was ambushed by the KGB indicates that he had already been compromised.

PETROV, VLADIMIR. Although spotted by the Australian Security Intelligence Organization (ASIO) in the company of prostitutes in Sydney, no attempt was made to **honeytrap** Vladimir Petrov, the NKVD *rezident* in Australia who had worked at the Soviet embassy in Canberra under diplomatic cover since February 1950. Instead, he was befriended by an ASIO informant, Dr. Michael Bialoguski, and when he was recalled to Moscow in May 1953, he procrastinated claiming dental problems, but actually he was worried about the reception he was likely to receive at NKVD headquarters. His concerns about his future increased considerably following the arrest of his sponsor, **Lavrenti Beria**, in June 1953, and Beria's subsequent execution at the end of December.

Finally, in April 1954, he opted to accept an offer of resettlement from ASIO's Ron Richards and defect. Although Petrov had been in contact with ASIO's Michael Thwaites for months, in an operation codenamed CABIN, he had not confided in his wife Evdokia; when he switched sides, the Soviets told her that he had been abducted and murdered, and attempted to escort her back to Moscow. However, when her plane landed at Darwin to be refueled, ASIO was able to reach her by telephone and she was able to speak to her husband. Persuaded by him that she faced certain death if she returned to the Soviet Union, and without children or other family at home, she agreed to defect too. As she was an experienced NKVD cipher clerk who had served with her husband during World War II at the Stockholm *rezidentura*, Evdokia was also an important catch for ASIO, and in 1965 her sister Tamara was allowed to migrate to Australia and join her. After staying in Palm Beach, Sydney, under the alias Cronides, Petrov was resettled at Bentleigh in Melbourne as Sven Allyson until he died in June 1991, and was survived by Evdokia until 2002.

The Petrovs' defection caused a political storm in Canberra when his evidence before a Royal Commission on Espionage revealed the existence of several Soviet agents inside the opposition Labour Party. Petrov's testimony, and the documents he provided, ensured the re-election of Sir Robert Menzies' Liberal government, and contributed to the Labour Party's failure in the polls for the next 17 years. Although no individual was prosecuted as a result of Petrov's disclosures, his impact on Australia was very considerable.

PHILBY, H. A. R. ("KIM"). Married four times, with six children, most of whom were born out of wedlock, Harold Adrian Russell Philby used his mild speech impediment to charm women. His affair in Spain with Lady Lindsay-Hogg, the Canadian divorcée and actress Frances Doble who had been married to Sir Anthony Lindsay-Hogg, enabled him to gain access to her wide circle of social contacts on the Nationalist side during the civil war, even though she was 10 years older than he.

His first wife was **Litzi Friedman**, the Communist daughter of his Viennese landlord, and she was followed by Aileen Furse, with whom he had two children, Josephine and John, before he divorced Litzi and married her. They then had three further children— Miranda, Tommy, and Harry—and he had a further son, Alan, by his mistress, a civil servant.

Aileen was a deeply troubled woman who, her husband learned in 1948, had suffered from a mental illness since her teen years when she had begun to mutilate herself and inject herself with her own urine. Because of her neuroses and instability, she had been disbelieved by her psychiatrist when she claimed her husband was plotting to kill her. After Aileen died in December 1957, in mysterious circumstances after a series of probably self-induced illnesses, Philby married **Eleanor Brewer**, the wife of a fellow journalist, Sam Pope Brewer, also based in Beirut. His tempestuous marriage to Eleanor, described in her autobiography, *The Spy I Loved*, continued after his sudden defection to Moscow in January 1963, but failed to survive his affair with Melinda Maclean, then married to his coconspirator Donald Maclean.

After divorcing Eleanor, Philby remained alone in Moscow, sinking into a haze of alcoholism and reportedly even contemplated suicide before being rescued by Rufina, the woman who would become his fourth wife.

Philby's first wife certainly knew of her husband's secret commitment to the NKVD as she had played a significant role in his recruitment, but there is no evidence that either Aileen or Eleanor knew of his espionage. Eleanor, of course, would learn after Philby's disappearance from their apartment in Beirut that he had decamped to Moscow, and would follow him there. Melinda Maclean, of course, had known of her husband's clandestine activities since he confided in her in Paris in May 1940, but her brief affair in Moscow with Philby served only to wreck her own marriage.

PITT, ROXANE. In her 1957 memoirs, *The Courage of Fear*, Roxane Pitt gave what she purported to be a factual account of her adventures as a British agent during World War II, and described in some detail how she had adopted the identity of Jacqueline Jaures, the niece of her former teacher in Paris, and had worked as a dancer in the Folies Bergère in Paris. She also claimed to have flirted with Field Marshal von Weitzleben to acquire information about a Nazi invasion of Spain and to have duped a staff colonel who was persuaded to be indiscreet about future German plans to a room of prostitutes dressed as schoolgirls.

Although Pitt followed up her autobiography 18 years later with a second volume, *Operation Double Life*, the contents of both books are so contradictory that it is unlikely either is authentic.

PITTS, EARL. In December 1996, Earl Edwin Pitts, a bisexual 43-year-old Federal Bureau of Investigation (FBI) special agent with 13 years' experience, was arrested at the Quantico training academy and charged with passing classified data to the Soviets between 1987 and 1992 for more than $224,000.

In July 1987, Pitts, a former army officer who had served in U.S. Special Forces, was assigned to the New York Field Office and approached Rollan Dzheikya, a Georgian and a suspected KGB officer at the Soviet mission to the United Nations, with the offer to sell him information, including a document entitled *Counterintelligence: Identifying Foreign Agents*. In fact, Dzheikya was a regular diplomat, but he agreed to a second meeting at which he introduced the FBI special agent to a KGB officer, Aleksandr Karpov.

The KGB accepted the offer, and Pitts met Karpov at least nine times but, having been paid $129,000, with another $100,000 allegedly placed in a foreign bank account, Dzheikya defected and revealed that Pitts had been recruited. Although Pitts had broken off contact with the KGB in 1992, a sting operation was mounted to entrap him into further acts of espionage, which was complicated at the outset by Pitts's wife Mary, an ex-employee of the FBI who reported her suspicions about her husband within two days of it being initiated. A man had called at their home claiming to be a real estate agent, and she had disbelieved him. Later, she searched her husband's desk and found a letter addressed to a Soviet. The FBI ran the operation for 15 months, during which Pitts was monitored making 22 drops of classified information, in exchange for $65,000. In February 1997, his personal computer was seized and found to contain a highly incriminating letter addressed to his supposed KGB case officer; Pitts pleaded guilty to two counts of espionage and in June was sentenced to 27 years' imprisonment. The prosecution conceded that all the material he had compromised had been below the level of top secret, so he did not have to face a life sentence.

At the time of his arrest, Pitts had been transferred to personnel security and security education, a position in which he was responsible for lecturing others on the importance of the bureau's security procedures. As an explanation of his own espionage, Pitts later claimed various grievances, including his posting to the expensive New York field office where, he complained, his living expenses were simply too high and thus forced him into selling secrets to maintain his lifestyle and pay for the male and female prostitutes he habitually used.

After his conviction, Pitts was interviewed by two FBI colleagues, Tom Kimmel and Pete O'Donnell, who noted that Pitts was convinced from the way the KGB had responded to his various offers, and their apparent disinterest in areas that ought to have been of great importance to them, that there was another mole at work inside the FBI. When asked for his candidate, Pitts named **Robert Hanssen**.

PLATON. The GRU **Second Chief Directorate** codename for a member of Italian embassy staff who was **honeytrapped** in Moscow by a **swallow** codenamed R, who moved into his apartment and subsequently pretended to be pregnant. Having persuaded him to pay for an abortion, PLATON was then blackmailed and arrangements were made to reestablish contact with him when he was posted to Belgium.

PLEVITSKAYA, LA. Twice divorced, the singer known as La Plevitskaya was married to General Nikolai Skoblin, a White Russian émigré living in Paris and a member of the Rossiiskii Obshchevoennyi Soyuz (ROVS), the international anti-Bolshevik movement, two of whose leaders, General Aleksandr Kutepov and General Evgenni Miller, had been assassinated. Kutepov had been seized off a Paris street at the end of January 1930 and died after he had been chloroformed for a journey back to Moscow to face interrogation. His successor, General Miller, was abducted, also off a Paris street in broad daylight, seven years later, in September 1937, but survived to face interrogation and execution in Moscow. In both cases, the assassinations were facilitated by Soviet agents who had penetrated the ROVS leadership, and suspicion fell on Miller's deputy, General Nikolai Skoblin, who promptly disappeared, apparently to Spain. After a long investigation conducted by the Sureté commissioner, Jean Belin, Skoblin's widow, La Plevitskaya, was charged with his murder. She confessed, was sentenced to 20 years' imprisonment, and died soon afterward.

POLIAKOVA, MARIA. A senior prewar and World War II GRU intelligence officer, Maria Poliakova was a Russian Jew who was known to British Communist Allan Foote by the codename VERA. She spoke several languages fluently and arrived in Switzerland in 1936 to supervise the network that would become known as the Rote Drei ("Red Three"), consisting of Alexander Rado in Geneva and Rachel Duebendorfer and Otto Puenter in Bern, even though her brother, husband, and father had perished in Josef Stalin's purges. In 1941, she returned to Moscow but her continued involvement in the network was evident from her distinctive Marxist style, which manifested itself in so many of the signals that were exchanged between Moscow and Switzerland, and which were intercepted. All the members of the network were arrested by the Swiss Bundespolizei during 1943 and 1944, and many of their sources were compromised. According to Foote, Poliakova was switched to head the GRU's Spanish section in 1944 and was probably liquidated "in about May 1946. The Centre has only one penalty for failure." Foote's memoirs, *Handbook for Spies*, is one of the very few reliable sources of information about Poliakova.

Before the war, Poliakova had served as the GRU's illegal *rezident* in Germany and Belgium, and had operated independently in France and Switzerland. When the senior GRU organizer Ismail Akhmedov undertook tours of inspection in Europe, Poliakova acted as his deputy in Moscow. Even though many of her colleagues disappeared during the purges, Poliakova survived, probably because her knowledge of the GRU's files was regarded as indispensable. When Foote reached Moscow in January 1945, he was interrogated by Poliakova, and she remained at her post until April 1946 when she fell ill. Soon afterward, she disappeared.

POLYGRAPH. Unlike the Federal Bureau of Investigation, the **Central Intelligence Agency** (CIA) has long depended on administering lie-detector tests to job applicants, assist internal investigations, support routine security clearances, and establish the veracity of sources. Although considered a controversial technique without much scientific support, polygraphs have acted as a significant deterrent to those who have compromised classified information. Fear of detection has been shown to be a powerful disincentive to persist in holding a security clearance.

One of the more invasive aspects of the polygraph are the so-called lifestyle questions, set to determine whether an individual might be vulnerable to pressure, and along with indebtedness and criminality, sexual behavior is a key component to distinguishing between truth and fiction. The imminent introduction of lifestyle polygraphs, which at the time excluded **homosexuals** from the National Security Agency, was a likely factor in the defection of **Bernon Mitchell** and William Martin in 1960.

The CIA introduced polygraphs in August 1948; after success with its use in background screenings for applicants in 1950, it was extended to test sources and assets for deception. A polygraph test uncovered CIA officers **Sharon Scranage**, charged in July 1985 with having passed classified material to her lover, and Jim Nicholson who failed three tests in October 1995 and was arrested as a spy 10 months later. Nicholson had undergone training by the KGB to defeat the polygraph, apparently using techniques recommended by a defector, Glen Rohrer, a polygraph operator employed by the Counter-Intelligence Corps who disappeared to Czechoslovakia in 1965.

A common problem for CIA case officers handling attractive agents is the temptation to engage in a sexual relationship, which, of course, is prohibited by the clandestine service. Such unprofessional conduct, though widespread, places at risk a CIA officer and his or her chain of command, and potentially compromises the quality of information emanating from the agent. No case officer in those circumstances can be expected to exercise independent judgment concerning his or her agent's product, and there could be a danger of an agent trimming or modifying reports to retain the attention of his or her handler. Once a case officer has concealed such an illicit relationship, he or she has been drawn into a deception that may easily be manipulated by others and have the severest consequences.

POPOV, DUSAN. A Yugoslav playboy and Abwehr agent, "Dusko" Popov reached London in December 1940 having already declared to the British Secret Intelligence Service in Belgrade that he had been recruited as a German spy. Popov's mission was to establish a network in Britain, and this he accomplished by recruiting his girlfriend, **Friedle Gaertner**. Upon his return to Lisbon in August 1941, he was given a new assignment by his Abwehr controller and sent to New York, where he acquired a mistress, French actress Simone Simone, and an English girlfriend, Terry Richardson.

Popov's immoral behavior in New York, as reported by the Federal Bureau of Investigation, outraged the organization's director, J. Edgar Hoover, who restricted his movements, so the double agent was unable to fulfill his task of reporting from Pearl Harbor in Hawaii. Lack of FBI cooperation led to Popov's withdrawal from the United States and his return to London, where he remained active until the end of the war. Publication of Popov's memoirs in 1975, *Spy/Counterspy*, which included details of his many amorous encounters, prompted speculation that Ian Fleming might have used Popov as a model for his fictional character **James Bond**.

POPOV, PIOTR. A Soviet GRU officer, Major Piotr Popov volunteered to supply the **Central Intelligence Agency** (CIA) with information in January 1953 while posted to Vienna. As well as a wife and family in Moscow, Popov also maintained a young Yugoslav mistress, Milica Kohanec, who had been his agent. Although politically motivated to help the CIA, Popov became dependent on the CIA for financial support until his arrest in October 1959. He was tried in January 1960 and executed.

Popov was the first GRU officer to be recruited as an agent in the postwar era and he supplied large quantities of information about his colleagues and their agents in the West. It proved impossible to communicate with him in Moscow, and he may have compromised himself when he reestablished contact with his American handlers through British channels upon his posting to East Germany. **Edward Smith**, a CIA officer sent to Moscow under diplomatic cover to plan a system of communicating with Popov, was himself compromised by his **UpDK** maid, and he may have compromised the GRU officer,

PRICE, MARY. Codenamed ARENA and DIR by the NKVD, Mary Price was a Soviet spy who worked in Washington, D.C., for newspaper columnist Walter Lippmann. A member of the **Communist Party of the United States of America** (CPUSA), she was initially implicated in a VENONA text dated 28 July 1944 from the Soviet embassy reporting a crisis that had arisen between her and **Elizabeth Bentley**:

> Your No. 3028. Some weeks ago CLEVER GIRL [Elizabeth Bentley] told MAYOR [Iskhak Akhmerov] that HELMSMAN [Earl Browder] as a result of a conversation with DIR [Mary Price] had apparently decided that DIR must be withdrawn completely from our work in order to employ her fully on FELLOWCOUNTRYMANLY [Party] work. In HELMSMAN's opinion DIR's nerves have been badly shaken and her health is poor, which renders her unsuitable for our work. In MAYOR's opinion it is possible to get HELMSMAN to change his opinion about

the advisability of this decision which MAYOR suggests was made under pressure from CLEVER GIRL, who for some reason dislikes DIR. MAYOR has informed CLEVER GIRL that if DIR is really ill she will need rather to be withdrawn for a rest, but afterwards be used on liaison with a conspirative apartment etc. She has been working for a long time and has acquired considerable experience. MAYOR proposes that she should not be employed on active FELLOWCOUNTRYMANLY work. Telegraph your opinion.

Later the same year, Elizabeth Bentley was to denounce Mary Price to the Federal Bureau of Investigation (FBI), identifying her as a source for whom she had acted as a courier, collecting extracts from Lippmann's confidential office files from her Georgetown house. "I would go to Washington once a month to pick up any material she had. She on her part would come up to New York once a month. Our traveling expenses would be paid by the Party. This meant that the information would be coming through every two weeks." In fact Price could not endure the strain, gave up her job in Washington, and took an extended holiday in Mexico. Upon her return Bentley had argued that Price, who was turned down for a job by the Office of Strategic Services (OSS) in the autumn of 1943 because of her past Communist connections, should be dropped from the network and allowed to rejoin the Party openly, which thereby provoked another furious disagreement. She also asserted that it had been the neurotic Mary Price who had enabled the NKVD to penetrate OSS by recruiting her lover, Major Duncan C. Lee, who was General Bill Donovan's assistant.

A Rhodes scholar who had worked for General Donovan's law firm in New York before the war, Duncan Lee had been born in China to missionary parents and had joined the CPUSA soon after he had graduated from Yale. As Bentley recalled for the FBI, "Although I succeeded in getting from him more than Mary, he almost always gave it to me orally and rarely would he give me a document, although under pressure he would hand over scraps of paper on which he had written down important data."

Mary Price's sister Mildred was also part of her network and provided an apartment in which the spy ring could meet. Married to Harold Coy, Mildred was the executive head of the China Aid Council, a Communist front organization. Bentley said that at first she had "regarded Mildred merely as an intermediary with Mary, but soon we discovered she would be a valuable adjunct to our apparatus in her own right." She was the organizer of the Communist unit that functioned in the Institute of Pacific Relations—a foundation for Far Eastern studies that had originally been set up by well-meaning philanthropists but had long since fallen under the domination of the Communists. The organization, because of its respectable past and high-sounding title, had been able to enroll in its ranks a vast number of "innocents," among them professors and businessmen who were interested in Pacific affairs. Hence it had become the center of all Communist activity in the Far Eastern field, offering a protective covering to a number of smaller, more obviously pro-Communist enterprises that clustered around it. Among these were the China Aid Council, of which Mildred was executive secretary, and their magazines *China Today* and *Amerasia*.

Thus Mildred Price helped her sister's espionage and used the Institute of Pacific Relations as a pool from which suitable recruits could be talent-spotted for the NKVD. However, because of the nature of the VENONA evidence, neither her lover nor the others implicated in Mary Price's network were ever prosecuted.

PRIEUR, DOMINIQUE. In July 1985, Captain Dominique Prieur of the French Direction Generale de Securité Extérieur (DGSE) was arrested in New Zealand following the sabotage of a Greenpeace ship, the *Rainbow Warrior*, which had been sunk in Auckland harbor by a pair of limpet mines. She and her companion, Commander Alain Mafart, had masqueraded as Swiss honeymooners and had participated in a lengthy DGSE operation to monitor antinuclear demonstrators protesting against French atomic tests in the Pacific, but had attracted unwelcome attention by not sleeping together, a fact noted by the chambermaid in their motel.

In reality Dominique Prieur was married to a Bordeaux firefighter, and she and Mafart were the support group for a much larger DGSE mission that had been planned by Christine Cabon, another DGSE officer posing as an archaeologist who had undertaken the preliminary local reconnaissance by working for Greenpeace as a volunteer. She had left New Zealand in May 1985, and had been replaced by Prieur and Mafart, who helped the wet-suited saboteurs launch their Zodiac dinghy on the night of their attack. However, a local resident had taken note of their rented Toyota campervan's registration number, and the couple was detained and questioned when they returned their vehicle to the airport. Although he claimed to be on vacation, Mafart had no explanation for why he had not shared his wife's bed but slept on a sofa, nor why, if he was not traveling on business and claiming his expenses, he had falsified his hotel receipts. The local police became convinced of their involvement in an official French plot when Prieur and Marfat made a telephone call to Paris to a number that the French authorities later claimed not to exist.

Mafart and Prieur were convicted of manslaughter for their complicity in the death of a Greenpeace photographer, Fernando Pereira, who had drowned aboard the *Rainbow Warrior*, and the DGSE's chief, Admiral Pierre Lacoste, was forced to resign. The couple was also convicted of carrying forged passports and making false statements.

As soon as Mafart and Prieur were imprisoned, the French government attempted to obtain their release by applying economic pressure on New Zealand through the European Economic community, and an agreement was reached allowing them to serve the remainder of their sentence in French custody. An initial suggestion of the resort of Mayotte in the Comoros Islands in the Indian Ocean was rejected by Prime Minister David Lange when it was realized that the island included a Club Méditerranée vacation village, and the final location was Hao Atoll, a military compound supporting the Mururoa test site. However, when Prieur became pregnant, following a visit from her husband, she was returned to France and released on medical grounds. An arbitration hearing at the United Nations concluded that France had breached the terms of its agreement, and ordered a fine of $2 million to be paid.

The remainder of the DGSE team responsible for the sabotage escaped to Norfolk Island on a yacht, the *Ouvea*, which was later scuttled at sea after the crew had been taken aboard a French submarine. Only one other DGSE officer, Gerard Royal, has been identified as a saboteur, and his name only emerged when his sister Segoline stood as the Socialist candidate for the French presidency in 2007.

PRIME, GEOFFREY. A former Government Communications Headquarters analyst and Russian linguist, Geoffrey Prime was working as a taxi driver in Cheltenham, Gloucestershire, when he was arrested in April 1982 on pedophile charges relating to a series of obscene telephone calls made to young girls in his neighborhood. The police eventually traced the calls to Prime's home, and he immediately admitted the offenses.

After he was detained, his wife Rhona discovered a quantity of espionage paraphernalia hidden in their home and it was seized by MI5. Under interrogation, Prime confessed that he had spied for the KGB between January 1968, when he had been posted to an intercept station in Berlin, and his resignation in 1977, when he was a section head in the sensitive J Division, GCHQ's Soviet signals intelligence branch. He was sentenced in November 1982 to 35 years' imprisonment and was released on license in 2003.

PROFILING. In an effort to identify the character traits that accompany treasonous behavior, several studies have been made in the United States of espionage case histories to establish whether those convicted of having betrayed their country conform to a type, in the expectation that profiles of suspects might be useful to molehunters. Within the **Central Intelligence Agency** (CIA), both of the two most senior serving officers to be imprisoned, **Aldrich Ames** and Harold J. Nicholson, appear to have been financially motivated, but their indebtedness was in part caused by a break-up of their marriage. A disgruntled CIA retiree, Edwin Moore, was also motivated by money but not, apparently, by any marriage issues, whereas the CIA's longest hostile penetration, Larry Wu-Tai Chin, claimed an ideological motive but definitely benefited financially from having passed information to the Chinese Ministry of State Security handlers, and eventually committed suicide to avoid his wife being financially disadvantaged by his imprisonment. Of the two other CIA officers known to have compromised classified information, **Edward Ellis Smith** was **honeytrapped** in Moscow, and **Ed Howard** seems to have been disgruntled but relied upon his wife Mary, also a former CIA officer, to assist in his escape.

No fewer than four senior Federal Bureau of Investigation (FBI) counterintelligence officers, **Earl Pitts**, **Robert Hanssen**, Richard Miller, and J. J. Smith, have engaged in espionage in which sex played a significant role.

Ronald Pelton, responsible for the most significant breach of security experienced by the National Security Agency, had parted from his wife and had declared bankruptcy when he volunteered classified information to the Soviets. All American intelligence agencies that suffered losses through their own personnel, from the well known to the rather more obscure Air Force Office of Special Investigations, conducted surveys to highlight common denominators and other factors that might signal a propensity to compromise secrets. The results were intended to assist polygraph operators in choosing their line of questions and to alert security specialists to hitherto underappreciated areas of potential concern. Of course, broken marriages, adulterous affairs, and illicit relationships between case officers and their agents were not necessarily indicators of criminal infractions, but could, when combined with other suspicions, amount to a reason to mount a security enquiry.

PROFUMO, JOHN. The secretary of state for war in Harold Macmillan's government, but not a member of his cabinet, Jack Profumo was introduced to **Christine Keeler** at a weekend party held at Cliveden by Lord Astor early in July 1961. Attracted to this ravishingly beautiful 19-year-old dancer, Profumo conducted a brief affair with her until a month later when he was invited by the cabinet secretary, Sir Norman Brook, to assist MI5 in an operation to entrap the Soviet naval attaché **Eugene Ivanov**. Profumo declined to do so and incorrectly interpreted the conversation as a warning that MI5 disapproved of his relationship with Keeler. He immediately wrote her a note terminating the relationship, but in January 1963 rumors circulated in London that suggested Keeler had sold the incriminating letter to a Sunday newspaper and had claimed to have had an affair with the minister while simultaneously sleeping with Ivanov, who had instructed her to extract information from the minister about the deployment of nuclear weapons in West Germany. Profumo responded to the allegations by suing the magazine for libel and denying in a statement to the House of Commons that there had been any impropriety in his relationship with Keeler. When he confessed his lie to his wife, actress Valerie Hobson, in June 1963, he resigned from Parliament and devoted the remainder of his life to charitable works. A subsequent inquiry conducted by Lord Denning concluded that Keeler had invented her affair with Ivanov, and there had not been any breach of security. Denning also heard testimony about rumors of other political scandals, including allegations that another minister, Duncan Sandys, had consorted with call girls, but these proved to be groundless. Nevertheless, evidence taken from **Mariella Novotny** and a showgirl from Murray's cabaret club, Mandy Rice-Davies, would have far-reaching implications, especially for President **John F. Kennedy**, and the political scandal would influence the general election held in October 1964 that returned a Labour government, the first for 13 years.

A wealthy man, having inherited control of an insurance company, Profumo retired from public life and devoted himself to the management of Toynbee Hall, a charity in London's East End. He died in 2005, having refused to make any public comment. *See also* DENNING REPORT, THE.

PROUTY, NADA NADIM. Convicted in November 2007 of gaining illegal access to **Central Intelligence Agency** (CIA) and Federal Bureau of Investigation (FBI) files, Nada Prouty had entered the United States on a student visa in June 1989 from Lebanon, where she had been born in 1970, and in August 1990 underwent a sham marriage to 24-year-old Chris Deladurantaye to remain in the country, gain citizenship as Nada Deladurantaye in August 1994, and work as a waitress at the La Shish restaurant in Detroit.

She obtained a degree from the Detroit School of Business and, while working as a receptionist in a medical clinic, a master's degree from Bloomsburg University, Pennsylvania. In 1995, she married Andrew Alley, the brother of the clinic's owner, but they were divorced five years later. Her third marriage was to 40-year-old Gordon Prouty, a State Department official.

She would later work for the FBI after April 1997 as an informant and as an interpreter, and in June 2003 was recruited by the CIA. However, a subsequent background security screening and polygraph failed to identify her brother-in-law as Talal Khalil Chahine, a well-known Hizbollah figure in Beirut, or that her sister, Eliat El-Aouar, was under investigation for a $20 million tax fraud, for which she would be convicted in 2006. Nada Prouty was charged with obtaining her citizenship by fraud, and of accessing FBI and CIA files on suspected members of Hizbollah, including those of her own family.

PSYCHOLOGICAL SEX OPERATIONS. Before and during World War II, both sides conducted psychological warfare operations intended to undermine the morale of frontline troops by asserting that their absence was being exploited by others who were taking advantage of their wives and sweethearts left at home. This impression was conveyed by "black radio" broadcasts transmitted from Pulborough, Sussex, to Europe by stations purporting to be based in Germany, and supported by air drops of suggestive postcards of vulnerable scantily clad women being molested by Nazi officials. However, Allied assessments concluded that the near-pornographic literature had little measurable impact apart from on the personnel engaged in preparing it, who much enjoyed their task. Similarly, in May 1939 the Nazi propaganda minister Dr. Josef Goebbels supervised the distribution of six versions of leaflets over the Maginot Line, illustrated with British soldiers bedding near-naked French women and captioned "*Ou le Tommy est-il reste?*" Other, more sophisticated cards revealed rape and other atrocities when held up against the light, but although the material quickly became collectors' items, there was no evidence that it had the desired effect. Truly pornographic pictures, prepared by the Japanese in Southeast Asia, were designed to sap the enemy's strength and make soldiers more willing to surrender, but surveys indicated that the recipients only manifested contempt for the tactics.

– Q –

QUEEN BEE. One of the three most expensive nightclubs in Tokyo, the Queen Bee employed high-class hostesses who were available to entertain clients off the premises so long as the club was compensated for their absence. In October 1957, a young U.S. Marine, Lee Harvey Oswald, began seeing one of the Japanese hostesses, and some of his fellow Marines were mystified at the source of his sudden wealth. At the time, Oswald was stationed at the Atsugi Naval Air Station, outside Tokyo, working as a radar operator in Marine Air

Control Squadron 1, which routinely handled U-2 flights. The U-2 reconnaissance aircraft, assigned to the Joint Technical Advisory Group at Atsugi, was part of a **Central Intelligence Agency** (CIA) program to fly clandestine missions into Soviet airspace at very high altitudes, far beyond the reach of Soviet air defenses. Oswald's knowledge of the aircraft's operating altitudes would have made him a very attractive target for the KGB, which was aware of the incursions but apparently powerless to prevent them.

When interviewed in Moscow by a consular official at the U.S. embassy in October 1959, Oswald attempted to renounce his citizenship, declaring that he had already offered to supply his Soviet hosts with classified information concerning his knowledge of radar.

Immediately after the assassination of President John F. Kennedy in Dallas in November 1963, Oswald was arrested, and when it was revealed that he had defected to the Soviet Union in October 1959, and then had returned to the United States in July 1961, some of his former fellow Marines speculated about the possibility that he had been recruited by the KGB when he had been stationed at Atsugi. Oswald was shot dead two days after his arrest so he was never interrogated on the subject.

QUORUM CLUB. Located in the Carroll Arms Hotel on Capitol Hill and owned by the secretary to the Senate, Bobby Baker, the Quorum Club provided a discreet venue for Washington, D.C., lobbyists to meet legislators. Baker was Lyndon Johnston's protégé and he gained a reputation, before being imprisoned for fraud and tax evasion, as a congressional fixer and influence peddler. He also ensured there was a ready supply of party girls to entertain the members, and this was where in 1962 **John F. Kennedy** was first introduced to **Ellen Rometsch**, a glamorous German call girl suspected by the Federal Bureau of Investigation of being an East German spy.

– R –

RAHAB THE HARLOT. One of the earliest documented examples of sexspionage, the Old Testament gives an account of Rahab the Harlot who sheltered Joshua's spies before the capture of Jericho. Betrayed to the king of Jericho, Rahab was interrogated and admitted only that a pair of Israelites had stayed with her but had left the city shortly before the curfew. As the king's agents pursued the pair, Rahab returned home and hid them under flax in her loft. She then enabled them to escape through a window, and left a scarlet thread in it to identify the house when Joshua attacked. The two agents returned safely to Joshua, submitted their report, and he was able to plan a successful assault on the city based on their information. When the Israelites sacked Jericho, Rahab's home, still bearing the scarlet thread, was spared.

RAKE, DENIS. A **Special Operations Executive** (SOE) radio operator who paddled ashore from a felucca at Juan-les-Pins in May 1942 on his first mission, Denis Rake, codenamed JUSTIN, was the son of *The Times* correspondent in Brussels, and having been brought up in Belgium spoke fluent French. He was also a **homosexual** who had an affair in Paris with a German officer, Max Halder, while on his first mission into France.

Having only recently escaped from prison in Dijon by hiding in a bin of swill, Rake met Halder in a nightclub, the Boeuf sur le Toit, where Rake had worked as a singer before the war, while attempting to make contact with another SOE agent, John Heslop, and had moved into Halder's apartment. An anti-Nazi aristocrat, Halder never had any idea that his lover was a British agent, and believed him to be an unemployed Belgian actor. Their affair continued until Rake was able to acquire a forged identity card with which he intended to return to Lyons and rejoin his circuit, but he was arrested by the Vichy police in Limoges and then transferred to a prisoner-of-war camp at Chambaran, where he was released with two British NCOs by a sympathetic prison commandant when the Allies landed in North Africa and the Nazis began to sweep south to occupy the whole of France. Together with the pair of soldiers, Rake traveled to Perpignan and eventually was guided over the Pyrenees to Spain, where he was interned at the Miranda del Ebro camp. Here, he encountered another lover, Alex Sholokovsky, who had served in the French Air Force and whom Rake would recommend to SOE as an agent. When Rake was eventually released from an internment camp at Jaraba, he made contact with the British embassy in Madrid and was escorted to Gibraltar where, almost exactly a year after his mission had begun, he was reunited with SOE and flown back to England.

After a further year acting as a conducting officer for SOE personnel in England, Rake went back into the field as a radio operator and found himself working alongside Alex Sholokovsky in the Chaeauroux area. However, Sholokovsky was killed in a firefight in May 1944. After the Normandy landings, Rake joined up with the local maquis and was the legendary Nancy Wake's radio operator until they were overrun by Allied troops in Clermont-Ferrand in August. Following a stay in the hospital, Rake rejoined the regular army to be posted to Germany and was decorated with the Military Cross.

In 1968, Rake, who worked as a butler for Douglas Fairbanks Jr., published his war memoirs, *Rake's Progress*, in which he gave a hilarious account of his adventures.

RASHEEDA, MARIYAM. In November 1994, two attractive women from the Maldives, Mariyam Rasheeda and Faujiya Hassan, were detained in Kerala, India, for having overstayed their visas. During the course of a routine local police enquiry into a breach of the immigration regulations, evidence emerged that both were agents of the Maldivian Security and Intelligence Service, and had been attempting to extract sensitive technical information from senior personnel working for the Indian Space Research Organization (ISRO) at Trivandrum.

The case was passed to the Indian Police's Intelligence Bureau (IB) and to India's external intelligence-gathering agency, the Research and Analysis Wing (RAW) of the Cabinet Secretariat, and under interrogation the suspects admitted that they had attempted to cultivate Doctors Sasikumar and Nambinarayan, a pair of ISRO scientists. At the time, there was considerable interest in the ISRO from the Pakistani Inter-Services Intelligence (ISI) because of a recent purchase by Islamabad of M-11 missiles from the People' Republic of China, and India's security agencies knew the ISI operated from bases at Male in the Maldives, and from Colombo in Sri Lanka, both cites visited recently by the two suspects, leading to the belief that they may have been ISI agents. Although the ISRO was engaged in civilian projects, the research on cryogenic rocket engines was believed to have military applications. As the investigation widened, it appeared that the IB had stumbled across a very extensive penetration of the ISRO by Pakistani, Russian, and possibly American spies.

The ISRO espionage case became a *cause celebre* in Delhi when transcripts of the interrogation showed that Prakhabkar Rao, the son of Prime Minister Narasimha Rao, had been implicated, and that Dr. Sasikumar appeared to enjoy considerable unexplained wealth from very extensive business interests outside his ISRO office at Valiamamala. However, as soon as word leaked that there were potential political ramifications to the investigation, it was taken out of the IB's hands and passed to the Central Bureau of Investigation in Delhi, which asserted that the videotaped statements made by the two suspects to the Kerala police had been made under duress. This verdict was subsequently repudiated by the High Court in Delhi when the tapes were viewed by judges, but by then the entire investigation had been discredited and the two women were released without charge. Although the IB was cleared of having fabricated a case of espionage against Prakhabkar Rao, the organization was purged and the joint director, Maloy Krishna Dhar, forced to retire.

RAVEN. The term applied to men who deliberately seduced vulnerable women to gain access to classified information. A technique pioneered by **Markus Wolf** of the East German Hauptverwaltung Aufkrarung, his victims invariably were lonely secretaries employed in sensitive posts in the German Federal Republic during the Cold War.

RED AVISTA. The codename of a Cuban espionage network in southern Florida arrested in September 1998 consisting of 14 spies led by Geraldo Hernández Nordelo. In June 2001, after a trial lasting six months, five defendants were found guilty of espionage. Four others had fled to Havana to avoid prosecution, including Major **Juan Pablo Roque**. Hernández, who had posed as a Puerto Rican named Manuel Viramontez, had sought to collect information on the Cuban émigré community and to penetrate the U.S. Army's Southern Command headquarters. The spy ring had been under surveillance by the Federal Bureau of Investigation (FBI) for years before Fernando González Llort, Rene González Schweret, Ramón Labanino Salazar, and **Antonio Guerrero** Rodriguez were detained. Hernández was convicted of convicted of contributing to the death of four Brothers to the Rescue aircrew whose aircraft was shot down by a Cuban MiG fighter in international airspace in February 1996.

Another member of the network, Alejandro Alonso, was sentenced to seven years' imprisonment in January 2000 after he confessed and led the FBI to a cache of false identification documents and enciphering equipment for communicating secret messages to Cuba. Two others, Joseph and **Amarilys Santos**, cooperated with the FBI and gave evidence for the prosecution.

Another couple, George and Marisol Gari, was arrested in Orlando in September 2001. He worked for the defense contractor Lockheed Martin while his wife was employed by the U.S. Postal Service. Codenamed LUIS and MARGOT, they had been trained by the Dirección General de Inteligencia before their arrival in the United States in 1991 and one of their tasks had been to monitor the Cuban American National Foundation.

REDFA, MUNIR. Designated *Fishbed* by NATO, the MiG-21 was an important intelligence objective when it was introduced into the Iraqi Air Force in July 1966. In August, a top Iraqi fighter pilot, Munir Redfa, the deputy commander of his squadron, flew his fighter to Israel, having been persuaded to do so by his lover, a Mossad agent purporting to be an American businesswoman, to whom he had been introduced in Baghdad but then met again for a weekend together in Paris. A Maronite Christian, Redfa had been motivated to defect because of the regime's indiscriminate bombing of Iraqi Kurds. Because of the plane's very short range, it was refueled in Turkey, and once in Israel was made available to U.S. Air Force intelligence experts so its manufacturing secrets and avionics could be studied. The movie *Steal the Sky* was made based on Redfa's experience.

REDL, ALFRED. Appointed the director of the Kundschaftsstelle, the Austrian counterintelligence service, in 1900, Colonel Alfred Redl was a professional soldier from humble origins born in 1864 who had graduated as an officer cadet from the Lemberg military academy. However, his **homosexuality** became known to the Russians, who supplied him with young men and then blackmailed him into disclosing the identities of Austrian agents in Russia, details of Austrian military codes, and the plans for the mobilization of the Austro-Hungarian army. In 1912, Redl was promoted and transferred to an army corps in Hungary but maintained contact with the Russians by opening a post office box in Vienna under the alias Nikon Nizetas.

Redl's activities were discovered in May 1913 when incriminating mail was intercepted in Vienna by his successor at the Kundschafstelle, Colonel Maximilian Ronge, and the post box traced to him. He was confronted with the evidence by a group of brother officers and, offered the opportunity to shoot himself, did so after writing a confession in which he asserted that he had been coerced into spying for the Russians.

REICH, WILHELM. As a controversial psychotherapist, Wilhelm Reich researched sexuality and neuroses, and claimed to have discovered "orgiastic potency" as the key to psychophysical health. His views were rejected by the medical establishment but were to have a profound impact on many of his adherents, including **Arnold Deutsch**, the NKVD illegal who successfully recruited numerous Soviet spies as moles during the 1930s, often exploiting their sexual preferences.

Reich, the author of *The Sexual Revolution* in 1930 and the founder of the Socialist Association for Sexual Counseling and Research, studied neurology in Vienna and was appointed deputy director of Sigmund Freud's Psychoanalytic Polyclinic. He fled Austria to Scandinavia in 1934 after he had been denounced by the Nazis as a Communist Jew. In fact, he had been expelled from the Kommunist Partei Deutschland the previous year because of his publications on the subject of fascism and never practiced Judaism. He moved to the United States in 1939 and was investigated by the Federal Bureau of Investigation in 1947 as a possible subversive, but no evidence was found against him. However, he was imprisoned in 1956 for breaking a federal injunction preventing him from peddling his invention, the Argone Accumulator, a metal box in which his patients sat to receive cosmic energy. Although Albert Einstein seemed impressed with the contraption, Reich was banned from making unsubstantiated claims for it, and he died in his sleep at Lewisberg Federal Penitentiary while serving a sentence of two years for contempt in December 1957.

Reich's highly progressive opinions about human sexuality made him attractive to the political left; one of his students, Arnold Deutsch, used his research into psychotherapy as a cover for espionage and the recruitment of agents such as **Kim Philby**, **Anthony Blunt**, and **Guy Burgess**, about whom he wrote very detailed psychological profiles.

REISS, IGNACE. Married to a fellow Soviet spy, Elisabeth Porestsky, the couple operated in Europe as illegals, but he was murdered on a road outside Lausanne in September 1937 by an experienced American-born gangster and hit man, Roland Abbiate.

Reiss had been initiated into the Comintern in Vienna, where he had been "centered in the Soviet Embassy. In later years, such open contact with Soviet diplomatic officials would have been unthinkable, but at the time there had not yet been police raids on Soviet trade missions and similar bodies so no precautions seemed necessary." On his first mission abroad, to Poland, he had been arrested and imprisoned on a charge of Communist subversion but he had escaped after 18 months, and then had been assigned to Holland, where, according to his widow, he had been given "a much more important assignment; he was to direct operations aimed at obtaining information in Great Britain. The headquarters were not to be in England but in the Netherlands." Reiss and his wife stayed in Holland, working with Dutch artist and accomplished illegal Henri Pieck, for "1928 and part of 1929" before leaving for Moscow. Three years later, Reiss was back in the West, operating in Berlin and then Paris, whence he had been obliged to flee in 1937 when the GRU *rezident*, Walter Krivitsky, defected. Reiss was assumed to have been compromised by Krivitsky, and so was recalled to Moscow, but Reiss suspected he would not last long if he returned. During the purges, neither wives nor children were exempt and the entire Reiss family had been sentenced to death.

Elisabeth knew only too well what was likely to happen and was quite aware that another murder squad would have been dispatched from Moscow to complete the "executive assignment." In July 1931, Georg Semmelmann, a former Soviet Intelligence Service (OGPU) agent who had worked in Germany under Handelsvertretung cover, had been shot in broad daylight in Vienna after he had threatened his old employers. He had been dismissed by the OGPU for having married a German regarded by Moscow as a security risk, and then he had compounded the error by publicly demanding his job back and hinting of sensational disclosures. Semmelmann's murder had been an unmistakable warning to others tempted to break the code of *konspiratsia*, and the lesson had not been lost on Elisabeth. She promptly went into hiding with friends in Holland, moving to America from Lisbon in 1940, and was later to write a bitter denunciation of Josef Stalin, *Our Own People*, and of her husband's murderers. She also cooperated with the Federal Bureau of Investigation and MI5, helping them to solve some of the more baffling puzzles of the illegal *konspiratsia*, including some of the assignments undertaken by her husband, who had spent 20 years as an illegal, operating in Berlin, Vienna, and Paris. Her sketches of personalities among the cosmopolitan illegals were also exceptionally useful, for they tended to corroborate much of what Krivitsky had disclosed.

REMBITSKY, LEONARD. In 1915, Leonard Rembitsky, then aged 12, was sent to a German-sponsored espionage academy in Warsaw, or so *Pravda* reported in November 2002 in an interview with the former child spy. According to his account, 300 girls and 72 boys graduated from the school and were deployed against the Russians, and he was arrested in Riga. Most of the women were selected for their looks and, in his recollection, were little better than prostitutes.

RHODES, ROY. Codenamed QUEBEC and ANDREY by the KGB, Roy Rhodes was born in 1917 in Oiltown, Oklahoma, and was caught in a classic **honeytrap** in Moscow just after Christmas 1951, when he was told that he had gotten a Russian girl pregnant at an encounter following a drunken orgy with two Russian mechanics. Blackmailed into cooperating, Rhodes revealed details of his previous training as a code clerk and information about other embassy employees.

Having worked as a mechanic and chauffeur in the U.S. embassy motor pool since 1951, Sergeant Rhodes returned to the United States in June 1953, having compromised himself further by taking various small sums of money from the KGB and having signed receipts for the payments. After six months at a signals base in San Luis Obispo, California, he was transferred to Fort Monmouth, New Jersey, and he lived in a house nearby, at Linden Place. Later, Rhodes was moved back to his unit's permanent base at Fort Huachuca, Arizona, where he received an honorable discharge at the end of his term of service, on 17 November 1955. In January the following year, he reenlisted, and was assigned back to Fort Monmouth as a code clerk with access to classified material. However, Rhodes declined to renew the contact, as he had been instructed, and this failure led to the KGB instructing the illegal *rezident*, **Willie Fisher**, to establish his current location. When confronted in June 1957 with a statement made by Fisher's assistant, **Reino Hayhanen**, who had defected to the **Central Intelligence Agency** in Paris, Rhodes confessed and appeared as a prosecution witness against Fisher. Later, at his own court-martial, he was sentenced to five years' hard labor at Fort Leavenworth. In total, Rhodes admitted to having met his Soviet contacts 15 times in Moscow, and to having been paid about $3,000.

RICHARD, MARTHE. Born Marthe Bettenfeld in Lorraine in 1889, she married wealthy businessman Henri Richer and learned to fly, but he was killed on the Western Front in 1915. Her attempts to become a military aviator rebuffed, Marthe instead was recruited as an intelligence agent by Captain Georges Ledoux of the Deuxième Bureau and sent to Madrid posing as an adventuress, to cultivate the German military attaché, Major von Krohn. Marthe was quickly recruited by Krohn and codenamed S-32, and she also became his mistress. According to an account of her activities published by Ledoux in 1932, Marthe succeeded in learning from her lover details of German operations in Morocco, discovering a clandestine route across the Pyrenees used to infiltrate spies into France, and foiling a plot to sabotage cargos of grain from Argentina destined for Britain. In a final coup, Marthe denounced von Krohn to his ambassador, handing him a packet of his love letters while claiming that she had been paid out of secret funds and had been entrusted with the combination of his office safe.

In 1935, after Ledoux had made his disclosures, Marthe Richard published *My Life as a Spy*, the first of four volumes of memoirs in which she described her wartime exploits in Spain.

RICHTER, KAREL. A 29-year-old Sudetan Czech who had lived in the United States before World War II, Karel Richter parachuted into Hertfordshire in May 1941 and was arrested the same day. He was interrogated by MI5 at Camp 020 and agreed to accompany his captors back to where he had hidden his parachute. He also surrendered a quartz valve he had been instructed to deliver to TATE, another spy then working for MI5 as a double agent.

Under interrogation, Richter explained he had been a marine engineer serving aboard the SS *Hansa* when the war started, and said his wife was still living in California. His sole objective, so he claimed, was to be reunited with his wife and daughter in the United States. His identity papers included a genuine Czech passport and documents naming him as "Fred Snyder." However, when confronted with Josef Jakobs, a spy who had been arrested the previous week and with whom he had trained, Richter's resistance collapsed. According to his confession, he had deserted his ship in Hamburg and had attempted to return to the United States through Sweden but had been arrested in Stockholm and deported to Germany, where he had been placed in a concentration camp until he had been offered the opportunity join the Abwehr. His mission had been to meet TATE to deliver the quartz crystal and check that he was not operating under the enemy's control.

While the Federal Bureau of Investigation traced his wife in California, Richter was tried at the Old Bailey in October 1941 and hanged at Wandsworth prison in December. *See also* NOMINAL AGENTS.

RITCHIE, RHONA. A junior diplomat at the British embassy in Tel Aviv in 1981, 30-year-old Rhona Ritchie shared some confidential cables with her lover, Rafaat El-Ansary, who worked at the Egyptian embassy. Their relationship was spotted by the Israelis, who reported the couple to London, and Ritchie was recalled, charged with breaches of the Official Secrets Act, and sentenced to a suspended prison sentence of nine months. The attorney general, Sir Michael Havers, described here as "more foolish than wicked" and noted that the content of the cables she had passed to her lover would eventually have been made public.

ROMEO SPIES. The term applied to men employed for the purpose of seducing and recruiting women with access to useful information. The strategy became known primarily in West Germany during the Cold War when a series of spies were identified as having entered into relationships with East German agents, often directed by Hauptverwaltung

Aufkrarung (HVA) chief **Markus Wolf**, who established a reputation as a shrewd manipulator of vulnerable women, often secretaries working for the Federal Republic.

Markus Wolf successfully penetrated Konrad Adenauer's chancellery with an agent codenamed FELIX who pretended to be a sales representative marketing beauty products to hairdressers, and who seduced NORMA, one of the chancellor's secretaries. Their relationship had lasted for years until the Bundesamt für Verfassungsschutz (BfV) started to take an interest in FELIX and he was withdrawn to safety in East Berlin. Typically, Wolf had been able to exploit the situation by learning from FELIX of another potentially vulnerable secretary who worked for Hans Globke, Adenauer's secretary of state. She was promptly targeted by Wolf's star Romeo, Hans Stöhler, and proved to be an excellent source, to the point that she was herself recruited as a spy and codenamed GUDRUN. She continued to supply valuable information until Stöhler, a former Luftwaffe pilot whose cover was that of an estate agent, fell ill and was brought home to die. After his death, GUDRUN, who thought she had been working for the KGB, gave up espionage, perhaps proving that she had been truly smitten by Stöhler and had only really spied for him. In this case, Stöhler had pretended to be Russian, but Wolf often recruited under a "false flag," which was a demanding role for any handler, and one relatively susceptible to discovery where someone masqueraded as a national of a foreign country. Ideally, the HVA needed to deploy authentic, suitable foreigners to play such parts, but they were in short supply in East Germany.

Wolf's best false-flag operator was Roland Gandt, who persuaded a German secretary working for Supreme Headquarters Allied Powers Europe, at Fontainebleau, that he was a Danish intelligence officer operating in France under journalistic cover. Accepting that Roland was a national of another NATO country, **Margarethe Lubig** fell for him in Vienna, but, as a devout Roman Catholic, insisted that she should confess her espionage to a priest. Ever the master of improvisation, Wolf arranged for a bogus priest to hear her confession at a remote Jutland church and give her an equally worthless absolution.

The women who spied for the HVA seem to have been motivated primarily by their almost blind devotion to their lovers, a common denominator that Wolf perceived as more important than ideology or nationality. At the time, few appreciated the potential of the Romeo, and it was only when the HVA's archives fell into Western hands and the **Central Intelligence Agency** acquired the cryptographic key, codenamed ROSEWOOD, to identify the individual sources, that it could be exploited fully.

Wolf's other agents included Ingrid Garbe, a member of the FRG's mission to NATO's headquarters in Brussels; **Ursel Lorenzen**, who worked in NATO's general secretariat; Imelda Verrept, a Belgian secretary in NATO; Inge Goliach, who penetrated the Christian Democrats (CDU); Christel Broszey, secretary to the CDU's deputy leader Kurt Biedenkopf; Helga Rödiger, a secretary in the FRG's Ministry of Finance; and Ursula Höfs, a secretary in the Christian Democrat Party. All these agents had been persuaded to spy by their Romeo lovers, but the BfV failed to grasp Wolf's strategy until 1979 when the new BfV president, Dr. Richard Meier, belatedly introduced a new vetting procedure, codenamed Operation REGISTRATION, to screen the partners of single women holding sensitive posts. This innovation precipitated the hasty withdrawal of several agents and their lovers, but the principle had been well established.

ROMETSCH, ELLEN. Born in Kleinitz in 1936, a village that was absorbed into the German Democratic Republic, Ellen Rometsch was a Young Pioneer who escaped to the West with her parents in 1955. After an unsuccessful marriage, she moved to the United States with her second husband Rolf, an NCO in the Federal German Air Force attached to the embassy in Washington, D.C. A breathtakingly beautiful brunette and a part-time call girl, she was introduced to **John F. Kennedy** in early 1963 while working at the **Quorum Club** on Capitol Hill, run by the Senate secretary Bobby Baker, a legendary congressional fixer who would eventually be convicted of fraud and tax evasion and spend 18 months in prison. Baker, a protégé of Lyndon B. Johnson, peddled influence in the Democratic Party and his friend Bill Thomson, a railway executive and close friend of the president's, acted as a procurer, supplying what were termed "party girls" for naked late-night frolics in the White House swimming pool on the many occasions when Jacqueline Kennedy was absent.

Rometsch's relationship with Kennedy was reported by an informant to the Federal Bureau of Investigation (FBI) in July 1963, which alerted the Department of Justice that she might have once worked for Walter Ulbricht, the East German leader. A formal FBI espionage investigation was initiated that suggested her home in Arlington and her expensive lifestyle could not have been supported by her husband's modest income. In August 1963, she was deported to Germany on an Air Force transport, accompanied by LaVern Duffy, one of Bobby Kennedy's closest friends, who had fallen for her and would act as a conduit for substantial payments made to her, apparently to buy her silence. A month after she left Washington, her husband divorced her on the grounds of her promiscuity, and then the Republican minority leader on the Senate's Rules Committee attempted to bring her back to Washington to give evidence about her activities and possible breaches of security. At the request of the White House, J. Edgar Hoover, following a private lunch with the president early in November 1963, reluctantly agreed to brief congressional leaders on the background of the case and explain the potential damage any further probing might inflict on the Oval Office.

ROQUE, JUAN PABLO. A Cuban Air Force officer, Major Juan Roque swam to the U.S. Naval Air Station at Guantanamo Bay in 1992 and was subsequently given political asylum in the United States. He settled in Florida and the following year was taken to a Bible study class by his cousin, a Federal Bureau of Investigation (FBI) special agent, where he met Ana Margarita Martinez, a woman with two teenage children from a previous marriage. After a romance lasting two years, the couple married, but on 23 February 1996, he disappeared. The following day, Cuban MiG fighters shot down two unarmed Brothers to the Rescue aircraft over international waters, killing four aircrew, and Roque appeared on a CNN broadcast from Havana two days later, revealing himself to have been a Cuban intelligence officer. Evidently, Roque, who had acted as a double agent, had worked as an FBI informant and had been part of the **RED AVISTA** spy network in southern Florida, infiltrating the Cuban émigré community.

Roque's wife, an executive secretary, obtained an annulment to terminate her marriage, which had lasted 11 months, and then brought an action against her former husband and the Cuban government for sexual battery, torture, and terrorism, claiming that she would never have allowed her relationship with him to develop if she had known his true allegiances. In March 2001, a Miami court found in her favor, ruling that he had committed sexual battery because he did not have her "informed consent to have marital relations" and awarded her $7,175,000 in compensatory damages, and $175,000 a year for the next 40 years, until she reached the age of 81.

The families of the Brothers to the Rescue aircrew also received awards of compensation in a separate action, amounting to $91 million, which was seized from Cuban government assets frozen in the United States.

ROSE, FRED. Born Fred Rosenberg to Russian parents in Lublin, Poland, Fred Rose was elected a member of the Canadian Parliament for the Cartier division of Montreal in 1932, soon after he had been released from prison on a charge of sedition. He worked as a GRU agent, running a large network of scientific and other sources with his mistress, **Freda Linton**. When his spy ring was compromised by defector Igor Gouzenko in September 1945, Rose went into hiding, but he was arrested by the Royal Canadian Mounted Police in March 1946 during a raid on his apartment. He was subsequently convicted of espionage and deported to Poland when he had served his sentence.

ROSENBERG, ETHEL. Identified in July 1950 as a Soviet spy by her brother David Greenglass, who had been arrested in May after he had been implicated by the NKVD courier Harry Gold, Ethel Rosenberg was taken into custody by the Federal Bureau of Investigation (FBI) in June 1950. Her husband Julius, codenamed LIBERAL, had been compromised by **Elizabeth Bentley** who had taken telephone messages from "Julius" for her lover, Jacob Golos.

As the FBI researched the links between LIBERAL's organization and other individuals and groups, and started building the legal case against the Rosenbergs, doubt was expressed about the wisdom of charging Ethel, for the proof against her, apart from testimony from Ruth Greenglass, was contained in a VENONA text to Moscow dated 27 November 1944 from Leonid Kvasnikov of the New York *rezidentura*:

> Your 5356. Information on LIBERAL's wife. Surname that of her husband, first name ETHEL, 29 years old. Married five years. Finished secondary school. A COMPATRIOT [Communist] since 1938. Sufficiently

well developed politically. Knows about her husband's work and the role of METER [Joel Barr] and NIL. In view of delicate health does not work. Is characterized positively and as a devoted person.

The text was of particular importance because the search for LIBERAL, formerly ANTENNA, and married to ETHEL had been under way since August 1947 when Meredith Gardner had identified the pair of spies in his first "Special Analysis Report." Cryptographically, the word ETHEL had been a special challenge, for Gardner had broken the spell code for "E" and "L," but initially had been baffled by a single value for "THE," for there is no definite article in Russian. However, he deduced that the NKVD must have anticipated enciphering masses of English text, and therefore had attributed a code group to THE, which is, after all, the most common word in the language.

The damning sentence about Ethel's knowledge of her husband's work was enough to persuade those who had been indoctrinated into VENONA who had doubted her involvement that she had played a role in Julius's organization. After her arrest, she proved rather more resilient than Julius, but the evidence that condemned her to the electric chair was strictly limited to what was admissible in court. According to those familiar with the FBI's recordings of their private conversations, Julius did express an interest in cooperating with the bureau but was talked out of his weakness by Ethel. The FBI's final attempt to save Julius, by establishing a specialist team in Sing Sing during the execution in June 1953, standing by in the hope he would agree to make a statement naming "names in up-state New York" at the last moment, was thwarted by the prison governor's decision to execute him first so as to avoid Ethel enduring the harrowing experience of walking past his cell to the execution chamber.

ROUSSEAU, MONIQUE. The daughter of the French military attaché's secretary, Monique was 16 years old when she was compromised in Belgrade by a young Yugoslav who seduced her and then insisted she undergo an abortion. She was then blackmailed into supplying information from her father's office, and as he was actually a Service de Documentation Exterieure et de Contre-Espionage (SDECE), she became a valuable spy before she moved to the United States and married a pastry chef in Los Angeles. In 1969, a Yugoslav defector named Monique's father, Eugene Rousseau, as a spy and in April 1970, aged 63, he was convicted of espionage at a secret trial and sentenced to 15 years' imprisonment. According to the defector, Rousseau had succumbed to pressure and had agreed to provide classified information to save his daughter. However, while serving his sentence at Mlun prison, Rousseau campaigned for his release and in December 1971 he was pardoned by President Georges Pompidou.

ROWSELL, IVOR. In March 1963, Ivor Rowsell, a transport clerk employed at the British embassy in Moscow, was the victim of an attempt by the KGB to **honeytrap** him. He reported the incident and was immediately withdrawn to London, but it was unclear precisely why he had been targeted. The most likely reason was his occupation of a flat that, until the previous June, had belonged to Lieutenant Commander John Varley, an assistant defense attaché whom the KGB suspected had been part of the support team deployed to manage Colonel **Oleg Penkovsky**, the GRU officer who had passed secrets to Secret Intelligence Service (SIS) and **Central Intelligence Agency** (CIA) personnel in Moscow since December 1960. This bonanza included details of the Soviet Strategic Rocket Force, headed by his indiscreet friend Marshal Sergei Vorentsov, and huge quantities of information about the GRU and its overseas *rezidenturas*.

Penkovsky was arrested in October 1962 after a lengthy period of surveillance during which the KGB saw Penkovsky contact Janet Chisholm, the wife of the local SIS station commander, Ruari Chisholm. When Chisholm was replaced by Gervase Cowell, he too was placed under observation, and gradually the KGB acquired sufficient evidence to intervene. The consequences of Penkovsky's espionage would be far reaching and would cost GRU Chief Ivan Serov his job, replaced by the KGB deputy chairman, Piotr Ivashutin. In this context, the attempt to compromise Rowsell may have been a reaction to the damage SIS and the CIA had inflicted on the Kremlin.

RUNGE, EVGENNI. A Ukrainian born of German parents who defected in Berlin in October 1967, Evgenni Runge underwent three years of preparatory training by the KGB in Moscow before working first in East Germany and then in Munich. His cover was that of the proprietor of a dry cleaning business that he ran with his East German "wife." When this enterprise failed, Runge, codenamed MAKS and run by the Karlshorst *rezidentura*, moved to Frankfurt where he operated rather more successfully as a salesman peddling automatic vending machines. Runge's illegal network included **Heinz Sutterlin**, who had cultivated and then married Leonore Heinz, a secretary in the Federal Republic's Foreign Ministry. Under her husband's influence, Leonore provided the KGB with a wealth of classified data from her office, but some suspicion must have arisen in Moscow for Runge was recalled unexpectedly for an extended interrogation. At its conclusion, he was told to return to his duties in Frankfurt, but without his wife. Runge appealed against the decision to leave his wife behind to the KGB's chairman, Yuri Andropov, who sympathized and rescinded the order. The Runges traveled back to the Federal Republic but, fearful of what they perceived as their bleak future as distrusted illegals, at the first opportunity surrendered to the **Central Intelligence Agency**. In return for betraying the Sutterlins and some other minor figures, including a source in the French embassy in Bonn, Runge was resettled.

RUPP, RAINER. Cultivated by a Hauptverwaltung Aufkrarung (HVA) talent-spotter he had met after attending a left-wing anti–Vietnam War demonstration in Mainz while studying economics at Düsseldorf in the 1960s, Rainer Rupp was 22 years old when he was invited to visit East Germany to be recruited as an agent by Colonel Jurgen Rogalla.

Born in 1959 in Saarlouis, Rupp studied in Mainz, Brussels, and Bonn, and after his graduation he worked for the International Relations Consulting Company before joining CEDIF Handelsbank in Brussels, where he was introduced to **Ann-Christine Bowen**, the daughter of a British Army officer. In 1971, she found a job at NATO headquarters, and a year later she married Rupp, but soon after the wedding Rupp revealed his relationship with the HVA and persuaded his wife to remove classified documents from her office so he could photograph them. He would then listen in to East German shortwave broadcasts to learn the location of the rendezvous or dead drop, often in Holland, where his films could be delivered to his HVA handlers, Colonels Klaus Roesler and Karl Rehbaum.

In 1977 Rupp applied successfully for a NATO job and started removing documents himself, and in 1984 persuaded his wife, who wanted to abandon espionage after the recent birth of their first son, to continue.

The couple was eventually identified as spies when the ROSEWOOD files were decrypted, and they were arrested at Rupp's parents' home in Saarburg at the end of July 1993. At their trial the following year, Rupp insisted he had played the leading role in their theft of NATO secrets, and he was sentenced to 12 years' imprisonment. His publications during that time include *Policy for the Next Decade* in 1984, *The Future of the European Alliance Systems* in 1992, and *Politics and Security in the Southern Region of the Atlantic Alliance* in 1998. On his release in 2000, he became a journalist.

– S –

SAAR-DEMICHEL, FRANÇOIS. A French paper merchant who bought wood pulp in Russia, François Saar-Demichel fought in the resistance during World War II and until 1947 served in the Direction General de Securité Exterieure, but was **honeytrapped** in Moscow in 1961. Codenamed NN, Saar-Demichel became close to the Elysée Palace and acted as an informal foreign policy adviser to President Charles de Gaulle on East-West relations.

SALON KITTY. A well-known bordello in prewar Berlin, Salon Kitty, owned and managed by Kitty Schmidt, was actually sponsored by the Sicherheitsdienst and used to compromise and exercise influence over its clientele, which included prominent businessmen, politicians, and foreign visitors, among them General Sepp Dietrich and the Italian foreign minister, Count Galeazzo Ciano. Opened in 1936, even though bordellos had been banned by the Nazi government, and supervised by Reinhard Heydrich, Salon Kitty's true role was first disclosed by Walter Schellenberg, who referred to it in his postwar memoirs, written after he had been interrogated by British intelligence personnel. In *The Labyrinthe*, he recalled that the establishment offered "the best service, food, and drink" while three technicians recorded every sound.

Located at Giebachstreasse 11, in premises riddled with microphones and recording equipment, Salon Kitty remained open for business until July 1942 when the building was damaged in an Allied air raid. According to one account, Kitty herself was arrested in 1939 and charged with having used her bank account to send funds abroad for Jewish friends. Thereafter she had been obliged to cooperate, and maintained a special stable of 20 especially attractive girls whose skills were reserved for friends of the regime.

SAMSON. A Judean of extraordinary strength who when a child had wrestled and killed a lion, Samson was tricked into revealing the solution to a riddle by his wife, a Philistine. Enraged by her betrayal, Samson killed 30 Philistines and deserted his wife. However, according to the Bible, Samson was later seduced by his wife's beautiful younger sister, **Delilah**, who attempted to extract from him the secret of the source of his remarkable strength. When he finally confided in her that his strength was in his hair, she cut it off, and he was arrested by the Philistines, who blinded him and then put him on display in the temple. Bound between two stone columns, Samson used his remaining reserves of strength to dislodge the pillars and cause the temple to collapse, killing him and a crowd of spectators that included Delilah.

SANSOM, ODETTE. The mother of three daughters and the widow of a British businessman whom she had married in Boulogne, Odette Sansom was recruited in June 1942 into **Special Operations Executive** and assigned to F Section for infiltration into Nazi-occupied France. The following October she was sent with the codename LISE to join SPINDLE, a network based in the Haute-Savoie near St. Jorioz, which had been penetrated by the Abwehr. A highly suspicious character claiming to be a disaffected German officer had made contact with the group and was negotiating a meeting. Improbably, he was the interrogator of a courier, André Marsac, codenamed END, who had been captured but had fallen for the German's claim that he wanted to switch sides. Marsac had fallen asleep on a train in November 1942 and had his briefcase stolen by an Abwehr agent. When the Germans examined the contents, they discovered the names and addresses of hundreds of CARTE's members, including Marsac himself, who was arrested instantly. When informed, London warned LISE that the same tactic had been adopted recently by the enemy to identify and arrest an entire circuit, and she was warned to break off the contact and consider herself contaminated until further notice.

While in France LISE conducted an affair with a former Commando officer and champion ice skater, Peter Churchill, codenamed MARCEL, and a member of the CARTE circuit. When she learned that he was due to return on another mission, LISE made arrangements to meet him, but just after midnight on the very day he landed by parachute the Germans raided the Hotel de la Poste and found her in bed with Churchill. It was the fourth time he had been infiltrated into France but, despite his orders to avoid LISE until she had shaken off her German contact, who was actually Sergeant Hugo Bleicher of the Paris Abwehr. Nevertheless, Churchill had agreed to spend a few days at the hotel with LISE, and he would later marry her in 1947, but his decision to stay in St. Jorioz was to prove disastrous for SPINDLE and CARTE. He survived his subsequent imprisonment by encouraging his captors to believe, falsely, that he was the prime minister's nephew.

After Bleicher had duped END, he had been put in touch with Roger Bardet (CHAILLAN) and LISE, supposedly to negotiate a Lysander flight to London; instead, he had arrested Bardet and then the following day traveled to St. Jorioz to find Sansom, never realizing that he would also ensnare Churchill.

SANTOS, AMARILYS. A self-confessed Cuban spy, Amarilys Silverio Santos was one of the **RED AVISTA** network arrested by the Federal Bureau of Investigation (FBI) in Florida in September 1998 and charged with espionage. She and her husband Joseph opted to cooperate with the FBI and gave evidence against five other members of the spy ring at their trial in Miami in January 2001. In return, he was sentenced to four years' imprisonment for conspiracy to act as an unregistered agent, and Amarilys received 42 months and a recommendation that she not be deported to Cuba upon completion of her sentence.

The couple's mission had been to infiltrate the U.S. Southern Command, the nerve center for all military operations in Latin America and the Caribbean, which was withdrawn from Panama to Miami.

Santos, who had been born in New Jersey, moved as a child to Cuba and later underwent intelligence training before moving first to

Puerto Rico and then to Miami, to work for GIRO, the codename of Geraldo Hernández, and head of the RED AVISTA.

Santos confessed that his mission had been to collect information about the area surrounding the Southern Command building, including details of local bus routes and planned restaurants, and pass it to Hernandez. When the complex had been completed, he was to find a job there, and in the meantime he worked as an electrician, and at a Goya Foods factory.

SCARBECK, IRWIN. The first postwar case of Soviet espionage within the State Department centered on Irwin C. Scarbeck, a career diplomat assigned to the U.S. embassy in Warsaw as second secretary. Twice married and with four children, three by his German second wife, Scarbeck was ensnared in a **honeytrap** by a **swallow** on Christmas Eve 1960 when he was photographed in bed with a beautiful Polish girl, Urszula Discher. Men purporting to be police officers burst into her apartment and took pictures that they later used to blackmail him, and he reluctantly put his signature on an agreement in which he undertook to supply them with information from the embassy. This he did, although he later insisted he had not compromised any secret material, and he also negotiated an exit visa for his girlfriend, who went to live in West Germany.

In June 1961, Scarbeck was questioned by a State Department security officer, Victor Dikeos, and then flown to Frankfurt for further interrogation. On 13 June, Scarbeck was arrested by the Federal Bureau of Investigation and the following month was indicted on charges of passing three documents to the Polish Urzab Bezpieczenstwa (UB): one was a summary of Polish-American relations written by the ambassador, Jacob Beam; the second was an estimate of the effectiveness of the Polish armed forces, prepared by the U.S. service attachés; and the third was a State Department report of an airfield located near the Czech frontier. After a trial lasting three weeks in October 1961, at which Urszula Discher gave evidence for the prosecution but denied ever having been a UB agent, Scarbeck was convicted and sentenced to the maximum, 30 years' imprisonment, although he was released after having served five years.

SCHALBURG, VERA. A German spy who was arrested soon after she had arrived in Scotland, Vera Schalburg rowed ashore at Portgordon from a Luftwaffe amphibious aircraft on 30 September 1940. She was of Danish extraction and was accompanied by Karl Drücke and Werner Wälti. Unlike them, she was never prosecuted and thus saved from the gallows. Instead, she was held at Holloway prison until the end of hostilities, and under interrogation at Aylesbury she claimed to have acted as a GRU agent in Paris, having been run by her lover, Serge Ignatieff, and admitted that her brother Christian was a leading figure in the Danish Nazi Party. They had both been brought up in Siberia, but their parents had later settled in Copenhagen, and Christian would later be killed fighting in a Danish Waffen SS battalion on the Russian front.

Before the war, she had lived in London and had been involved with the **Duchesse de Chateau-Thierry** and another Abwehr agent, the Countess Costenza, who had set up a salon to entertain prominent people, with an emphasis on ambassadors. At the time, while being the mistress of a man named Mackenzie, she had been married to a GRU agent in Paris, Serge Ignatieff, who had sent a gunman to London to kill her, although she had only been wounded in the chest.

During her initial interrogations by MI5, Vera claimed to know nothing of Wälti, who refused to make any statement, but eventually acknowledged that de Deeker's real name was Karl Drücke, who was Jewish and with whom she was deeply in love. She claimed that he was a figure of considerable status in Germany, and for a short period she was released into the custody of Klop Ustinov, who extracted more information from her during the course of many lengthy conversations. In one, Schalburg revealed that her previous lover had been a well-known Abwehr officer, Hans Dierks, who had been killed recently in a car accident.

Drücke proved as obdurate as Wälti, although he compromised himself when he entrusted a letter to a Belgian stool pigeon who told him that he was due for repatriation imminently. Drücke took the bait and wrote a very incriminating letter to a friend, another known German agent in Brussels. In a further effort to gain his cooperation, MI5 arranged for the Camp 020 medical officer to pretend to exchange notes between Drücke and Schalburg, and in one of them Schalburg claimed to be expecting his baby and urged him to make a full confession. The ruse failed, for Drücke replied that he was resigned to spending the rest of his life in prison, but advised her to do whatever was necessary to save herself. Although MI5 thought Vera's ploy was an ingenious method of applying pressure on her lover, it turned out that she really was pregnant, and this saved her from the gallows.

After the war, Schalberg, released from prison, reportedly moved to the Isle of Wight where she brought up her son under an assumed name.

SCHILBECK, GERTRUDE. In 1937, two NKVD illegals, **Ignace Reiss** and his wife Elisabeth Poretsky, chose to take refuge in Switzerland rather than obey orders and return to Moscow to face execution for the crime of having supported **Leon Trotsky**. Reiss had known Walter Krivitsky, the GRU *rezident* in Holland, since their childhood, and came from the same small town in Galicia, at the edge of the Austro-Hungarian Empire; before he defected, he tipped off Reiss to his likely fate. Accordingly, Reiss and Porestsky had gone into hiding but had been tracked down to Lausanne, where she was contacted by an old friend, Gertrude Schilbeck, a German Communist of long standing.

Schilbeck arranged to meet Poretsky and intended to give her a box of chocolates as a gift, but at the last moment quickly snatched it back, not revealing that the contents had been laced with strychnine. Poretsky then sought a rendezvous with her husband, but when they met in September 1937, he was gunned down by the side of the road by an accomplice, Roland Abbiate.

SCHNEIDER, KARL-HEINZ. A **Romeo spy** working for the East German Hauptverwaltung Aufkrarung (HVA), Karl-Heinz Schneider seduced a 31-year-old divorcée, **Marianne Lenzkow**, in 1960 while pretending to be a Danish intelligence officer, and recruited Roland Gandt to play a supporting role, and Gandt soon became engaged to Marianne's younger sister, **Margarethe Lubig**. Both women were employed as secretaries in sensitive positions in the Federal German government and agreed to provide classified information to their lovers, whom they believed to be Danes.

In 1968, Schneider turned his attention to a future Bundesnachrichtendienst (BND) analyst, Gabrielle Gast, while she was completing her doctorate in Karl-Marx-Stadt. She later applied for a job with the BND at its headquarters in Pullach and by 1987 was deputy chief of the BND's Soviet Bloc political branch, and a dedicated convert to Communism. Three years later, Gast was betrayed by Colonel Heinz Busch, a senior HVA officer anxious to ingratiate himself with the Federal Republic, who knew only that **Markus Wolf** had been running a woman inside the BND for years, and she had adopted a handicapped child, but this was enough information for the Bundesamt für Verfassungsschutz to identify Gast and she was imprisoned.

SCHULENBURG, WERNER VON DER. Appointed the German ambassador to Moscow in 1934, the Graf von der Schulenburg was a career diplomat who previously had served as his country's ambassador in Bucharest. An anti-Nazi aristocrat, von der Schulenburg acquired a young ballerina, Olga Lepeshinskaya, as his Russian mistress in Moscow, in 1935. However, she was employed by the NKVD's Leonid Raykhman, who earned his promotion to deputy chief of his organization's counterintelligence department. The ambassador's recruitment by his lover brought Raykhman to Stalin's attention and in 1938 Raykhman sought and received **Lavrenti Beria**'s permission to marry Lepeshinskaya. Von Schulenburg withdrew from the Soviet Union in June 1941 and retired to Austria, but he was implicated in a plot to assassinate Adolf Hitler and was executed.

SCHULER, RUBY. The girlfriend of an electronic engineer, James Harper, Ruby Schuler was an executive secretary employed by Systems Control Inc. in Palo Alto, California, with access to a safe containing classified information about the company's ballistic missile research. A former U.S. Marine discharged in 1955, Harper was in touch with a pair of Polish intelligence officers to whom he had been introduced in Geneva in November 1975. On that occasion, he had been paid $5,000 for some information. In June 1980, he attended a rendezvous in Warsaw at which he was paid $100,000 for a large quantity of secret documents removed by Schuler. Further meetings took place in September in Warsaw and in December in Mexico City, but the following year, fearing exposure by his girlfriend, he contacted a lawyer to negotiate with the Federal Bureau of Investigation

(FBI). Coincidentally, the FBI was already aware of the loss of ballistic missile information to the Polish Sluzba Bezpieczenstwa, which had passed it on to the KGB, and Harper was arrested in October 1983, Schuler having died in June. Harper was convicted of espionage and sentenced to life imprisonment.

SCHULTZE, SONJA. Sonja Schultze and her husband Reinhard were arrested in August 1985 at their home at Cranford, near Heathrow. Both were illegals; Reinhard had adopted the identity of Bryan Waldemar Strunze, the son of a former prisoner of war who had remained in England after the war.

They arrived in England in 1980 on Federal German passports, and while Sonja took classes to qualify as an interpreter, her husband worked as a kitchen salesman. Although there was no evidence that they had ever spied, their house was filled with espionage paraphernalia, one-time pads, and aviation maps of local airports. They were sentenced to 10 years' imprisonment each and recommended for deportation after their release.

SCHULZE-BOYSEN, LIBERTAS. A stunningly beautiful blonde, Libertas Eulenburg was brought up on her family's ancestral estate at the Schloss Liebenberg, and after attending a finishing school in Zurich, she joined Metro-Goldwyn-Mayer in Berlin as an assistant in the press department. When she married Harro Schulze-Boysen in 1936, she was a member of the Nazi Party, but under his influence she became a Communist. Although he had joined the Luftwaffe's intelligence branch in April 1934, Schulze-Boysen, codenamed SENIOR, was already part of a Soviet network that would later report to Alexander Korotkov, alias Erdberg, the NKVD *rezident* at the Soviet embassy in Berlin, through Arvid Harnack, codenamed CORSICAN. In his position as an intelligence analyst, often briefing Hermann Göring, he had access to a mass of classified material, including reports from attachés overseas.

Although Schulze-Boysen was stationed at Wildpark Werder, near Potsdam, he and Libertas enjoyed a very active social life at their apartment in the Altenburger Allee, Charlottenburg, and gained a reputation for hosting very Bohemian parties. These gatherings were not political meetings, but because so many of their fellow conspirators attended them, the Gestapo would later label them orgies, asserting that Libertas had seduced numerous men to entice them into espionage. Actually, Libertas did pose naked for photographer Elisabeth Schumacher and her husband, Kurt, who was a sculptor.

The Soviet spy ring, dubbed the Rote Kapelle by its Gestapo investigators, was eventually broken up when the GRU sent an agent from Brussels to reestablish contact with the organization that, after the closure of the Soviet embassy in June 1941, had lost its conduit to Moscow. In August 1941, Anatoli Guryevich received a wireless message instructing him on how to find CORSICAN and SENIOR, and he traveled to Berlin in October to deliver new ciphers, radio schedules, and mailing addresses in Stockholm, Paris, and Brussels. This crucial message was intercepted by the Funkabwehr but not decrypted until July 1942, just two weeks after Johann Wenzel, a GRU radio operator, was caught as he communicated with Moscow. From that moment, the entire network in Germany was doomed because the German cryptographers were able to read Guryevich's signal and quickly identify CORSICAN as Arvid Harnack and SENIOR as Schulze-Boysen.

Libertas was arrested by the Gestapo as she attempted to leave Berlin by train in August 1942, a week after her husband had been seized while at his office. By March 1943, 129 suspects had been taken into custody, of whom 19 were women who were sentenced to death for a variety of crimes, ranging from war treason to the distribution of subversive leaflets. Libertas was guillotined in Plotzensee prison, minutes after her husband had been hanged on a meathook.

After her death, Libertas was portrayed as a promiscuous traitor, one story claiming that she was so seductive that Gestapo officers were only allowed to interrogate her in pairs.

SCOTT, EDWARD. In March 1961, Edward Scott resigned from the Foreign Office after he admitted that he had been entrapped into cooperating with the Czech **Statni Bezpecnost** (StB) while he had been *charge d'affaires* at the British embassy in Prague in 1958. Educated at Eton and Magdalene College, Cambridge, Scott joined the Foreign Office in 1947 and was posted to Tehran and then Tangier before his transfer to Czechoslovakia in 1956. Infatuated with a maid at the embassy, he was caught attempting to smuggle her out of the country, and when he returned to London in December 1958 he was contacted by the StB. Scott was interrogated over a weekend at Littlehampton police station, near his country home, but was never charged with any offense.

SCRANAGE, SHARON M. In July 1985, a **Central Intelligence Agency** (CIA) operations support assistant, Sharon Scranage, based at Accra, was arrested and charged with leaking information to her Ghanaian boyfriend, Michael Soussoudis. In November 1985, she pleaded guilty to one offense under the espionage statute and two counts under the Intelligence Identities Protection Act, and was sentenced to five years' imprisonment, later reduced to two on appeal. Of major concern for the CIA was the suspicion that Scranage's information had been passed by the Marxist head of Ghana's intelligence agency, Kojo Tsikata, to the East Germans. Soussoudis, who was arrested when he visited the United States in July 1985, was sentenced to 20 years' imprisonment, suspended on condition he leave the country immediately and that eight Ghanaians compromised by Scranage were released from jail.

Scranage had been identified as a potential security risk during a routine inspection of the station in Accra when one of the visiting teams noticed a photograph in Scranage's apartment that suggested she had become involved with a foreign national. Such a relationship requires official consent and it was decided that when she next returned to the United States on home leave, and before she took up her next scheduled foreign assignment, she should undergo a reinvestigation **polygraph**. The test, conducted by the CIA's Office of Security Special Activities Division, revealed deception and over a period of four days her polygraph operator teased a confession from her. The Federal Bureau of Investigation was then called in and she was charged with 18 counts of espionage, although she would subsequently only be convicted on one.

SECOND CHIEF DIRECTORATE (SCD). The designation of the KGB branch responsible for maintaining surveillance on foreigners inside the Soviet Union and running operations against foreign diplomatic missions in Moscow. Information about the SCD came primarily from **Yuri Nosenko**, the KGB defector who had served in the

SCD's First Department, which monitored the U.S. embassy and American diplomats. *See also* GRIBANOV, OLEG.

SHAOMIN, LI. In July 2001, an American academic, Li Shaomin, was convicted in Beijing on charges of having spied for Taiwan. Born in China, Li had a doctorate from Princeton University and was employed as a teacher at a Hong Kong university when he was arrested, according to the *People's Daily*, which referred to his guilty plea and to recent examples of Taiwanese agents using sex as demonstrations of intent to lure Chinese students to adopt "a hostile ideology."

SHUSTER, ANTON. An experienced Soviet intelligence officer of Polish origin, Anton Shuster was posted to the NKVD's *rezidentura* at the London embassy between 1936 and 1937. Also a **homosexual**, Shuster worked as a case officer for several important spies, among them **Guy Burgess** and **Anthony Blunt**. His withdrawal to Moscow may have been a precaution, following the defection in France of a senior GRU officer, Walter Krivitsky, who may have been thought by Moscow to have been in a position to identify Shuster, who had not adopted an alias, as an intelligence officer working under diplomatic cover. Reportedly he was posted to an NKVD training academy upon his return and died in a road accident in Moscow in 1946.

SIEVERS, SUSANNE. A freelance West German journalist, and one of Chancellor Willy Brandt's many former lovers, Susanne Sievers was arrested while attending the annual Leipzig Trade Fair in 1951 and served eight years' imprisonment in East Germany. However, upon her release she agreed to spy for the Hauptverwaltung Aufkrarung (HVA) and, codenamed LYDIA, she established herself as an influential political hostess in Bonn. She continued to supply information to the HVA until August 1961, when the Berlin Wall was constructed, and later she appeared in the Far East with Major Fred Sagner who was employed as a military attaché. Subsequently Sievers served as the Bundesnachrichtendienst head of station in Hong Kong, and apparently remained in the organization until 1968.

SIMPSON, WALLIS. The twice-married mistress of the Prince of Wales, who was crowned King Edward VIII following the death of his father in January 1936, Wallis Simpson was an American resident in London who had lived previously in Shanghai. The Security Service was requested by Prime Minister Stanley Baldwin in 1935 to place her under physical and technical surveillance but MI5 initially demurred, concerned that the demand went beyond MI5's remit to restrict its activities to the protection of the realm. MI5's director-general was eventually persuaded that a watch should be maintained on Mrs. Simpson and it was established in June 1935 that as well as being the future king's mistress, she was also sleeping with Guy Trundle, a 36-year-old car salesman employed by the Ford Motor Company, at his home in Mayfair's Bruton Street.

Although rumors had circulated that Mrs. Simpson had been Count Ciano's mistress in China and may have been recruited as a spy for the Italians or the Nazis, no evidence of espionage was ever found by MI5 or the Metropolitan Police Special Branch. The king abdicated in December 1936 and married Mrs. Simpson in France in June 1937.

Edward, known to his family as David, had previously kept other mistresses, among them the wives of friends: Marion Coke, Freda Dudley Ward, and Thelma Furness. It was Lady Furness who first introduced the Prince of Wales to Simpson in 1931 at a party held in her London home, and then was replaced by her as his mistress in 1934. He died in 1972 and she survived him for a further 14 years.

SKRIPOV, IVAN F. A KGB First Chief Directorate officer who had spent five years in London under air attaché cover between 1953 and 1958, Ivan F. Skripov was expelled from Australia in February 1963 after he had been entrapped by the Australian Security Intelligence Organization (ASIO). In June 1959, Skripov had been sent as first secretary, accompanied by his wife and son, to reopen the Soviet embassy in Canberra, which had been closed since the defection of **Vladimir Petrov** and his wife Evdokia in 1954. Soon after the restoration of diplomatic relations, Skripov recruited a young woman, actually the wife of a serving MI5 officer who had been sent to Australia for the specific purpose of being "dangled" before the KGB officer. She pretended to be a lonely immigrant with a dull job in the passport office while the convivial Skripov, who cultivated a reputation as a gregarious figure on the diplomatic social scene, took the bait, never realizing that all his meetings were taped by a miniature recorder hidden in her purse. He entertained her at expensive restaurants, gave her small gifts and, over a period of two years, cash totaling $425. Skripov was also filmed by ASIO while he emptied dead-letter drops in Sydney's Botanical Gardens and Taronga Park Zoo, and although he never handed his agent over to an illegal, he did arrange for her to act as an intermediary or "cut-out" between himself and an illegal supposedly based in Adelaide. After a series of exercises, in which she practiced secret writing and recovered a metal canister from a dead drop in a park near Sydney Harbour Bridge, Skripov had instructed her to collect two items left in a drop at a cemetery and to deliver them to him: a single photo and a genuine Canadian passport that had been issued in September 1960 in the name of Andrew Huha. ASIO examined and photographed both before they were passed on to Skripov. Later, after the agent who was being used as bait had apparently gained his trust, Skripov produced a high-speed transmitter concealed inside a hairdryer and told her to take it to a contact who would meet her at a rendezvous in Adelaide. Unfortunately, although an elaborate trap had been prepared, Skripov's elusive illegal failed to materialize and consequently the KGB officer demanded the return of the radio. This placed ASIO in a dilemma, as it was unwilling to give back the valuable transmitter and was equally reluctant to sever the promising link between its double agent and Skripov. Eventually, ASIO was obliged to abandon the case and settle for Skripov's much-publicized formal expulsion in February 1963.

SMEDLEY, AGNES. Originally from a poor family in Missouri, Agnes Smedley committed herself to anticolonialism when she met Laipat Rai, an Indian nationalist at Columbia University in New York in March 1917. Thereafter, she was constantly in the vanguard of campaigns for radical, feminist causes and, in particular, schemes to undermine the British Empire. She was indicted on espionage charges in March 1918 after the arrest of a group of Indian nationalists who had established contact with the German government and had planned to smuggle weapons and propaganda to India. She was an active member of the Socialist Party and a regular contributor to its newspaper, the *Call*. After her release from prison, she moved to Berlin, where she continued her close association with Indian nationalists.

In November 1928, she traveled to China as a correspondent for the *Frankfurter Zeitung* and immersed herself in the Chinese revolutionary movement. In her absence, she was tried in the marathon Meerut conspiracy trial that began in March 1929 following the arrest of the leading members of the outlawed Indian Communist Party. Later the same year, she moved to Shanghai and soon afterward became the mistress of **Richard Sorge**, the famous Soviet GRU agent. She introduced Sorge to a Japanese journalist, Ozaki Hotsumi, who was translating her best-selling autobiography, *Daughter of the Earth*, and in 1941 both men were arrested in Japan on espionage charges, and executed in 1944.

Between June 1933 and April 1934, Smedley was in the Soviet Union, recovering her health and working on her journalism, but by October 1934, following a brief return to the United States, she was reporting for the *Manchester Guardian* from the Sino-Japanese front. For 18 months, she lived among the Communist guerrillas and became close to their leader, Mao Tse-Tung. In August 1940, her health failed and she was evacuated by air to Hong Kong, where she was placed under house arrest by the British authorities. After her release, she became a vocal critic of the colony's administration and in May 1941 she arrived by ship in California. Her account of the war against the Japanese, *Battle Hymn of China*, was published in 1943 and regarded as a masterpiece of war reporting, even if the political bias was strident and she omitted any reference to her lover and recruiter, Richard Sorge. In July of that year, she entered an artists' retreat, the Yaddo Foundation near Saratoga Springs, New York, but continued her political campaigning in support of the Chinese Communists.

By August 1944, Smedley had attracted the attention of the Federal Bureau of Investigation, although her political views had been well known for many years, not least because they had been noted in the report issued in 1938 by the House Committee on Un-American Activities (HCUA), chaired by Martin Dies. In March 1948, she was obliged to leave Yaddo. Early the following year, she was named as a Soviet spy by General Charles Willoughby, the former director of military intelligence in Japan who had edited a report on the Sorge case, based on the interrogation of his Japanese captors. Willoughby's allegations were given additional weight by testimony of **Hede Massing** and **Whittaker Chambers**, who both identified

Smedley as a Soviet agent, as well as the confession written for the Japanese by Richard Sorge. Smedley indignantly denied the charges but experienced considerable difficulty in obtaining a renewal of her American passport because the HCUA intended to subpoena her as a witness. Smedley settled for a travel document limiting her movement to Britain, France, and Italy. In December 1949, she arrived in London and moved in with friends she had made in Hong Kong.

In April 1950, Smedley was admitted to a hospital in Oxford for surgery on the duodenal ulcer that had been responsible for her poor health, but she died on 6 May, the day after her operation.

SMITH, EDWARD ELLIS. The first **Central Intelligence Agency** (CIA) officer to be posted under diplomatic cover to the American embassy in Moscow, Edward Ellis Smith attempted to handle **Piotr Popov**, but his agent complained that the sites he had selected for dead drops were far too dangerous. Ellis subsequently admitted to his ambassador, Chip Bohlen, that he had been compromised by Valya, a beautiful Russian maid, and he was dismissed from the CIA. According to defector **Yuri Nosenko**, Smith had been blackmailed into supplying the KGB with information. Eventually, he became an academic in San Francisco, where he died in a car accident in February 1982.

SOCIAL AGENTS. Uniquely in the Soviet bloc during the Cold War, the Czech **Statni Bezpecnost** (StB) developed a category of informants known as "social agents" who might not have had access to classified information but did maintain contact with potentially useful foreigners. This hitherto unknown category was revealed when the StB's archives were opened for public scrutiny and Margaret ("Margot") Milner was exposed as having acted as the organizer of a network of expatriates living in Prague whose task was to collect compromising information that could be used as a lever to extract the cooperation of individuals who otherwise would not contemplate entering into any kind of a relationship with the regime. Margot Milner was married to Dr. **Ian Milner**, formerly an Australian diplomat who had defected to Czechoslovakia in June 1950 after he had been incriminated by several VENONA decrypts indicating he was a long-term KGB mole.

According to the StB files, while her husband was teaching at Charles University, Margot Milner was targeting members of the foreign diplomatic community, using both men and women to cultivate vulnerable individuals. One dossier identified the wife of a British diplomat who had an affair with a suave Czech in 1959 in the hope of applying pressure on her husband, but when she confessed her infidelity the couple was withdrawn.

SOKOLOV, ALEXANDRE. Surveillance on a GRU officer attached to the United Nations in New York, Alexandre Sokolov was identified in 1963 by a defector, Kaarlo Tuuomi, as an illegal support officer. Surveillance on Tuuomi led the Federal Bureau of Investigation (FBI) to Robert K. Baltch and Joy Ann Garber, who had been living on Greenmount Avenue, Baltimore, since March 1962. Baltch taught French at a Berlitz language school and she was a hairdresser in a local beauty salon, and on the weekends they stayed at a cabin in Dulaney Valley, a forested area north of the city. Soon after the FBI operation began, the Baltches moved to 27th Street NW in Washington, D.C., where he found a job lecturing in French at George Washington University. Baltch also enrolled as a part-time student of German at the university, while his wife continued to work as a hairdresser. The FBI's surveillance of the Baltches was to last two years, during which they were spotted making contact with their GRU case officers. In May 1963, Baltch was watched while he conducted a fruitless search for a small container that had been hidden under a railway bridge in Queens by Ivan D. Egerov, a first secretary at the Soviet Delegation to the United Nations, who had served previously as a diplomat in Ottawa and New Delhi. On that occasion, the connection failed but a month later Egerov, accompanied by his wife Alexandra, succeeded in using the same site to communicate with Baltch. This particular episode seemed to prompt a change in the Baltches' behavior, for they sold their car and were seen to make preparations to move home, thus prompting the FBI to raid their apartment on 9 July. A search revealed a mass of espionage paraphernalia, including a pair of forged American passports, a Hallicrafters shortwave receiver, a wireless schedule, and a one-time cipher pad. The forged passports, in the names of James O. Jackson and Bertha R. Jackson, were entirely false, although when checked the actual details proved authentic. The genuine James Jackson, an athletics coach living in Texas, had been issued with a passport bearing the same number on the same date, and he had used it to travel across Eastern Europe in May 1961. Bertha's passport had been issued to a Harry Lee Jackson, an advertising executive from Maryland who had visited Europe in July 1961, and apparently had inadvertently provided the GRU with an opportunity to copy the contents.

From the documentary material recovered from various ingenious hiding places, the FBI were able to reconstruct some of the Baltches' background. Evidently, they had arrived separately in the States on false documentation sometime in late 1958. He then rented an apartment in New York on West 48th Street, and she lived alone at 105 Riverside Drive. In his original job application to the Berlitz branch at the Rockefeller Center, Baltch claimed that he had been born in the United States but had been brought up and educated in Canada and France. In April 1959, he married Joy Ann Garber and they moved to an address on East 139th Street, in the Mott Haven neighborhood of the Bronx. When they moved to Baltimore in March 1962, they stayed temporarily in Mount Royal Terrace while Joy Ann qualified as a cosmetologist and received a New York State certificate at that address.

While tracing the Baltches over the past three years proved a straightforward task for the 80 FBI special agents assigned to the investigation, who simply followed the paper trail left deliberately by the two illegals in New York while they had created a past for themselves, the question of their true identities was to be rather more complex. For example, the real Robert K. Baltch turned out to be a Catholic priest from Dormont, Pennsylvania, whose parents had been immigrants from Lithuania. They had returned home in 1933, having acquired American citizenship, and had taken their son and daughter with them. After the war, in March 1947, the entire family had traveled back to America where Robert had been ordained, and had even applied for a renewal of his U.S. passport. At the time the imposter was obtaining a marriage license in lower Manhattan, the real Robert Baltch was serving his congregation in Amsterdam, an industrial town in upstate New York.

As for Joy Ann Garber, she also existed, as a married woman in Norwalk, Connecticut. While it was evident how the GRU had obtained details of Robert Baltch's passport details, probably in Moscow soon after his father had applied for passports for his family at the U.S. embassy in Moscow back in 1940, the use of Joy Garber's identity was rather more unusual. In the various official papers she had signed since her arrival in the United States, the illegal masquerading as Joy Ann Garber had correctly given her birth details as 16 May 1930, in Springfield, Massachusetts. When the FBI checked the original record, it was discovered that Joy Ann's parents had been Ossip and Sonia Garber, and her father was the photographer who had been convicted with eight others in 1949 in a fraudulent passport racket in New York run by the **Communist Party of the United States of America**. He had been released from prison in 1940 and had died in 1951.

One item recovered by the FBI from Baltch's apartment was to be the key to his true identity. A name and address in France was found among his belongings, and when the French Direction de la Surveillance du Territoire (DST) eventually traced the person listed, she instantly recognized the FBI's photograph of Baltch as being that of Alexandre Sokolov, a childhood friend. Having established Baltch's true identity, his family background was relatively easy to research for Alexandre, born in Tiflis on 26 February 1918, had already earned a substantial DST dossier for his political activities in Paris. Under interrogation, "Robert K. Baltch" admitted that he was really Alexandre V. Sokolov, the eldest of four children born to Vincent, a White Russian Army officer who had been a liaison officer with the British forces in southern Russia. A skilled interpreter of Far Eastern languages, he had fled to France not long after the revolution. His unit had been disbanded on the Persian front and he had been taken aboard a British ship to Constantinople, where his wife Nadeshjda had been delivered of a second son, Igor. Vincent, who had found work in a German shipping company in Paris run by a czarist family, had died of tuberculosis in 1932, causing his children to be split up, with one of Alexandre's younger brothers, Misha, placed with a guardian in England. At the end of the war Alexandre, a committed Socialist, persuaded his mother, sister Moura, and brother Igor, who had joined the French Army and had fought with the resistance during the Nazi occupation, to return to the Soviet Union. Alexandre met his wife, Lise-Lotte, in the Soviet zone of Germany and subsequently both were recruited by the GRU as illegals. Like his brothers, he spoke French and English as well as Russian, and with his ideological zeal, which was not shared by the rest of the family, he must have been a natural for the GRU. He remained in Potsdam for a period and then had been infiltrated into America where he pretended to meet and marry Lise-Lotte, the woman who was already his wife. Further details of the Sokolov family background were added by Misha, Alexandre's brother who had moved to England and later had been educated at HMS *Conway*, and had served in the Royal Navy on HMS *Conway*. The British Security Service traced Misha without difficulty because he had worked in the Intelligence Division of the Control Commission for Germany after the war. Later, he had trained for Massey-Ferguson, the agricultural machinery manufacturer, before taking up farming. His wife, Sheila Grant Duff, whom he had married in 1952, was related to Clementine Churchill and she had headed the BBC's Czech Department. Before the war, she had traveled widely in Europe as a journalist and had written several books. When the Sokolovs were interviewed at their farm in Stowmarket, Suffolk, they were, not surprisingly, horrified to discover that Alexandre, the brother Misha had not seen since he had seen him off to the Soviet Union after the war, was a Soviet spy.

Almost immediately after the Baltchs were arrested, Ivan and Alexandra Egorov were detained at their home in Flushing, Queens, and charged with conspiracy to commit espionage. As an employee of the United Nations, Egorov was not entitled to diplomatic immunity, despite the protests of the Soviet authorities. Also named on the indictment were Alexei I. Galkin, first secretary of the Bylorussian delegation to the UN; Piotr E. Maslennikov, a first secretary at the Soviet mission; and "various others." Galkin and Maslennikov returned to Moscow in May, but when pressed by the defense lawyers, the prosecution confirmed that the "various others" included Anatoli B. Senkin, Lev V. Sosnovski, a certain Dmitri F. Polyakov, and a witness named Kaarlo Tuomi.

The State Department released the Egerovs on 12 October 1963 and swapped them for two Americans held in Soviet labor camps. In October 1964, when the trial opened against the other defendants, the government attorneys offered no evidence and the case was dismissed. Their excuse was the Brooklyn federal court's ruling that accepted the defense's inconvenient demand for the public disclosure of the addresses of every prosecution witness. The prosecution asserted that the court order would endanger Kaarlo Tuomi's life, and pretended there was no choice but to protect its witness by dropping the case. As the jubilant Baltches congratulated themselves on this surprising development, they were arrested by agents of the Immigration Service and deported, at their request, to Prague. Alexandre, the idealist who was to become disenchanted with Communism after his return to the Soviet Union, died of a heart attack on a station platform in Moscow in 1973; his widow, Lise-Lotte, continues to live and work in Nizhni Novgorod (formerly Gorky), not far from the foreign languages institute where her sister-in-law Moira teaches English and French.

SOLOMATIN, PIOTR. In 1998, the headquarters of the Sluzhba Vnezhney Razvedki (SVR) was rocked by a scandal when it emerged that the officer intended for the post of deputy *rezident* in New York, Piotr Solomatin, had been disgraced by his wife who had conducted an indiscreet affair with an SVR cipher clerk while on holiday in the Crimea. The cipher clerk had mentioned the affair to a counterintelligence officer at the *rezidentura* in New York, and the matter was reported to Moscow where Solomatin's appointment was canceled on the grounds that if the unpopular officer could not command the loyalty of his wife, he would never achieve the respect of his subordinates.

SORGE, RICHARD. A charismatic Soviet intelligence officer, Richard Sorge was born in Germany in 1895 and graduated from the University of Hamburg. Having served in the Kaiser's army during World War I, and married the wife of his economics professor at Aachen, Christiane Gerlach, Sorge moved with her to Moscow in 1924 and thereafter undertook numerous military intelligence operations for the GRU, working under his own name as a foreign correspondent for the *Frankfurter Zeitung*. However, Sorge's clandestine life and his many affairs did not suit Christiane, who divorced him and immigrated to the United States.

While in Shanghai for three years beginning in 1930, Sorge built a spy ring and exercised his considerable personal charm over **Ursula Kuczynski** and the American journalist **Agnes Smedley**, both members of his organization. Later he would return to Moscow where he moved in with the beautiful Katchka Maximova, with whom he remained until his next assignment overseas.

In September 1933, Sorge moved to Tokyo and created a large network that collected valuable information about Japanese intentions and transmitted it to Moscow. Sorge himself penetrated the local German embassy and after the outbreak of war, having gained the trust of the ambassador, was appointed the press attaché. He also acquired a pair of mistresses—Kiyomi, an exotic dancer at a notorious nightclub, the Fuji Club, and Miyake Hanako, a waitress working at the same establishment—but this led to Kiyomi denouncing her lover to the Kempe'tai. When the police went to his home, early in the morning of 18 October 1941, they waited for an hour so as to allow the unidentified owner of a vehicle with diplomatic plates to leave.

Sorge was taken into custody with some 40 other spies, and after a lengthy interrogation was hanged in November 1944, leaving Hanako to tend his grave. After the war, Kiyomi was shot dead in the street and her murder went unsolved. In Moscow, rumors circulated that at the moment of his arrest, Sorge had been in bed with Helma, the wife of his friend Eugen Ott, the German ambassador, and that under interrogation Sorge had betrayed his entire network.

SPECIAL OPERATIONS EXECUTIVE (SOE). The revelation immediately after World War II, as disclosed by the citations for posthumous gallantry awards, that large numbers of women had been engaged in secret operations behind enemy lines and had been captured and suffered execution took both the public and politicians alike by surprise. A movie made by the Royal Air Force's film unit and sponsored in 1946 by the Ministry of Information, *Now It Can Be Told* (distributed in the United States as *School for Danger*), gave a documentary account of Jacqueline Nearne's training in radio techniques, sabotage, parachuting, and unarmed combat, and confirmed that large numbers of women had been infiltrated into Nazi-occupied France to undertake secret missions.

In 1958, Jean Overton Fuller wrote *Double Webs*, raising serious questions about SOE's integrity. Having been the executor of the will left by her friend Noor Inayat Khan (codenamed MADELEINE), she had researched her biography. Her investigations took her to Germany, where she met many of SOE's wartime adversaries, and unearthed the appalling truth that an SOE Air Movements officer, Henri Dericourt, had worked as a double agent for the Sicherheitsdienst. Because he was still alive and had been convicted of no serious crime, she could only refer to him by his SOE nom de guerre, GILBERT. Miss Fuller's discovery, combined with the severe criticisms of the way SOE had recruited and run seven women agents who had been betrayed to the Nazis made by Elizabeth Nicholas in *Death Be Not Proud*, caused questions to be tabled in the Commons.

The admission that some of them had suffered appalling privations while in enemy hands, and that a substantial proportion had failed to return, led a Member of Parliament, the redoubtable Dame Irene Ward, to campaign for a proper accounting of what had happened to them.

That the fairer sex should have been employed in a clandestine role by a covert arm of the British government provoked considerable attention, in part because the universal revulsion surrounding the execution of **Edith Cavell** by the Germans in World War I had led to what amounted to a policy decision by the Secret Intelligence Service (SIS) to avoid hiring women as agents. Nurse Cavell's death in October 1915, following a trial at which she had been found guilty of assisting Allied evaders reach neutral Holland, proved to be a propaganda disaster for the Kaiser, but the episode had prompted a debate about the wisdom of deliberately placing women in jeopardy. Of course, foreigners recruited overseas as members of existing networks, such as the railway-watching organizations monitoring enemy movements in France and Belgium, often included women, but as a rule no British women were put at risk. The predictable reaction to what was perceived, and exploited, as typical brutality of the Hun was a reluctance, at least on the part of the British, to engage women in anything other than support duties, and certainly not in the field. In the interwar period, SIS promoted a handful of women, Rita Winsor among them, to officer rank and deployed them overseas. In her case, Winsor worked at the Geneva station before spending the remainder of hostilities in Lisbon, proving herself to be a remarkably gifted intelligence officer, and played a key role in the defection and exfiltration of Otto John. However, she was an unusual exception; as an organization, however, SIS was dependent on a large secretarial staff.

Special Operations Executive, in contrast to SIS, decided at the outset to send women into hostile territory, and accordingly the most unfeminine courses were developed to provide them with the attributes they would need to survive in Axis-held Europe. Of the various country sections responsible for running agents in the field, only F and RF Sections actively recruited, trained, and dispatched women from Great Britain, as opposed to the other units that opportunistically adopted self-recruited volunteers or personnel acquired by active networks. Of the better-known examples, RF Section dropped Alix d'Unienville into France in 1944, and N Section parachuted Jos Gemmeke into her native Holland in March 1945. In SOE's Middle East theater, centered in Palestine, Hannah Sanash, aged 23, was executed in Budapest in October 1944, having been arrested as she attempted to cross into Hungary, and Lela Karyanni was arrested in Greece in March 1944 and executed in September.

F Section's women were vetted by Vera Atkins, a Women's Auxiliary Air Force squadron officer recruited in March 1941. By the end of hostilities, 52 agents had been sent by her to France. Determined to learn of the fate of the 12 who failed to return, Atkins took it upon herself to research what had happened to the 17 who had been arrested, and she compiled the harrowing statistics that 12 had suffered death at the hand of their captors, often after extended periods of dreadful maltreatment.

The public acknowledgment that so many brave women had perished proved controversial and led to the government's decision in December 1958 to commission an official history into SOE's activities in France from Professor M. R. D. Foot, and this was released in April 1966, a testament to the memory of 12 brave agents who gave their lives to liberate Europe.

The first two F Section women agents in France, both of whom had official permission to be in the Vichy zone, were Giliana Balmaceda, a Chilean actress, and Virginia Hall, an American journalist with a wooden leg working for the *New York Post*, who ran a safe house in Lyons. The first woman agent to be infiltrated into France was 45-year-old Yvonne Rudelatt, who adopted the field name JACQUELINE. Separated from her Italian husband, in civilian life JACQUELINE had been a receptionist in a West End hotel, but in July 1942 she was put ashore in the south of France from a felucca and went to work as a courier for the PHYSICIAN network. She operated successfully for a year, participating in the sabotage of a power station at Chaigny and the railway goods yard in Le Mans in March 1944. She was arrested in June 1943 while waiting for an air drop.

Although Balmaceda survived the war and Hall would later join the **Central Intelligence Agency**, Rudelatt died of typhus at Belsen just after the concentration camp had been liberated on 15 April 1945.

SQUILLACOTTE, THERESE. Aged 39, Theresa Squillacotte was a retired Defense Department analyst when she was arrested in October 1997 and charged with having engaged in espionage for the East Germans for the previous decade and a half. According to files recovered from the Hauptverwaltung Aufkrarung (HVA) archive in Berlin, she had been recruited in 1981 in Wisconsin by her husband Kurt Stand, whom she had married the previous year. Stand, the son of a German immigrant, had been an HVA spy since 1972, when, at the age of 18, he had adopted left-wing politics and had been approached by the HVA while on a visit to East Germany.

The Federal Bureau of Investigation (FBI) began a search for the HVA spies codenamed JACK and JUNIOR in 1996, following access to the ROSEWOOD files, the key to the encrypted HVA agent dossiers recovered by the **Central Intelligence Agency** from a former KGB officer who had been trusted with the material when the German Democratic Republic collapsed in 1989. The FBI eventually closed in on James Clark and Karl Stand. Both men had met Squillacotte while students at the University of Wisconsin, and Clark later became a paralegal for the U.S. Army, having been recruited as a source by Stand in 1976. Always a political activist, he passed Stand documents he obtained from friends in the State Department but in 1996 joined a private security company. Meanwhile, Squillacotte bore her husband two children, Karl and Rosa, took a law degree, and after working for the House Armed Services Committee, accepted a post at the Pentagon.

Surveillance on the trio revealed incriminating evidence, including an offer by Squillacotte in August 1996 to supply information to Ronnie Kasirilis, a former Communist Party of South Africa leader and then minister of defense in Pretoria. With South African approval, an undercover FBI special agent operating under a false flag, whom Squillacotte believed to be a South African intelligence agent, contacted her and recorded numerous compromising conversations in New York. In January 1999, she was sentenced to 22 years' imprisonment while her husband received 17 years and Clark, who testified against them, was imprisoned for 12 years. Under interrogation, Clark was revealed to have been JACK, who had received $17,500 for photographs of classified documents he had mailed to a cover address in Germany. He also identified his HVA handler as Lothar Ziemer and his evidence ensured the conviction of Squillacotte and Stand.

STAHL, LYDIA. Born Lydia Chkalov in Rostov in 1885, Lydia's husband was an aristocrat who lost his estates in the Crimea in the Russian revolution, prompting the couple to immigrate to the United States with their child. Following the death of her son in 1918 and having acquired an American passport, Lydia moved to Paris, where she was recruited by the Soviets and, under their sponsorship, opened a photographic studio that was used to copy secret documents. She took as her lover Professor Louis Pierre Martin, a Latvian émigré working for the French Naval Ministry, and often traveled to Berlin as a courier to deliver secret documents concealed in a belt. She remained active until 1928 when she was ordered back to New York. In 1933, she returned to Paris, her role in the United States having been taken by a husband-and-wife team, Robert and **Marjorie Switz**.

In December 1933, Lydia was arrested by the Sureté, having been identified as a Soviet spy by Ingrid Bostrom, one of her closest friends who had been charged with espionage in Helsinki. During her interrogation, Bostrom implicated Lydia, who was placed under surveillance that revealed her relationship with Professor Martin, and exposed her links to a wider spy ring headed by Robert and Marjorie Switz. Altogether, 29 Soviet agents were detained, and a further 200 suspects were investigated. Under interrogation, Robert Switz and five others made full confessions, but Lydia refused to make any admissions; at her trial in 1935, she was sentenced to five years' imprisonment, reduced on appeal to four.

STASHINSKY, BOGDAN. The defection of Bogdan Stashinsky in 1961 was prompted not by his revulsion of his murder of the Ukrainian politician Stefan Bandera, whom he killed with an ingenious cyanide gas gun in October 1959, but by his love for Inge Pohl, a young German hairdresser who had married him and later persuaded him to surrender to Federal authorities. Originally a KGB informer around Lvov, where he had been brought up, Stashinsky had operated as a low-level penetration agent targeted against local nationalists, and in particular the Organization of Ukrainian Nationalists (OUN) resistance movement. His cover survived until early in 1952 when the murderers of Ukrainian writer Yaroslav Galan were arrested on his tip. Regarded as a traitor by the nationalists, Galan had been assassinated by members of the Narodnyi Trudovoi Soyuz (NTS) cell Stashinsky had cultivated, which effectively terminated his future in Lvov.

As a consequence of the Galan murder, Stashinsky had been sent to Kiev to learn German, and subsequently had been sent to Karlshorst for training as an illegal. There he adopted the authentic identity of Josef Lehrmann, a German born in Lukowek, Poland, and until January 1956, when he was entrusted with minor tasks in the West, such as mailing letters, he built up his legend as a metalworker in Zwickau. On his first assignment, he traveled to Munich to service a KGB mole, an émigré journalist on the Ukrainian anti-Communist paper *Ukrainski Samostinik*. He held four further meetings with the agent, supplying him with money and messages from his wife who was still in the Ukraine, until the strain became too much for the agent and he was repatriated in the late autumn of 1956. Stashinsky replaced this source by recruiting another on the same newspaper, using a combination of bribery and blackmail, for the agent both received cash for his information and was left in no doubt that his wife and family in the Ukraine were vulnerable to reprisals.

In the spring of 1957 Stashinsky was given a new identity, that of Siegfried Drager, from Rehbrucke near Potsdam, and armed with his authentic identity card, was sent to Munich to watch Lev Rebet, the exiled Ukrainian nationalist leader. Stashinsky kept his quarry under almost continuous surveillance from April until 12 October when, armed with a specially designed weapon, he encountered Rebet outside his apartment and sprayed prussic acid into his face. By the time

Stashinsky had returned to Karlshorst, his victim's body had been found and the cause of death declared to be a heart attack.

While preparing for his second assassination, that of the NTS leader Stefan Bandera, and under the influence of his German fiancé, Stashinsky had begun to lose his commitment to the cause but nevertheless he fired a second, double-barreled gas gun directly into Bandera's face outside his home in Munich on 15 October 1959. Like Rebet, Bandera inhaled a lethal dose of prussic acid and died. Once again, Stashinsky returned by train and air to Karlshorst and reported the success of the operation to his KGB handler. The following month he was summoned to Moscow where he was decorated with the Order of the Red Banner by Aleksandr N. Shelepin, the chairman of the KGB. He was also granted permission to marry Inge Pohl, which he did in Berlin in April 1960. Their baby son was born a year later but died in August, prompting Inge and Bogdan to evade their KGB escort and, on the day before the wall was erected, flee to West Berlin where they surrendered to the German authorities. At his subsequent trial at Karlsruhe in October 1962, Stashinsky confessed to the murders of Rebet and Bandera, and received a sentence of eight years' imprisonment, but he was released after less than four and resettled in South Africa.

STATNI BEZPECNOST. At the end of the Cold War, the Czech Statni Bezpecnost (StB) was restructured, and Western intelligence agencies were invited to advise the new organization. During a review of the StB's archives, a Canadian Security Intelligence Service (CSIS) officer of Czech parentage discovered the file of a clerk in the Canadian diplomatic service who had been compromised in a **honeytrap** more than 20 years earlier and had supplied information to the StB. When interviewed, the man, who had long since retired from the Department of External Affairs, gave a slightly different account of what had happened, but no further action was taken and he moved to England. *See also* SOCIAL AGENTS.

STEIN, LILY. In June 1939, Willam H. Sebold, a 40-year-old married engineer working for the Consolidated Aircraft Corporation in San Diego, returned from a visit to his family in his native Germany, his first for fifteen years, and revealed to the Federal Bureau of Investigation (FBI) that he had been approached to spy for the Nazis. He had succumbed to an implied threat from officials purporting to be from the Gestapo and, for the sake of his mother, two brothers, and a sister in Mülheim, Sebold reluctantly had agreed to be signed on by the Hamburg Abstelle in June 1939 with the codename TRAMP. However, dismayed by this episode, which occurred so soon after he had disembarked from the SS *Deutschland*, and the theft of his passport, Sebold had alerted the American consulate in Cologne of his predicament, and had been advised by the vice consul, Dale W. Maher, to pretend to cooperate with the Nazis.

Once safely back in the United States in February 1941, aboard the SS *Washington* from Genoa, and traveling on a new passport, Sebold made a detailed statement to the FBI and identified one of the German spies he had been instructed to contact. She was Lily Stein, an Austrian model of Jewish descent, of East 54th Street, Manhattan, and formerly the mistress of an American consul in Vienna, Ogden Hammond Jr., whose father was the ambassador in Madrid. She had been recruited in Germany under duress after she had fled from Vienna during the Anschluss in 1938 and was unenthusiastic about the mission for which she had been trained in Hamburg, but she was short of money; the apartment to which she had moved, on East 79th Street, acted as a postbox for other members of the Abwehr's organization in the United States.

Another key figure in the spy ring was Frederick Duquesne and his mistress, Evelyn Lewis, who was a sculptress from a wealthy Southern family, at West 76th Street. Calling themselves "Mr. and Mrs. James Dunn," Duquesne had also volunteered his services to the Abwehr as a professional spy. His offer had been accepted and he had established himself in a small, one-room office at 120 Wall Street operating under the name Air Terminal Associates. It was here that he received Sebold, two days after the *Washington* had docked, and took delivery of his microfilmed questionnaire, which had been read and copied already by the FBI.

Duquesne was an extraordinarily colorful character whose career bordered on the bizarre. Among his many extravagant assertions was his claim that he had once been young Winston Churchill's jailer, and had witnessed British troops maltreat his mother and sister during the

Boer War. Originally from the Cape Colony in South Africa, where allegedly he had spied against the British, Duquesne claimed in a sensational book published in New York in February 1932, *The Man Who Killed Kitchener: The Life of Fritz Joubert Duquesne 1891*, written by a journalist, Clement Wood, that he had been responsible for the loss of the cruiser HMS *Hampshire* in the North Sea in June 1916, while carrying the field marshal to Petrograd. Although the British Admiralty had always believed that the cruiser had hit a mine, Wood reported that Duquesne had slipped aboard, disguised as a Russian officer, to signal a U-boat waiting to torpedo her, and then had made his escape before she sank.

The FBI's lengthy case ended after two years of surveillance in April 1941 with arrests and prison sentences totaling 300 years, and fines of $18,000. Duquesne received the longest sentence, of 18 years, while his mistress, Evelyn Lewis, received a year and a day, and Lily Stein received 10 years. One of Stein's friends and also a member of Duquesne's ring, Else Weustenfeld, worked as a secretary in the German consulate's legal branch on Battery Place, and she was sentenced to five years' imprisonment. A middle-aged divorcée born in Essen who had been a naturalized citizen for the past 15 years, she had been implicated by Sebold, and it turned out that she was living in New York with the brother of Major Nikolaus Ritter, a senior Abwehr officer who had recruited Sebold in Hamburg. Ritter's textile business in America had collapsed in the Depression, so after 10 years in the United States he had returned to Germany, where he had followed a new career as an intelligence officer with excellent English and a skill for talent-spotting suitable agents. On the pretext that Weustenfeld had contaminated the consular offices, President Franklin D. Roosevelt announced that all German consulates would have to close.

STIEBER, WILHELM. The famous Prussian spymaster of the 1860s allegedly established the Green House in Berlin to entrap the unwary and blackmail them into supplying him with information. The brothel was staffed by beautiful women and Stieber's victims invariably succumbed to his demands. He was so successful that he was invited by the Chinese to advise them on establishing a similar venture, the Hall of Pleasurable Delights, in Hankow in 1867.

STILLER, WERNER. In January 1979, Senior Lieutenant Werner Stiller, then in the Hauptverwaltung Aufkrarung's (HVA) Scientific and Technological Department, defected to West Berlin via the Friedrichstrasse station. An expert on nuclear and chemical technology, he was a physics graduate and as soon as he was debriefed by the Bundesnachrichtendienst (BND), with whom he had been in contact during the previous year, he identified the 22 HVA and KGB sources he knew of in the West, including Rolf Dobbertin in Paris, Johannes Koppe in Hamburg, Reine Fuller of the National Research Center at Karlsruhe, Arnulf Raufeisen in Hanover, and Professor Karl Hauffe of Göttingen University.

Brought up as one of three children near Leipzig, Stiller joined the Young Pioneers while still at school and remained an activist when he started to study physics, aged 19, at the city's Karl Marx University in August 1966. While in his final year, Stiller was approached by the Ministry of State Security and invited to undergo training as an agent in the Federal Republic of Germany (FRG). In December 1970, he was sworn into the organization and assigned the task of reporting on various acquaintances, and continued to maintain contact with the HVA's Science and Technology Directorate after his graduation and appointment to a post in the Physics Society in Berlin. Stiller attended the HVA's training school at Belzig and after completing the course concentrated on recruitment and running agents in the scientific community. In February 1976, he was promoted to first lieutenant and soon afterward established contact with the BND. A method of communicating was agreed and continued for two years until he underwent an emotional crisis resulting from his affair with Helga, a dissident living in Oberhof.

Motivated by his love for Helga, a waitress with a brother in the West, who had acted as an intermediary with the BND, Stiller was in an unhappy marriage and wanted to be resettled in the FRG. He also provided 20,000 HVA documents. In January 1979, he engineered the escape to the West of Helga and her son, and he then caught a train into West Berlin. At Tegel airport, he identified himself as a defector to the police and he was passed on to the BND. He was given a death sentence in absentia from the German Democratic Republic. Following a divorce from his wife, he married Helga and now lives in the

United States. His autobiography, *Beyond the Wall*, was published in Germany in 1986.

STOEBE, ILSE. The prewar mistress of Rudolf Herrnstadt, a well-known *Berliner Tageblatt* journalist who defected to Moscow in 1933, Ilse Stoebe had been a correspondent for several Swiss newspapers until World War II, when she went to work for a senior German Foreign Ministry official, Theodor Wolff. However, in November 1942 an Abwehr cryptographer, Dr. Wilhelm Vauck, succeeded in retrospectively decrypting about 200 Soviet GRU wireless messages, and one of them referred to a woman named Ilse at an address in Berlin, Saalestrasse 36, which was Stoebe's home. Another signal, dated 28 August 1941, stated, "An important agent known as Ilse will in the future be designated under the covername ALTE."

This appalling lapse of security led the Gestapo straight to Stoebe who, under interrogation, admitted that she had remained in contact with Hernnstadt, who had become a senior GRU officer and had organized parachutists for missions into Nazi Germany. She also acknowledged that her apartment had been used as a safe house for some of the Soviet agents. Before she was executed on 22 December 1942, she had implicated the three most important members of the Rote Kapelle, Harro Schulze-Boysen of the Air Ministry, university lecturer Arvid von Harnack, and a Foreign Ministry official, Rudolf von Sheliha. All were arrested and interrogated, and up to 80 members of their network were subsequently executed.

A lengthy Reichsicherhauptamt investigation into the Rote Kapelle concluded that the three ringleaders betrayed by Ilse Stoebe had only become active as spies after the Soviet Trade Delegation, the GRU's main cover in Berlin, had been withdrawn in June 1941. The GRU *rezident*, Alexander Erdberg, had provided the network with a radio before he left for Moscow, but they had failed to make contact. Instead, another transmitter had been delivered in August 1941 by a GRU agent, Viktor Guryevitch, but when that channel failed, the spy ring had been forced to communicate by passing messages to the Soviet embassy in Stockholm, and occasionally sending material to Johann Wenzel, a German Communist engineer living illegally in Brussels. Wenzel had been caught while transmitting in the attic of a villa in Laeken by a German radio direction-finding team on 30 July 1942, and a search of the house had revealed copies of many of his past messages, enabling Vauck and his colleagues to solve the GRU's cipher and read some of the back traffic, thus compromising Ilse Stoebe.

STONEHOUSE, JOHN. Elected the Labour Member of Parliament for Wednesbury at a by-election in February 1957 and appointed a junior aviation minister in 1964, rising to postmaster-general in 1968 and then minister for posts and telecommunications in 1969, John Stonehouse was identified by a **Statni Bezpecnost** (StB) defector, Josef Frolik, as a Czech spy who had been recruited in February 1960, after he had been ensnared in a **homosexual honeytrap** in Prague. When confronted with the allegations by MI5's Charles Elwell, in the presence of Prime Minister Harold Wilson at 10 Downing Street, Stonehouse denied having done anything aside from lunching with Robert Husak, whom he claimed to have known only as a Czech diplomat, and claimed to have submitted an official report of the encounter.

Codenamed KOLON and then TWISTER by the StB, Stonehouse faked his own death in Florida in November 1974 when overwhelmed by debt and the failure of his Bangladeshi bank. He had checked into the Fontainebleau Hotel in Miami and left his clothes on the beach, suggesting he had disappeared while swimming, and then had switched to his alternative identity at another hotel nearby before leaving the country. He was discovered in Australia living under the aliases Donald Muldoon and Joseph Muldoon, the names of two of his deceased constituents.

The only person who knew of his deception was his mistress and former secretary, Sheila Buckley, who was almost 20 years younger than he. However, by the time she had flown to Melbourne to join him, he had been arrested by New South Wales police who suspected he might be the fugitive peer Lord Lucan. There, they were joined by Stonehouse's wife Barbara, to whom he had been married for the past 26 years, and the beneficiary of his life insurance policy.

Six months after his arrest, Stonehouse was returned to Great Britain to face trial for theft, fraud, and deception, and he was convicted in August 1976 and sentenced to seven years' imprisonment.

He then resigned his seat in the Commons, and at the same trial Buckley received two years' suspended for having participated in his frauds. He served only three years, and died while making an appearance on live television in 1988, aged 63, having written his autobiography, *Death of an Idealist*, in 1975.

STOOL PIGEONS. During World War II, the Germans employed women to persuade Allied prisoners of war (POWs) to act as stool pigeons and inform on their fellow soldiers. One in particular, John White, confined at Lamsdorff after being captured at Dunkirk in 1940, made a detailed statement to investigators at the end of hostilities and described how in his isolation he had succumbed to the charms of a girl provided for him by the camp's intelligence officer, who had then threatened him with execution for fraternizing with the local population unless he cooperated. White agreed to supply information about the other prisoners, and so did two Canadians, John Galaher and Edwin Martin, both captured at Dieppe in 1942. All three were prosecuted and convicted of collaboration. White was sentenced to 10 years' imprisonment, Galaher to life, and Martin to 25 years.

STRAIGHT, MICHAEL. A self-confessed Soviet spy before and during World War II, Michael Straight came from a wealthy background and in 1961 admitted to the Federal Bureau of Investigation that he had been recruited as a spy at Cambridge University. This news was eventually imparted to MI5's Arthur Martin in March 1964, following the latter's interview with Cambridge spy John Cairncross, who was then living in Cleveland, Ohio. Straight admitted that he had been recruited as a Soviet spy by his lover at Cambridge, **Anthony Blunt**, and revealed that he had remained in touch with the Soviets after he had returned to Washington, D.C., to take up a post in the State Department.

The son of a prominent American family, Michael Straight was educated in England at Dartington Hall, the London School of Economics, and at Cambridge where he studied under John Maynard Keynes. Among his circle of friends at the university were Tess Mayor, later to marry Victor Rothschild; **Guy Burgess**; James Klugmann; and Anthony Blunt. He became a member of the Communist

Party and the elite Apostles but after the death of John Cornford in the Spanish Civil War he was drawn into clandestine activity, "a world of shadows and echoes," by Blunt who instructed him to abandon the Party and break off contact with those on the left.

Having graduated from Cambridge, Straight returned to America and joined the State Department as an unpaid volunteer in the Office of the Economic Adviser. Soon afterward, in April 1938, he was approached by a mysterious stranger with a European accent whom he referred to as "Michael Green" who suggested that "when interesting documents crossed my desk, I should take them home 'to study.'" In fact Straight recognized Green "as a cog in the Soviet machine" and continued to meet him secretly in Washington and give him State Department documents to copy. The liaison persisted when Straight moved to a post in the Department of the Interior although nothing he had passed "had contained any restricted material" so Green encouraged him to return to the State Department. Instead, in 1940, Straight went to work for *New Republic*, the weekly journal founded by his parents, and wrote *Make This the Last War*, which was published in January 1943, two months after he had joined the U.S. Army Air Reserve. Straight was trained as a bomber pilot and became a flight instructor but, because of heart problems, never flew in combat.

After the war, Straight returned to radical politics as editor of *New Republic*, and published articles by various individuals investigated by Senator Joseph McCarthy, but it was not until he was offered a federal post in Kennedy's administration in 1963 that he revealed to the FBI what he knew about British Communists. His statement led to an interview with MI5. On his evidence, Anthony Blunt was confronted with the charge that he had recruited Straight as a Soviet agent. The knowledge that Straight had identified him proved enough for Blunt to confess to his lifetime of espionage. Five months later, the two men met again but there were no recriminations, for they were both to act as informers for the next decade or so, denouncing their former friends to the authorities. As he recalled in his autobiography, *After Long Silence*, published in 1983, Straight simply accepted his new role.

> In his autobiography *Witness*, Whittaker Chambers describes the anguish he suffered when he became an informer against the Soviet agents who had been his accomplices and friends. He found his justifi-

cation in the conviction that he was acting as an instrument of The Almighty in a titanic struggle between communism and Christianity. I do not picture myself in any such grandiose role. I believed simply that the acceptance of individual responsibility is the price we must all pay for living in a free society.

Straight identified his contacts as his former brother-in-law, Michael Greenberg, who had been mentioned by the NKVD defector **Elizabeth Bentley**, and one other, later confirmed as Iskhak Akhmerov, the NKVD illegal *rezident* in the United States. Codenamed NIGEL by the NKVD, Straight died in January 2004.

STREATER, ISABEL. A young English teacher living with her parents in Istanbul, Isabel Streater fell in love with one of her students, Georges Agabekov, who turned out to be a Soviet intelligence officer based in Turkey. He defected to Paris in 1930, where the following year he published his memoirs, *OGPU: The Russian Secret Terror*. His true name was Arutyanov but he adopted the new identity when he was assigned to Istanbul (then Constantinople) as the illegal *rezident*, a task he had fulfilled previously in Tehran. After they were married, Agabekov and Isabel settled in Brussels, but in July 1937, he was lured to the Franco-Spanish frontier in a scheme involving smuggled works of art looted during the Spanish Civil War. He was never seen again and it is presumed that he was assassinated by the NKVD. His wife returned to England and died in New York in November 1971 while working for the British mission to the United Nations.

STREFFER, IGON. In 1969, Igon Streffer, a senior civil servant in the Federal German Ministry of Defense, was persuaded by his **homosexual** lover, Dieter Poppe, to pass him classified information. Poppe was a long-term Hauptverwaltung Aufkrarung (HVA) agent who remained active after Streffer died in 1989, aged 43, but he was betrayed in 1990 by an HVA defector, Colonel Heinz Busch, and sentenced in December 1991 to six years' imprisonment.

SUHARTO, PRESIDENT. The president of Indonesia from 1967 to 1998, Suharto came from a farming family in central Java before joining the army and commanding a battalion of Japanese-backed troops during the World War II occupation. He participated in the suppression of a Communist coup in 1966 but a year later seized power from President Sukarno. Born in June 1921, Suharto established an authoritarian regime, the New Order, and ruled with an iron grip, oppressing all Communist opposition, until he resigned following mass demonstrations in Djakarta.

Part of his anti-Communism may be explained by a heavy-handed attempt to blackmail him while on a visit to Moscow. He was shown a movie of himself cavorting in bed with a pair of KGB **swallows**, but, according to stories circulating at the time, far from being dismayed or intimidated by the film, he is alleged to have remarked, "My people will be so proud of me!" He had invited some of the air hostesses on his Soviet plane to visit him at his Moscow hotel, and the resulting orgy had been recorded by cameras concealed behind a two-way mirror. Suharto died in January 2008.

SUKHOMLINOV, VLADIMIR. The wife of the Czar Nicholas II's minister for war appointed in 1909, General Vladimir Sukhomlinov, proved to be the source of Russian military information passed to a German spy, Colonel Sergei Myaoedev, who was hanged in March 1915 having been convicted of espionage. Allegedly his lover's role in the scandal was hushed up so as to avoid embarrassment to the imperial court, but Sukhomlinov was replaced in June 1915 by General Alexei Polivanov, who proved more competent. In May 1918, Sukhomlinov went into exile in Finland, published his memoirs in 1924, and died in Berlin in February 1926, aged 77.

SUMMERSBY, KAY. The British driver assigned to General Dwight D. Eisenhower when he arrived at Prestwick in Scotland in May 1942, Kay Summersby was a young Irish redhead who became his mistress and constant companion. Formerly a movie actress and Worth of Paris model, born Kathleen McCarthy-Morrogh in County Cork, she had married Gordon Summersby in 1939 before starting an affair with an American Corps of Engineers officer, Dick Arnold. Having volunteered to drive an ambulance in Lambeth during the Blitz, she was assigned by the Auxiliary Transport Corps to a group of chauffeurs for the American embassy in Grosvenor Square.

There was a widespread belief among those Americans who knew of the affair that she exercised influence over many of his decisions, perhaps even his unexpected selection of General Kenneth Strong as his chief intelligence officer. Eisenhower's relationship with Summersby remained a closely guarded secret, although she was constantly photographed with the Supreme Allied Commander, much to his wife's irritation. Mamie Eisenhower remained in the United States throughout the war and saw him only twice during his brief visits home. Meanwhile, Summersby spent increasing amounts of time with Ike in his suite in the Dorchester Hotel and then at Hay's Lodge, his house off Berkeley Square. To those who were dismayed by her attendance at top-level staff meetings, Eisenhower would remark, "We have no secrets from Kay," and a journalist once remarked that he had never before seen a chauffeusse kiss her general each morning.

The vivacious Kay Summersby was commissioned into the U.S. Women's Auxiliary Army Corps as a lieutenant, although she was not an American citizen, and later served as one of Eisenhower's secretaries. In her memoirs, *Past Forgetting: My Love Affair with Dwight D. Eisenhower*, published posthumously in 1976, she recalled that when they shared Telegraph Cottage, on the edge of his headquarters in Bushey Park, "his kisses absolutely unraveled me"; although their affair was passionate, it apparently was unconsummated. After her American fiancé was killed by a land mine in Tunisia, Summersby accompanied Eisenhower on his overseas visits to Algiers and Cairo, and was at his side when he lunched with Churchill and met King George VI. She also drove him across France in his armored Cadillac and was present in Rheims when General Alfred Jodl signed the surrender. In March 1945, she went to a London restaurant in London with Ike, his first such public appearance since July 1942, and was seen later in his box at the theater when the audience cheered him and asked him to make a speech.

By the time Summersby moved to the United States in October 1945 to take out American citizenship, the relationship had cooled. She broke off an engagement in New York in 1947, published *Eisenhower Was My Boss* in 1948, and married a stockbroker, Reginald Morgan, in 1952. Harry Truman revealed in his autobiography *Plain Speaking* that Eisenhower had considered divorcing his wife to marry Kay, and this so infuriated Mamie that she instructed her son John to release *Letters to Mamie* in 1978 to demonstrate that her husband had been in constant contact by letter throughout his absence.

SUSCHITSKY, EDITH. Born in Vienna in 1908 to William Suschitsky, a radical Socialist who advocated birth control and sex education and owned a bookshop in the working-class district of Petzvalgasse, Edith trained as a Montessori kindergarten teacher and in 1925 traveled to England to work as a teacher. Two years later she was back in Vienna and studied photography under Walter Peterhans at the Bauhaus in Dessau. In 1933, at the height of the political turmoil in Vienna, she married Dr. Alex Tudor Hart, a left-wing medical practitioner at the British consulate, and moved to Brixton in south London, and then to the Rhondda Valley. As well as an active member of the banned Austrian Communist Party, she was also a Soviet illegal who had completed two undercover missions, to Paris and London, in 1929, and she was activated in London by the *rezident*, **Arnold Deutsch**, soon after his arrival in 1934.

Upon their return from South Wales, Alex Tudor Hart joined the Republican forces in Spain as a surgeon, while his wife opened a studio in Acre Lane in south London and began to specialize, after the birth of her son in 1936, in child portraits. It was during this period, while active in the Workers Camera Club, contributing to *Picture Post*, and organizing the Artists against Fascism and War exhibition that she maintained contact with her friend from Vienna, **Litzi Friedman**, who was by then separated from **Kim Philby**, and liaised closely with Bob Stuart of the **Communist Party of Great Britain** (CPGB), who was himself acting as a clandestine link between the CPGB headquarters and the Soviet embassy. In March 1938, having divorced Alex after his return from Spain, a Leica camera originally purchased by her was discovered in a police raid on the home of Percy Glading, who was subsequently convicted of organizing the Woolwich Arsenal spy ring, but when questioned by Special Branch detectives she simply denied any involvement. At that moment MI5 had no reason to be suspicious of her and was unaware that as a talent-spotter in June 1934 she had cultivated Kim Philby and introduced him to Deutsch for recruitment.

After the war Edith worked as a commercial photographer and briefly for the Ministry of Education, but her mental condition deteriorated and she suffered a breakdown, her son already having been institutionalized. She later opened a small antiques shop in Brighton, and died of liver cancer in 1973.

SUTTERLIN, HEINZ. A KGB illegal codenamed WALTER, Heinz Sutterlin cultivated and then in December 1960 married 30-year-old Leonore Heinz, a secretary in the Federal Republic's Foreign Ministry. Sutterlin, who had been recruited by the KGB in Freiburg in 1957, had been guided to her by a spy in the Foreign Ministry's Personnel Department, **Gisela Herzog**. Under her husband's influence, and codenamed LOLA, Leonore provided the KGB with a wealth of classified data from her office, for which he was paid 1,000 Deutsche marks a month, although initially he deliberately did not identify the organization "working for peace" who received her material. The couple was betrayed finally in 1957 by a KGB defector, **Evgenni Runge**. Sutterlin was arrested by the German authorities, but his wife, filled with remorse, hanged herself in her prison cell.

SWALLOW. The term applied to women used by the KGB to seduce Western men in an effort to compromise them in a **honeytrap**. Among their victims were the French Ambassador **Maurice Dejean** and the British Ambassador Sir **Geoffrey Harrison**.

SWITZ, MARJORIE. Aged just 19 when she married Robert G. Switz, a salesman for MacNeill Instruments from East Orange, New Jersey, Marjorie Tiley quickly became an important Soviet spy who underwent a Moscow training course in photography in 1931 to serve a spy ring operating in the Canal Zone in Panama. In July 1933, Robert and Marjorie moved from Greenwich Village, New York, to Paris but they were compromised when they were spotted meeting an NKVD agent named Markovich who himself had been placed under surveillance by the Sureté after he had been implicated by **Lydia Stahl**. When the police came to arrest the Switzes in December 1933, Marjorie casually lit a cigarette containing miniaturized photographs of secret documents removed from the French Ministry of War by Colonel Octave Dumoulin, the editor of a technical military journal, *Armée et Démocratie*. Although initially they denied any involvement with espionage, when the Switzes were confronted with damning evidence linking them to other secret French War Ministry documents they both confessed, claiming to have become disillusioned with Communism.

The day after they made their statement, Dumoulin was arrested, together with a chemical engineer and poison gas expert named

Aubry and Vatroslav Reich, also employed in a secret French germ warfare research laboratory. Codenamed AVIATOR, Robert Switz named a businessman, Benjamin Burkowitz, and his wife as coconspirators, and incriminated a schoolteacher, Madeleine Mermet, as his radio operator and photographer. All were arrested, and Aubry, Reich, and Mermet made confessions. At their trial in 1935, Dumoulin and Berkoitz were sentenced to five years' imprisonment, and Mermet to three, while the Switzes were freed and went into hiding in Salzburg before returning to the United States in 1938, where Robert died in 1951. A further 10 named defendants were also convicted in absentia and received five-year sentences.

SYMONDS, JOHN. Detective Sergeant John Symonds of the Metropolitan Police's Criminal Investigation Department left England in 1972 to start a new life as a mercenary in Africa. A former army officer, he had been charged with corruptly receiving £150, and when two colleagues were given lengthy prison sentences for similar offenses, on equally dubious evidence, he went abroad and prepared a dossier on police corruption that caught the attention of the KGB *rezident* in Tangier, who tried to interest him in assassinating a recent defector, **Oleg Lyalin**. His affair with a German woman while on holiday in Bulgaria led to his recruitment by the KGB to undertake a mission that involved Gunter Guillaume, the spy inside Chancellor Willi Brandt's private office. Later he was given sex training in Moscow as a **Romeo spy** and sent to India by Oleg Kalugin to seduce the wives of certain **Central Intelligence Agency** officers, but when his girlfriend in Bulgaria was persecuted by the secret police he abandoned his assignment to protect her. Symonds also undertook a mission to Australia to collect authentic passports for use by KGB illegals.

After eight years working for the KGB, Symonds returned to London where he faced trial and was sentenced to two years' imprisonment for corruption. Upon his release he was granted immunity from prosecution for his evidence concerning corruption at Scotland Yard, although MI5 disbelieved his claims to have spied for the KGB.

In 1992 KGB defector Vasili Mitrokhin identified Symonds as the KGB's star British agent, prompting Symonds to write his autobiography. This proved an embarrassment for MI5, which had rejected his offers of information on advice from Scotland Yard, which was anxious to bury his allegations of widespread corruption. He was finally vindicated and was the subject of a Parliamentary enquiry conducted by the Parliamentary Intelligence and Security Committee.

SZYMANSKA, HALINA. The wife of Colonel Antoni Szymanski, the prewar Polish military attaché in Berlin, Halina Szymanska tried to make her way home when war broke out and her husband was detained and then deported to the Soviet Union. Already acquainted with Admiral Wilhelm Canaris, chief of the Abwehr, she was able to make contact with him and he arranged for her to be escorted to Bern with her three daughters. There, she was visited by Canaris who supplied her with information that she passed on, apparently with his encouragement, to the Polish intelligence service and to the British Secret Intelligence Service, which supplied her with false documents identifying her as Marie Clenat. Canaris later met Szymanska in Italy and asked her to relay a warning that Hitler intended to invade the Soviet Union in June 1941.

After the war, Madame Szymanska was resettled by the British Secret Intelligence Service in England, where her daughters attended a convent. In later life, she moved to Mobile, Alabama, where she died in 1988.

– T –

TAIROV, IGOR A. In October 1957, **Piotr Popov**, a GRU officer selling information to the **Central Intelligence Agency** (CIA) in Berlin, revealed that he had been selected to escort an illegal on the first stage of her mission to the United States. Popov told his Russian-speaking CIA case officer, George Kisevalter, about an illegal named Igor A. Tairov, codenamed JACOB, who had already completed a mission in England and had been infiltrated into the United States. He was now to be joined there by his wife, Margarita N. Tairova, whom he described as an experienced GRU officer who had adopted the identity of an American of Polish extraction and had already acclimatized herself to the role in Vienna. As Popov had been designated her conducting officer while she passed through Berlin, he had been able to supply Kisevalter with all Tairova's details, including the two names she had intended to use to travel to New York, and these were duly passed to the Federal Bureau of Investigation (FBI), which kept her under surveillance from the moment her flight arrived at Idlewild. "Mary Grodnik" was trailed to a hotel in Manhattan, where her luggage was searched surreptitiously; her room was bugged and she was watched when, soon afterward, she made contact with her husband in a Yonkers cinema. According to Popov, they planned to pretend to meet for the first time, and then undergo a marriage ceremony in New York to cement their documentation.

Margarita's meeting with her husband led the FBI to investigate "Walter A. Soja," ostensibly a bookkeeper for a wholesaler of women's accessories who lived alone in a dingy apartment in Manhattan's Upper West Side. He, too, had been placed under surveillance but the pair continued to act normally, with her working as a manicurist, until mid-March 1958, when, with no warning, they both vanished. The FBI later denied that either had shown any sign of having spotted the surveillance, but when Popov reported their return to the CIA in Berlin, he disclosed that Margarita Tairova had claimed that she had been kept under observation from the moment she had arrived at Tempelhof to catch her flight to New York the previous December. The KGB had taken her complaint seriously and had initiated an intensive postmortem, but although Popov had been obliged to undergo an uncomfortable interrogation, he appeared to have avoided suspicion. Nevertheless, the interagency recriminations between the CIA and FBI over the handling of the Tairovs were to last for years. Although on this occasion Popov experienced a narrow escape, he was eventually to be arrested by the KGB in a Moscow bus in October 1959 in the act of passing a message to his CIA contact, and executed.

THOMSON, BASIL. Appointed the assistant commissioner of the Metropolitan Police in 1913, Sir Basil Thomson personally supervised the activities of the Special Branch. During World War I, he participated in several of the important espionage investigations and interrogated **Eva de Bournonville**, **Lizzie Wertheim**, and **Mata Hari**, and in April 1919 adopted the title director of intelligence. However, he was forced to resign in October 1921 by the commissioner, Sir William Horwood, when a summer house at the prime minister's country home, Chequers, in Buckinghamshire, was defaced by a group of Irish Sinn Fein supporters, and Lloyd George complained about the breach of security. This was a severe blow to Thomson's colorful career, which had included service as the prime minister of Tonga and the governor of Dartmoor and Wormwood Scrubs prisons. However, worse was to follow in December 1925 when he was arrested in Hyde Park with a known prostitute, Thelma de Lava. Both were charged at the Cannon Row police station and released under bail, to appear two days later at Marlborough Street Magistrates Court. On the appointed day, Thomson went to the wrong court and de Lava failed to turn up at all, resulting in a warrant for her arrest. Having given the false name of "Hugh Thomson" to the police, Sir Basil's offense was given widespread publicity, and his assertion that he had gone to Speaker's Corner after dinner to meet a confidential source in the Communist Party was disbelieved, as was his claim that he had felt sorry for the prostitute and so had given her a few shillings out of pity, and merely had been adjusting his clothing at the time the two police constables had encountered them seated on a park bench. Thomson's appeal against conviction was dismissed, as was his insistence that the entire incident had been stage-managed by Sir William Horwood to frame him. His reputation in ruins, Thomson was supported by his friends, including the former director of naval intelligence, Sir Reginald Hall MP, and the former home secretary who had appointed him in 1913, Reginald McKenna MP. He died in 1939.

THORPE, JEREMY. Jeremy Thorpe was elected the leader of the Liberal Party in January 1967. In October 1975, he conspired to have Norman Josiffe, his former lover, killed, after the latter began blackmailing him. A hit man, Andrew Newton, was hired for £20,000 to murder Josiffe, who was a male model, but bungled the assignment and instead only shot Josiffe's dog. After his release from a two-year prison sentence in 1977, Newton was granted immunity to give evidence against Thorpe, who went on trial in May 1979.

In the meantime, the South African Bureau of State Security (BOSS) had taken a close interest in Thorpe and had employed an agent, Gordon Winter, to pose as a journalist and interview Josiffe, a man supposedly in possession of proof of his relationship with the

Liberal leader who for years had been an outspoken opponent of apartheid. Winter attempted unsuccessfully to publicize Thorpe's past involvement with Josiffe, thereby implicating BOSS and inadvertently supporting Thorpe's subsequent claims that he was the victim of a South African plot to smear him. Many believed Thorpe's version of a political plot, including Prime Minister Harold Wilson, and the jury acquitted him after deliberating on a verdict for 52 hours.

Thorpe, who resigned from the Liberal leadership, lost his North Devon seat in the 1979 general election and soon afterward developed Parkinson's disease, although this did not prevent him from campaigning for a peerage. He always denied ever having been a **homosexual**, and insisted that Josiffe's allegations had been fabricated by a mentally fragile acquaintance. However, the evidence presented in court, while insufficient to secure a conviction on the charges he faced, showed that he had for years employed intermediaries to pay off his blackmailer and had diverted official party funds to pay for Josiffe to be silenced permanently. The South Africans played no part in the plot, apart from seeking to expose Thorpe's duplicity.

TILLO, IRINA. A tall, beautiful, blue-eyed, 35-year-old blonde, Irina Tillo had a French father and a Russian mother, and was fluent in French and German, working occasionally as a translator of novels. Supposedly, she also worked in the Foreign Exchange Department of the Moscow State Bank in 1939 when she married Victor Kravchenko, a Ukrainian engineer with a checkered past. Although he had been a member of the Communist Party for more than a decade, he had been convicted of sabotage and counterrevolutionary activity in the pipe-fabricating factory he managed, and had been reprimanded. A divorcé, Kravchenko survived the purges and fell for Irina Tillo, apparently initially unaware that she was a senior, well-connected NKVD official. Despite the blot on his Party record, Kravchenko was selected for an attachment to the Soviet Purchasing Commission in Washington, D.C., as a specialist in metals, and he traveled there alone in August 1943, leaving Irina in Moscow. She was unaware that Kravchenko had decided to defect, and in March 1944 he was granted political asylum and resettled in Manhattan as "Peter Martin." There he was under constant surveillance by the NKVD, which planted two agents close to him. One was Sara Veksler, codenamed OLA, a Latvian who had been his interpreter at the Purchasing Commission, and the other was Christina Krotkova, codenamed JEANNE, a Russian translator who subsequently returned to Moscow, where she died in 1965. The nature of Kravchenko's relationship with OLA is unclear, but they were certainly very close, and according to some of the VENONA texts referring to her as a source, she was submitting regular reports on his activities and movements to the local *rezidentura* in 1944.

Kravchenko married for a third time in 1947 when his girlfriend, Cynthia Kuser, a wealthy 35-year-old heiress, bore him a son and divorced her husband, Theodore Herbst. Kravchenko would later seek his fortune investing in lead and silver mines in Peru, but eventually committed suicide in a friend's Manhattan apartment in February 1966.

In his autobiography, *I Chose Freedom*, Kravchenko sought to protect his first wife Zinaida, their 10-year-old son Valentin, and his second wife Irina, then still in a Moscow apartment, omitting all mention of Irina's covert NKVD role. In interviews with the FBI in March 1954, he suggested that she should be approached in Moscow, perhaps while she attended church at Sokolniki on Sundays, and invited to defect, too.

Irina's fate remains unclear; her family is convinced she was shot in 1949. According to Valentin, she had also had a son, Vladimir, who was born in 1932 when she was 28.

TROTSKY, LEON. The murder of Leon Trotsky at his heavily fortified home in Mexico City in August 1940 was the culmination of a long surveillance and penetration operation conducted by the NKVD to identify the weaknesses in his protection. After Trotsky's death at the hands of a Spanish assassin, Ramón Mercader, the Mexican police learned that a brothel, the Casa Chiquita, had been established and run by two women married to Mexican Communists for the purpose of attracting business from Trotsky's guards and collecting information from them about precautions that had been taken to screen visitors, liaise with the local authorities, and build physical barriers in the compound to prevent a repetition of the unsuccessful attack that previously had been mounted on his home.

The first attempt on Trotsky's life took place on the night of 23 May 1940 when the leader of the Mexican Communist Party, Marteo

Martinez, led two others wearing army uniforms and called at Trotsky's borrowed home at Coyoacan outside Mexico City. The trio seized Trotsky's American private secretary, Robert Sheldon Harde, as he opened the gate, and his body was later recovered from a nearby shack. The villa's interior was raked with machine-gun fire and damaged by an incendiary grenade. Trotsky and his wife Natalya dove for cover in an upstairs bedroom as the bullets flew, but the only casualty was their 11-year-old grandson who was slightly grazed. When Trotsky's bodyguards returned fire, a dozen or more gunmen fled, the Mexican police in pursuit.

The Mexican government was embarrassed by the incident, and the first to be arrested was a painter, David Siqueiros, a veteran of the Spanish Civil War who had commanded the 82nd Brigade. Siqueiros, who had once served as the Mexican military attaché in Paris, admitted his role in the attack but insisted that he and his supporters had been seeking evidence of Trotsky's anti-Soviet activities. Released on bail, Siqueiros, who was known to Josef Stalin personally, was promptly smuggled out of the country by a Chilean diplomat, Pablo Neruda.

Also implicated in the attack was Siqueiros's brothers-in-law, Luis and Leopoldo Arenal. Siqueiros was married to Angelica Arenal, and she and her brothers were from a prominent Mexican family with strong Communist links. Indeed, Luis was married to Rose Biegel, who lived in Prospect Park, Brooklyn, and was to play a key role acting as a conduit for mail exchanged between the local NKVD *rezidentura* in Manhattan and its agents south of the border.

Three months later, on 20 August 1940, Trotsky invited a young man calling himself Frank Jacson into his study, his purpose being to help him with an article he had written. As Trotsky leaned over the document Jacson, who was standing behind him, pulled a small mountaineer's pickaxe from his raincoat pocket and plunged it into the back of the older man's head. The blade went straight into Trotsky's brain, and he died in the hospital the following day. As for Jacson, who was detained immediately by Trotsky's bodyguards, he never denied the murder but went to elaborate lengths to conceal his true identity and his motive, spuriously claiming to be a disgruntled supporter who had been personally offended by the embezzlement of his contributions to the movement and dismayed at Trotsky's plans to kill other Communist leaders. Indeed, even after his true identity was established, Ramón never admitted that he was part of an NKVD plot.

When interrogated by the Mexican police, Jacson initially identified himself as a Belgian named Jacques Van den Dreschd, but this proved to be false, and when he was convicted at his trial in April 1943, few knew who he really was, although some of his recent background became known. His introduction into Trotsky's household had been facilitated by his 28-year-old lover, Sylvia Angelov, Trotsky's Brooklyn-born secretary and a close friend of his wife, and she had met him in Paris just before the Fourth International in September 1938 when he had used the name Jacques Mornard and had posed as the son of a wealthy, aristocratic Belgian diplomat. Sylvia had acquired her post from her sister Ruth. When she moved to New York early in 1939, Jacson had followed in September on the *Ile de France*, using a Canadian passport that had been issued originally in Ottawa in March 1937 to a naturalized Yugoslav from Lovinac named Antoni Babich. According to the Canadian authorities, Babich had taken up citizenship in 1929 and had used his passport to travel to Spain in 1936, where he had fought with the International Brigade and had been killed in action. Evidently, Babich's passport had been altered to accommodate "Jacson." His explanation for his change in name was his wish to avoid being called up in France for military service. When Angelov went down to Mexico City, Jacson accompanied her, and she took her wealthy young suitor to meet Trotsky. Although extremely cautious about encountering strangers, Jacson won the confidence of the Trotsky family and initially made no move against the exile, masquerading as a wealthy, nonpolitical businessman. Later, writing from New York, Jacson thanked Trotsky for his hospitality and suggested a further visit, at which the attack took place, all suspicions having been allayed.

Jacson's true identity only became known in 1950, five years after his mother, Caridad Mercader, arrived from Moscow to begin a series of regular prison visits to her son. She was a well-known Catalan Communist and mother of five children who had abandoned her husband, a wealthy railway magnate, and taken her children to Paris, where they lived in relative poverty until she had returned to Barcelona at the outbreak of the Spanish Civil War to join the anarchists. She was injured in an air raid, one of her sons was killed in action, and her middle son, Ramón, fought with a guerrilla unit. The identification of Caridad revealed her surprising antecedents, and among her aristocratic predecessors was a governor of the then-Spanish possession of Cuba; another had been the Spanish ambassador to the czar's court in St. Petersburg.

Ramón would remain in prison, comforted by visits from his girlfriend Raqella Moralez, until his release in May 1960 to Havana, where he died in October 1978.

TRUDI. The codeword attributed by Security Intelligence Middle East (SIME) to an Austrian dancer working in a Nicosia cabaret in June 1943 when she was nominally recruited by a German spy. The Abwehr agent, codenamed LITTLE LEMON by SIME, was a radio operator and the son of an Athens restaurateur who had turned himself in with his leader, a Greek from Istanbul, codenamed BIG LEMON, to the British when they reached Beirut. BIG LEMON was imprisoned until the end of hostilities but LITTLE LEMON promoted himself as a womanizer and claimed to his German controllers that he had recruited TRUDI as a useful source of information. He also claimed to have recruited the other members of her troupe: the Hungarian GABBIE, the Austrian HELGA, and the Romanians MARIA and SWING-TIT. Together the group, codenamed LEMONS, was used by SIME to convey deception material until September 1944.

TSHOMBE, MOISE. In an effort to learn more about the leader and intentions of the Katanga rebels who had seceded from the Congo upon independence from Belgium in July 1960, the **Central Intelligence Agency** (CIA) station chief in Elizabethville, David Doyle, attempted to recruit Moise Tshombe's European secretary. As she seemed noncommittal, Doyle persuaded another of his agents, a United Nations officer attached to the peacekeeping force who had a reputation as a ladies' man, to seduce her and encourage her cooperation with the CIA. His task, according to Doyle, was "to woo and win the secretary's favours in bed and to get her to talk about Tshombe's real character and plans." Crestfallen, the agent later described the experience as being like trying "to stuff a marshmallow into a piggy-bank."

TURING, ALAN. Elected to a fellowship at King's College, Cambridge, in 1935 at the age of 23, Alan Turing was one of the most innovative mathematicians of his generation, and the author of *On Computable Numbers*. He worked at Princeton's Institute of Advanced Studies before joining the Government Code and Cipher School in 1938 at Bletchley Park to assist in the development of electromechanical aids designed to race through the permutations of German Enigma cipher machine keys. His device, the Bombe, consisted of 30 drums that replicated Enigma rotors, could race through tens of thousands of the possible Enigma settings, and proved a cryptographic breakthrough. Then Turing turned his attention to the more sophisticated 10-rotor, high-speed Geheimschreiber enciphered teleprinter, and in 1944 his programmable analog computer, the Colossus, enabled Anglo-American code breakers to solve significant quantities of the enemy's most secret messages.

The success achieved at Bletchley in reading some of the Axis traffic resulted in the distribution of ULTRA summaries based on signals intelligence, and probably shortened World War II by up to two years. Nevertheless, the vital contribution of academics such as Peter Twinn, Gordon Welchman, and Alan Turing would go unrecognized for decades because of their work's sensitivity, and Turing continued to be employed after the war on classified projects at Hanslope Park. Neither Turing's mathematical genius nor his part in the complex calculations that had led to the test of the first atomic weapon could save him from prosecution in 1954 when he was charged with having committed an act of gross indecency with another man in a public conveyance in Manchester. Having concealed his **homosexuality**, Turing opted for suicide and took his own life in his mother's garden shed by biting into an apple laced with cyanide.

TURNBERRY ISLAND. This popular golf resort in Miami, Florida, acquired some notoriety in 1988 when one of the residents, Donna Rice, was photographed sitting on the lap of an American presidential candidate, Senator Gary Hart, aboard the motor yacht *Monkey Business*, which was owned by the resort's developer. The incident effectively ended Hart's bid to achieve the Democratic nomination.

At the time, there were suspicions that the Mafia had invested in Turnberry Island after it had been chased out of Havana by Fidel

Castro, and that the number of glamorous models who had been offered accommodation on very preferential terms corresponded to the mob's wish to entertain and influence senior political figures and others deemed potentially helpful. The subsequent investigation proved inconclusive and the resort remained popular with Hollywood celebrities but lost its appeal for politicians.

– U –

UNITED NATIONS SPECIAL COMMISSION (UNSCOM). Following the liberation of Kuwait in 1991, a Special Commission was set up by the United Nations to supervise the dismantling of Iraq's heavy weapons. UNSCOM inspectors were deployed to sites across the country to ensure compliance, but gradually Saddam Hussein's Mukhabarat became increasingly aggressive in attempts to penetrate UNSCOM to learn the sites scheduled for unannounced visits. In 1993, the German Luftwaffe aircrew assigned to flying the UNSCOM teams on their inspection tours found that they were the subject of concerted **honeytrap** operations conducted at the Al-Hyatt Hotel in Baghdad, where their deputy commander was presented with a videotape of his late-night encounter with a glamorous member of the hotel's domestic staff and threatened with publication unless he compromised details of UNSCOM's plans. The officer reported the incident to UNSCOM, adding that his wife in Germany had very liberal ideas about such matters and would enjoy viewing the tape. The Luftwaffe withdrew the pilot, and the rest of the UNSCOM team was given the appropriate advice.

UpDK. The Russian acronym for Upranlenie podelam Diplomatichestogo Korpusa, the Soviet Foreign Ministry's Main Directorate for Services to the Diplomatic Corps, the organization responsible for providing domestic and clerical staff to foreign missions in the Soviet Union, but actually subordinate to the KGB's **Second Chief Directorate** (SCD), and staffed by KGB SCD personnel. Ostensibly, UpDK was little more than a state-sponsored employment agency but in reality it undertook surveys of embassy premises; provided opportunities for the installation of technical surveillance systems; supplied qualified maids, clerks, janitors, and cleaners; and made assessments of potentially vulnerable foreigners. In example after example of entrapments in Moscow, it was UpDK-supplied staff who were implicated in each scenario.

– V –

VANDENBERG, ARTHUR. The Republican senator from Michigan since March 1928, Arthur Vandenberg was a committed isolationist whose second wife, Hazel, stayed in Grand Rapids while her husband occupied an apartment in the Wardman Park Hotel next to his British mistress, Mitzi Sims, whose husband Harold was a diplomat at the British embassy in Washington, D.C., until his death from a stroke in May 1940.

Vandenberg's improbable but dramatic conversion to the British cause, announced in a radio broadcast on 9 June 1940, was attributed to Mitzi's influence; her lover was often described as "the senator from Mitzi-gan." When Mitzi returned to Montreal after her husband's death, her place was taken by 30-year-old **Betty Pack**, whose mother, Cora Thorpe, had been Hazel Vandenberg's friend and contemporary at the University of Michigan. Pack turned her charms to the senator, and his isolationism continued to recede. By the time the controversial Lend-Lease Bill came to be debated in Congress, before it was enacted in March 1941, Pack's role had been taken by Eveline Paterson, a 32-year-old statuesque blonde working for British War Relief whose husband John was in Malaya. Reportedly their relationship continued until at least June 1948 when the Vandenberg Amendment enabled the Truman administration to join the North Atlantic Treaty Organization.

VANUNU, MORDECAI. The son of an immigrant family from Marrakesh, Morocco, Mordechai Vanunu abandoned his studies as a physicist and joined the Dimona nuclear research center in 1977, working as a technician. He was made redundant in 1985, having applied to join the Israeli Communist Party, but in 1986 attempted to sell information and photographs he had taken from inside the plant to a journalist in Australia. He was brought to London by the *Sunday*

Times to have his story verified, and a rival newspaper, the *Sunday Mirror*, identified him as a hoaxer and claimed that his supposedly illicit photographs of a secret underground plutonium processing unit were actually of a car wash or an egg-packing factory. Dismayed but undeterred, the *Sunday Times* obtained independent corroboration of Vanunu's bona fides and in September 1986 published his assertion that Israel had developed a sizable atomic arsenal of free-fall bombs and nuclear land mines.

Meanwhile the Australian Security Intelligence Organization had learned of Vanunu's intention to make disclosures regarding his former employment and informed Mossad, which conducted an operation in London to lure him to Italy. He apparently accidentally encountered an attractive 26-year-old American blonde named Cindy while window shopping, and she invited him to Rome where, she claimed, an apartment belonging to her sister, an airline stewardess, would be available for a weekend of lovemaking. However, upon his arrival with Cindy at her sister's address, Vanunu was abducted and returned on a ship to Israel for trial. He was convicted in March 1988 of treason and sentenced to 18 years' imprisonment. Released on license in 2004, he converted to Christianity but was quickly rearrested for breaching the terms of his parole, which included a ban on interviews with foreign journalists and on travel abroad.

Cindy was later revealed to be an American-born Mossad agent, Cheryl Hanin, who would later marry another Mossad veteran and move to a golf resort near Orlando, where she lives today as Cheryl Bentov with her two daughters.

VASSALL, JOHN. The grandson of a Church of England clergyman, John Vassall served in the Royal Air Force during the latter part of World War II and trained as a photographer. In 1954, he applied for a clerk's post in the Admiralty and he was sent to the British embassy in Moscow as secretary to the naval attaché.

In Moscow, he was befriended by a Pole, Sigmund Mikhailski, who worked at the embassy as an interpreter, and he was responsible for drawing the hapless Vassall into a **homosexual honeytrap**. Mikhailski, about whom a security warning was circulated in December 1955, was invited to dine with some of Vassall's friends at a restaurant near the

Bolshoi Ballet and Vassall, having been plied with alcohol, lost his inhibitions and was photographed in bed with a young man. Hopelessly compromised, Vassall succumbed to the KGB's blackmail and, in an attempt to prevent pictures of his indiscretion being circulated, started supplying classified material to his Russian contact. This methodology was the classic handiwork of General **Oleg Gribanov**, of the KGB's **Second Chief Directorate**; two defectors, Anatoli Golitsyn and **Yuri Nosenko**, later confirmed Gribanov's role in the operation.

In June 1956 Vassall's tour of duty ended and he was posted back to the Admiralty where he worked in the secretariat to the naval staff. A rendezvous with his KGB handler, known to him as Grigori, quickly followed, and they remained in touch until the arrest of **Harry Houghton** in January 1961, when Vassall was told to temporarily discontinue his meetings. When they resumed, he was handled by a new contact named Nikolai. Despite being the victim of coercion, Vassall developed a reliance and even friendship with his Soviet contacts, one of whom was later identified as a skilled professional, Nikolai Karpekov, who had masqueraded as a diplomat.

An early clue to Vassall's espionage had been provided by Anatoli Golitsyn during one of his first interviews, conducted in May 1962 by Geoffrey Hinton, the Secret Intelligence Service station commander in Washington, D.C., but an initial investigation, conducted by MI5's Ronald Symonds, had concluded that he was an unlikely candidate as a spy because he enjoyed a private income from his father, a wealthy cleric.

Once the public furor about the Portland spy ring had subsided, Vassall was activated again and he held regular meetings with his KGB case officer until his arrest in September 1962. After a lengthy MI5 investigation, which had been initiated the previous April after the CIA had imparted information from Yuri Nosenko, Vassall's flat in Dolphin Square was searched, and he was charged with offenses under the Official Secrets Act and sentenced to 18 years' imprisonment. He was released from Maidstone prison in October 1972 and, after staying in a Catholic monastery, wrote a book, *Vassall: The Autobiography of a Spy*. He then lived in north London under an assumed identity and worked for a firm of solicitors before his death in November 1996.

VETROV, VLADIMIR. A senior KGB officer in the Science and Technology Directorate who had served abroad in Canada and France, Vladimir Vetrov was married with a son when he conducted an affair with a 47-year-old married KGB secretary, Ludmilla, who was well known for her extramarital office relationships. Vetrov was aware of her reputation but was drunk when he and his lover were challenged by a colleague while they sat arguing in his car parked in a notorious lover's lane in Moscow. Apparently the second KGB officer had followed the couple to the remote area and a scuffle had ensued after he had interrupted Vetrov. In the fight his KGB rival was stabbed, and Vetrov then attempted to run down a distraught Ludmilla as she tried to flee the scene. When he sobered up, Vetrov confessed to his wife Svetlana and gave himself up to the police.

In November 1982 Vetrov was convicted of manslaughter and imprisoned while the KGB circulated various cover stories to hide the embarrassing tale, unaware that in fact Vetrov was also a spy who had been passing information to the French Direction de la Surveillance du Territoire (DST), codenamed FAREWELL. The DST had circulated Vetrov's material to the **Central Intelligence Agency**, which had placed a high value on it. Only after Vetrov had been imprisoned did the KGB learn from a DST source that he had been a mole inside the organization, so he was charged with treason and executed.

– W –

WALKER, BARBARA. The sexual politics of the Walker family were extraordinarily complex, but at the heart of them was Barbara Walker, who had been married to John Walker, a U.S. Navy warrant officer, since she was 19 years old. As well as having his four children, of whom two would also become Soviet spies, she would have an affair with her brother-in-law, Arthur Walker, while he in turn would have an adulterous relationship with his daughter-in-law Rachel, of which his wife was aware.

In her statement to the Federal Bureau of Investigation (FBI), Barbara claimed that she had learned her husband was a spy in 1968 when she discovered $2,000 in a drawer at a time when the bar they owned in Charleston, South Carolina, was in financial difficulties. She subsequently acquiesced in his espionage and on one occasion, in June 1972, collected $35,000 from a dead drop and carried it on her body on a flight from Washington, D.C., to San Francisco. In 1979, she revealed to her son Michael, then 17 years old and about to begin a navy career in December 1981, that his father was a Soviet spy.

In 1984, she threatened to denounce her husband unless he fulfilled his promise to pay her $1,000 a month in alimony, and when he ignored her, she approached the Hyannis Port FBI office in November while drunk and claimed her ex-husband was a spy. She was also drunk when she was interviewed in December 1984, but as she named her daughter Laura as having been approached to spy, she, too, was interviewed, at her home in Buffalo, New York. Both women passed a polygraph examination, but Barbara then telephoned Arthur to say she had turned in his brother John. The conversation was wiretapped by the FBI, which then persuaded Barbara to visit her ex-husband and persuade him that she had been drunk when she had talked to Arthur and had not really contacted the FBI. She was later granted immunity in return for her testimony.

When interviewed by the FBI, Arthur, a retired submariner who had joined the U.S. Navy in 1952, claimed that he had only engaged in espionage in 1981 and 1982 when he had been employed as a defense contractor in Chesapeake, Virginia, and that the three compromised documents were classified as confidential and concerned ship construction. He was arrested on 29 May 1985. In October of the same year, he was sentenced to life imprisonment and a fine of $250,000.

Barbara's husband John was indicted in May 1985 on six counts of espionage, along with his son Michael. Born in Washington, D.C., in 1937, and the son of an alcoholic, bankrupt father, Walker had a burglary conviction as a youth and had joined the U.S. Navy in May 1955 as an alternative to prison. Thirty years later, he was accused of having spied for the Soviets for 18 years, during which period he had held top secret crypto clearances, served on two ballistic nuclear submarines, the USS *Arthur Jackson* and *Simon Bolivar*, and had handled the most sensitive coding equipment. Walker had experienced financial difficulties in December 1967 and had even contemplated suicide before he visited the Soviet embassy in Washington, D.C., where his offer to sell information was accepted by the KGB *rezident*, Boris

Solmatin, who interviewed him for two hours. A month later, he met Yuri Linkov in a shopping mall in Alexandria, Virginia, and was promised a salary of $4,000 a month, given a Minox camera, a schedule of dead drops, and a rotor reader for a KL-47 cipher machine. He would not hold another personal meeting with a Soviet contact for 10 years, but over the 17 years of his espionage he made some 30 drops.

Anticipating his retirement in 1976 and a new career as a private detective, Walker recruited his son Michael who, at the time of his arrest, was a petty officer serving on the carrier USS *Nimitz* and was found to have 15 pounds of classified material in his locker. When arrested, Michael's wife Rachel, who conducted an affair with her father-in-law John, and had only been married to her husband since December 1984, persuaded her husband to make a full confession.

John Walker had also recruited his brother, Lieutenant Commander Arthur Walker, and another navy friend, Jerry Whitworth. In October 1985, father and son pleaded guilty, and received two life terms plus 10 years' imprisonment and 25 years' imprisonment respectively, in return for John Walker's testimony against Whitworth, who surrendered to the FBI in June 1985. He confessed that he had been recruited as a spy by John in September 1974, and given an initial payment of $4,000. At his trial, on charges of espionage and evading tax on $140,000 of undeclared income, Whitworth was accused of having received $325,000 from John between 1975 and 1982 in return for classified data, and he was sentenced in August 1986 to 365 years' imprisonment and a fine of $410,000.

Although Arthur, Michael, and John Walker were imprisoned, Barbara, Rita, and Rachel were never charged. President Ronald Reagan noted in his diary for 24 July 1985 that he had received a top secret report on the Walker family's espionage.

WANNENMACHER, HELGA. According to her autobiography, *Red Spy at Night*, published in 1977, Helga Wannenmacher-Pohl was Polish but of German extraction, whose family had fled from Daliatin, in Galicia, to Strehlin, near Breslau, in 1939, where she joined the Hitler Youth. At the end of World War II, aged 17, she moved again, fleeing the Soviets, to Güsten where, during the occupation, she was employed by the Red Army as an interpreter. However, having resisted the advances of a Soviet officer, she had been arrested on espionage charges and sent to a labor camp near Novosibirsk in Siberia. There she had managed to exchange identities with a dead prisoner and start a new life as Jelena Pushkova, a student at Moscow University, where she married the doctor who had saved her. However, he turned out to be already married so after an annulment she wed an army officer, Andrei Sidrov. She accompanied him to Kirovabad, a missile research establishment in the Caucasus, but in September 1949, while heavily pregnant, she attempted to cross the frontier into Iran, accompanied by a pair of German rocket engineers. They were all caught and Pushkova was interrogated at the Lubyanka, incarcerated in the notorious Butirka prison, and then sentenced to six years' hard labor. Although her husband was unaware of his wife's plan, he too was sentenced to a long term of imprisonment in Novaya Zemlya.

In March 1950 Wannenmacher appealed her conviction before President Nikolai Shvernik and the chief of Soviet foreign intelligence, Viktor Abakumov, won her release, and was recruited reluctantly into the NKVD by Pavel Sudoplatov who described her future duties as entertaining foreign visitors. "They are looking for feminine charm and affection—which you will be able to offer them." He went on to explain that "KGB agents must trust nobody. Our work begins with searching waste-paper baskets and ends with . . . well, in your case, darling, it may end in somebody's bed. All in the interests of the Communist Party, you understand."

Wannenmacher attended a police college for six months and then was posted to Vienna to persuade an Austrian Communist to provide the NKVD with passports and other identification documents. Having accomplished this task, she was given a new mission, to seduce a U.S. Army lieutenant, Charlie Rudford, whom she had encountered in a nightclub. The proposal, made by Colonel Shalatov in Sudoplatov's presence, was that she should "be employed for a few months at the Soviet embassy in Vienna" and set up in a flat wired for sound and equipped with a hidden camera to entrap Rudford in bed with her. On this occasion, "rage and disgust took hold of" her and she "crossed the room and hit Colonel Shalatov hard in the face."

Wannenmacher was then sent in November 1950 to Vladivostock to investigate the disappearance of some military equipment but ended up penetrating a smuggling racket and arresting the merchant seaman who was running it. Then she was given an assignment in

Paris to murder "two men who were proving an embarrassment" using "fountain-pens with lethal charges" but she warned the two victims, one of whom was a KGB officer, and they fled to Copenhagen. When the NKVD learned of what she had done, through a listening device installed in her home, she was threatened with a court-martial, but narrowly escaped punishment by persuading Ivan Serov that she had been poorly trained and was ill prepared for her mission.

Wannenmacher then had a brief affair with **Lavrenti Beria**'s son Semyon, and in March 1951, aged 23, was posted to the Dzerzhinsky Military and Diplomatic Faculty before volunteering for a posting to Kazan to monitor the foreign students and supervise the prisoners at Zelenodolsk. During a visit back to Moscow, she was seduced by Viktor Abakumov who arranged for her to be reunited with her husband Andrei, who was moved to Pertovka prison in Kazan in November and released the following month after the intervention of Nikolai Shvernik.

In May 1954, having graduated from Kazan Institute, Wannenmacher attended a further course at the Dzerzinsky Academy and in November was posted to Potsdam, on the outskirts of Berlin. In May 1955, she moved to a house in Karlshorst where, reunited with her mother and son Alik, she worked with the trade delegation at the Soviet embassy in Unter den Linden. Posing as a Russian teacher, she participated in entrapment operations against American personnel, one of whom turned out to be a **Central Intelligence Agency** (CIA) officer named Smith, who recruited her as an agent. However, instead of supplying him as intended with false information carefully fabricated by the KGB, she succeeded in passing him genuine material, and seized the opportunity to defect just when she was about to return to Moscow with her son. On 16 June 1956, having identified herself to the CIA as a KGB officer with the rank of captain, she and her son were flown from Tempelhof to West Germany, where she underwent a debriefing.

In Wannenmacher's tale, *Red Spy at Night*, she describes how she had been an athlete at a display attended by Adolf Hitler, shaken hands with Stalin in the Kremlin, performed a striptease for Pavel Sudoplatov, bedded both Semyon Beria and Viktor Abakumov, and danced with Stalin's son Vasili. Although billed by her publishers as "a true story of espionage and seduction behind the Iron Curtain," there is considerable doubt about its authenticity. If the book were true, then it is the first by a KGB officer who was trained to seduce foreign visitors to the Soviet Union, and although there are plenty of references to real people, such as Viktor Abakumov, Ivan Serov, and Pavel Sudoplatov, the story is so improbable that it is more likely a work of fiction. According to Wannenmacher, she had been virtually coerced into becoming a KGB officer, having been reminded that there were nine years of a prison sentence outstanding, even though she was a foreigner and a former member of the Hitler *Jugend*. To anyone with any experience of Soviet intelligence training, it would have been unthinkable for any officer to have been sent abroad on a mission without several years of experience, yet Wannenmacher claimed to have been sent to France and Vienna after only a few weeks in the KGB, an organization that, incidentally, did not come into existence with that title until 1954. Nor is there any record of a KGB defector escaping to Copenhagen in 1950.

There is no external confirmation that Wannenmacher's story is anything other than fiction, and there is certainly no record of any KGB captain defecting to the CIA in 1956. Such an event would have been major news at the time and would have provoked a hideous scandal within the KGB, yet the episode appears to have gone unnoticed by the many KGB retirees who have described in detail the events of that era of the Cold War in Vienna and Berlin.

WARD, STEPHEN. A well-known society osteopath and artist in London, Stephen Ward was recruited by MI5 in June 1961 in an attempt to **honeytrap** his acquaintance, **Eugene Ivanov**, a GRU officer under assistant naval attaché cover at the Soviet embassy in London. Ward's MI5 handler was Keith Wagstaffe, but when it was learned that the secretary of state for war, **John Profumo,** had been conducting an affair with Ward's flatmate, **Christine Keeler,** the relationship was terminated. When Ward was charged with the criminal offense of living off immoral earnings, relating to Keeler's activities as a call girl, Ward attempted to contact Wagstaffe, whom he knew only under the alias of "Woods" but was unable to reach him. Apparently abandoned by MI5, Ward committed suicide in July 1963 by taking an overdose of Nembutal on the last day of his trial. Keeler would be sentenced to nine months' imprisonment at Holloway for perjury.

MI5 belatedly realized that Ward was quite unsuitable as an agent, partly because he was notoriously indiscreet, but mainly because he reveled in his espionage role, and during the Cuban missile crisis of October 1962 became an embarrassment in his attempts to act as a back channel to the Soviet embassy, claiming to be an intermediary between the governments. As well as being a talented artist, erotic photographer, stiletto shoe fetishist, amateur spy, and collector of pornography, Ward developed a coterie of young women, known in the then-current slang as "popsies" whom he introduced to his society friends at parties in London or at his weekend cottage on Lord Astor's Cliveden estate. Although not full-time prostitutes, they accepted "pillow-money" and passed on some of the proceeds to him, a practice that would lead to his arrest by Scotland Yard on vice charges. Ward shared his flat in Wimpole Mews with Christine Keeler, knew Mandy Rice-Davies, **Mariella Novotny**, and Suzy Chang, and faced evidence for the prosecution from Ronna Riccardo, Vickie Barrett, and Frances Brown, all professional prostitutes who testified that he had lived off their income.

Originally from an Irish family who settled in Torquay where his father was a vicar, Ward studied osteopathy in Missouri and during World War II served as an officer in the Royal Army Medical Corps, although his American qualifications were never recognized by the British authorities. At the end of the war, following a nervous breakdown, he was returned to England from India, where he had treated Mahatma Gandhi's neck. In London, he campaigned for osteopathy to be accepted by a skeptical medical establishment and developed a practice in the West End that included **Averell Harriman**, King Peter of Yugoslavia, Winston Churchill, and numerous film stars among his patients. After a failed brief marriage to a beauty queen, Ward came to prefer the company of dancers he gave physiotherapy to and of prostitutes, and he made them available to his high-society friends with whom he gained a reputation for making such introductions. These connections, when they extended to the Soviet embassy, made Ward attractive to MI5 as a means of gaining access to Ivanov, but the plot would eventually unravel with disastrous consequence, especially for Ward, who took his overdose in a flat belonging to a journalist friend in Mallord Street, Chelsea.

WATKINS, JOHN. A former Canadian ambassador to Moscow between 1954 and 1956, John Watkins was identified by a KGB defector, **Yuri Nosenko**, as having succumbed to a **homosexual honeytrap**. Codenamed ROCK BOTTOM, Watkins had just retired from the Department of External Affairs when he was questioned for 26 days by the Royal Canadian Mounted Police (RCMP) in October 1964 after the information had been confirmed by another defector, **Yuri Krotkov**. He recognized Anatoli Gorsky as his blackmailer but died of a heart attack in a Montreal Holiday Inn during a break in the interviews.

During the course of the ROCK BOTTOM investigation, the RCMP learned that Watkins' successor in Moscow, David Johnson, was also a homosexual, and Johnson was dismissed.

WEBSTER, WILLIAM. In June 1988, the U.S. Supreme Court ruled in *Webster v. Doe* that the director of the **Central Intelligence Agency** (CIA), William Webster, could not dismiss an employee simply on the basis of sexual orientation. The CIA officer, named only as John Doe in the litigation, insisted that because he had been open about his **homosexuality** he was not a candidate for blackmail and therefore was not a security risk.

WEINMANN, ARIEL. Broken-hearted when he was dumped by his girlfriend, 21-year-old Ariel J. Weinmann, originally from Salem, Oregon, enlisted with the U.S. Navy in July 2003. After he completed submarine school in October 2004, he joined the Connecticut-based USS *Albuquerque*, a Los Angeles–class attack submarine. However, after six months aboard the *Albuquerque* as a fire control technician 3rd class, he deserted in July 2005, having already attempted to sell classified documents to Russian diplomats in Bahrain.

Weinmann was arrested at Dallas/Fort Worth Airport in March 2006. Having pleaded guilty at a court-martial in Norfolk, Virginia, in December 2006 to six charges of larceny, desertion, and espionage, Weinmann was sentenced to 12 years' imprisonment for the theft of a laptop. He admitted having approached the Russian embassy in Vienna, Austria, when he was living there in October 2005, where he had offered to sell classified material, including a ring binder containing a

Tomahawk cruise missile manual, and of then calling on the Russian embassy in Mexico City in March 2006.

WERTHEIM, LIZZIE. In July 1915, reports were received in London from the Royal Navy base at Rosyth of an inquisitive German woman who had taken an interest in naval officers serving on ships of the Grand Fleet. Accordingly, the Metropolitan Police Special branch placed Mrs. Lizzie Wertheim under observation, having established that she was a German separated from her husband, a naturalized British subject.

Almost as soon as the surveillance on Wertheim began, she left Scotland and traveled down to London where she joined a young American, Reginald Rowland, at a hotel in Bloomsbury. Coincidentally, a letter posted in Rosyth and mailed to a foreign address had been tested by the Censorship Department for secret writing and found to contain a concealed message about the movements of HMS *Tiger*, a warship about to sail to Scapa Flow in the Orkneys. The handwriting appeared to match Wertheim's, so she was arrested in Regent's Park Road and interrogated at Scotland Yard. Meanwhile Rowland was also questioned and confronted with evidence that he had been mailing copies of the London evening newspapers to overseas addresses, and that the "stop press" columns had contained secret writing. When interviewed by Assistant Commissioner **Basil Thomson**, who had established that Rowland's American passport was a forgery, he admitted that his true name was Georg Breeckow, and that he was a German who had lived in the United States since 1906, and had attended a German espionage school in Antwerp, where he had been supplied with secret ink disguised as hair tonic.

Breeckow and Wertheim were tried at the Old Bailey in September 1915, and both were found guilty of espionage. Breeckow was shot in the Tower of London at the end of the following month, while his companion was sentenced to 10 years' imprisonment. She served five years at Aylesbury Gaol but died insane at the Broadmoor hospital for the criminally insane in 1920.

WICHFELD, MONICA DE. Born Monica Massy-Beresford at her Anglo-Irish parents' palatial home in London's Eaton Square in July 1894, she would marry Jorgen de Wichfeld, a Danish nobleman 12 years her senior working as an attaché at the Danish legation, in June 1916. The death of her younger brother Jack two years later, during the Marne offensive, turned her profoundly anti-German, and gave her depression, but in 1921, heavily pregnant with their second child, she accompanied her husband to Engestofte, a large but impoverished ancestral estate at Maribo on the Baltic coastal island of Lolland that he had inherited from his father, where she met her German neighbor, Kurt Haugwitz-Reventlow, and promptly fell in love with him. Their undisguised affair, which would last nine years, scandalized society in London and Copenhagen. Aged 26, two years younger than she, Haugwitz-Reventlow had served in the Kaiser's army during the war and seemed an unlikely lover for Monica. Nevertheless, she spent an increasing amount of time with him on his neighboring farm at Rosenlund, and traveled with him frequently to London and to her mother's villas at Cannes and Rapallo. Their circle of friends included Max Beaverbook, Clementine Churchill, Edwina Mountbatten, and Noel Coward, but in 1930 she ended the relationship, even though he continued to pursue her to Italy, France, and Monaco, until he married the 24-year-old American Woolworth's heiress Barbara Hutton in 1935. Their stormy marriage only lasted two years and ended in acrimony and sensational press reports of the divorce, allowing Haugwitz-Reventlow to renew his friendship with Monica.

When Denmark was invaded in April 1940, the de Wichfelds were in Italy, where they remained until they were able to return to Engestofte in September 1941, via Berlin. Once back in Denmark, Monica contacted the resistance through one of her tenants, Communist writer Hilmar Wulff, and made the Engestofte estate available as a safe house for fugitives, arranging with Flemming Muus, who had parachuted into Jutland in March 1943, to have **Special Operations Executive** (SOE) make drops into the Maribo Lake. One of the members of her network who stayed at Engestofte was Jacob Jensen, an SOE-trained saboteur who had been working on a trawler in the Persian Gulf when his country had been occupied. Jensen was arrested by the Gestapo in Arhus in December 1943 and under interrogation identified 44 members of the network, including Monica, who was taken into custody in January 1944, along with her husband who had absolutely no knowledge of her clandestine activities. She was imprisoned at the notorious Vestre Faengsel and questioned at Dagmar

House, the Gestapo headquarters, and in May 1944 put on trial before a German military tribunal, accompanied by an SOE wireless operator and two other members of her network. All four were condemned to death, and her sentence was the first on a woman in Denmark for 300 years.

Within a fortnight, with the threat of growing civil unrest, Monica's sentence had been commuted to life imprisonment in Germany, and in June she was transferred to Kiel, Hamburg, Leipzig, and then finally Cottbus. However, in January 1945, as Soviet troops approached the town, Monica and the other foreign prisoners were evacuated to Waldheim, but she barely survived the journey by railway in cattle trucks. Upon arrival she developed pneumonia, and on 27 February died in the prison's hospital ward.

As an Englishwoman married into one of Denmark's oldest families, Monica and her beauty had always attracted considerable attention, but her long affair with her German neighbor ensured her fame spread far beyond London and Copenhagen. Few, however, suspected that she had engaged in espionage, and her name would become synonymous for patriotism in her adopted country. Her lover, Haugwitz-Reventlow, married another American heiress soon after Barbara Hutton married Cary Grant in July 1942, and died in 1969 in New York. Monica's husband Jorgen remained at Engestofte until his death in July 1966.

WILKY, HELEN. The mistress of Captain John King, a senior Foreign Office cipher clerk of Irish extraction, Helen Wilky was identified in 1993 by a GRU defector, Walter Krivitsky, as being the source of stolen British codes. Wilky was placed under surveillance, was followed from her home in Ravenscourt Park to her job at the Chancery Lane Safe Deposit Company, and was arrested in September 1939. When her safe was opened, it was found to contain an envelope holding £1,300 in notes that were traced to the Moscow Narodny Bank, via an account in Rotterdam held by a suspected Soviet spy. Under interrogation King stated that his mistress had never known what was in the envelope, or its source. He admitted having sold information during an official posting in Geneva to a Dutch acquaintance, Henri Pieck, and then to a man he had known as "Mr. Petersen" since 1934. MI5 recognized Pieck as a well-known Soviet spy, while "Petersen" was a mysterious figure who had been implicated in the Woolwich Arsenal case but had escaped abroad in 1938. Codenamed MAG, King had sold huge quantities of telegrams and other documents he had removed from his office and taken to a room rented in Buckingham Gate for copying by the NKVD, until 1937 when he lost contact with Petersen. His stated motive was the desire to provide for his son.

Also found in Wilky's safe were Foreign Office documents that were traced to her sister Nora, who turned out to be the lover of another cipher clerk, a Major Grange, but no action was taken against either of them. On the basis of King's evidence, Wilky was released, but King was imprisoned for 10 years.

WILLIAMS, NELLIE. Married to a carpenter, 39-year-old Albert Williams, Nellie was a member of the **Communist Party of Great Britain** (CPGB) and an active Soviet spy. After her husband's arrest and conviction on espionage charges in 1938, she acted as a courier, maintaining a link between Williams, who had headed a spy ring based in the Woolwich Arsenal, and the CPGB. Their home, at 24 Albion Road, included a photographic studio and darkroom, and Williams had been considered "a very dangerous Communist" since he first came to the attention of Special Branch in September 1927. Born in 1899, Williams had enlisted in the Royal Field Artillery in June 1915 and had served with the British Expeditionary Force in France and Flanders as a gunner, and with the North Russian Expeditionary Force. Demobilized in June 1919, he had joined Woolwich Arsenal as a laborer and had been promoted to a gun examiner. He was also elected secretary of the local branch of the CPGB and gained a reputation as an uncompromising revolutionary. It was only after his conviction, when regular reports were submitted about him to MI5 by a stool pigeon named Parkinson at Parkhurst prison on the Isle of Wight that he, not Percy Glading, had really directed the spy ring. Of particular interest to MI5 was an overheard conversation with another convict, George Whomack, in which Williams had mentioned that an important senior Foreign Office official was being paid £15,000 a year for his espionage. He had also boasted that he had been very lucky, for if MI5 had acted a week earlier or a week later, he would have been in possession of some very incriminating material that would have earned him a much longer sentence. MI5 paid close attention to

Williams and his wife Nellie, and noted that he considered Glading, incarcerated separately at Maidstone, to be the weakest link. Even in prison he kept up his links with the CPGB, apparently through the owner of the Victoria Tea Shop in Cowes High Street, which Nellie visited on her trips to Parkhurst, and Frank Munday, another visitor whose brother also had been convicted. Williams was released in November 1940 and, unrepentant about his conviction, found work as a carpenter with a corn merchant. When he attended a government-sponsored training scheme in Croydon to learn engineering, MI5 intervened discreetly to ensure that, as an ex-convict, he was not offered a government job, and instead he spent the remainder of the war working for a building contractor repairing bomb-damaged property in south London. *See also* GRAY, OLGA.

WOLF, MARKUS. The chief of the Hauptverwaltung Aufkrarung (HVA) for 34 years, Markus Wolf was educated by the Comintern in Moscow and returned to Germany in 1946 to cover the Nuremberg War Crimes trials as a journalist. He later became a diplomat and was posted to Moscow but in 1951 was recalled to East Berlin to join the fledgling "Institute for Economic Scientific Research," headed by a veteran revolutionary, Richard Stahlmann, who had fought in the Spanish Civil War. Advised by an experienced NKVD officer, André Graur, who had served in the London and Stockholm *rezidenturas* before the war, the organization was renamed the Hauptverwaltung Aufklärung in 1956. Initially employed as an analyst and deputy to Robert Korb, who had previously worked as a correspondent for Radio Moscow, Wolf was promoted to be deputy to Gustav Szinda and commence operations against West Germany. His principal tactic was to blackmail potential sources, and he later refined this strategy to ensnare vulnerable secretaries with **ravens**, taking a close personal interest in the handling of **Romeo spies**.

Increasingly disenchanted with East Germany's repressive nature, and having left his second wife for a dissident who had spent four months in prison for attempting to flee to the West, Wolf retired from the HVA in 1986 and became a political activist, campaigning for Mikhail Gorbachev's reforms. After the reunification of Germany, Wolf was indicted for treason and espionage, but his conviction was quashed by the Federal Constitutional Court in October 1995, and he died in 2006.

WOLKOFF, ANNA. Convicted of breaches of the Official Secrets Act in November 1940, Anna Wolkoff was the daughter of the czar's last naval attaché in London and worked as the proprietor of the Russian Tea Room in Harrington Gardens, South Kensington. A well-connected seamstress, she made dresses for society ladies, and among her clients were **Wallis Simpson** and Pamela Mitford.

She was also suspected by MI5 of being a Nazi sympathizer and member of the Right Club, a group dedicated to distributing anti-Semitic literature, and of being in contact with Italian assistant naval attaché Colonel Francesco Maringliano. One of her letters, intercepted by the censorship authorities and addressed to the broadcaster William Joyce in Berlin, revealed that she communicated with him in a rather primitive code. Further surveillance on Wolkoff suggested that she had acted as an intermediary for the American cipher clerk **Tyler Kent**; several MI5 agents, among them Mrs. Marjorie Mackie (alias Mrs. Amos), Helene Munck, and Joan Miller, gave evidence against her at her Old Bailey trial. Released from prison in June 1946, Wolkoff died in a car accident in 1969.

– X –

X, MISS. The name under which the MI5 informant **Olga Gray** gave evidence for the prosecution in the Woolwich Arsenal trial at the Old Bailey in May 1938. *See also* WILLIAMS, NELLIE.

XX COMMITTEE. The subcommittee of the Wireless Board created to run MI5's controlled enemy agents, the XX (Twenty) Committee consisted of representatives of the various British service intelligence branches, and other liaison personnel. Chaired by the Christ Church, Oxford, academic John Masterman, the XX Committee met on a weekly basis from January 1941 until the end of hostilities, and accumulated more experience of the management of double agents than probably any other group of individuals. Naturally, as sex was inevitably a significant motivation for espionage, MI5 handled several cases involving women, and men involved with women. Some, such as TREASURE, **BRONX**, GELATINE, and THE SNARK, were agents in their own right, whereas others were entirely **nominal**, such as TATE's girlfriend Mary, who supposedly was an Admiralty cipher clerk, and GARBO's subsource **Theresa Jardine**, who was eventually transferred to Ceylon. Their importance ranged from the provision of political gossip by GELATINE and BRONX who were socially well connected in London, to relatively insignificant information about food prices and availability, supplied by THE SNARK, a Yugoslav domestic servant. Following experience with TREASURE, who proved notoriously difficult to handle, a woman case officer, Gisella Ashley, was recruited by MI5 to manage women agents. Because of TREASURE's temperamental behavior, MI5 learned either to invent notional women sources or to adopt existing personalities and attribute to them entirely fictional roles. Thus in Cyprus SWING-TIT and TRUDI were authentic chorus girls working at various Nicosia cabarets, although they had no knowledge of the espionage they supposedly engaged in for their Axis spymasters. *See also* GAERTNER, FRIEDLE.

– Y –

YURCHENKO, VITALI. Convinced that he was suffering from the cancer that had killed his mother and could only be cured in the United States, Vitali Yurchenko defected to the **Central Intelligence Agency** (CIA) in Rome in August 1985 while on a mission to find Vladimir Alexandrov, a Soviet nuclear physicist who had gone missing. Upon his arrival at Andrews Air Force Base, he was interviewed by **Aldrich Ames** and then debriefed by Bob Wade of the Federal Bureau of Investigation.

Formerly the security officer at the Soviet embassy in Washington, D.C., Yurchenko had been disciplined for calling the police when a CIA retiree, Edwin Moore, tossed a package of secrets over the fence at the Mount Alto compound. Having discussed the incident with the *rezident*, Boris Yakushin, they had decided the package was probably a bomb, when in fact it contained classified documents. Yurchenko was estranged from his wife and found it hard to support Piotr, his mentally handicapped adopted son.

Yurchenko redefected on 31 October 1985 but not before he had given sufficient information for the FBI to identify a spy in the National Security Agency, Ronald Pelton, and learn the full details of how a defector, **Nikolai Artamonov**, had perished in Austria. He also mentioned that a KGB colleague, Oleg Gordievsky, had been recalled to Moscow recently because he was suspected of being a traitor, and named a source codenamed ROBERT as having supplied CIA secrets to the KGB. He was also able to clear up dozens of loose ends on other counterintelligence cases and reveal the KGB's latest tradecraft, including the deliberate brushing of CIA personnel in Moscow with a radioactive spy dust to enable their movements to be monitored.

Unusually, the director of central intelligence Bill Casey met Yurchenko several times during his debriefings, entertaining him to dinner twice, but was quite unable to resist spreading the good news of the CIA's impressive coup. However, Yurchenko was alarmed when he was told that he might be obliged to appear as a witness in an action brought against the U.S. government by Ewa Shadrin, the widow of the naval defector Nikolai Artamonov. Yurchenko, who had been promised total discretion, was understandably dismayed by the leaks and disappointed by his treatment by his CIA Security Division handlers who had failed to show him the respect he felt he deserved, so he redefected to the Soviet embassy in Washington, D.C., and called a press conference four days later to complain that he had been abducted by the CIA and drugged.

The heavy-drinking counterintelligence expert had an exaggerated view of what was in store for him and was bitterly disappointed when he was rejected by his former girlfriend, Dr. Valentina Yereskovsky, a beautiful blonde pediatrician and the wife of the Soviet consul-general in Montreal. The CIA concluded that it was highly likely that Aldrich Ames, who had been part of his debriefing team, had tipped off the KGB to Yurchenko's continuing interest in the woman with whom he had previously conducted a lengthy and passionate affair and in whom he remained besotted. Accordingly, when Yurchenko unexpectedly turned up on the doorstep of her apartment in Canada, she had almost certainly been warned to throw him out, which is precisely what she did, protesting that she had no intention of defecting with her two daughters.

Yurchenko's ludicrous claim to have been abducted and drugged was highly reminiscent of the assertions made by the journalist Oleg Bitov who had gone unpunished after he abandoned his recent defection to England. Although Yurchenko's ploy fooled nobody in the KGB, Vladimir Kryuchkov found it expedient to accept his version of events. After his retirement from the KGB, Yurchenko found work as a bank guard in Moscow.

– Z –

ZARUBINA, ELIZAVETA. Originally from Bukovina in Romania, Elizaveta Rosenzweig adopted the surname Gorskaya and in the mid-1920s found a job as a secretary in the Soviet embassy in Vienna, where she was recruited by Soviet intelligence. She had a degree in philology and spoke several languages, including French, German, English, and her native Romanian. On one of her first missions, she went to Turkey as an illegal where she encountered Yakov Blumkin, who was the chief illegal in the region. Under orders from Moscow, she seduced Blumkin to establish the nature of his contact with **Leon Trotsky** in 1929, and on her evidence Blumkin was recalled and executed. She then worked as an illegal with Roland Abbiate and her future husband, Vasili Zarubin, in Belgrade against Germany, Britain, and France. As cover the trio ran a small French restaurant, Le Petit Caporal, and later in the 1930s they moved to France where Zarubin adopted the cover of a businessman while Abbiate became a bartender in a fashionable restaurant on the Riviera where he cultivated and recruited young secretaries and typists on vacation from European foreign ministries. From France, Zarubina traveled extensively in Europe, Britain, and the United States to maintain contact with NKVD agents. Her husband was a former banker, codenamed MAXIM, who adopted the alias Colonel Zubilin. He had been in Finland since 1926 before moving to Berlin, and had red hair and "despite the heavy accent . . . spoke French, English and German fairly well."

According to her declassified KGB file, she was codenamed VARDO and had been recalled from Germany in April 1941 to cultivate the wife of a senior German diplomat in Moscow, and later successfully ran a code clerk in the German Foreign Ministry. In January 1942, Zarubin was appointed the *rezident* in New York under consular cover, and the following year was transferred to head the Washington, D.C., *rezidentura*. Meanwhile his wife was recruiting sources inside the Manhattan Project, mainly in California. Pavel Sudoplatov recalled that

> She hardly appeared foreign in the United States. Her manner was so natural and sociable that she immediately made friends. Slim, with dark eyes, she had a classic Semitic beauty that attracted men, and she was one of the most successful agent recruiters, establishing her own illegal network of Jewish refugees from Poland, and recruiting one of Szilard's secretaries, who provided technical data. She spoke excellent English, German, French, Romanian and Hebrew. Usually she looked like a sophisticated, upper-class European, but she had the ability to change her appearance like a chameleon.

One of her agents, Boris Morros, who later was also a double agent working for the Federal Bureau of Investigation, recalled that she was a "frail, pretty, middle-aged woman with an aristocratic manner" who often appeared to Morros to be in charge:

> I often heard of other Communist women talking of Elizabeth Zubilin as though she was a sort of Red Joan of Arc, a saint whose faith in the Soviet was pure and bottomless. They also had great respect for her intellect and judgment. Often I heard these wives of other spies say, while in the midst of a dispute over some matter of strategy, "Well, what did she say about it?" or "Let's ask Liza," or "Don't argue, Helen said so!" as though Madame Zubilin had the last word. She was generally acknowledged to be the real brain behind whatever shrewd moves her blustering husband made.

Recalled to Moscow in 1944 to answer allegations sent direct to Josef Stalin by a subordinate, Zubilin was appointed deputy chief of the NKVD's foreign intelligence branch, and retired on grounds of ill health three years later.

Bibliography

INTRODUCTION

The literature on the narrow topic of sexspionage is indeed limited, although there are plenty of books that refer obliquely to the subject. Broadly, they can be seen to fall into three distinct categories: the firsthand memoirs of those who have participated in the operations described in this book, the nonfiction accounts of intelligence operations that have included references to entrapments, and the case histories of individual incidents.

Because of the potentially sensational nature of sexspionage, its treatment—especially by journalists—has bordered on the lurid, with authors opting for supposition and speculation, for example when dealing with Mata Hari, in preference to fact. Thus, her first biographer, Richard Rowan, wrote about her in *Spy and Counter-Spy* in 1928 and Major Thomas Coulson, without the benefit of her trial papers, wrote a further account of her activities in 1930 that contained few verifiable facts. Three years later, her French interrogator, Pierre Bouchardon, gave a more detailed version in his memoirs *Souvenirs*, but thereafter numerous authors have rewritten her story with varying degrees of accuracy. Unfortunately, the principal areas of her life that have suffered most have been the three most important in intelligence terms, namely, her actual involvement in espionage, her precise movements during World War I, and the evidence upon which she was convicted.

The tale of an exotic, oriental dancer extracting military secrets from her indiscreet lovers proved irresistible, and Bernard Newman embroidered Coulson's version in 1956 with *Inquest on Mata Hari*; it was followed by Arch Whitehouse in 1964 with *Heroes and Legends of World War I* and his second book, *Espionage and Counterespionage*, and by Sam Waagenar's *Mata Hari* in 1965 and Kurt Singer's *Mata Hari* two years later. Curiously, Kurt Singer had written about Mata Hari in 1953 in *Women Spies*, in which he also gave an account of her beautiful daughter Banda, a spy for the Americans who was allegedly shot without a trial in Korea after she settled there in 1950.

Then Ronald Millar released *Mata Hari* in 1970 and Erika Ostrovsky produced *Eye of Dawn: The Rise and Fall of Mata Hari* in 1978. A year later, Edward Heubsch published *The Last Summer of Mata Hari* and an anonymous author produced *The Diary of Mata Hari* in 1984. In 1986, Russell Howe released *Mata Hari*, and in 1987 Julia Keay wrote *The Spy Who Never Was: The Life and Loves of Mata Hari*. Finally, in 1992, Julie Wheelwright explored Mata Hari's life in *The Fatal Lover: Mata Hari and the Myth of Women in Espionage*.

This minor literary cottage industry has been enhanced by further contributions by Hugh Cleland Hoy in *40 O.B.*, by Basil Thomson in *Queer People*, and by Sir William James in *The Eyes of the Navy*, not to mention the novels supposedly based on Marguerite MacLeod's remarkable life.

The tragedy of Mata Hari and the myths surrounding her have served as a foundation upon which several other authors have made some extravagant claims about the role of manipulative women engaged in espionage. For example, J. Bernard Hutton wrote two books, *Schools for Spies* in 1961 and *Women Spies*, to exposé Soviet spies at work in England and America, "with documented facts straight from the Soviet Secret Service files." German-educated author Josef Heisler was a graduate of Berlin University, a Czech journalist on a Communist newspaper in Prague, and a member of the Party's Central Committee who went to Moscow in 1934 to spend fours years at the Lenin School and work on the evening paper *Vecherniaya Moskva*. In 1939, as Czechoslovakia was occupied, Heisler fled to London and later, having anglicized his name to Joe Bernard Hutton, served as press attaché in Jan Masaryk's Czech government-in-exile. As a Communist convert, Hutton was apparently well placed to write about espionage and subversion, but in *School for Spies* he gave a detailed description of five KGB training schools in the Soviet Union, concentrating on Gaczyna, a hundred miles southwest of Kuibyshev, where illegals destined to work in the West spend 10 years in a sealed-off area covering 425 square miles in which Western towns had been faithfully reconstructed with a "true replica of streets, buildings, cinemas, restaurants and snack bars" so as to acquaint future agents with life in the West. Graduates from the decade-long course included "Soviet Secret Service operators like . . . William Arthur Mortimer." Supposedly Karakov had been assigned to Gaczyna in 1942 and had adopted the identity of William Mortimer to work as a pianist in a Boston nightclub. In July 1953, he had moved to New York where he sang with a jazz band. Between the summer of 1954 and the autumn of 1957, he managed a nightclub, ran a photographic business in the Bronx, and continued to recruit agents, among them Erzhika, the "Hungarian-born fiancée of an American government official" and his fiancée Pamela, a "personal secretary to a senior executive in a government department." However, following the arrest of Rudolf Abel in June 1957, an unnamed army officer from Alabama became convinced he had come under surveillance by the Federal Bureau of Investigation and was shot dead. Similarly, Pamela took an overdose because of the attention this incident had drawn to her private life, and William Mortimer "discreetly disappeared and was safely returned to Russia" in February 1961. Although plausibly narrated, the entire book is a fabrication.

Ten years later, Hutton returned to the subject in *Women Spies*, but described Gaczyna as "covering an area of some forty-two square miles" and named Rita Elliott and Eileen Jenkins as agents. Apparently, these women were actually Esfir G. Yuryna and Tanya M. Radyonska, and Hutton had mentioned them briefly in his earlier book. Trained as a high-wire artist, Elliott had been smuggled into Australia in October 1955, after the mandatory decade of preparation at Gaczyna and, as "one of the Soviet Secret Service's top agents, she managed to set up in a comparatively short time a widespread spy-ring." Her method of obtaining information from sources was dependent on hypnosis and drugs, and after five years she came to "the attention of the Australian Counter-Intelligence." Despite being under secret round-the-clock surveillance, she "managed to contact her informers, go-betweens, and other agents, and to dispose of all the incriminating equipment" she had used for her clandestine communications with Moscow. Finally, having "discovered limpet microphones hidden in her home," she left the country in February 1961, ostensibly to fulfill engagements in India and Pakistan, and disappeared. According to Hutton's second version of her case history, Elliott "met government officials and influential people who had first-hand knowledge of work in progress on the Woomera range and in research centers."

As for Eileen Jenkins, not previously mentioned by Hutton, she was smuggled into England in May 1958 and found lodgings in King's Cross before immigrating to Canada in March 1959. There, she worked in a Montreal bakery for six weeks, and then moved to Ottawa, where she found a job in a lingerie shop and "successfully established herself as a master spy." She "not only operated an espionage set-up, but maintained a terror group, which kidnapped and murdered." One of her victims was "a Slovak immigrant working as a draughtsman in an aircraft design company" who was abducted off the street when he refused to cooperate, drugged, and smuggled aboard a ship bound for Russia.

At Christmas 1959, she met "a police official" buying a gift for his mother in her shop who was well informed about the GRU defector Igor Gouzenko, and became his fiancé. The police official apparently described how Gouzenko had stolen a quantity of incriminating documents from the embassy's *referentura*, and these had been sufficient to put "a dozen diplomat spies behind bars." However, having concluded that her lover either did "not know or is too careful to divulge Western counter-intelligence methods," Jenkins received orders to leave Canada and was redeployed to another English-speaking country.

Neither of these two stories bears any scrutiny whatsoever. The Australian Security Intelligence Organization (ASIO) has no record of any circus performer who was suspected of being a Soviet master spy, and the proposition that Eileen Jenkins had "first heard about Igor Gouzenko" from her Canadian fiancé suggests that her 10 years of training at Gaczyna had been far from complete, as Gouzenko had defected more than 14 years earlier, and all the counterintelligence details of the case had been included in the Royal Commission Report, published in March 1947. Incidentally, not a single diplomat had been arrested, let alone convicted, as a result of Gouzenko's testimony.

Hutton not only invented most of the case histories to which he referred in *School for Spies*, but he adopted the same approach with *Women Spies*, published 10 years later, which was a catalog of female espionage. He returned to a slightly embellished version of the Eileen Jenkins case, and revealed that during his research he had been told of Anne, a clairvoyant with "a good working knowledge of German" who had been employed by British intelligence during World War II to "mind-travel" to "Nazi headquarters in Berlin." There she had "picked up a certain amount of information about military movements" and "the information she brought back to British secret service headquarters was treated as respectfully as information provided by other spies. British political and military strategy was influenced and helped by Anne's reports."

This splendidly fanciful tale could be written off as an example of the author being hoaxed, but he insisted that he was "able to trace Anne and meet her unofficially" to test the story and confirm the old lady's paranormal powers.

Hutton also disclosed that "one of the United States' spies who spied on Britain had the code name of Patricia" and she had been the manager of a dry-cleaning establishment in London's West End, and was thus well placed in the heart of Britain's metropolis and within a stone's throw of Whitehall where all important political and military decisions are made." Patricia "was efficient and over a period of many months her network of informers and agents ferreted out every detail of the specific subject that interested U.S. Intelligence Headquarters."

According to Hutton, "the British Secret Service is equally capable of treachery towards their friends across the Atlantic" and he revealed that an American woman named Gene had been carefully cultivated and recruited by a "young man who was, of course, a British Secret Service agent." She supplied him with "classified information from Washington's files" and when she returned home she "established a spy web of agents and informers and, over a period of years, supplied London with much secret information about the United States. What particularly interested Gene's superiors in London was not what was entered in official inter-governmental and inter-military communications but what was omitted from those communications, and also the behind-the-scenes reasons for these omissions."

All the cases of women spies described in such detail by Hutton were entirely invented, and this characteristically low standard of accuracy was emulated by others, such as Miles Copeland, a former Central Intelligence Agency (CIA) officer. In *The Real Spy World*, Copeland referred to two cases of what might be termed sexspionage, the first being "Emily," an "active but shy" personal assistant to an assistant secretary of state, who in 1950 had been cultivated and recruited by a Soviet intelligence officer posing as a life insurance salesman. He had "disappeared early in her career of espionage, but an attractive, independently wealthy, intelligent woman can always uncover romantic possibilities even when she has entered her fifties."

Emily passed the Soviets classified information for 14 years but, according to Copeland, Moscow "analysts, after many years, had come to the conclusion that much of the information was fake." When she was eventually identified, with the help of a defector, she confessed and returned the $100,000 that had accumulated in her Beirut bank account. Apparently, no further action was taken and she was allowed to retire to be "a librarian in some small New England town."

Actually, Copeland's tale about Emily was entirely fabricated, thereby proving that whatever an author's credentials—and Copeland had indeed been an authentic CIA officer until his retirement in the mid-1950s—the temptation to manufacture tales of seduction and espionage are irresistible.

Nor is such mischief confined to a single gender, for plenty of women have been willing to write books in which they invented espionage adventures during World War II for themselves. Elizabeth Denham started the genre with *I Looked Right* in 1956, describing her infiltration into Nazi-occupied France, and was followed by Roxane Pitt who wrote *The Courage of Fear* in 1957 and *Operation Double Life*, in 1975, recalling her clandestine assignments in Italy. In 1983, Josephine Butler described her covert visits to France in *Churchill's Secret Agent* and followed with a sequel in 1991, *Cyanide in My Shoe*. However, none of these authors could match Aline, the Countess of Romanones, who between 1987 and 1994 published four books, *The Spy Wore Red, The Spy Went Dancing, The Spy Wore Silk*, and *The Well-Mannered Spy*, recording her involvement in espionage, beginning with Operation BULLFIGHT in Spain at the end of 1943. Although Alines had served as a cipher clerk in Madrid for the Office of Strategic Services, her supposedly factual accounts were completely fictional.

Understandably, there are relatively few firsthand accounts written either by the perpetrators of sexual espionage or their victims, and apart from Christine Keeler's *The Truth at Last* and Eugene Ivanov's *The Naked Spy*, are largely authentic. Anthony Courtney and John Vassall detailed their experiences as targeted victims of sexual espionage, and Eugene Ivanov might also be included in this category, even if his memoirs, *The Naked Spy,* are largely fiction. *Red Spy at Night*, the autobiography of Helga Wannenmacher-Pohl, also appears to be a mixture of a few authentic names set in highly improbable tableau of espionage, bigamy, and sexual exploitation. If true, the book would have been a major contribution to the literature as the first detailed account written by a Soviet intelligence defector from her personal experience of Soviet entrapment operations. Unfortunately, there is neither internal nor external evidence to suggest the author ever served in any Soviet intelligence organization.

With so much of the available literature demonstrably unreliable, is there any material that is above suspicion? There is, but it is limited. Anthony Courtney used *Sailor in a Russian Frame* (1968) to describe his ordeal as a victim of KGB coercion, and John Vassall's *Autobiography of a Spy* (1975) offers a candid account of the blackmail he endured after he had been honeytrapped in Moscow. Understandably, few of those who have been ensnared in this way have much of an incentive to prolong the agony, and these two examples remain the only ones of their kind. While plenty of observers would write about the Profumo affair, the former minister himself remained silent on the matter, leaving it to his son David to publish his memory of those events in a book highly critical of both his parents.

Nor is anyone really likely to boast of having masterminded honeytrap operations, so apart from the participants mentioned previously, the field is limited. Denis Rake wrote engagingly and humorously about his love affair with a German officer in Paris, but he felt genuine affection for the man and did not attempt to extract information from him. Equally, the German had no idea that his lover was a British agent, and in any event Rake's superiors at SOE's headquarters had never instructed him to sleep with the enemy.

There is also a paucity of firsthand accounts written by those responsible for having participated in operations that have proved so controversial. Nikolai Khokhlov's memoirs are an exception, and so perhaps is the biography of Pavel Sudoplatov, the NKVD general who masterminded Leon Trotsky's assassination, although its authorship, by two American writers and Sudoplatov's son, remains controversial because of some of their unsubstantiated assertions concerning Soviet spies in the United States. For example, they claimed that the distinguished physicists Enrico Fermi, Leo Tzilard, Bruno Pontecorvo, George Gamow, and J. Robert Oppenheimer had all been invaluable Soviet spies inside the Manhattan Project, while simultaneously ascribing NKVD codenames to the wrong agents. When, a year after *Special Tasks* had been published, the VENONA material was declassified and released, there were rather too many contradictions in what were purported to be Sudoplatov's recollections. Admittedly, he had not been given the benefit of access to the KGB's archives, but nevertheless his version seemed rather too flawed to be taken at face value.

Although there have been plenty of titles penned by KGB veterans, most have concentrated on revealing details of operations conducted with willing participants rather than coerced victims. Thus, Igor Damaskin's *Kitty Harris: The Spy with Seventeen Names* recounted the tragic life of the NKVD agent who ran Donald Maclean in London and Paris and who was also his lover, but even after the collapse of the Soviet bloc and the brief opening of the KGB's archives, such disclosures are the exception. The Russians prefer to remember their ideological adherents, and their victims invariably opt for anonymity.

BIBLIOGRAPHY

Reference Works

Blackstock, Paul, and Frank Schaf. *Intelligence, Espionage, Counterespionage and Covert Operations.* Detroit, Mich.: Gale Research, 1978.

Constantinides, George. *Intelligence and Espionage: An Analytic Bibliography.* Boulder, Colo.: Westview Press, 1983.

Kross, Peter. *The Encyclopedia of World War II Spies.* Fort Lee, Va.: Barricade, 2001.

Mahoney, M. H. *Women in Espionage: A Biographical Dictionary.* Santa Barbara, Calif.: ABC-Clio, 1993.

McLaren, Angus. *Sexual Blackmail: A Modern History.* Cambridge, Mass.: Harvard University Press, 2002.

Minnick, Wendell L. *Spies and Provocateurs.* London: McFarland, 1992.

O'Toole, G. L. A. *The Encyclopedia of American Intelligence and Espionage.* New York: Facts on File, 1988.

Parrish, Michael. *Soviet Security and Intelligence Organizations 1917–1990.* Westport, Conn.: Greenwood, 1992.

Polmar, Norman, and Thomas Allen. *Spy Book.* New York: Random House, 1997.

Europe

Accoce, Pierre, and Pierre Quet. *The Lucy Ring.* London: W. H. Allen, 1967.
Andrew, Christopher. *Secret Service.* London: Heinemann, 1985.

Anonymous. *The Diary of Mata Hari*. New York: Carroll & Graf, 1984.
Bazna, Elyesa. *I Was Cicero*. London: André Deutsch, 1962.
Booth, Nicholas. *Zigzag*. London: Portrait Books, 2007.
Borovik, Genrihk. *The Philby Files*. London: Little, Brown, 1994.
Bouchardon, Pierre. *Souvenirs*. Paris: Albin Michel, 1933.
Bower, Donald. *Sex Espionage*. New York: Knighsbridge, 1990.
Bower, Tom. *The Perfect English Spy*. London: Heinemann, 1995.
Butler, Josephine. *Churchill's Secret Agent*. London: Metheun, 1983.
———. *Cyanide in My Shoe*. London: This England Books, 1991.
Carter, Miranda. *Anthony Blunt: His Lives*. New York: Farrar, Straus & Giroux, 2001.
Cookridge, E. H. *Sisters of Delilah*. London: Oldbourne, 1959.
Costello, John. *Mask of Treachery*. London: Collins, 1988.
Coulson, Thomas. *Mata Hari: Courtesan and Spy*. New York: Harper Brothers, 1930.
Courtney, Anthony. *Sailor in a Russian Frame*. London: Johnson Books, 1968.
Damaskin, Igor. *Kitty Harris: The Spy with Seventeen Names*. London: St Ermin's Press, 2001.
Denham, Elizabeth. *I Looked Right*. New York: Doubleday, 1956.
Driberg, Tom. *Guy Burgess*. London: Weidenfeld & Nicolson, 1956.
———. *Ruling Passions*. London: Jonathan Cape, 1977.
Farago, Ladislas. *Game of the Foxes*. New York: McKay, 1973.
Foot, M. R. D. *SOE in France*. London: HMSO, 1966.
Foote, Alexander. *Handbook for Spies*. London: Museum Press, 1964.
Gisevius, Hans-Berndt. *To the Bitter End*. London: Jonathan Cape, 1948.
Heubsch, Edward. *The Last Summer of Mata Hari*. New York: Crown Books, 1979.
Hill, George. *Go Spy the Land*. London: Cassell, 1932.
Hodges, Andrew. *Alan Turing: The Enigma*. London: Burnett Books, 1983.
Hoehling, Adolph. *Women Who Spied*. New York: Dodd, Mead, 1967.
Höhne, Heinz. *Canaris: Hitler's Master Spy*. New York: Doubleday, 1979.
———. *Codeword Direktor*. London: Secker & Warburg, 1971.
Höhne, Heinz, and Herman Zolling. *The General Was a Spy*. New York: Coward McCann, 1972.
Howe, Russell. *Mata Hari*. New York: Dodd Mead, 1986.
Hoy, Hugh Cleland. *40 O.B.* London: Hutchinson, 1932.
Hutton, J. Bernard. *School for Spies*. London: Neville Spearman, 1961.
———. *Women in Espionage*. London: W. H. Allen, 1971.
Hyde, H. Montgomery. *Cynthia*. New York: Farrar, Strauss & Giroux, 1965.
Ivanov, Eugene. *The Naked Spy*. London: Blake, 1992.
James, William. *The Eyes of the Navy*. London: Metheun, 1955.

Keay, Julia. *The Spy Who Never Was: The Life and Loves of Mata Hari*. London: Michael Joseph, 1987.
Keeler, Christine. *Scandal*. London: St. Martin's Press, 1989.
———. *The Truth at Last*. London: Sidgwick & Jackson, 2001.
Knightley, Philip. *Philby: KGB Masterspy*. London: Jonathan Cape, 1997.
Koehler, John O. *Stasi*. Boulder, Colo.: Westview Press, 1999.
Laville, Helen. *Cold War Women*. Manchester: Manchester University Press, 2002.
Lewis, David. *Sexspionage*. New York: Harcourt Brace, 1976.
Lovell, Mary S. *Cast No Shadow*. New York: Pantheon Books, 1992.
Macintyre, Ben. *Agent ZIGZAG*. London: Bloomsbury, 2007.
Masterman, J. C. *The Double Cross System of the War of 1939–46*. London: Pinloco, 1995.
Masters, Anthony. *The Man Who Was M*. Oxford: Basil Blackwell, 1984.
Meissner, Hans-Otto. *The Man with Three Faces*. New York: Rinehart, 1955.
Millar, Ronald. *Mata Hari*. Geneva: Heron Books, 1970.
Modin, Yuri. *My Five Cambridge Friends*. London: Headline, 1994.
Moyszich, Ludwig. *Operation Cicero*. London: Wingate, 1950.
Mure, David. *Master of Deception*. London: William Kimber, 1980.
———. *Practise to Deceive*. London: Sphere, 1979.
———. *The Last Temptation*. London: Buchan & Enright, 1984.
Newman, Bernard. *Inquest on Mata Hari*. London: Robert Hale, 1956.
Ostrovsky, Erika. *Eye of Dawn: The Rise and Fall of Mata Hari*. New York: Dorset Press, 1978.
Pacepa, Ion. *Programmed to Kill*. Chicago: Ivan R. Dee, 2009.
Page, Bruce, Phillip Knightley, and David Leitch. *The Philby Conspiracy*. New York: Doubleday, 1968.
Penrose, Barry, and Simon Freeman. *Conspiracy of Silence*. London: Grafton, 1986.
Philby, Eleanor. *The Spy I Loved*. London: Hamish Hamilton, 1967.
Philby, Kim. *My Silent War*. London: McGibbon & Kee, 1968.
Philby, Rufina. *The Private Life of Kim Philby*. London: St. Ermin's, 1999.
Pitt, Roxane. *Operation Double Life*. London: Racghman & Turner, 1975.
———. *The Courage of Fear*. London: Jarrolds, 1957.
Popov, Dusko. *Spy/Counterspy*. London: Weidenfeld & Nicolson, 1974.
Putlitz, Wolfgang zu. *The zu Putlitz Dossier*. London: Allan Wingate, 1957.
Rake, Dennis. *Rake's Progress*. London: Lesliie Fewin, 1968.
Rowan, Richard. *Spy and Counter-Spy*. New York: Viking, 1928.
Rupp, Rainer. *Policy for the Next Decade*. Boston: 1984.
———. *Politics and Security in the Southern Region of the Atlantic Alliance*. New York: Houndsmill, 1998.

———. *The Future of the European Alliance Systems*. Berlin: Das schweigekartell, 2003.
Seale, Patrick, and Maureen McConville. *Philby: The Long Road to Moscow*. London: Hamish Hamilton, 1973.
Silber, Jules. *The Invisible Weapons*. London: Hutchinson, 1932.
Singer, Kurt. *Mata Hari*. London: Tandem, 1967.
———. *Women Spies*. Toronto: Harlequin Books, 1953.
Stiller, Werner. *Beyond the Wall*. Washington, D.C.: Brassey's, 1983.
Strong, Kenneth. *Men of Intelligence*. London: Cassell, 1970.
Sudoplatov, Pavel. *Special Tasks*. Boston: Little, Brown, 1994.
Summers, Anthony, and Stephen Dorril. *Honeytrap*. London: Weidenfeld & Nicolson, 1987.
Sutherland, Christine. *Monica: Heroine of the Danish Resistance*. London: Canongate, 1991.
Thomson, Basil. *Queer People*. London: Hodder & Stoughton, 1922.
Vassall, John. *Autobiography of a Spy*. London: Sidgwick & Jackson, 1975.
Waagenaar, Sam. *Mata Hari*. New York: Appleton-Century, 1965.
Werner, Ruth. *Sonia's Report*. London: Chatto & Windus, 1991.
Wheelwright, Julie. *The Fatal Lover: Mata Hari and the Myth of Women in Espionage*. London: Collins, 1992.
Whitehouse, Arch. *Espionage and Counterespionage*. New York: Doubleday, 1964.
———. *Heroes and Legends of World War I*. New York: Doubleday, 1964.
Whymant, Robert. *Stalin's Spy*. London: I. B. Tauris, 1996.
Willoughby, Charles. *Shanghai Conspiracy*. New York: E. P. Dutton, 1952.
Wright, Peter. *SpyCatcher*. New York: Viking, 1987.

United States

Albright, Joseph, and Marica Kunstel. *Bombshell*. New York: Random House, 1997.
Anonymous. *British Security Coordination*. London: St. Ermin's, 1998.
Batvinis, Raymond. *The Origins of FBI Counterintelligence*. Lawrence: University of Kansas Press, 2007.
Bentley, Elizabeth. *Out of Bondage*. New York: Ivy Books, 1988.
Bord, Belle. *Belle Boyd in Camp and Prison*. New York: Saunders, Otley, 1865.
Breindel, Eric, and Herbert Romerstein. *The Venona Secret*. New York: HarperCollins, 1999.
Breuer, Willaim B. *War and American Women*. Westport, Conn.: Praeger, 1997.
Brook-Shepherd, Gordon. *The Storm Petrels*. London: Collins, 1977.

Chavez, Judy, with Jack Vitek. *Defector's Mistress*. Collingwood, Vic.: Unicorn Books, 1980.
Copeland, Miles. *The Real Spy World*. London: Weidenfeld & Nicolson, 1975.
Dallek, Robert. *An Unfinished Life: John F. Kennedy 1917–1963*. Boston: Little, Brown, 2003.
Dallin, David. *Soviet Espionage*. New Haven, Conn.: Yale University Press, 1955.
De Pauw, Linda Grant. *Battle Cries and Lullabies*. Lantham, Md.: University Press of America, 1992.
Deriabin, Piotr. *The Secret World*. New York: Doubleday, 1959.
Dulles, Allen. *The Craft of Intelligence*. New York: Harper & Row, 1963.
Eisenhower, John. *Letters to Mamie*. New York: Doubleday, 1978.
Haynes, John Earl, and Harvey Klehr. *Venona: Decoding Soviet Espionage in America*. New Haven, Conn.: Yale University Press, 1999.
Hersh, Seymour. *The Dark Side of Camelot*. Boston: Little, Brown, 1997.
Hyde, H. Montgomery. *Room 3603*. New York: Farrar, Straus, 1962.
Kessler, Lauren. *Clever Girl*. New York: HarperCollins, 2003.
Klehr, Harvey, and John Haynes. *The Secret World of American Communism*. New Haven, Conn.: Yale University Press, 1995.
Markle, Donald E. *Spies and Spymasters of the Civil War*. New York: Hippocrene Books, 2000.
Massing, Hede. *This Deception*. London: Sloane & Pearce, 1951.
Olmsted, Kathryn. *Red Spy Queen*. Chapel Hill: University of North Carolina Press, 2002.
Romanones, Aline. *The Spy Went Dancing*. New York: Putnam's, 1990.
———. *The Spy Wore Red*. New York: Random House, 1987.
———. *The Spy Wore Silk*. New York: Jove Books, 1992.
———. *The Well-Mannered Spy*. New York: Jove Books, 1994.
Summersby, Kay. *Eisenhower Was My Boss*. New York: Prentice-Hall, 1948.
———. *Past Forgetting: My Love Affair with Dwight D. Eisenhower*. New York: Simon & Schuster, 1976.
Thomas, Evan. *Robert Kennedy*. New York: Simon & Schuster, 2000.
Vise, David A. *The Bureau and the Mole*. New York: Atlantic Monthly Press, 2002.
Weinstein, Allen, and Alexander Vassiliev. *The Haunted Wood*. New York: Random House, 1999.

Historical Dictionaries

Kahama, Ephraim. *Historical Dictionary of Israeli Intelligence*. Lanham, Md.: Scarecrow Press, 2006.

Pringle, Robert W. *Historical Dictionary of Russian/Soviet Intelligence*. Lanham, Md.: Scarecrow Press, 2006.
Trenear-Harvey, Glenmore. *Historical Dictionary of Air Intelligence*. Lanham, Md.: Scarecrow Press, 2008.
Turner, Michael A. *Historical Dictionary of United States Intelligence*. Lanham, Md.: Scarecrow Press, 2006.
West, Nigel. *Historical Dictionary of British Intelligence*. Lanham Md.: Scarecrow Press, 2005.
———. *Historical Dictionary of Cold War Counterintelligence*. Lanham, Md.: Scarecrow Press, 2007.
———. *Historical Dictionary of International Intelligence*. Lanham, Md.: Scarecrow Press, 2006.
———. *Historical Dictionary of World War II Intelligence*. Lanham, Md.: Scarecrow Press, 2008.

Websites

The National Women's History Museum, www.nwhm.org/spies.

Index

-A-

Abakumov, Viktor, 305, 307
Abbiate, Roland, 58, 162, 238, 254, 318
Abbott, G. W., 47
ABC, 11
Abel, Rudolf I, 84
Abwehr, xvii, 11, 26, 39, 45–47, 52, 71, 92, 98, 106, 118, 135, 137, 182, 190, 198, 214, 241, 250–51, 253, 276–77, 279, 289, 296–97; Chief of. *See* Wilhelm Canaris Defectors from, *See* Otto John, Willi Hamburger, William Sebold, Erich Vermehren
ADA, 56, 107
ADAM, 79
ADEN, 103
Adenauer, Konrad, 242
Afrika Korps, 197
After Long Silence, 282
Agabekov, Georges, 283
Agee, Phillip, xiv, xxi, 1–4
Agiraki, Anna, 4
Agnelli, Marella, 144
The Angry Exile, 153
AIER, 142
Air Force Office of Special Investigations, 229
Aitken, Agnes, 55
Akhmerov, Iskhak, 56, 71, 162, 224, 283

Akhmedoc, Ismail, 222
ALARIC, 135
Albin, Gabrielle, xx, 4–5
ALEC, 190–91
ALEK, 175
ALES, 52, 117
Alexandrov, Vladimir, 316
ALICE, 169
Allami Vedelmi Hatosag (AVH), xiv, 81
Allen, W. E. D. ("Bill"), 39
Allyson, Sven, 217
Alonso, Alejandro, 235
Alsop, Kenneth, xviii, 5
ALTE, 279
Alvarez, Carlos, xxi, 5
Alvarez, Elsa, xxi, 5
Amerasia, 200, 226
American Girl, 40
Ames, Aldrich, xx, xxi, xxv, 5, 160, 204, 228, 316
Ames, Rosario, xx, xxi, xxv, xxviii, 5, 6, 9
Amos, Mrs., 315
Amtorg, 38, 54, 105
Andersen, Helene, 10
Andersen, Svend, 10
Anderson, Helen, 10–11
Anderson, Jack, xx, 11
Andreev, Vladislav, 164
ANDREY, 239
ANDRIES, 135

336 • INDEX

Andropov Institute, 8
Andropov, Yuri, 248
Androsov, Stanislav, 5
Angelov, Sylvia, 295
Angleton, Cicely, 177
Angleton, James J., 177
ANITA, 140
ANTENNA, 246
Antheil, Henry W., xvii, xxvii, 11
Anton, Natasha, 11
Apostles, 282
Apresyan, Stepan, 58
ARABEL, 135
ARENA, 224
Arenal, Leopoldo, 294
Arenal, Luis, 294
Argone Accumulator, 237
Argylle, Duchess of, 65
Armstrong, Sir Robert, 207
Arnold, Dick, 284
Artamonov, Ewa, 12, 317
Artamonov, Nikolai, 12, 317
Arthur Jackson, USS, 303
ARTICHOKE, 177
Arvad, Inge, 142
Arvad, Inga, xvii, 12–14
Ashenden, 173
ASIO. *See* Australian Security Intelligence Organisation
ASKO, 110
Astor, Hon. Hugh, 40
Astor, Lord ("Bill"), 141, 195, 229, 308
Astor, Viscount, 133
ATILLA, 69
Atkins, Vera, 271
Atsugi Naval Air Station, 231
Aubry, 288
Auden, W. H., 120, 122
Australian Defence Intelligence Organisation (DIO), 156, 157
penetration of. *See* Simon Lappas
Australian Department of External Affairs, penetration of. *See* Ian Milner
Australian Security Intelligence Organisation (ASIO), xxiv, 157, 164, 178, 217–18, 260–61, 300, 324
Autobiography of a Spy, 16
AUTOGIRO, 45–48
AVH. *See* Allami Vedelmi Hatosag
AVIATOR, 288
Ayres, Peter, 188
Ayriss, Paddy, 95
Azpillaga, Florentino, xiv, 14

-B-
Babich, Antoni, 295
Bagley, Tennent ("Pete"), 200
Bailey, Kimberley, 203, 205
Baillie-Stewart, Norman, xvi, 14–15
Baker, Bobby, 232, 243
Baker, Josephine, 15–16
Balch, Robert K., 264–68
Baldwin, Stanley, 260
Balmaceda, GIliana, 271
Bancroft, Mary, xvii, 16
Bandera, Stefan, 275
Baranowsky, Lucia, xviii, 96
Barczatis, Elli, xviii, 16–17
Bardet, Roger, 251
Barkowitz, Benjamin, 287
Barnett, David H., xx, 8
Barr, Joel, 246
Barrett, Vickie, 308
Bart, Pierre, 27
Baruch, Bernard, 14
Bates, Charlie, 144
Batissky, Gen., 21
Battle Hymn of China, 262
Baucq, Phillipe, 50
Bay of Pigs, 77
Beam, Jacob, 252

Beams, Dovie, xiv, 17–18
Bearden, Milton, 7
Beardsley, Mimi, 143
Beaumont, Lia, de, 65
Beaverbrook, Lord, 72, 311
Beck, Joseph, 210
Beck, Louis, 11, 145
Beck, Rudolf, 4, 5
Becker, Franz, 119
Becker, Maggie, 100
Bedell Smith, Walter, 40
Bedford, Duke of, 66
Begué, Georges, 46
Behar, George, 22
Bele Boyd in Camp and Prison, 36
Belin, Jean, 221
BELLA, 139
Belyakov, Evgenni, 92
Benedict, Clara, 172
Benkendorgg, Count Johann, 41
Bennett, Paddy, 180
Bentley, Elizabeth, xvii, 18–20, 52, 57, 161, 162, 224–25, 245
Benvenuto, Ludmilla, 167
Berger, Helge, xiv, 20
Beria, Lavrenti, 20, 21, 67, 89, 217, 255, 306
BERTHA, 92, 93
Beurton, Leon, xvii, 154
Beyond the Wall, 279
BfV. *See* Bundesamt für Verfasstungsschutz
Bialoguski, Dr. Michael, 217
Biegel, Rose, 294
BIG LEMON, 296
BILL, 135
Bishop, Maurice, 3
Bissell, Richard, 77
Bitov, Oleg, 318
Black, Helen, 170
Black, Ivan, 47
Black Sheep Club, 202

Blake, George, 21–26, 31, 93
Bleicher, Hugo, 45–48, 251
Bletchley Park, 297
Blits, Helena, 26–27
Bloch, Felix H., xx, xxi, 27–29, 160
Bloch, Georges, 46
Bloch, Lucille, 27
Blok, Niks, 14
BLUE WREN, 193
Blumkin, Yakov, 318
Blunt, Anthony, xvi, xx, 29–31, 42, 56, 69, 73, 112, 120–22, 142, 196, 199, 238, 259, 281
BND. *See* Bundesnachrichtendienst
Bobarev, Evgenni, 31
Boeckel, Lisa, 154
Bohlen, Chip, 263
Bokhan, Sergei, 6
Bond, James, 31–33, 214
BORDEAUX, 162
Bossard, Frank, xviii, 33
Bostrom, Ingrid, 273
Bothwell, John, 102
Bouchardon, Pierre, 172, 321
Bournonville, Eva de, xv, 33–34, 290
Boursicot, Bernard, xiv, 34, 35
Bowen, Ann-Christine, xiv, xxi, 35, 248–49
BOW TIE, 144
Boyce, Ernest, 42
Boyd, Belle, xv, 36
Boy-Ed, Karl, 75
Boyer, Dr. Raymond, 158
Bra Camera, 35
Bracey, Arnold, 159
Bradwell, Lord, 73
Brandes, Willie, 146
Brandt, Hilda, 36, 37
Brandt, Willy, 259, 288
Breeckow, Georg, 310
Brennan, Charles D., 149
Bretton Woods Conference, 161

Brewer, Eleanor, xiv, 37, 122, 218
Brewer, Sam Pope, 37, 218
Brik, Evgenni, 38, 134
Briscoe, Nora, xvii, 38, 39, 115
British Agent, 41
British Broadcasting Corporation (BBC), 5, 42, 267
British Information Service, 210
British Security Coordination (BSC), 44, 156, 211–12; Director of. *See* William Stephenson
British Security Service (MI5), xxviii, 10, 11, 17, 30, 42, 45, 52, 56, 62, 65, 70, 72, 90–92, 95, 96, 112, 115, 118, 122–32, 135, 141, 142, 144–46, 150, 153, 167, 168, 175, 179, 182, 186, 195, 196, 198, 199, 202, 209, 239, 241, 253–54, 260, 281–82, 286, 288, 301, 307–08, 312–16; Director-General. *See* Roger Hollis, David Petrie
Penetration of. *See* Anthony Blunt, Guy Burgess
Watcher Service, 124
British Union of Fascists (BUF), 38, 39, 115, 132
Broda, Engelbert, 175
Broda, Hildegard, 175
BROKEN ARROW, 101
BRONX, 39, 40, 198, 316
Brook, Sir Norman, 141, 229
Brooke, Sir Alan, 47
Brooke, Gerald, 190
Brooks, Tony, 165
Broszey, Christel, 243
Brothers to the Rescue, 236, 244–45
Brousse, Charles, 211
Brousse, Kay, 211
Browder, Earl, 56, 162, 224
Browder, Marguerite, 56, 107

Brown, F., 18
Brown, Frances, 308
Browning, Freddie, 114
Bruce, David, 144
Bruce Lockhart, Robert, xvi, 41
Brunet, Gilles, 31, 38, 63, 165
Brunger, Anita, 157
Bryhn, Asbjorn, 166, 167
BSC. *See* British Security Coordination
Bucar, Annabelle, xvii, xviii, 40, 41, 100
Buckley, Edward J., 19
Buckley, Sheila, 280
Budberg, Moura, xvi, 41
Budenz, Louis, 19
Buechner, Elfriede, 112
BULLFIGHT, 326
Bundesamt für Verfassungsschutz (BfV), 67, 112, 119, 140, 164, 242, 354; Chief of. *See* Otto John, Roland Meier
Defector from. *See* Otto John
Bundesnachrichtendienst (BND), 17, 117, 118, 158, 163, 192, 254–55, 278; Director of. *See* Reinhard Gehlen
Bundespolizei, 222
Bureau of State Security (BOSS), 291–92
Burgess, Guy, xviii, 29, 30, 42–44, 69, 73, 112, 120–22, 146, 168, 169, 196, 199, 238, 259, 281
Burgess, Nigel, 43
Burhop, Dr. Eric, 179
Burnside, Gen. Ambrose, 194
Burobin, 166
Busch, Heinz, 158, 163, 283
Bush, George W., 214
Burton, Richard, xv, 44
Busch, Heinz, 255

Butkov, Mikhail, 102
Butler, Josephine, 326
Bystrolyotov, Dmitri, 309

-C-
CABIN, 217
Cabon, Christine, 226
Cadet, Madame, 44
Cairncross, John, 30, 31, 69, 122, 281
Calvo, Luis, 11–12
Cambridge Five, 168
Camp 020, 10, 12, 70, 92, 93, 240, 253
Camp Peary, 201
Campbell, William, 76
Canadian Department of External Affairs, penetration of. *See* Herbert Norman
Canadian Security Intelligence Service (CSIS), 139, 275
Canaris, Wilhelm, 117, 289
Cape Matapan, 212
Capiau, Herman, 50
Capone, Al, 76
Cardin, Lucien, 195
Carlson, Olaf, 110
Caros, Gen. Michael, 70
Carré, Mathillde, 45–48
CARTE, 250–51
Carter, Jimmy, 140
Casa Chiquita, 293
Casement, Sir Roger, xv, 48–50
 Black Diaries, 49
Casey, William ("Bill"), 317
Casino Royale, 32
Castro, Fidel, 77, 193, 298
CAVALRYMAN, 103
Cavell, Edith, xv, 50, 270
CD, 141
Central Bureau of Investigation, 235

Central Intelligence, Director of. *See* Bill Casey, Bill Colby, John Deutsch, Allen Dulles, Richard Helms, William Webster
Central Iintelligence Agency (CIA). xvii, xx, xxi, xxiii, xxv, 1–3, 5, 11, 17, 27–29, 35, 50, 70, 77, 83, 90, 91, 93, 97, 99, 102, 109, 120, 121, 123, 131, 143, 144, 147, 159, 166, 167, 176, 192, 200, 202, 203, 205, 216, 222, 224, 228 230–32, 240, 258, 263, 272, 288–90, 296, 301–02, 306, 316–18; Directorate of Operations, 6
Counterintelligence Staff, 7, 160, 201
 defector from. *See* Edward Lee Howard
 Latin America Division, 47
 penetration of. *See* Aldridge Ames, Larry Wu-Tai Chin, Karl Koecher, Edwin Moore, Harold Nicholson, Nada Prouty, Sharon Scranage
 Security Division, 258, 317
 Soviet/Eastern European Division, xx, 6, 51, 150–51
Chahine, Talal Khalil, 230
CHAILLAN, 251
Chalet, Maurice, 64
Chambers, Whittaker, 51–52, 83, 116, 171, 262, 282
The Champagne Spy, 197
Chang, Suzy, 202, 308
Chankung, Yang, 213
Chaplin, Charlie, 206
Chapman, Eddie, 202
Chateau-Thierry, Duchesse de, 52, 253
Chaudoir, Elvira, 40

Chavchavadze, David, 143
Chavez, Judy, 52–53
CHEESE, 197
Cheka, 114
Cheng, Isabelle, 146
Chequers, 291
Cherkashin, Viktor, 9
Chernyak, Yakov, 176
Chernyavsky, Genrykh, 216
Chernyavsky, Irina, 216
Chertov, Nikolai, 33
CHICKWIT, 177
Childs, Jack, 149
Childs, Morris, 149
Chin, Larry Wu-Tai, 228
China Aid Council, 225
China Today, 226
Chinese intelligence service. *See* Ministry of State Security
Chisholm, Ruari, 247
Chulkov, Pavel, 53
Chung, Johnny, 213
Church, Frank, 79
Churchill, Clarissa, 43
Churchill, Clementine, 311
Churchill, Peter, 251
Churchill, Randolph, xxvii, 107
Churchill, Sarah, xxvi
Churchill, Winston, xxvi, 39, 42, 145, 276, 285, 308
Ciano, Count Galeazzo, 249, 260
CICERO, 141
Cissey, General de, xv, 53
Clark, James, 272–73
Cleveland, William, xx, xxi, 213
CLEVER GIRL, 18, 224–25
Clinton, Bill, 70, 214
Close, Dave, 135
Cochran, Charles H., 114
Cohen, Leontina ("Lona"), xxviii, 53–55, 61, 89, 103, 131, 134, 185

Cohen, Morris, xxviii, 53–55, 61, 131, 134, 185
COINTELPRO, 149
Coke, Marion, 260
Colby, Bill, 11
Colchester, Halsey, 208
Collins, Martin, 84, 111
Colossus, 297
Comintern, 96, 170, 238
Communist Party of Australia (CPA), 178
Communist Party of Austria, xvi, 68, 286
Communist Party of Canada, 199
Communist Party of Denmark, 164
Communist Party of Great Britain (CPGB), 30, 31, 42, 55–56, 60, 72, 95, 96, 150, 170, 178, 179, 194, 286, 291, 313; National Organiser. *See* Percy Glading Secretary-General. *See* Harry Pollitt
Communist Party of India (CPI), 96, 262
Communist Party of Mexico, 293
Communist Party of South Africa, 272
Communist Party of the United States of America (CPUSA), 18, 51–53, 56–57, 71, 81, 82, 103, 107, 146, 149, 224, 266; Secretary General. *See* Earl Browder
Conquest, Robert, 74
Conrad, Clyde, xxi, 8
Control Commission for Austria, 134
Control Commission for Germany, 267
Cooper, Lady Diana, 40
Cooper, Afred Duff, 41
Copeland, Miles, 325–26
Coplon, Judith, xviii, 57–60
Cornford, John, 282

CORSICAN, 256–57
Costello, Paddy, 60, 128
Costenza, Countess, 253
Cot, Pierre, 157
Cottenham, Earl of, 132
Cottin, Roger, 47–48
Coulson, Thomas, 321
Counter-Intelligence Corps, 223
CounterSpy, 3
The Courage of Fear, 219
Courtney, Anthony, xvii, xiv, 61–62, 326–27
Courtney, Elizabeth, 62
Covert Action Information Bulletin, 1, 3
Cowan, Jill, 143
Coward, Nöel, 311
Cowell, Gervase, 247
Coy, Harold, 225
Cram, Cleveland, 144
Crosby, Bing, 143
CRONIN, 6
Crough, Mr., 215
CROWN, 118
Crump, Ray, 177
Cuban American National Foundation, 236
Cuban intelligence service. *See* Direccion General de inteligencia
Cummingham, Randy, 90
Cushman, Paulene, xv, 62, 63
Currie, Lauchlin, 19, 161
Curzon, Grace, 39
CX, 206
Cynthia, 212
Czech intelligence service. *See* Stanti Bezpecnost

-D-
DAEDALUS, 157
DAISY, 17

Daladier, Edouard, 42, 157
Dalrymple-Champneys, Lady, 30
Damaskin, Igor, 328
DAMSEL, 63
Danielson, Christian, 98
Danischewsky, Irene, 145
Danish Intelligence Service, 158, 163
Danish Nazi Party, 253
Daughter of the Earth, 262
Davis, Jefferson, 97
D-Day, 40, 80
Deacon, Richard, 120
Death of an Idealist, 281
Deeker, Francois de, 253
DEEP ROOT, 63
Defector's Mistress, 53
Defense Intelligence Agency (DIA), 192–93
penetration of. *See* Ana Montes
Dejean, Marie-Claire, 64, 99
Dejean, Maurice, xxvii, 64, 153, 287
Deladurantaye, Chris, 230
Delilah, xxvi, 64, 250
DELTA, 177
Demaris, David, 79
Denham, Elizabeth, 326
Denning, Lord, 65, 142, 229
The Denning Report, 64–65
DENZIL, 4
D'Eon, Charles, 65, 66
Departamentul de Informatii Externe (DIE), 152
DERBY HAT, 177
Deriabin, Piotr, xviii, 66, 67
Dericourt, Henri, 270
Deutsch, Arnold, xvi, 67–70, 122, 237, 286
Deutsch, John M., 70
Deutsch, Oscar, 68
Deutsch, Sylvia, 69
Deuxieme Bureau, 15, 172, 240

Devaux, Rolf-Peter, 35
Devonshire, Duke of, 133
DGI. *See* Direccion General de Inteligencia
Dhan Maloy Krishna, 235
Diamond, Suzy, 202
Diamonds Are Forever, 32
Diaz, Viviana, xvii, 70, 71
Dibben, Hod, 202
DICK, 135
Diefenbaker, John, 195
Dierks, Hans, 253
Dies Committee, 83, 262
Dietrich, Sepp, 249
Dietze, Frank, 4,
Digby, Pamela, xxvii, 107
Dikeos, Victor, 252
Dinger, Richard, 215
Diomede, HMS, 22
DIR, 224
Dirección General de Inteligencia (DGI), 5, 14, 100, 192, 193
Defector from. *See* Florentino Azpillaga
Direction de la Surveillance du Territoire (DST), 27, 34, 64, 266, 302; Director of. *See* Maurice Chalet
Direction Generale de Securité Extérieur (DGSE), 226, 249
Chief of, *See* Pierre Lacoste
Directorate of Operations (DO), 6
Dirty Work, 3
Discher, Urszula, 252
Discredit Operations, 71
Dobertin, Rolf, 278
Doble, Frances, 218
Dobrova, Maria, xiv, 71
Doctor No, 32
Dodd, Martha, 71–72, 106
Dodd, William, 71

Doe, John, 309
Donahue, Dan, 176
Donegan, Leslie, 1
Donovan, William, 12, 19, 225
DONNY, 136
Dowling, Sherryll, xxi, 156
Doyle, David, 296
Dozhdalev, Vasili A., 26, 131
Drager, Siegfried, 274
DRAKE, 136
Dreadnought, HMS, 129
Dreschel, Jacques Van den, 295
Driberg, Tom, xvi, xviii, 31, 43, 72–73, 150
Drücke, Karl, 253–54
DST. *See* Directon de la Surveillance du Territoire
Dubanova, Larissa, 101
Dubcek, Alexander, xxiii
Dubendorfer, Rachel, 221
Ducimetiere, Rose, 73
Ducquesne, Frederick, 276–77
Dudley Ward, Freda, 260
Duffy, LaVern, 244
Duggan, Laurence, 80–81, 171
Dulles, Allen, xvii, 16, 81
Dulles, Clover, 16
Dumoulin, Octave, Col., 287
Dunbarton Oaks Conference, 116
Duncan, Andrew, xxi, 74
Dunn, James, 276
Duranty, Walter, xviii, 74–75
DVORAK, 179
Dzheikya, Rollan, 220

-E-
East German Intelligence Service. *See* Hauptverwaltung Aufklarung
East India Company, 44
Eden, Anthony, 42, 47
Edmonds, Emma, xv, 75

EDWARD, 135
Edwards, Mena, 75, 76
Effingham, Earl of, 132
Egerov, Alexandra, 267
Egerov, Ivan D., 264, 267
Einstein, Albert, 152, 238
Eisenhower, Dwight D., xxvii, 284–85
Eisenhower, John, 285
Eisenhower, Mamie, 285
Eisler, Gerhardt, 169
Eitel, Carl, 118
Eitingon, Leonid, 89
El-Ansary, Rafaat, xx, 241
El-Aouar, Eliat, 230
Elwell, Charles, 183, 184, 189, 280
ELZA, 162
Emig, Marianne, 93
END, 250
ENERO, 76
Enigma, 297
ENORMOZ, 20
Erdberg, Alexander, 256, 279
Erikson, My, 52
Ernst, Carl Gustav, 215
ETHEL, 246
Eulenburg, Libertas, 256
Exner, Dan, 76
Exner, Judith Campbell, 76–79, 143

-F-
Fairbanks Jr., Douglas, 65, 234
Falk, Elke, 79
FAREWELL, 302
Farrell, Elizabeth, 194
FBI. *See* Federal Bureau of Investigation
Federal Bureau of Investigation (FBI), xvii, xx, xxiii, xxv, 5, 11, 12, 19, 33, 52–55, 57, 71, 72, 77, 82–85, 90, 91, 98–100, 103, 109–11, 118, 121, 122, 131, 132, 134, 138, 139, 148, 151, 152, 155, 168–70, 183, 192, 193, 204, 205, 212–14 219–20, 222–25, 228, 230–32, 235–36, 238–39, 241, 243–44, 251, 255–56, 262, 272–73, 275–77, 281–82, 289–90, 293, 302–03, 316, 319, 323;
Chinese source: J. J. Smith
Director of. *See* J. Edgar Hoover
Legal Attaché in London, 144
penetration of. *See* Robert Hanssen, Robert Miller, Nada Prouty, Earl Pitts
Special Surveillance Group, 9, 147
Fedoreko, Sergei, 6
Fejos, Paul, 13
Feklisov, Aleksandr S., 11, 181
Feldman, Armand, 146
FELIX, 242
Fellner, Consul, 11
Fermi, Enrico, 327
Ferrera, Salvatore, 1
Feuchtinger, Edgar, 79–80
Field, Herta, 81–84, 170
Field, Noel, xvi, 80–84, 170, 171
Filipov, Aleksei V., 166
Filton, George, 146
Fincken, Jack, 46–48
FISH, 55
Fisher, Evelyn, 84–86
Fisher, Genrykh, 89, 90
Fisher, Ilya, 84–86
Fisher, Willie, 54, 84–90, 111, 134, 169, 240
Fitin, Pavel, 69
Fleming, Ian, 31–33, 214
Fleming, Peter, 136, 137
Fletcher, Harold, 89
Foggo, Kyle ("Dusty"), 90, 91

Fomin, Aleksandr, 11
FOOT, 165
Foot, M. R. D., 271
Foote, Alexander ("Allan"), 145, 221–22
Ford, Gerald, 50
Forden, David, 102
Foreign Office, penetrations of. *See* Guy Burgess, John King, Donald Maclean, Ernest Oldham, Rhona Ritchie, Edward Scott
Forrest, Gen. Nathan, 194
Forster, E. M., 113
Foster Hall, Miss, 30
Francillard, Marguerite, xv, 91
FRANK, 118
Freud, Sigmund, xvi
Freyberg, Bernard, 61
Friedman, Litzi, 31, 91, 122, 218, 286
Froberville, Philip de, 52
Frolik, Josef, 280
From Russia with Love, 32
Fruhailova, Jarmila, 179
Fuchs, Klaus, 37, 57, 154, 155, 178
Fuentes, Elvira de la, 39, 40
Fuller, Jean Overton, 269
Fuller, Reine, 278
Furness, Thelma, 260
Furse, Aileen, 122, 218

-G-
GABBY, 296
Gaertner, Friedle, 91–92, 214
Gaertner, Lisel, 91
GALA, 4
Galaher, John, 281
Galan, Yaroslav, 274
Galey, Priscilla, xxi, 105
Galkin, Alexei I., 267
Galore, Pussy, 32
Gandt, Roland, 158, 163, 254

Gane, Capt., 45
Garber, Joy Ann, 264
Garber, Ossip, 266
GARBO, 135–37, 199, 316
Garbo, Greta, 172
Garby-Czerniawski, Roman, 45
Gardner, Meredith, 246
Gari, George, 236
Gari, Marisol, 236
Gandt, Roland, 242
Gaskin, John, 31
Gast, Gabrielle, 254–55
Gaulle, Charles de, 42, 64, 157, 249
Gee, Ethel ("Bunty"), 124
Geheimschreiber, 297
Gehlen, Reinhard, 191
Geiller, Lotte, 15
GELATINE, 91, 316
General Dynamics Corp., 78
George, Clair, 7
GEORG, 79
GEORGE WOOD, 16
Gerber, Burton, 7, 51
GERHARD, 4
Gerhardsen, Einar, 92
Gerhardsen, Varna, 92
Gerlach, Christiane, 268
Gertier, Malwina, 132
Gestapo, 98, 257, 279, 311
Ghanaian intelligence service, 258; Chief of. *See* Kojo Tsikata
Giancana, Sam, 76–78, 143
Gibney, Frank, 67
GIDEON, 38
Gikman, Reino, 27–28
GILBERT, 270
Gilbert, Hubert ("Bill"), 164
GIRO, 252
Gisevius, Hans Bernd, 16
Glading, Percy, xvii, 56, 95, 150, 286, 313

Glaser, Eric, 118
Glass, Ann, 183
GLEAM, 135
Globke, Hans, 242
Gobin, Josef, 92
Goebbels, Dr. Josef, 231
Goertz, Herman, 93, 94
Gold, Harry, 245
Gold, Helen, 170
GOLDFINCH, 165
Goldfus, Emil, 84, 111
Goleniewski, Michal, 93, 123
Goliach, Inge, 243
Golitsyn, Anatoli, xxiii, 26, 107, 205, 301
Gollnow, Herbert, 106
Golos, Celia, 18
Golos, Jacob, xvii, 18, 56, 245
Golos, Milton, 18
Gomulka, Wladislaw, 81–83
Gonzalez, Fernando, 100, 235
Gonzalez, René, 100, 235
Goodnight, Mary, 32
Gorbachev, Mikhail, 314
Gordievsky, Oleg, xxiv, xxiv, 6–7, 148, 188, 317
Gordievsky, Leila, xxiv
Gordon, Lucky, 141
Göring, Herman, 13, 119, 256
Gorkin, Aleksandr, 135
Gorkina, Maya, 135
Gorky, Maxim, 41
Gorskaya, Sofia, 21
Gorsky, Anatoli, 19, 29, 30, 117, 162, 310
Goslar, Peter, 140
Gottlieg, Dr. Sidney, 177
Gould, Frederick, 94, 95
Gould, Maud, xv, 94, 95
Gouzenko, Igor, xvii, xxiii, 175, 200, 245

Government Code and Cypher School (GC&CS), 90, 95
Government Communications Headquarters (GCHQ), 125–27, 227–28, 297
Grange, Maj., 313
Grant, Sir Alfred, 23
Grant, Cary, 311
Grant, George, 172
Grant, Guinevere, 23
Grant-Duff, Sheila, 267
Graur, André, 314
Gray, Olga, xvii, 55, 95, 96, 150
Grayevsky, Victor, xviii, 96, 97
Green, Michael, 282
Greenberg, Michael, 283
Greenglass, David, 245
Greenglass, Ruth, 57
Greenhow, Rosie, xv, 97
Greenpeace, 226
GREGORY, 20
Greibl, Ignatz, xvii, 98, 99, 118, 193
Grenyke, Bill, 162
Gribanov, Oleg M., 53, 64, 99, 163, 201, 301
Gridina, M. M., 108
Griebl, Maria, 98
GRIGORI, 201
Grigovin, 99, 100
Grimes, Sandy, 160
Gromov, Anatoli, 29, 30
Gromova, Galina, 102
Grotehohl, Otto, 16
Grow, Robert, 100
GRU, xxiii, xxv, 6, 20–21, 33, 43, 52, 71, 80, 104, 117, 135, 139, 154, 157–59, 175, 216, 222, 224, 245, 247, 253–54, 259, 264–65, 279, 289; Chief of. *See* Ivan Serov

Defectors from. *See* Sergei Bokhan, Igor Gouzenko, Walter Krivitsky
Gruner, Jay, 120
GRÜNSPAN, 17
GT/ACCORD, 8
GT/BACKBEND, 7
GT/COWL, 8
GT/EASTBOUND, 8
GT/GLAZING, 7
GT/JOGER, 8
GT/MEDIAN, 8
GT/TAME, 7
GT/TWINE, 8
GT/VEST, 7
GT/VILLAGE, 8
Guatemalan Intelligence Service, 176
Gubitchev, Valentin, xviii, 60
GUDRUN, 242
Guerrero, Antonio, 100, 235
Guevara, Che, 1
Guibaud, Louis, xiv, 99, 101
Guillaume, Gunter, 288
Guindon, Roy, 101
Guinness, Bryan, 39
Gundarev, Viktor, xx, xxiv, 101–02
Guns of a Stranger, 18
Guryevich, Anatoli, 257
Guryevitch, Viktor, 279
Guy Burgess: A Portrait with Background, 73
G. W., 12

-H-
Haavik, Gunvor, xx, 102, 166
Haganah, 197
HAGEN, 119
Haldane, J. B. S., 42–43
Halder, Max, xvii, 233
Hall, Joan, 55, 102–04
Hall, Sir Reginald, 291

Hall, Robert, 146
Hall, Theodore, xvii, 55
Hall, Virginia, 271–72
Hall of Pleasurable Delights, 277
Halperin, Israel, 200
Hambleton, Hugh, 206
Hamburger, Paul, 154
Hamburger, Willi, xvii, 182
Hammond, Ogden, 276
Handbook for Spies, 154, 222
Handelsvertretung, 238
Hanin, Cheryl, 300
Hanslope Park, 297
Hanssen, Robert P., xx, xxi, xxv, 29, 104–05, 221, 228
Hao Atoll, 227
Harde, Robert Sheldon, 294
Hardinge, Lt., 36
Hardt, Paul, 96
Hardy, George, 95
Hare, John, 65
Harmer, Christopher, 40
Harnack, Arvid von, 105, 106, 256, 279
Harnack, Mildred von, xvii, 105–07
HARP, 38
Harper, James, 255–56
Harriman, Averell, xvi, xxvii, 107, 308
Harris, Hennie, 107
Harris, Kitty, 56, 107
Harris, Tilly, 107
Harrison, Sir Geoffrey, xiv, xxvii, 108, 287
Hart, 170
Hart, Gary, 297
Hartington, Lord, 133
Harvey, Bill, 78
Hassan, Faujiya, 234
Hathaway, Gus, 7
Hauffe, Prof. Karl, 278

Haugwitz-Reventow, Kurt, 311–12
Hauptverwaltung Aufkrarung (HVA), xiv, 4, 35, 111, 119, 140, 158, 162–65, 215–16, 235, 241, 248, 254–55, 259, 272–73, 278, 283, 314; Chief of. *See* Robert Korb, Marcus Wolf Defectors from. *See* Heinz Busch, Werner Stiller
Havemann, Wolfgang, 106
Havers, Sir Michael, 241
Haxton, Gerald, 174
Hayhanen, Reino, 84, 108–11, 240
Heath, Ted, 206
Hees, George, 195
Heilmann, Horst, 106
Heinz, Leonore, 112, 248, 287
HEIR, 69
Heisler, Josef, 322
Helfmann, Heinz, xviii, 111, 112
HELGA, 296
Helms, Richard, 178
HELMSMAN, 56, 107, 224
Henley, Tony, 26
Henri, Ernst, 100
HENRY, 203
Henry-Haye, Gaston, 211
Henze, Hans Jurgen, 119
Herbst, Theodor, 293
Herman, Karl, 98
Hernandez, Geraldo, 100, 235, 252
Hernandez, Linda, xxviii, 112
Hernandez, Nilo, 112
Herrnstadt, Rudolf, 279
Herzog, Gisela, 112, 287
Heslop, John, 233
Hewit, Jack, 30, 112–13, 122
Hewitt, Ada, 194
Heydrich, Reinhard, 249
Hill, Christopher, 43
Hill, George A., xvi, 113–15

Hill, Jim, 178, 179
Himmler, Heinrich, 119
Hinton, Geoffrey, 301
Hiscox, Mollie, xvii, 38, 39, 115, 116
Hiss, Alger, 51, 80, 116, 117, 170, 171
Hiss, Priscilla, 52, 116
Hitler, Adolf, 13, 39, 118, 255, 289, 306
Hizbollah, 230
Hobson, Valerie, 229
Hofa, Ursula, 243
Hofer, Heldrun, 117, 118
Hoffmann, Joanna, 118
Höhenloe, Princess Stephanie von, 119
Höke, Margarete, xx, 119, 120
Hollis, Sir Roger, 62, 142
Holm, Richard L., xxi, 120
Holmes, Oliver Wendell, 116
Homintern, 120
homosexuality, 31, 42, 49, 51, 72, 74, 112, 121–23, 146, 149, 153, 161, 180, 196, 199, 201, 205, 222, 233, 236, 259, 280, 292, 297, 300, 309–10; Moscow entrapments. *See* John Vassall, John Watkins Prague entrapment. *See* John Stonehouse
honeytrap, 11, 31, 44, 53, 64, 65, 71, 74, 101, 102, 108, 122, 133, 135, 153, 159, 164, 196, 200, 215, 217, 221, 228, 239, 247, 249, 252, 275, 280, 298, 300, 307, 310; Moscow entrapments. *See* Anthony Courtney, Maurice Dejean, Louis Guibaud, Gunvor Haavik, Geoffrey Harrison, Clayton Lonetree, Roy Rhodes, Francois Saar-Demichel, Edward Ellis Smith

Warsaw entrapment. *See* Irwin Scarbeck
Hoover, J. Edgar, 77, 99, 143, 149, 192, 214, 244
Horwood, Sir William, 290–91
Hoschouer, Jack, 105
Houghton, Harry, 24, 55, 93, 122, 182, 301
Houghton, Peggy, 122
House Committee on Un-American Activities (HCUA), 262
Houston, Jack, 115
Howard, Brian, 30
Howard, Edward Lee, xxi, xxiii, 131, 132, 228
Howard, Mary, 132, 228
Howard of Effingman, Lady, 132
Howe, Russell, 322
Hoy, Hugh Cleland, 322
Hughes, Howard, 1
Huha, Andrew, 261
Hungarian intelligence service. *See* Allami Vedelmi Hatosag
Hunloke, Henry, 132, 133, 195
Hunt, John, 204
Hüppe, Heinz, 164
Hurran, Christopher, 121
Husak, Robert, 280
Hussein, Saddam, 298
Husted, Helen, 143
Hutton, Barbara, 311–12
Hutton, J. Bernard, 322–25
HVA. *See* Hauptverwalrung Aufklarung
Hyde, Harford Montgomery, 212

-I-
I Chose Freedom, 293
Ignatieff, Serge, 253
IKAR, 133
Illegals Directorate. *See* KGB
ILONA, 134
Ilovaiskaya, Tanya, 145, 146
Indian Intelligence Bureau, 234
Indian Space Research Organisation (ISRO), 234
Immoor, Joseph, 76
INGE, 140
Inside the Company: A CIA Diary, 1
Institute of Pacific Relations, 226
Intelligence Crops, 205
In the Name of Conscience, 147
INTERALLIÉ, 45–47
International Commission of Jurists, 167
International Labor Organization, 1
International Monetary Fund, 161
Inter-Services Intelligence (ISI) 74, 234
Invisible Weapons, 34
Irish Republican Army, 93
Isherwood, Christopher, 113
ISI. *See* Inter-Services Intelligence
ISOS, 11, 92
ISPAL, 133
Israeli Communist Party, 299
ITALIAN, 106
Ivanov, Boris, 41
Ivanov, Eugene, xiv, 21, 65, 135, 141, 229, 307, 326
Ivanova, Rufina, 121, 218–19
Ivashutin, Sergei, 247

-J-
JACK, 135, 272
Jackson, Bertha R., 264–65
Jackson, James O., 264–65
JACOB, 289
JACQUELINE, 271
Jacson, Frank, 294–95
Jaffe, Philip, 199
Jahnke, Kurt, 90, 145

INDEX • 349

Jakobs, Josef, 241
James, Jimmie, 208
James, Sir William, 322
Jansky, A., 179
Jardine, Theresa, xvii, 135–37, 199, 316
JAVELINE, 135
JEANNE, 293
JEROME, 157
Jewish Brigade, 197
Ji, Gen. Shengde, 213
Jirousek, Tina, 27, 28
Jodl, Gen. Alfred, 285
John, Otto, 67, 270
Johnson, David, 310
Johnson, Florence, 93
Johnson, Lyndon B., 149, 232
Johnson, Robert, xiv, 137–38, 180
Joint Broadcasting Committee, 42
Joint Intelligence Bureau, 33
Joint Technical Advisory Group, 232
JOKER, xiv, 63
Jones, Brian, 202
Jordan, Jesse, 118
Jordan, Thomas, 97
Joshua, 233
Josiffe, Norman, 291
Judd, Alan, 138
JULIA, 57
JULIET, 2, 71
JUNIOR, 272
JUSTIN, 233

-K-
KABAN, 138, 139
Kahle, Wilhelm, 139, 140
Kahlig-Scheffler, Dagmar, xx, 140
Kakhotkin, Vladimir A., 63
Kalle, Maj. von, 172
Kalugin, Oleg, 12, 288
Kama Sutra of Vatsyayana, 44

Kamensky, 62
Kapp, Nellie, xvii, 140, 141
KAREV, 141
Karlin, George, 153
Karpekov, Nikolai, xxviii, 189
Karpov, Aleksandr, 220
Karsten, Maj., 71
Kasirilis, Ronnie, 272
Katyanni, Lela, 271
Katz, Joseph, 19
Kaulle, Baroness de, xv, 53
Kazachenko, Diana, 76
Keay, Julia, 322
Keeler, Christine, xiv, 65, 135, 141, 142, 229, 307–08, 326
Kekkonen, Urho, xvii, 142
Keller, Heinz, 4
Kelley, Brian, 29
Kempe'tai, 269
Kennedy, John F., xvii, 13, 76–79, 107, 142–45, 148, 176, 201, 202, 230, 232, 243, 282
Kennedy, Joseph, 144
Kennedy, Kathleen, 12–13
Kennedy, Robert F., 78, 143, 148, 244
Kent, Tyler, xvii, xxvii, 144, 145, 315
Kercsik, Dr. Sandor, 8
Kerensky, Alexander, 174
Kessler, Eric, 43, 146
Keynes, John Maynard, 161, 281
Keyser, Donald, xxi, 146, 147
KGB, xiv, xx, xxiii, xxiv, xxv, 1, 5, 12, 21, 29, 31, 38, 64, 71, 73, 76, 79, 89, 92, 97, 99–101, 105, 109–12, 117–20, 123, 126, 130, 132, 138, 139, 153, 159, 164, 165–67, 169, 180, 181, 186, 203, 232, 239–40, 247–48, 256, 263, 274, 278, 284, 287–88, 301,

305–06, 316–18; archives, 328; Chairman of. *See* Yuri Andropov, Aleksandr Shelepin; defectors from. *See* Mikhail Butkov, Anatoli Golitsyn, Oleg Gordievsky, Viktor Gundarev, Reino Hayhanen, Yuri Krotkov; Vladimir Kuzichkin, Oleg Lyalin, Vasili Mitrokhin, Yuri Nosenko, Evdokia Petrov, Vladimir Petrov, Bogdan Shashinsky, Kaarlo Tuomi, Vitali Yurchenko; Directorate K, 1; Directorate S, 133; Illegals Directorate, 133, 134, 140, 169, 189; Line N, 195; Science & Technology Directorate, 302; First Chief Directorate, 94, 102, 148, 260; Fourteenth Department, 99; Second Chief Directorate, xxvii, xxviii, 40–41, 53, 67, 71, 76, 99, 133, 141, 163, 196, 200–01, 216, 221, 258–59, 298, 301
Khan, Noor Inayat, 269
Khlopkova, Olga, 57
Khokhlov, Nikolai, xviii, 147, 148, 327
Khorumsky, Nikita, 147
KHOSYAIN, 162
Khovanskaya, Lydia, 64
Khrushchev, Nikita, xviii, 20, 96
Kieper, Aldred, 171
Kiffer, Raoul, 45
Kim, Suim, 148
Kimmel, Tom, 220
KIN, 162
King, John, xvii, 312–13
King, Martin Luther, 148–50
Kinsman, Richard, 3
KIRILL, 138
Kirk, Alan G., 142

Kisevater, George, 200, 289
Kita, Nagao, 156
Kiyomi, 269
KL-47 cipher machine, 304
Klein, Caroline, 18
Klugmann, James, 121
Knight, Maxwell, xvi, xxix, 39, 72, 73, 92, 95, 96, 150
Koecher, Hana, xiv, xx, xxix, 150–52
Koecher, Karl F., xiv, xx, 150–52, 204
Koedel, Marie, 152
Koedel, Simon E., 152
Koehling, Moritz, 92
Kohanee, Milica, 224
Kohlman, Israel, 91
KOLON, 280
Kommunist Partei Deutschland (KPD), 81, 169, 170, 238
Kondrashev, Sergei, 26, 62
Konenkova, Margarita, 152
KONRAD, xviii, 152, 153
Koppe, Johannes, 278
Korb, Robert, 314
Korda, Alexander, 41
Korotkov, Alexander, 256
Korovin, Nikolai B., 24–26, 131, 189
Kostov, Traicho, 81
Kotov, Vladimir, 100, 142
Kovalik, Ivan M., 169
Kowarski, Lev, 176
Krakover, Joan, xvii, 103
Krause, Peter, xiv, 20
Kravchenko, Victor, xvii, 292–93
Kravchencko, Valentin, 293
Kravchenko, Zinaida, 293
Krelik, Vesek, 151
Krepkogorsky, Col., 1
Kreshin, Boris, 30, 69
Krivitsky, Walter, 55, 69, 170, 209, 238–39, 254, 259, 312

INDEX • 351

Kroger, Helen, 55, 61, 127–31, 185
Kroger, Peter, 55, 61, 127–31, 185
Krohn, Maj. von, xv, 240
Kronberg-Sobolevskaya, Larissa, 64
Krotkov, Yuri, xiv, 64, 101, 153, 310
Krotkova, Christina, 293
Krutki, Bernard, 45
Kryuchkov, Vladimir, 318
Kuczynski, Ursula, xvii, 154–55, 268
Kube, Wilhelm, 147
Kühn, Dr. Bernard, 155
Kühn, Friedl, 155
Kühn, Ruth, 155, 156
Kukin, Konstantin, 26
Kulikowski, Edward, 210
Kunk Kook, Lee, 148
Kurkovich, Hans, 147
Kurnakow, Sergei, 103
Kurrika, Hanna, 108
Kuser, Cynthia, 292
Kutepov, Aleksandr, 221
Kuzichkin, Vladimir, xxiv
Kuznetsov, I. I., 76
Kvasnikov, Leonid, 245

-L-
Labanino, Ramón, 100, 235
Labarthe, André, 42, 157
The Labyrinth, 249
Lacoste, Adm. Pierre, 227
Lais, Alberto, xvii, 156, 211
Lamphere, Robert, 59
Landowne, Lord, 48–49
Lange, David, 227
Lappas, Simon, xxi, 156–57
Lapshin, Konstantin, xvii, 40
Largo, Emilio, 31
LAST ACT, 125
Laty, Amir, xxi, 157
Lauder, John, 28
Laurenz, Karl, xviii, 16–17

Lava, Thelma de, xvi, 291
LAVINIA, 124
Lawford, Peter, 77, 202
Lawrence Livermore National Laboratory, 213
Lecky, Terence, 25, 26
Lecoutre, Alta, 157
Ledoux, Georges 172, 240
Lee, Duncan, 19, 225
Lee, Helen, 40
Legacy, 138
Legh, Diana, 23
Legh, Sir Piers, 23
Legion of St. George, 15
Lehrmann, Josef, 274
LEMONS, 296
LENA, 79
Lenzkow, Marianne, xviii, 157, 254
LEPAGE, 73
Lepeshinskaya, Olga, 255
Lerner, Bella, 60
LESLIE, 54
Lesser, Dr. Annamarie, 158
Leung, Katrina, xx, xxi, 212–14
Levi, Renato, 197
Levison, Stanley, 148
Lewis, David, xxiv
Lewis, Evelyn, 276
Liaison, 34
LIBERAL, 245
Liddell, Guy, 105, 146, 196
LINA, 17
Lincoln, Evelyn, 176
Lindsay-Hogg, Sir Anthony, 218
The Link, 150
Linkov, Yuri, 304
Linse, Dr. Walltter, 67
Linton, Freda, 158, 159, 245
Liossis, George, 4
Lippmann, Walter, 224–25
LISE, 250

LITTLE LEMON, 296
Live and Let Die, 31
LIZA, 71
Ljuskiv, Igor, 159
Ljuskova, Natalia, 159
Lloyd George, David, 174, 291
Lockwood, Rupert, 179
LOLA, 287
Lonetree, Clayton, xx, xxi, 159, 160
LONG, 61
Long, Leo, 30
Lonkowsky, Willy, 98, 118
Lonsdale, Gordon, 124–31, 182
Lopokova, Lydia, 160–61
Lorenzen, Ursel, xx, 161–62, 243
LORIENT, 100
Lotz, Wolfgang, 196–97
LOUISA, 162
Lowry, Helen, 56, 162–63
Lubienski, Count Michael, 210
Lubig, Margarethe, xiv, xxi, 158, 163, 164, 242, 254
Lucan, Lord, 280
Luibimov, Mikhail, xxiv
LUIS, 236
LUKAS, 152
Lummer, Heinrich, 164
LUO, 213
Lutsky, E. P., xviii, 164
Lutz, Renate, xx, 165
Lyalin, Oleg, xiv, 165, 166, 288
LYDIA, 269
Lygren, Ingeborg, 166–67
Lynd, Vesper, 31

-M-
M-21, 150
MacArthur, Gen. Douglas, 199
Macdermott Niall, 167
MacGibbon, James, 42
Mackie, Marjorie, 150, 315
Mackinder, Sir Halford, 114
Maclean, Donald, 43, 69, 73, 107, 121, 167, 168, 219, 328
Maclean, Melinda, 38, 167, 168, 219
MacLeod, Margarethe, 171, 322
Macmillan, Harold, xxvi, 64, 141
MADAM, 309
MADCHEN, 42
MADELEINE, 269
Mafart, Alain, 226
MAG, 313
MAGNATE, 107
Maher, Dale W., 276
Maheu, Robert, 77
Mailer, Norman, 3
Maisky, Ivan, 42, 161
Makarov, Semen, 178
Makayev, Valeri M., 134, 169
Makhotina, Natasha, xiv, 63
Maki, Eugene, 108
MAKS, 248
Maksimilishvili, Vardo, 21
Maly, Theodore, 68
Manhattan Project, 37, 57, 102, 175, 319
The Man Who Never Was, 180
MAO, 213
Mao Tse Tung, 262
Marchetti, Victor, 2
Marcos, Ferdinand, xiv, 17
MARGARET, 57
MARGOT, 236
Maringliano, Francesco, 315
Marini, Ferruccio, 18
Markin, Valentine, 170
MARLENE, 112
Maroff, Vadim, 172
Marples, Ernest, 65
Marsac, André, 250
MARTHA, 157
Martin, Arthur, 281
Martin, Edwin, 281
Martin, Pierre, xvi, 273

Martin, William, xviii, 125, 181, 222
Martin, Maj. William, 180
Martinez, Ana Margarita, 144
Martinez, Marteo, 294
Martynov, Valeri, 7
MARY, 10
Masaryk, Jan, 322
MASK, 95, 96
Maslennikov, Piotr E., 267
Mason, Mrs., 194
Maspero, Francois, 1
Massing, Hede, xvi, 83, 169–71, 262
Massing, Paul, 83, 170
Massow, Gen. Gerd von, 80
Massy-Beresford, Jack, 311
Masterman, John C., 315
Masterton, Jill, 32
Mata Hari, xv, xxvi, 171, 172, 290, 321–22
Matthews, J. B., 83
Matthias, Ludwig Ernst, 145
Maugham, Willie Somerset, 173–75
MAX, 30
MAXIM, 318
Maximova, Katchka, 269
Maxwell, Susan, 30
May, Allan Nunn, 175, 176, 178
Mayer, Cord, 143, 176, 177
Mayer, Mary, 143, 176, 177
Mayer, Otto, 50
MAYOR, 224
Mayor, Tess, 281
MAZER, 118
McAfee, Marilyn, 176
McCarthy, Joseph, 282
McCarthy-Morrogh, Kathleen, 284
McCleary, Don, 195
McClellan, Gen. George, 75
McCoy, Tim, 14
McBride, Maichael, 120
McKenna, Reginald, 291

McNeil, Hector, 43
Meier, Dr. Roland, 243
Menzies, Ian, 91
Menzies, Sir Robert, 218
Menzies, Stewart, 91–92
Mercader, Caridad, 295–96
Mercader, Ramon, 293
Mermet, Madeleine, 288
Mers el Kebir, 211
Metcalfe, Alexandra, 39
Metcalfe, Maj. "Fruity", 39
METER, 246
Metkov, Lt., 134
Meyer, Mary, xiv
MfS. *See* Ministerium fur Sicherheit
Miami International University (MIU), 5
Michael, Gwyndr, 180
Michaelson, Eric, 158
Michalek, Karl-Heinz, 11
MIDNIGHT CLIMAX, xiv, 177
MI5. *See* British Security Service
MI6. *See* Secret Intelligence Service
MI19, 80
MiG-21, 236
Mikhailski, Sigmund, 300
Miles, Geoffrey, 61
Millar, Ronald, 322
Miller, Gen. Evgenni, 221
Miller, Joan, 150, 315
Miller, Richard, xx, 204, 228
Milne, Tony, 91
Milner, Ian, 178–79, 263
Milner, Margot, 263–64
Milner, Ted, 179
MIMI, xviii, 152
MINCEMEAT, 179, 180
Ministerium fur Sicherheits (MfS), xviii, 16
Ministry of State Security (MSS), xxi, 34, 213, 228
Defector from. *See* Yu Zhensan

Mintkenbaugh, James, xviii, xiv, 138, 180, 181
Miranda del Ebro, 22, 233
Mitchell, Bernon S., xviii, 125, 181, 182, 222
Mitchell, Galya, 182,
Mitchell, Dr. W. E., 183
Mitford, Diana, 39
Mitford, Pamela, 315
Mitrokhin, Vasili, 28, 55, 73, 140, 163, 288
MIU. *See* Miami International University
Miyake, Hanako, 269
MLAD, 103
MK/ULTRA, 177
Molnar, Adrienne, xvii, 182
Molody, Galyusha, 134, 185
Molody, Konon, 134, 182–92
Molody, Liza, 185
Molody, Trofim, 184
MONA, 139
Monk, Margaret, 39
Monkey Business, 297
Monroe, Marilyn, 143
Montagu, Ewen, 180
Montes, Ana, xxi, 192
Moog, Kay, xvii, 98, 193
Moon, Ginnie, xv, 193, 194
Moon, Lottie, xv, 193, 194
Moore, Edwin, 228, 316
Moore, Joanna, 194
Moralez, Raqella, 297
Morgan, John Hunt, 63
Morgan, Reginald, 285
MORRIS, 69
Morris, Augusta, xv, 194
Morros, Boris, 72, 319
Morrow, Susan, 76
Morton, Desmond, 42
MOSEL, 162

Mosley, Cynthia, 39
Mosley, Sir Oswald, 38, 39
Mossad, 97, 157, 236, 300
Motorin, Sergei, 7
Mountbatten, Edwina, 311
Mountbatten, Lord Louis, 40, 135
Moyne, Lord, 39
Muggeridge, Malcolm, 74
Mukhabarat, xxi, 298
Muldoon, Donald, 280
Muller, Peter, 79
Mullinas, Dep, 105
Munck, Helene, 150
Munsinger, Gerda, 194, 195
Munsinger, Michael, 194
Murdoch, John, 15
Mure, David, 195, 196
Muroroa, 227
Murphy, Carol, 176
Muselier, Emile, 42
Mussolini, Benito, 39
Muus, Flemming, 311
Myaoedev, Sergei, 284
MYRNA, 18
My Story, 79
My Three Years in Moscow, 40

-N-
Nambinarayan, Dr., 234
NAOMI, 177
Napier, Gen. Sir Charles, 44
Narodnyi Trudovoi Soyuz (NTS), 147, 274–75
NATASHA, 63, 196
National Intelligence Service, 194
National Security Agency (NSA), 125, 151, 181, 193, 222, 229, 317; Defectors from. *See* William Martin, Bernon Mitchell
NATO. *See* North Atlantic Treaty Organization

Naval Intelligence Division, 49, 61, 198
Naval Investigative Service, 159
Naval Security Group, 181
Nemeth, Anna Marie, 159
Neruda, Pablo, 294
Neubacher, Aglaya, 16
Neumann, Waldrutt, 196, 197
Newman, Bernard, 321
Newton, Andrew, 291
New Zealand Security Intelligence Service (NZSIS), 61
New Zealand Security Service, 164; Director of. *See* Bill Gilbert
Nichiporenko, Oleg, 1
Nicholas, Elizabeth, 270
Nichols, Donald, 145
Nicholson, Harold J. ("Jim"), 223, 28
NICNAC, 33
Nicossof, Paul, 197
NIGEL, 283
NIL, 246
Nizetas, Nikon, 237
NKVD, xvi, xxvii, 11, 19–21, 36, 40, 41–42, 54–55, 66–71, 73, 81, 91, 103, 107, 115, 121, 134, 138, 142, 145, 152, 162, 167, 178, 209, 217, 219, 225, 238, 245–46, 255, 259, 283, 292–93, 295, 305–06, 313; Chief of. *See* Lavrenti Beria Defectors from. *See* Piotr Deriabin, Allan Foote, Nikolai Khokhlov, Victor Kravchenko, Alexander Orlov
NN, 249
Nominal Agents, 198
Nordic League, 115
Norfolk Island, 227
NORMA, 242
Norman, Herbert, 199–200

North Atlantic Treaty Organization (NATO), 10, 35, 92, 139, 158, 162, 163, 206, 236, 248–49, 299
Norwegian Military Intelligence Service, 166; Head of. *See* Wilhelm Evang
Penetration of. *See* Ingeborg Lygren
Norwegian Security Service, 166; Head of. *See* Asbjorn Bryhn
Norwood, Melita, 127
Nosenko, Yuri, xiv, 51, 99, 200, 201, 258, 263, 301, 310
Notional Agent, 197
Novotny, Mariella, 144, 201–03, 229, 308
Now It Can Be Told, 269
NTS. *See* Narodnyi Trudovoi Soyuz
Nurse and Spy in the Union Army, 75
Nye Committee, 116
NZSIS. *See* New Zealand Security Intelligence Service

-O-

Ochals, Edward, 96
Octopussy, 31
O'Donnell, Pete, 220
Office of Naval Intelligence (ONI), 13, 142
Office of Strategic Services (OSS), xvii, 12, 16, 19, 81, 119, 140, 141, 182, 211, 225, 326; Chief of. *See* William Donovan
Office of War Information, 37
The Officer in the Tower, 15
Official Secrets Act, 241, 301
Ogorodnik, Aleksandr, xxv, 6, 51, 151, 203, 204, 216–17
Ogorodnikov, Matvei, 204
Ogorodnikov, Nikolai, xiv, xxix, 204, 205

Ogorodnikova, Svetlana, xx, xxix, 204, 205
OGPU, 238
 Defector from. *See* Georges Agabekov
OGPU: The Russian Secret Terror, 283
Okolovich, Georgi S., 147
Okun, Oleg, 147
OLA, 292–93
Oldfield, Maurice, 121, 205–09
Oldham, Ernest, xvi, 309
Oldham, Lucy, 309
Olson, Jim, 14, 159
On Her Majesty's Secret Service, 31
On the Warpath, 100
ONI. *See* Office of Naval Intelligence
Operation Double Life, 219
Oppenheimer, J. Robert, 327
ORANGE, 146
OREL, 55
Organization of Ukrainian Nationalists (OUN), 273
Orlov, Alexander, 40, 68
Orta, Juan, 78
Osprey, HMS, 130
OSS. *See* Office of Strategic Services
Osterreider, Gerda, 140, 209, 210
Ostrovsky, 38
Ostrovsky, Erika, 322
Ott, Eugen, 269
Ott, Helma, 269
Our Own People, 239
Out of Bondage, 19
Ouvea, 227
Oswald, Lee Harvey, xviii, 201, 231–32
Otsama, Hotsumi, 262
Owen, Dr. David, 208

-P-
Pacepa, Ion, xviii, 152
Pacheco e Cuesta, José, 70
Pack, Arthur, 210, 212
Pack, Elizabeth ("Betty"), xvii, 156, 210–12, 299
Pack, Troy, 212
Pakistani intelligence. *See* Inter-Services Intelligence
Pakkanen, Ivan, 142
Palme Dutt, Rojani, 179
Panfilowska, Halina, 186
PAPADOPOULOS, 4
Papen, Franz von, 75, 76
PAP News Agency, 97
Paques, George, 206
Parliamentary Intelligence and Security Committee, 289
PARLOUR MAID, 212–14
Parrott, George, xv, 215
Paterson, Eveline, 299
Paterson, John, 299
Pauli, Ludwig, 215
Pavlovna, Fini, 68
Pavlovsky, Grigori, 196
PCD. *See* Postal Censorship Department
Peace Corps, 51
Peake, Iris, 23
Peake, Sir Osbert, 23
Pearl Harbor, 155, 214
Peatfield, James, 159
Pelton, Ronald, 229, 317
Penkovsky, Oleg, xviii, 67, 135, 205, 216, 247
The Penkovsky Papers, 67
Pepper, John, 211
Pereira, Fernando, 227
The Perfumed Garden, 44
Perelli, Count Ladislas, 309
Perlo, Katherine, 52

Perlo, Victor, 19, 51
Peterhans, Alter, 286
Petersen, Kai, 157, 163
Peterson, Martha, 203, 216–17
Petrie, Sir David, 42
Petrov, Evdokia, xviii, xxiv, 217–18, 260
Petrov, Vladimir, xviii, xxiv, 217–18, 260
Petty, Alan, 138
Pfeffer, Gula von, 90
Pfieffer, Edouard, 42
Philaja, Arnold, 183
Philby, Aileen, 37, 121
Philby, H. A. R. ("Kim"), xvi, xiv, 37, 42–43, 69, 91, 115, 122, 141, 168, 169, 189, 196, 218–19, 238, 286
  wives of. *See* Litzi Friedman, Aileen Furse, Rufina Ivanova, Eleanor Pope Brewer
Philby, Harry, 218
Philby, John, 218
Philby, Josephine, 218
Philby, Miranda, 218
Philby, Tommy, 218
PHYSICIAN, 272
Pieck, Henri, 238, 312
Piguzov, Vladimir, 8
Pinkerton, Allan, 63, 97
Pitovranov, Gen., 41
Pitt, Roxane, 219, 326
Pitts, Earl, xx, xxv, 219–21, 228
Pitts, Mary, 220
PLATON, 221
Plevitskaya, La, xvii, 221
Pohl, Inge, 274
Poincaré, Raymond, 73
Poleshuk, Leonid, 7
Poliakova, Maria, 221–22
Police Journal, 190

Polish intelligence service. *See* Urzab Bezpieczenstwa
Polivanov, Gen. Alexei, 284
Pollitt, Harry, 95
Pollock, Peter, 30
Polyakov, Dmitri, xiv, 8, 71, 267
Polygraph, xvii, 131, 139, 181, 214, 258
Pompidou, Georges, 247
Pontecorvo, Bruno, 327
Popov, Dusan ("Dusko"), xvii, 92, 223–24
Popov, Piotr, xviii, 224, 263, 289–90
Poppe, Dieter, 283
Poppel, Maj. von, 26–27
Poretsky, Elisabeth, 238, 254
Postal Censorship Department (PCD), xvi, 33–34
Potashov, Vladimir, xx, 8
Powers, Dave, 177
Powers, F. Gary, 89
Pravdin, Vladimir S., 58, 162
Pravdina, Olga, 57
Pribytkov, Vladimir, 66
Price, Mary, 224–26
Price, Mildred, 225
Prieur, Dominique, 226–27
Prime, Geoffrey, xx, 227–28
Prime, Rhona, 228
Proctor, Dennis, 31, 43
profiling, 228–29
Profumo, David, 327
Profumo, John, xiv, xxvi, 64–65, 135, 141, 142, 144, 196, 201, 229–30, 307, 327
The Property of a Lady, 31
Prouty, Gordon, 230
Prouty, Nada Nadim, xxi, 230–31
Provisional Irish Republican Army (PIRA), 206–07
Psychological Sex Operations, 231

Puenter, Otto, 221
Pujol, Juan, 135
Pushkova, Telena, 305

-Q-
Quantum of Solace, A, 31
QUEBEC, 110, 239
Queen Bee, xviii, 231–32
QUICKSILVER, 4
Quien, Gaston, 50
The Quiet Canadian, 212
Quine, John, 25
Quorum Club, 232, 243

-R-
Radio Liberty, 83
Rado, Alexander ("Sandor"), 221
RAFTER, 127
Rags, 136
Rahab the Harlot, 232–33
Rainbow Warrior, 226–27
Rajk, Laszlo, 81, 82
Rake, Denis, xvii, 233–34, 327
Rake's Progress, 234
Rao, Narasintha, 235
Rao, Prakhabkar, 235
Rasheeda, Martyam, 234–35
Rau, Suzanne, 164
Raufersen, Arnulf, 278
Raven, 92, 209, 235, 314
Ray, James Earl, 150
Raykhman, Leonid, 41, 255
RCMP. *See* Royal Canadian Mounted Police
Reagan, Romald, 304
Rebet, Lev, 274
RED AVISTA, xxi, 100, 112, 235, 245, 251–52
Redding, Claude, 47
Redfa, Munir, xiv, 236
Redl, Alfred, xv, xxvi, 236, 237

Redmond, Paul, 160
Redesdale, Sir Julian, 180
Red Orchestra, 106
Red Spy at Night, 304–06
Reed, Ronnie, 175
REGISTRATION, 243
Rehbaum, Karl, 248
Reich, Vartoslav, 288
Reich, Wilhelm, xvi, 68, 237–38
Reif, Ignaty, 68
Reishsicherheitshauptamt, 182, 279
Reilly, Sidney, 114
Reiss, Ignace, xvii, 80, 170, 238–39, 254
Rembitsky, Leonard, 239
RENATA, 120
Research and Analysis Wing (RAW), 234
Rhee, Singman, 148
Rhodes, Roy, xviii, 110, 239–40
Ribbentrop, Joachim von, 119
Riccardo, Ronna, 308
Rice, Donna, 29
Rice-Davies, Mandy, 230, 308
Richard, Marthe, xv, 240
Richards, 196
Richards, Sir Brooks, 207
Richards, Ron, 217
Richardson, Terry, 214
Richer, Henri, 240
Richter, Herbert, 140
Richter, Karel, 240–41
Right Club, 38, 145, 150, 315
Ritchie, Rhona, xx, 241
Ritter, Nikolaus, 52, 277
RIVER CITY, 160
ROBERT, 317
Roberts, Douglas, 205
ROCK BOTTOM, 310
Rodiger, Helga, 243
Rodin, Nikolai, 26

Roemer, Irmgard, xviii, 111
Roesler, Klaus, 249
Rogalla, Jurgen, 248
Rohrer, Glen, 223
ROLAND, 117
Rolling Stones, 202
Romanones, Aline, Countess of, 326
Romeo Spies, 79, 139, 140, 162, 163, 165, 241–43, 254, 288, 314
Rometsch, Ellen, 143, 232, 243–44
Rometsch, Rold, 243
Ronge, Maximilian, 237
Roosevelt, Archie, 202
Roosevelt, Franklin D., xxvii, 12, 107, 145,211, 277
Roosevelt, Kermit, 144
Roque, Juan Pablo, 235, 244
ROSE, 158, 163
Rose, Fred, xvi, 158, 245
Rosenberg, Ethel, 54, 57, 131, 245–46
Rosenberg, Julius, 54, 57, 131, 245–46
ROSEWOOD, 243, 249, 272
Rosselli, Johnny, 77, 143
Rossiiskii Obshchevoennyi Soyuz (ROVS), 221
Rote Drei, 221
Rote Kapelle, 106, 257, 279
Rothermere, Lord, 119
Rothschild, Victor, 281
Rousseau, Eugene, 247
Rousseau, Monique, xiv, 246–47
Rousseau, Xavier, 171
ROVS. *See* Rossiiskii Obshchevoennyi Soyuz
Rowan, Richard, 321
Rowland, Reginald, 309–10
Rowsell, Ivor, xiv, 247
Royal, Gerard, 227
Royal, Segoline, 227

Royal Canadian Mounted Police (RCMP), xiv, 31, 38, 63, 101, 182, 195, 199, 200, 245, 310
Royal Commission, 324
Royal Ulster Constabulary (RUC), 207
Ruddock, Caitlin, 157
Ruddock, Philip, 157
Rudellat, Yvonne, 271–72
Rudford, Charlie, 305
Ruling Passions, 73
Rumrich, Gunther, 98, 118
Runge, Evgenni, xiv, 247–48, 287
Rupp, Rainer, xiv, xxi, 35, 248–49
Rusk, Dean, 144
Russell, Clement, 30
Russian Foreign Intelligence Service. *See* SVR
Rustin, Bayard, 149
Ryder, Honeychile, 32

-S-
Saar-Demichel, Francois, 99, 249
Sagner, Fred, 259
Sailor in a Russian Frame, 62
Salinger, Pierre, 143
Salon Kitty, xvi, xxvi, 249–50
Samson, 64, 250
Samach, Hannah, 271
Samson, David, 9
Sandys, Duncan, 65, 230
Sansom, Odette, 250–51
Santos, Amarilys, xxviii, 236, 251–52
Santos, Joseph, 236, 251–52
Sarkisov, Ruben, 21
Sasikumar, Dr., 234–35
Sax, Saville, 103
Scarbeck, Irwin, xviii, 94, 252
SCAR TISSUE, 193
Schalburg, Christian, 253

360 • INDEX

Schalburg, Vera, xvii, 52, 253–54
Schellenberg, Walter, 249
Schilbeck, Gertrude, xvii, 254
Schmidt, Helmut, xx, 140
Schmidt, Kitty, 259
Schneider, Karl-Heinz, 158, 163, 254–55
Schoter, Herbert, 209–10
Schramm, Kalle, 157
Schroeder, Adolf, 94
Schroter, Herbert, 140
Schulenburg, Werner Von der, 255
Schuler, Ruby, 255–56
Schultze, Reinhard, 256
Schultze, Sonja, 256
Schulze-Boysen, Harro, 256, 279
Schulze-Boysen, Libertas, 256–57
Schumacher, Elisabeth, 257
Schumacher, Kurt, 257
Schurmacher, Dietmar, 10
Scott, Edward, xvii, xviii, 257–58
Scranage, Sharon M., 223, 258
SDECE. *See* Service de Documentation Exterieure et de Contre Espionage
Sebold, William H., 275–76
Second Chief Directorate (SCD), xxvii, xxviii, 40, 53, 67, 71, 76, 99, 133, 141, 163, 196, 200, 216, 221, 258–59, 298, 301; American Department, 41
  Foreign Tourist Section, 201
Secret Intelligence Service (SIS), xviii, xxiv, 4, 20, 31, 38, 42, 45–46, 114, 121, 138, 146, 165, 173, 195, 197, 205–09, 210–11, 216, 223, 247, 270, 289, 301; Chief of. *See* Stewart Menzies
  Defectors from. *See* George Blake, Kim Philby
  Dutch Section, 22

Secret Service, 144
The Secret War of Josephine Butler, xviii, 16
Security Intelligence Middle East (SIME), 132, 195, 205, 296
Segebarth, Nancy, 6
Seina, Violette, 159
Selborne, Lord, 47
Sellers, Michael, 8
Semmelmann, Georg, 238
Senate Internal Security Subcommittee, 149, 200
SENIOR, 256–57
Senkin, Anatoli B., 267
SERB, 103
Serov, Ivan, 247, 307
Service de Documentation Exterieure et de Contre Espionage (SDECE), 118, 246
Servicio di Informazione Militar (SIM), 4, 197
Sevigny, Pierre, 195
Seymoniczky, Stanislas, 157
Shadrin, Ewa, 317
SHAH, 127, 190
Shalatov, Col., 305
Shaomin, Li, 259
Shapiro, Harold, 59–60
Shaw, George Bernard, 41
Shcharansky, Anatoli, 151
Shei Pei Pu, 34, 35
Shelepin, Aleksandr N., 275
Sheliha, Rudolf von, 279
Shelley, Jack, xvii, 210
Shergold, Harold, 25
Shevchenko, Arkadi, xx, xxi, 6, 52–53
Shin Beth, 101
Shivers, Robert L., 155
SHMELOV, 201
Sholokovsky, Alex, 233–34

INDEX • 361

Shtykov, Nikolai, 164
Shurygin, Sergei, 10
Shuster, Anton, 259
Shvernik, Nikolai, 305
Sicherheitsdienst, 140, 155, 270;
    Chief of. See Reinhard Heydrich
    Defector from. See Nellie Kapp
Sidrov, Andrei, 305
Sievers, Susanne, xviii, 259
Sikorski, Wladislaw, 45
Silber, Jules, xvi, 34
Silverman, George, 161
Silvermaster, Helen, 19
Silvermaster, Nathan Gregory, 18–19
SIM. See Servicio di Informazione Militar
SIMA, xvii, 57–59
Simon Bolivar, USS, 303
Simon, Kurt, 79
Simone, Simone, 214
Simpson, Wallace, xvi, 259–60, 315
Sims, Harold, 299
Sims, Mitzi, 299
Sinatra, Frank, 77
Singer, Kurt, 35, 36, 321–22
Sioeng, Ted, 214
Siqueros, David, 294
SIS. See Secret Intelligence Service
Sites, Eric, 8
Skachkov, Anatoli I, 67
Skardon, W. James, 175, 179
Skoblin, Gen. Nikolai, xvii, 221
Skortskov, Nikolai, 134
Skripov, Ivan F., xiv, 164, 260–61
Skvotsov, Gennadi, 180
Sluzba Bezpiecezenstwa (SB), 94, 256
    Defectors from. See Michal Goleniewski, Josef Swiatlo
Sluzhba Vnazhney Razvedki (SVR), 139, 159, 268

Defector from. See Sergei Tretyakov
Slansky, Rudolf, 81, 82
Smedley, Agnes, xvi, 261–63, 268
SMERSH, 31
Smetanin, Gebbadi, 7
Smetanin, Svetlana, 7
Smith, Edward Ellis, xx, 201, 224, 228, 263
Smith, Ferguson, 129
Smith, George, 129, 190
Smith, Jane M., 130
Smith, J. J., xxi, 212–14, 228
Smith-Cumming, Mansfield, 207
SMOLENSKAYA, 100
SNARK, THE, 316
Snellman, Anne-Marie, xvii, 142
SNIPER, 94, 128
Sobell, Helen, 110
Sobell, Morton, 110
Soble, Jack, 72
Soboloff, David, 38
Social Agents, 263–64
Socolov, Albert H., 60
Sokolov, Alexandre, xxviii, 134, 264–68
Sokolov, Gennadi, 135
Sokolov, Lise-Lotte, 134
Sokolov, Misha, 266–67
Solmatin, Boris, 304
SOLO, 149
Solomatin, Piotr, 268
SONIA, 154
SOPHIE, 92, 93
Sorge, Richard, xvi, x4vii, 169, 262–63, 268–69
Sosnovski, Lev, 267
Soussoudis, Michael, 258
Soviet/Eastern European Division (SE), 6
Soviet intelligence service. See KGB, NKVD

Soviet military intelligence service. *See* GRU
Soviet Strategic Rocket Force, 247
Spanish Civil War, 53, 81, 89, 146, 154, 282–83, 294–95, 314
Special Branch, 26, 38, 128, 132, 207, 215, 260, 286, 309, 313
Special Operations Executive (SOE), 46, 113, 233, 269–72, 311–12, 327; F Section, 47, 250, 271 Minister for. *See* Lord Selborne
Spence, Wishart, 195
Spencer, Arthur, 126, 127
Spencer, Victor George, 195
SPINDLE, 250
SpyCatcher, 99
SpyCounterspy, 214
The Spy I Loved, 37, 218
The Spy Who Loved Me, 31
Squillacotte, Therese, xxi, 272–73
Squires, Richard, 100
Staatsicherheit (Stasi), 36
Stahl, Lydia, xvi, 273, 287
Stahlmann, Richard, 314
Stalin, Joseph, 20, 41, 67, 74, 82, 96, 255, 294
Stand, Karl, 272
STAR, 103
Stashinsky, Bogdan, 274–75
Stasi. *See* Staatsicherheit
State Department, penetration of. *See* Henry Antheil, Felix Bloch, Laurence Duggan, Alger Hiss, Donald Hiss, Tyler Kent, Donald Keyser, Noel Field, Irwin Scarbeck, Therese Squillacotte, Michael Straight
Statni Bezpecnost (StB), 73, 179, 202, 257–58, 263–64, 275, 280
STEVEN, 4
Stieber, Wilhelm, xv, xxvi, 53

Stein, John, 7
Stein, Lily, 275–77
Steinauer, Gustav, 94
Stephens, Terence E., 146
Stephenson, 212
Stern, Alfred, 71
Stettinius, Edward, 116
Stewart, Annie, 55
Stewart, Bob, 31, 55, 56
Stewart, Margaret, 55
Stewart, Michael, 91
Stieber, Wilhelm, xxvi, 277
Stiller, Helga, 278
Stiller, Werner, xx, 278
Stoebe, Ilse, xvii, 279–82
Stöhler, Hans, 242
Stonehouse, Barbara, 280
Stonehouse, John, xviii, xx, 280–81
stool-pigeons, 281, 313
Strachey, John, 95
Straight, Michael, xxi, 30, 69, 122, 199, 281–83
Strand, Evelyn, 146
Streater, Isabel, 293
Streffer, Igon, 283
Strickland, Janet, xiv, 1
Strokov, Gleb, 40
Strong, Gen. Kenneth, 285
Strunze, Bryan Waldemar, 256
Stufflebeam, Robert, 160
Styles, Roger, 186
Sudoplatov, Pavel, 89, 152, 305, 307, 319, 327
Suharto, President, 283–84
Sukhomlinov, Vladimir, 284
SUKHOVA, 76
Sullivan, William J. ("Bill"), 71
Summersby, Gordon, 284
Summersby, Kay, xxvii, 284–85
Supreme Headquarters Allied Powers Europe, 243

Suschitsky, Edith, xvi, 31, 68, 91, 122, 286
Suzuki, Kissy, 32
Sutterlin, Heinz, 112, 248, 287
Svirin, Mikhail N., 109
SVR. *See* Sluzhba Vnazhney Razvedki
swallow, 76, 196, 252, 284, 287
Swedish Security Service, 8
SWING-TIT, 296, 316
Switalo, Josef, 83, 84
Switz, Marjorie, xvi, 273, 287–88
Switz, Robert, xvi, 273, 287–88
Symonds, John, xiv, 166, 288–89
Symonds, Ronald, 301
Szabo, Zoltan, xiv, 8–9
Szinda, Gustav, 314
Sztanko, Enud, 143
Szymanska, Halina, xxvi, 289
Szymanski, Col. Antoni, 289

-T-
Tabet, Henri, 46
Tairov, Igor A., xxix, 134, 289–90
Tairova, Margarita N., xxix, 134, 289–90
TAKIS, 4
Task Force W, 78
TASS News Agency, 7–8, 69, 108, 153
TATE, xvii, 198, 199, 241, 316
Teamsters Union, 78
Templyakova, Irina, 165
Tenet, George, 70
Thatcher, Margaret, 31, 207
Their Trade Is Treachery, xxviii
Thieme, Gerhard, 79
THIRD CHANCE, 177
Thomas, Elizabeth, 210
Thomson, Sir Basil, xvi, 34, 172, 290–91, 310

Thomson, Bill, 243
Thorpe, Cora, 299
Thorpe, Jeremy, xx, 291–92
Thwaites, Michael, 217
Tiger, HMS, 310
Tillo, Irina, 292–93
Timashkevits, Yania, xviii, 147
TIMO, 142
Timofayev, Nikolai, 196
Tolhurst, George, 4
Tolkachev, Adolf, 7, 132
TOLLUS, 4
TONY, 30
TOPAZ, 35
TOP HAT, 104
TOURIST, 178
Towers, Harry, 202
Trafficante, Santos, 77–78
TRAMP, 276
TREASURE, 198, 316
Treholt, Arne, 102
Trent Park, 80
Tretyakov, Sergei, 139
Trie, Charlie, 213
TRIGON, xv, 203–04
TRIPLEX, 113
Trotsky, Leon, 114, 254, 293–96, 327
Trotsky, Natalya, 294
Trudeau, Pierre, 139
TRUDI, 296, 316
Truman, Harry S., 285, 299
Trundle, Guy, 260
The Truth about American Diplomats, xviii, 40
Tsikata, Kojo, 258
Tshombe, Moise, 296
Tsuru, Shigeto, 199
Tube Alloys, 175
Tudor Hart, Dr. Alex, 286
Tuomi, Kaarlo, 264, 267–68

Turing, Alan, 297
Turnberry Island, 297–98
Turnure, Pamela, 143
TURQUOISE, 35
Turrou, Leon, 98, 99, 118
Twinn, Peter, 297
TWISTER, 280
Tzilard, Leo, 327

-U-
U-2, 232
Ulbricht, Walter, 244
ULTRA, 297
Union Corse, 32
United Nations Special Commission (UNSCOM) xxi, 298
Unrau, Ivan D., 117
UNSCOM. *See* United Nations Special Commission
Upranlenie Podelam Diplomatichestogo Korpusa (UpDK), xxvii, 224, 298–99
UpDK. *See* Upranlenie Podelam Diplomatichestogo Korpusa
Urzab Bezpieczenstwa (UB), 82, 253–54
Ustinov, Klop, 42, 253

-V-
VADIM, 29
Vandenberg, Arthur, 211, 299
Vandenberg, Hazel, 299
Vanunu, Mordechai, xx, 299–300
VARDO, 318
Varenik, Gennadi, 7
Varley, John, 247
Varona, Tony, 78
Vasiliev, Vladimir, 8
Vassall, John, xviii, xiv, xxvii, 32, 99, 200, 300–01, 326
Vauck, Dr, Wilhelm, 279–80

Vegh, Diana de, 143
Veksler, Sara, 292
VENONA, 20, 52, 57–60, 103, 107, 117, 157, 168, 178, 224–26, 245–46, 263, 293, 327; Soviet spies in, *See* Roland Abbiate, Iskhak Akhmerov, Stepan Apreyyan, Joel Barr, Elizabeth Bentley, Earl Browder, Lona Cohen, Judith Coplon, Pierre Cot, Laurence Duggan, Klaus Fuchs, Aleksandr Feklisov, Ruth Greenglass, Ted Hall, Kitty Harris, Jim Hill, Alger Hiss. Olga Khlopkova, Christina Krotkova, Sergei Kurnikow, Leonid Kvasnikov, André Labarthe, Alta Lecoutre, Donald Maclean, Ian Milner, Boris Morros, Victor Perlo, Kim Philby, Olga Pravdina, Mary Price, Fred Rose, Ethel Rosenberg, Julius Rosenberg, Saville Sax, Sara Veksler, Harry Dexter White, Vasili Zubilin
VENSKE, 158, 163
VERA, 120, 158, 221
Vermehren, Dr. Erich, 182
Verrept, Imelda, 243
Vertefeille, Jeanne, 160
Vetrov, Svetlana, 302
Vetrov, Vladimir, 302
Vicenzo, Teresa di, 31
VIK, 108
Vitali, Dominetta, 31
VLADIMIR, 117
Vlasov, Anatoli, 21
Vogel, Wolfgang, 151
Volkova, Zinaida, 61–62
VOLUNTEERS, 54
Vomecourt, Pierre de, 46–48
Voronin, Yuri, 142

INDEX • 365

Vorontsov, Sergei, 7–8, 247
Voss, Otto, 118
Vyshinsky, Andrei, 116

-W-
Waagenar, Sam, 321
Wade, Bob, 316
Wagstaffe, Keith, 307
Wake, Nancy, 234
Wales, Prince of, 259
Walker, Arthur, 302–04
Walker, Barbara, 302–03
Walker, John, 6, 302–03
Walker, Michael, 303
Walker, Rachel, 302, 304
Walker, Rita, 304
Wallinger, John, 173
Walsh, Patrick, 200
Walter, Leon, 48
Wälti, Werner, 253
Wannenmacher-Pohl, Helga, 304–07, 326
Ward, Dame Irene, 270
Ward, Stephen, xiv, 65, 135, 141, 142, 196, 202, 307–08
Warner, Sir Fred, 43
WASP, 57
Watkins, John, 153, 200, 310
Wear, Priscilla, 143
Weber, Kurt, 147
Webster, William, 309
Weinmann, Ariel J., xxi, 309
Weisblatt, Edward, 132
WEISE, 36
Weisz, George, 29
Weitzleben, Field-Marshal von, 219
Welch, Richard, 3
Welchman, Gordon, 297
Wells, H. G., 41–42
Wenner-Gren, Axel, 13
Wenzel, Johann, 279

WERNER, 139
Wertheim, Lizzie, xv, xvi, 290, 309–10
West, Rebecca, 42
Weustenfeld, Else, 277
Weyl, Nathaniel, 52
Wharton, Harry, 165
Wheatley, Dnnis, 114
Wheelwright, Julie, 322
White, Harry Dexter, 19, 51, 161
White, John, 281
Whitehouse, Arch, 321
Whitelaw, Willie, 62
Whitworth, Jerry, 304
Whomack, George, 313
Wichfeld, Jurgen, 310, 312
Wichfeld, Monica de, xvii, 310–12
Widemann, Fritz, 119
Wigg, George, 62
Wijk, Knut, 30
Wilcott, Elsie, 3
Wilcott, Jim, 3
Wild Wheels, 17
Wilkins, Elizabeth, 50
Wilkes, Brent, 90
Wilky, Helen, 312–13
Will, Dieter, xx, 162
Williams, Albert, 55, 313–14
Williams, Nellie, xvi, 55, 313–14
Willoughby, Gen. Charles, 199, 262
Wilson, Harold, 62, 167, 280, 292
Wilson, James H., 130
Winant, John, xxvi
Winchell, Walter, 13
Winsor, Rita, 270
Winston, Alan, 54
Winter, Gordon, 291–92
Wiseman, Sir William, 174
Wolf, Markus, xvii, xxi, xxviii, 165, 210, 235, 242, 254, 314
Wolff, Theodor, 279

Wolkoff, Anna, xvii, 39, 144, 150, 315
Women Spies, 36
Wood, 277
Woolwich Arsenal, 56, 57, 146, 286, 313
Workers Camera Club, 286
World Bank, 161
World Council of Peace, 179
World Tourists Inc., 56
Wright, Peter, 31, 43, 99, 100, 189
Wylie, Tom, 30, 112
Wynne, Greville, 186

-X-
X, Malcolm, 202
X, Miss. *See* Olga Gray
XX Committee, 315–16
XXXI Committee, 195

-Y-
Yaddo Foundation, 262
Yakushin, Boris, 316
Yalta Conference, 116
Yefimov, Aleksei G., 159
Yeliseyev, Petr, 180
Yereskovsky, Dr. Valentina, 317
Yezhov, Nikolai, 20
Young Communist League, 72, 149
Yugoslavia, King Peter of, 308
Yurchenko, Piotr, 317
Yurchenko, Vitali, xxiii, 12, 132, 316–18
Yuzhin, Boris, xx, 8

-Z-
Zakrevsky, Count Ignaty, 41
Zarubin, Vasili, 170, 318–19
Zarubina, Elizaveta, 170, 318–19
Zehe, Alfred, 6
Zelle, Adam, 171
Zhensan, Yu, 34, 35
Ziemer, Lothar, 273
ZR/RIFLE, 77
Zubilin, Col., 318–19

About the Author

Nigel West is a military historian specializing in intelligence and security issues. While still at the university, he worked as a researcher for two authors: Ronald Seth, who had been parachuted into Silesia by SOE, and Richard Deacon, a former wartime naval intelligence officer and later the foreign editor of the *Sunday Times*. He later joined BBC TV's General Features Department to work on the *SPY!* and *ESCAPE* series.

His first book, coauthored with Richard Deacon in 1980 and published by BBC Publications, was the book of the *SPY!* series, and was followed by other nonfiction: *British Security Service Operations 1909–45* (1981); *A Matter of Trust: MI5 1945–72* (1982); *MI6: British Secret Intelligence Service Operations 1909–45* (1983); *The Branch: A History of the Metropolitan Police Special Branch* (1983); *Unreliable Witness: Espionage Myths of the Second World War* (1984); *GARBO* (coauthored with Juan Pujol, 1985); *GCHQ: The Secret Wireless War* (1986); *Molehunt* (1987); *The Friends: Britain's Postwar Secret Intelligence Operations* (1988); *Games of Intelligence* (1989); *Seven Spies Who Changed the World* (1991); *Secret War: The Story of SOE* (1992); *The Faber Book of Espionage* (1993); *The Illegals* (1993); *The Faber Book of Treachery* (1995); *The Secret War for the Falklands* (1997); *Counterfeit Spies* (1998); *Crown Jewels* (with Oleg Tsarev, 1998); *VENONA: The Greatest Secret of the Cold War* (1999); *The Third Secret* (2000); *Mortal Crimes* (2004); *The Guy Liddell Diaries* (2005); *MASK* (2005); *Historical Dictionary of British Intelligence* (2005); *Historical Dictionary of International Intelligence* (2006); *On Her Majesty's Secret Service* (2006); *Historical Dictionary of Cold War Counterintelligence* (2007); and *Historical Dictionary of Word War II Intelligence* (2008).

In 1989, he was voted the "Experts' Expert" by a panel of spy writers selected by the *Observer*. He is currently the European editor of the *International Journal of Intelligence and Counterintelligence* and teaches the history of postwar intelligence at the Centre for Counterintelligence and Security Studies in Alexandria, Virginia. In October 2003, he was awarded the U.S. Association of Former Intelligence Officers first Lifetime Literature Achievement award.